THE HOLY SPIRIT AND THE EAGLE FEATHER

ADVANCING STUDIES IN RELIGION
Series editor: Sarah Wilkins-Laflamme

Advancing Studies in Religion catalyzes and provokes original research in the study of religion with a critical edge. The series advances the study of religion in method and theory, textual interpretation, theological studies, and the understanding of lived religious experience. Rooted in the long and diverse traditions of the study of religion in Canada, the series demonstrates awareness of the complex genealogy of religion as a category and as a discipline. ASR welcomes submissions from authors researching religion in varied contexts and with diverse methodologies.

The series is sponsored by the Canadian Corporation for Studies in Religion whose constituent societies include the Canadian Society of Biblical Studies, Canadian Society for the Study of Religion, Canadian Society of Patristic Studies, Canadian Theological Society, Société canadienne de théologie, and Société québécoise pour l'étude de la religion.

8 Identities Under Construction
Religion, Gender, and Sexuality among Youth in Canada
Pamela Dickey Young and Heather Shipley

9 Prayer as Transgression?
The Social Relations of Prayer in Healthcare Settings
Sheryl Reimer-Kirkham, Sonya Sharma, Rachel Brown, and Melania Calestani

10 Relation and Resistance
Racialized Women, Religion, and Diaspora
Edited by *Sailaja V. Krishnamurti and Becky R. Lee*

11 Sacred as Secular
Secularization under Theocracy in Iran
Abdolmohammad Kazemipur

12 Under Siege
Islamophobia and the 9/11 Generation
Jasmin Zine

13 Sacred Cyberspaces
Catholicism, New Media, and the Religious Experience
Oren Golan and Michele Martini

14 Caught in the Current
British and Canadian Evangelicals in an Age of Self-Spirituality
Sam Reimer

15 Prophets of Love
The Unlikely Kinship of Leonard Cohen and the Apostle Paul
Matthew R. Anderson

16 The Holy Spirit and the Eagle Feather
The Struggle for Indigenous Pentecostalism in Canada
Aaron A.M. Ross

The Holy Spirit and the Eagle Feather

The Struggle for Indigenous Pentecostalism in Canada

AARON A.M. ROSS

McGill-Queen's University Press
Montreal & Kingston • London • Chicago

ISBN 978-0-2280-1765-3 (cloth)
ISBN 978-0-2280-1766-0 (paper)
ISBN 978-0-2280-1811-7 (ePDF)
ISBN 978-0-2280-1812-4 (ePUB)

Legal deposit third quarter 2023
Bibliothèque nationale du Québec

Printed in Canada on acid-free paper that is 100% ancient forest free (100% post-consumer recycled), processed chlorine free

This book has been published with the help of a grant from the Canadian Federation for the Humanities and Social Sciences, through the Awards to Scholarly Publications Program, using funds provided by the Social Sciences and Humanities Research Council of Canada.

Financé par le gouvernement du Canada | Funded by the Government of Canada | Canada

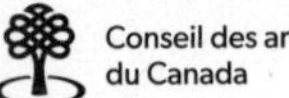

Canada Council for the Arts

We acknowledge the support of the Canada Council for the Arts.

Nous remercions le Conseil des arts du Canada de son soutien.

Library and Archives Canada Cataloguing in Publication

Title: The Holy Spirit and the eagle feather: the struggle for Indigenous Pentecostalism in Canada / Aaron A.M. Ross.

Names: Ross, Aaron A. M., author.

Series: Advancing studies in religion; 16.

Description: Series statement: Advancing studies in religion; 16 | Includes bibliographical references and index.

Identifiers: Canadiana (print) 20230205046 | Canadiana (ebook) 20230205186 | ISBN 9780228017653 (hardcover) | ISBN 9780228017660 (softcover) | ISBN 9780228018117 (ePDF) | ISBN 9780228018124 (ePUB)

Subjects: LCSH: Indigenous peoples—Canada—Religion. | LCSH: Pentecostalism—Canada. | LCSH: Pentecostals—Canada. | CSH: First Nations Pentecostals.

Classification: LCC BR1644.5.C3 R67 2023 | DDC 269/.408997071—dc23

This book was typeset by Marquis Interscript in 10.5/13 Sabon.

Contents

Figures

All images are from the PAOC archives and are used with permission.

Acknowledgments

In 2012, my denomination (the Pentecostal Assemblies of Canada, or PAOC) issued an apology and statement of reconciliation regarding the treatment of Indigenous ministers throughout its history. Early in my career as a minister, and not thoroughly versed in the history of events referred to, I found that the apology and statement sent me along a path of intrigue and interest. What is more, I was not the only one unaware of the issues addressed in 2012. Now, over a decade later, it is my hope that the pages of this volume shed some light on aspects of that story, as well as its present-day outcomes. I hope that others who asked the same questions I did will find some answers within this monograph.

The journey of writing a history such as this one is seldom undertaken alone. There were many who came alongside me, and encouraged me along the way. I wish to express my thanks to them. I am deeply grateful to my wife Annabel for her love and never-ending patience. By her own admission this project has been our "constant companion" throughout our entire relationship. I thank her for seeing it through to completion with me. I thank my parents Patrick and Ruth for depositing within me life's most valuable and longest-lasting lessons. I thank them for their loving support through the years, gently guiding me to this point. I extend thanks to the many family members and friends whose conversations encouraged me throughout the writing of this history.

I wish to thank my mentors who have guided me in the historian's craft: Phyllis D. Airhart, Alan Hayes, and Stuart Macdonald. Not least, I am grateful to James Craig, archivist of the Pentecostal Assemblies of Canada. I thank James for his commitment to his discipline and his passion for the preservation of the historical record.

Without James's acute archival instinct and discipline, and the PAOC's vast archival collection, this project never would have been feasible. I thank George Gunner (Moose Cree First Nation; Moose Factory, Ontario), Dan Collado (Kanien'kehá:ka; Tyendinaga Mohawk Territory, Ontario), and Levi Samson Beardy (Anishinini; Bearskin Lake, Ontario) for giving generously of their time and sharing their reflections and insights with me over the course of several conversations through the years. I wish to thank Kyla Madden, senior editor at McGill-Queen's University Press, for her support and her efforts in bringing this book to publication. Finally, to the many Indigenous people whose accounts and words appear within these chapters, I express how great an honour it is to carry the memories, stories, and testimonies shared. I hope they are well reflected within these pages.[1]

Aaron A.M. Ross
Richmond, British Columbia (situated on the unceded traditional territories of the Tsawwassen, Kwantlen, and Musqueam First Nations)
2023

Abbreviations

AFN	Assembly of First Nations
AG USA	Assemblies of God United States of America
APM	PAOC WOD Aboriginal Pentecostal Ministries
BCYD	PAOC British Columbia and Yukon District
CMS	Church Missionary Society
CPBC	PAOC Central Pentecostal Bible College (Saskatoon, Saskatchewan)
DHMBC	PAOC Department of Home Missions and Bible Colleges
DIAND	Canadian federal Department of Indian Affairs and Northern Development
EOQD	PAOC Eastern Ontario and Quebec District
EPBC	PAOC Eastern Pentecostal Bible College (Peterborough, Ontario)
MNWOD	PAOC Manitoba and Northwestern Ontario District
NLM	PAOC Northland Mission
NLMBC	Northland Mission Bible College
NNLC	PAOC National Native Leadership Council
PAOC	Pentecostal Assemblies of Canada
SPG	Society for the Propagation of the Gospel in Foreign Parts
TEE	Theological Education by Extension (travelling NLM Bible College)
Testimony	*The Pentecostal Testimony* (PAOC periodical)
TRC	Truth and Reconciliation Commission of Canada
UNDRIP	United Nations Declaration on the Rights of Indigenous Peoples
WOD	PAOC Western Ontario District

THE HOLY SPIRIT AND THE EAGLE FEATHER

INTRODUCTION

The Indigenous Principle

The Pentecostal Assemblies of Canada and Its Missiology

> Our endeavor shall be to establish a self-supporting native church and from the beginning, each work … should be made self-supporting to the very limit possible.
>
> Pentecostal Assemblies of Canada 1932 Missionary Policy[1]

On 12 July 2000, Matthew Coon Come (Eeyou; Mistissini, Quebec), former Grand Chief of the Northern Quebec Cree, was elected to the position of National Chief of the Assembly of First Nations (AFN), the highest office among First Nations. That midsummer Ottawa day, Coon Come, clad in a buckskin jacket, delivered his acceptance speech. The dynamic and celebrated First Nations leader and now newly minted National Chief doubled down on his confrontational campaign promises, vowing to take Ottawa to task over Indigenous treaty rights. Coon Come declared, "I want Canada to respect the treaties it has signed with us, for they are also the rule of law," and emphasized that he "strongly believed in the freedom of religion for all people." The day prior, Coon Come drew "thunderous applause" from his fellow AFN delegates for stating, "I want to be national chief, but [one] that lobbies and opens doors and facilitates. I don't want to be a national chief that competes with our chiefs and councils for programs and funding dollars."[2]

At Coon Come's inauguration, former National Chief Ovide Mercredi (Néhinaw; Grand Rapids, Manitoba) passionately proclaimed to the roomful of chiefs that it was "Coon Come's destiny to succeed … as national chief, and that it was important to the future of Canada's native bands that he be allowed to fulfill that destiny." When Mercredi finished speaking, a procession of chiefs formed from the back of the room, and one by one they publicly confirmed their support for Coon Come. Armand McKenzie (Innu; Northern Quebec) recalled, "It was a powerful moment ... The chiefs were moved."[3]

Coon Come's election was significant, not least because he was the first eastern chief named to the top post of the largest Indigenous organization in Canada,[4] but also because of Coon Come's religious affiliation. It was well known that Coon Come was Pentecostal, had attended Bible college, and was a member of a prominent Pentecostal Assemblies of Canada (PAOC) congregation in Ottawa.[5] In fact, Coon Come was the first Pentecostal to hold the national chief position. Coon Come recalled of the event, "I was prepared to lose this election, but I am not prepared to abandon the gospel of Jesus Christ."[6] The overtness of Coon Come's Pentecostal association was lost on neither his fellow chiefs nor the international media, with *The New York Times* reporting that Coon Come's "strong conviction stems in part from his beliefs as an evangelical Christian."[7]

The national chief's inauguration serves as an historically culminating moment, illustrating the rise to prominence of Indigenous Pentecostal affiliation and influence. Canadian historian of Christianity Robert K. Burkinshaw wrote:

> The election of Matthew Coon Come ... raised questions about religious faith among indigenous people ... [T]he election of a Pentecostal to the highest office among Canada's First Nations unexpectedly brought attention to the quiet, but extensive, growth of Pentecostalism among the native peoples of Canada.[8]

Still, the story of Indigenous Pentecostalism is one that remains largely untold. Although currently the largest neo-evangelical (hereafter Evangelical) denomination in Canada, the PAOC came from humble roots. The annals of the PAOC's history often provide a "who's who" of church founders – typically Euro-Canadian men. Yet, unfortunately, casual observers can easily overlook the significant contributions to Canadian Pentecostalism of non-Euro-Canadians and women. Thus the historian should consider the perspectives of the denomination's breadth of constituents.[9] Contemporaneous to the development of social history, it is important for religious history also to examine the accounts of groups generally excluded from the

Canadian nation-building, political-enterprise, and even ecclesial narratives.[10] Although not providing a comprehensive ethnographic overview of the PAOC, this monograph sheds light on a lesser-known aspect of its story: that is, the history of Pentecostalism among Indigenous people.

SYNOPSES OF INDIGENOUS PENTECOSTALISM AND THE NORTHLAND MISSION

While historically many denominations and faith groups missionized Indigenous people, by the twenty-first century, the most rapidly growing religious group among them was not Catholic, Anglican, Baptist, United Church of Canada, nor Christian and Missionary Alliance. It was Pentecostal. Rivalled only by the rapid resurgence of Indigenous traditional spiritualities,[11] Pentecostalism, increasingly led by local individuals and frequently a focal point of community life, has become a prominent religious force in most Indigenous communities.[12]

In addition to being rapid, the growth of Pentecostalism among Indigenous people has also been recent. According to Canadian census data, in 1971, 6,650 Indigenous people identified as Pentecostal. By 1981, that number was 13,890.[13] In 2001, 19,000 "Registered/Treaty Indians" identified as Pentecostal. This figure accounts for 3.4 per cent of "Registered/Treaty Indians." By 2011 that figure had increased to 36,360 respondents who identified as both "Aboriginal" and Pentecostal, accounting for 7.6 per cent of respondents identifying as "Aboriginal." An additional 35,000 Canadians with some Indigenous ancestry claimed to be Pentecostal. The rate of subscription to Pentecostalism among "Registered/Treaty Indians" is almost three times that of Canada's overall population, the latter being 1.2 per cent. In particular, the 1981–2001 period of increase in Indigenous Pentecostal adherents compares favourably to the rate of practice of Pentecostalism among the general population, which plateaued during the same timeframe. By comparison, roughly one in ten Pentecostals in Canada are Indigenous. Pentecostalism is particularly prevalent in the Arctic and subarctic regions of Canada, where anthropologists Christopher Fletcher and Aaron Denham claim it forms "the single most important social movement ... for the past 30 years."[14] Approaching the dawn of the third millennium, the rate of growth of Pentecostalism among Indigenous people had outpaced the rate of growth of the Indigenous population overall.[15]

Indeed, Indigenous Pentecostals are a substantial group numerically, but also symbolically as they occupy an increasingly significant socio-political position and status, with many filling leadership roles. Some have been band and council chiefs, such as Billy Diamond (Eeyou; Waskaganish, Quebec, and the first grand chief of the Grand Council of the Crees), Reggie Neeposh (Eeyou and former chief of Oujé-Bougoumou First Nation, Quebec), and of course Matthew Coon Come, who ascended to the AFN's national leadership.[16] Indigenous Pentecostalism has evolved into a movement that influences religious, social, and political spheres. Today, Indigenous Pentecostals are major players within religious life, but also in culture, economy, and society.[17]

Given the prevalence of Indigenous Pentecostalism, it is important to explain the rationale for looking specifically at the PAOC. The PAOC is the largest Pentecostal organization in Canada. Of Pentecostal and Evangelical organizations in that country, the PAOC maintains the highest level and rate of Indigenous adherence.[18] Further, the PAOC has a well-articulated and well-documented Pentecostal missiology (philosophy of Christian mission) that is accessible for research purposes.[19] Within the PAOC, the Northland Mission (NLM) provides a helpful case study on the spread of Pentecostalism among Indigenous people, because it was one of the most prominent, best funded, and most popularly supported PAOC domestic missions. Further, the NLM leadership's struggle to implement the PAOC's oft-trumpeted missiological ideals provides a purposeful focus for this monograph.

Founded in 1943, the NLM was based primarily within the regions adjacent to James Bay and Hudson Bay in Manitoba, Ontario, Quebec, and to a lesser extent the Northwest Territories. Throughout the thirty-three years following its establishment, the NLM existed as the brainchild of its missionary pilot founder, John Spillenaar, who initially itinerated from the Timmins, Ontario area. These decades saw the mission evolve from a generic, Eurocentric evangelistic organization into an aviation-based mission targeting an Indigenous audience.

By the 1950s, aviation allowed the NLM to enjoy newfound opportunities among Indigenous people in north-central Canada, and the mission practised extensive evangelism among Nehiyawak (the exonym for which is Cree), Anishininiwag (the exonym for which is Oji-Cree), and Ojibweg Anishinaabeg (the exonym being mainline Ojibway). At a time when an absence of roads limited Spillenaar's conventional efforts at northward itineration, aviation allowed the

PAOC to realize that the "heavens have become a highway."[20] By the 1960s, there were approximately fifteen Indigenous PAOC congregations in Ontario, predominantly under NLM management.[21] Spillenaar was better known for his itineration than his administration. It was not uncommon for Spillenaar's aircraft to stray off course to the far north, where he periodically worked among Inuit communities.[22] In the late 1970s, Spillenaar's successor, Dale Cummins, established a central mission station in Pickle Lake, Ontario, where it remained until the early 1990s. At that time, the NLM's third director, Ian Winter, moved the mission to Sioux Lookout, Ontario.

An important aspect of the PAOC's attempt to generate Indigenous leadership was the Northland Mission Bible College (NLMBC), which trained candidates for ministry. The rationale for founding the college was explained thus:

> The Pentecostal Assemblies of Canada challenged by the cry of Native Christians for their own Bible Training Centre developed the practical school setting ... Here students come from all parts of Canada to learn the word of God and develop their own Christian character and ministry. This distinctive Pentecostal Bible School is committed to meeting the needs of Christian Native people.[23]

According to another report, the PAOC's aim was to establish "a Bible College to educate and train native students in the north. These native students will then become the native pastors and leaders of the mission in the future."[24] Nowhere was the attempt at the missiological ideal known as the "indigenous principle" more prominent and obvious than in the creation and development of the NLMBC. Through the college, the PAOC sought to train Indigenous leadership to continue the NLM's work.

THE INDIGENOUS PRINCIPLE

From the day it was founded in 1919, the PAOC placed high priority on mission work, a hallmark of classical Pentecostalism in general.[25] The PAOC has a distinct and unique missiology owing to classical Pentecostalism's eschatological (Christian doctrine regarding the world's end) and pneumatological (Christian doctrine pertaining to God the Holy Spirit) emphases.[26] These factors contribute to Pentecostal missionaries' sense of urgency, and influence them to be pragmatic. In many denominations, mission work's reputation has suffered from its association with the colonial enterprise, and the missionary movement has garnered criticism and even stigma. In some cases, well-established denominations have responded to said criticism by ceasing missionization altogether. By contrast, numerous Pentecostals pride themselves in their movement's ongoing commitment to spreading their message. Further, many Pentecostals believe that their approach to the task of evangelism is unique within the history of Christianity in its motivation, and unprecedented in its results.[27] Many would extend this claim to the PAOC's mission work among Indigenous people.

An important feature of that claim has been steadfast subscription to what missiologists customarily referred to as the indigenous principle,[28] whereby the first wave of indigenous adherents to Christianity was to be trained to replace the missionaries in the ongoing task of ministry and local church leadership. The PAOC's missiology strongly embraced the indigenous principle. As early as 1926, PAOC Missionary Secretary Robert McAlister suggested that mission work "ought to be self-supporting and self-governing." In 1928 McAlister appealed for the "self-propagation" of the Pentecostal message, stating that "there are scores of native workers available if they had support to step out into the work."[29] It would seem the Missionary Secretary's words appealed to his contemporaries, as the denomination's 1932 constitution proclaimed: "Wherever on the foreign field it is workable and practical, our endeavor [*sic*] shall be to establish a self-supporting native church and from the beginning, each work on the foreign field should be made self-supporting to the very limit possible."[30]

At first glance, the timing of the PAOC's missionary policy appears to imply fiscal pragmatism surrounding mission, ostensibly coinciding with the Great Depression. Still, McAlister's descriptions of the "Three-Self" mission policy in 1926 and 1928 predate the Wall Street Crash of 1929. It is furthermore worth noting that economic circumstances did not prevent the PAOC from expanding. During the Great Depression, the denomination was one of the fastest-growing in the country. During the 1930s, the number of PAOC churches increased from 65 to 300.[31] Thus, while there likely was an element of economic pragmatism surrounding this missionary policy, it was not brought on by the Great Depression – at least not exclusively. More likely it was a result of the characteristically Pentecostal sense of urgency and pragmatism surrounding mission.

Simply put, the basis of the indigenous principle was to root Christianity in the culture of the mission's hosts. In order to make this possible, the missionary needed to do everything he or she could to create a "self-perpetuating indigenous church among the converts." The missionary's goal was to equip local adherents to run, finance, and support the mission. Additionally, the indigenous principle required the missionary to remove any colonial and ethnocentric vestiges. In other words, the missionary could not view Western culture as being superior, but rather must accept an indigenous culture as being equally valid.[32]

PAOC historian Thomas Miller recorded the moment the PAOC adopted the indigenous principle.

> A landmark decision which still characterizes PAOC missions policy was taken in 1933 at the Toronto General Conference: it involved the adoption of "the indigenous church idea" which was to be recommended "to all our missionaries on the field." The goal ... was to develop a "self-governing, self propagating and self-supporting native church." The source of this philosophic concept of missions in PAOC ranks is difficult to locate, but it is evident that the Fellowship was decades ahead of many other evangelical denominations in its approach.[33]

The minutes from the General Conference to which Miller referred specifically described the PAOC "as being in full sympathy with the indigenous church idea."[34] Although Miller could not pinpoint the origins of the indigenous principle within the PAOC's echelons, it is obvious that the denomination did not invent the concept. Various other denominations and missionary organizations historically had employed similar models earlier than did the PAOC. The idea of a church drawing its leadership from the culture within which it was based is a scriptural concept, particularly present in the writings of Paul the Apostle.[35] Eighteen centuries after Paul wrote his epistles, and on a different continent, Rufus Anderson, the secretary of the American Board of Commissioners for Foreign Missions in the 1830s, proposed such a model for American Protestant missions. Anderson's model prescribed the strict sequence of missionary church foundation among indigenous adherents as: 1) the missionary training indigenous ministers; 2) the missionary handing over the responsibility of running the church to them; 3) the missionary giving complete control over the church to the local population; and finally 4) the missionary departing. Ideally, all of this was managed within one generation, or during the career of the missionary.[36]

A few decades after Anderson, Henry Venn, secretary of the England-based Church Missionary Society (CMS) between 1841 and 1872, proposed a native church policy that envisioned missionary work as a progression toward an autonomous, indigenous church. CMS missionaries missionized indigenous peoples throughout the regions occupied by the British Empire, with the intention of training national pastors and churches.[37] Venn proposed the famous and oft-quoted "Three-Self" mission policy of a self-supporting, self-governing, and self-propagating indigenous church.[38] In this sense, Venn was a pioneer of the indigenous principle. Even in Canada, churches sought to exercise Venn's indigenous church ideal,[39] and ordained Indigenous people to lead self-governing, autonomous churches.[40]

Anglican Roland Allen followed in Anderson's and Venn's footsteps, in 1912 publishing his seminal volume, *Missionary Methods: Saint Paul's or Ours*. Allen challenged the traditional and prevalent Western approach to mission, proposing a missionary prototype whereby mission posts transitioned into churches led by local indigenous acolytes. After an initial period of service, a missionary was expected to withdraw, leaving the continuing work to a local designate.[41] Later, Assemblies of God (AG USA) missionary and missiologist Melvin Hodges wrote the popular volumes *The Indigenous Church* and *The Indigenous Church and the Missionary*. Hodges's books were highly regarded and widely read, and functioned as some of classical Pentecostalism's earliest and most enduring volume-length missiological treatises.[42] In each of these cases – Anderson, Venn, the Church of England's Roland Allen, and the AG USA's Hodges – their similar proposals of implementing an indigenous church proved popular, but also radical for their time, recommending a marked departure from the colonial missionary status quo of the periods.[43] Each proved influential within the PAOC's emerging missionary methods.

Notwithstanding missionaries' best intentions, the indigenous principle had struggled (but had not entirely failed) in Canada – even before the PAOC adopted and attempted it. For instance, the CMS native church policy allegedly "fell by the wayside." Domestic missions generally were less successful than international missions in transferring churches to Indigenous control. This trend is attributable to Euro-Canadian missionaries' general tendencies toward Eurocentrism and paternalism. Venn's vision was stifled in settler-occupied regions such as the Americas and Oceania but was far more successful in Africa and Asia. The latter, although generally under colonial subjugation, unlike the former maintained an overwhelmingly majority indigenous population.[44] The native church policy was further challenged by the Canadian nation-building enterprise, in full force by the turn of the twentieth century. By then the Catholic Church and several of the Protestant churches had partnered with governments, generally altering their Indigenous policies from those of implementing Indigenous clergy to those of assimilation, a process to be described in chapter 1.[45] For these reasons and others, indigenous autonomy was challenged in the New World while it generally fared better in the Old.

The shortcomings of the PAOC-preceding Anglican, Catholic, and United Churches and of its antecedent denominations (hereafter referred to as the longer-established churches) relative to the indigenous principle are provided not to suggest that these denominations all employed identical missiological methods, nor that ecclesial indigenization in Canada is impossible. Rather this example is given to provide historical context for the PAOC's missionization. The task for the PAOC would be to make good on what their longer-established denominational predecessors had already attempted for generations. This was a challenge PAOC missionaries were willing to accept, confident their message was unique among denominations. PAOC missionaries believed they practised the indigenous principle, and as such they confidently claimed that they were proponents of Indigenous autonomy, thereby resisting charges that their activity was a force for assimilation. Such criticism surfaced in the modern era with the claim that Western missionaries of the longer-established churches had occasionally functioned as agents of colonialism, expressing a rhetoric of civilizing and Westernizing in their dealings with Indigenous host cultures.[46]

Contrastingly, in what little scholarly attention has been given to the history of Euro-Canadian Pentecostal and Indigenous encounter in Canada, historians generally have declined to accuse Pentecostals of attempting to assimilate their Indigenous participants. For instance, Canadian historian John Webster Grant argued that Indigenous people became disillusioned with the longer-established churches' missions. Many believed Pentecostalism allowed greater autonomy and lay leadership than the longer-established churches did, thus enabling Indigenous people's initiative within the movement. Allegedly Indigenous people's agency resulted, giving rise to counter-movements and the reassertion of religious independence that contributed to Pentecostalism's rapid expansion among Indigenous people in Canada.[47]

In a similar fashion, Canadian historian of Christianity John Stackhouse articulated that Pentecostals

> grew in their recognition of a concern for the social needs of the natives. Generally untrammelled by a burden to 'civilize' the natives and characteristically concerned with a simple gospel presented by white or native leaders trained in Bible schools … Pentecostals made significant inroads into this field of mission.[48]

Stackhouse argued that since Pentecostal missionaries did not seek to "civilize" their audience, they may not have attempted to assimilate Indigenous people.[49]

While Grant and Stackhouse are reputable scholars, their contribution to Canadian Pentecostal historiography concerning Indigenous people comprises only a few paragraphs amid hundreds of pages. They cannot be faulted for their claims about Pentecostalism among Indigenous people, but neither can their claims about this subject be upheld as authoritative. A thorough examination of source materials reveals that Pentecostal missionaries at first claimed the goal of training Indigenous people, and in some quarters involved them in ministry leadership more than the longer-established churches did. Still, this monograph challenges the assumption that Pentecostal missionaries universally allowed more autonomy to Indigenous adherents than did the longer-established churches. Throughout most of the NLM's existence, its Euro-Canadian leadership claimed to support the indigenous principle yet subtly undermined it, doubting and ignoring Indigenous ministers, and opposing the integration of Indigenous culture with Pentecostalism. Part of the difficulty resulted from nomenclature. Although they spoke a language of "indigenization," realistically the PAOC's leaders could not effectively indigenize the NLM. Only the NLM's Indigenous ministers could do that. Still, doing so would require the PAOC to allow autonomy, something that could only come about through significant investment and trust on the part of PAOC leadership. In short, indigenizing and autonomizing are different but related processes, a concept to be developed throughout this monograph. Under the best of circumstances, the consistency of PAOC leadership's autonomizing efforts was mixed.

Effectively, Pentecostal missionaries were not that different from their longer-established church peers. After all, in presenting the Christian religion to Indigenous people, Pentecostal missionaries built upon a foundation already established by the other-denominational missionaries who preceded them, a theme to be examined in chapter 1. Neither is it universally true that Pentecostal missionaries and their motives were innocent of attempting to assimilate Indigenous mission participants. Although not referring directly to Pentecostals, Terry LeBlanc (Mi'kmaq and Acadian, with family roots in the Listuguj First Nation, Quebec) articulated an apt critique, describing the dangers implicit in a church "allowing its eschatological impulse to drive its mission endeavors, [whereby] … bigotry and racism, structural oppression and corruption, conquest and colonization, were expressed in the guise of ushering in the reign of God and the fulfillment of all things."[50] In the Pentecostal missionary historical record, the indigenous principle readily morphs into inculturation. Rather than accepting Indigenous culture as equally valid to Euro-Canadian Pentecostal culture, PAOC missionaries often opposed Indigenous culture and advocated their own, demonstrating colonial and paternalistic behaviours.[51]

While the PAOC repeatedly articulated and attempted to implement the indigenous principle, the ideal would prove quite difficult for the denomination to achieve. Although the PAOC's Bible colleges trained Indigenous candidates for ministry, the Euro-Canadian NLM missionaries themselves found it nearly impossible to hand over leadership and resources to Indigenous people. The PAOC was ultimately reluctant to make good on its indigenous principle ideal, and for fifty years failed to surrender leadership to Indigenous ministers.[52] The NLM came about a century after Venn's native church policy, yet the PAOC's shortfall with the indigenous principle is reminiscent of the longer-established denominations' shortcomings in implementing their own native church policies in Canada. Thus, it is beneficial to briefly compare the PAOC's missionizing efforts to those of non-Pentecostal denominations, which chapter 1 will address.

Pentecostal missionaries, believing they practised the indigenous principle, arrived at mission destinations claiming that local adherents eventually would take ownership of the ongoing work. Simply put, they believed their best energies would result in working themselves out of a job. Indeed, some described their efforts exactly that way. To answer the question of how well this principle worked in practice, this monograph explores the NLM's history, spanning fifty-three years from its founding under Pentecostal evangelist John Spillenaar – the PAOC's first missionary pilot – in 1943 to its dissolution in 1996. This monograph argues that decisions made by PAOC leaders (including the missionaries who operated the NLM), and certain systems of the PAOC's governance structures, contributed to the incomplete transfer of the mission to Indigenous control, and resulted in the NLM's ultimate dissolution before it was redeveloped into Aboriginal Pentecostal Ministries (APM) in 1996. Among the factors that led to this prolonged outcome was Euro-Canadian leadership's lack of confidence in emerging Indigenous leaders, demonstrated in such areas as succession planning for Indigenous leadership, resource management, and empowering Indigenous candidates for ministry.

SOURCES (SECONDARY AND PRIMARY) AND METHODOLOGY

In order to provide answers to the questions underlying this monograph's core argument, the first task is to identify volumes exploring similar themes. There is no comprehensive, book-length treatment of the history of Pentecostalism among Indigenous people in what is now Canada preceding this one. However, there are a few related publications respecting Indigenous people in what is now North America. One example is Kirk Dombrowski's *Against Culture: Development, Politics, and Religion in Indian Alaska* (2001). Dombrowski's work provides an ethnographic approach to analyzing Pentecostalism's influence upon Native American public life in Alaska. He chiefly argues that Native American Pentecostals in Alaska rejected Native American culture in favour of a Holiness-influenced Pentecostal identity.[53]

Against Culture is a respected study of Native American Pentecostalism, yet its thesis has not gone unchallenged. Clinton N. Westman, archaeologist, anthropologist, and ethnographer at the University of Saskatchewan, conducted research and fieldwork among Nehiyawak Pentecostals in the communities of Trout Lake and Peerless Lake, five hundred kilometres north of Edmonton, Alberta.[54] Westman contested Dombrowski's central argument, stating that Pentecostalism is not against Indigenous culture but, quite to the contrary, embraces it.[55] Westman further hypothesizes that Pentecostalism has been indigenized and incorporated into Nehiyaw cultural expression.[56] There is evidence of both embrace and rejection of Indigenous culture in NLM history, as will be addressed in chapter 4.

Westman's monograph *Cree and Christian: Encounters and Transformations* (2022) draws from and expands on his doctoral thesis, itself titled *Understanding Cree Religious Discourse* (2008). Both volumes are based on findings resulting from Westman's fieldwork in northern Alberta. Focusing on independent Pentecostal evangelists and networks, Westman's fine scholarship likewise lends valuable insights to this monograph, and to the telling of the story of Indigenous Pentecostalism.

Another germane study is Angela Tarango's *Choosing the Jesus Way: American Indian Pentecostals and the Fight for the Indigenous Principle* (2014), a history of AG USA missions among Native Americans in what is now the contiguous United States (predominantly the Southwest region). Tarango argues that Native American Pentecostals asserted their right to indigenization, thereby securing their autonomy and denominational significance.[57] Related to Tarango's work is an earlier publication, *American Indian College: A Witness to the Tribes* (2007), containing articles about the AG USA's American Indian College, written by alumni. Both volumes' emphasis on the indigenous principle, and on the role played by the American Indian College in its implementation, provide a comparative model for the analysis of PAOC strategy that follows.

A further work of significance is American anthropologist Kimberly Jenkins Marshall's *Upward, Not Sunwise: Resonant Rupture in Navajo Neo-Pentecostalism* (2016), which provides a thorough ethnography of the Oodlání Pentecostal movement among Diné (the exonym for which is Navajo Nation) in what is now the United States Southwest. Neo-Pentecostalism is differentiated from Pentecostalism in that it is typically non-denominational and is a derivative of later revivals taking place during the 1950s and 1960s. There is not a firm distinction between Neo-Pentecostalism and Pentecostalism, and the movements and their members tend to blend with one another and across networks.[58] Accordingly, Marshall's analysis of Diné Neo-Pentecostalism is relevant to this monograph, and for its purposes, Marshall's most significant contributions pertain to the indigenization of Pentecostalism and the transnational implications of the Indigenous Pentecostal movement in North America.

Lastly, Mark Clatterbuck, Associate Professor of Religion at Montclair State University, edited *Crow Jesus: Personal Stories of*

Native Religious Belonging (2017). This volume compiles the voices of several Indigenous (Apsáalooke, the exonym for which is Crow) and non-Indigenous participants in southwestern Montana. The stories contained therein combine to reshape understandings surrounding the complex tale of encounter and interaction between Christianity and Indigenous traditional spiritualities. The narratives shed light on both the diversity and at times the seeming contradictions that exist within Indigenous Christian adherence, devotion, and practice. Clatterbuck's findings furthermore complicate the shifting dimensions of terminology surrounding the subjects of conversion and doctrinal orthodoxy, otherwise so frequently relied upon in missionary correspondence and literature.[59] Finally, Clatterbuck's volume presents parallels to some of the accounts contained within this monograph, as the definitions and distinctions between Pentecostalism and Indigenous traditional spiritualities are rarely as clear-cut as they might otherwise be (and historically have been) portrayed.

These volumes all have a bearing on this monograph because they explore the encounter between Pentecostalism and Indigenous cultures and traditions, analyzing and highlighting their interactions.[60] This range of perspectives is crucial for the purposes of exploring the space between and shared by Pentecostalism and Indigenous cultures, and where the indigenous principle's ideals are most applied and most tested. Unrelated directly to either Canadian or Pentecostal histories (but worth noting here because of its familiarity to many) is Andrea Smith's *Native Americans and the Christian Right: The Gendered Politics of Unlikely Alliances* (2008). Smith draws attention to the role of religion in certain Native American social movements, highlighting the exchanges taking place with the Christian Right in matters of culture, gender, nationalism, and Scripture. Her underlying goal is to demonstrate the alliance of these seemingly unlikely parties.[61]

Although without an Indigenous emphasis, particularly important secondary sources pertaining to the history of Canadian Pentecostalism include Gloria Kulbeck's *What God Hath Wrought* (1958) and Gordon Atter's *"The Third Force"* (1962). The most comprehensive PAOC denominational history (with respect to the amount of detail it contains) is Thomas William Miller's *Canadian Pentecostals* (1994). The PAOC Western Ontario District (WOD) – the district primarily responsible for overseeing the NLM – provided the helpful volume *Fifty Years of Pentecostal History* (1983). Similarly, the PAOC Alberta and Northwest Territories District (ABNWT) published the helpful denominational history *Rejoice: A History of the Pentecostal Assemblies of Canada Alberta and the Northwest Territories (MacKenzie) District* (1983), part iii of which provides extensive information on what became the PAOC's Sub-Arctic Mission among Dene and Inuit communities in the Northwest Territories and what has since become the territory of Nunavut. Douglas Rudd contributed the predominantly testimonial *When the Spirit Came Upon Them* (2002). This collection of PAOC denominational histories is rounded out by *Picture This! Reflecting on 100 Years of the PAOC* (2018), a collection of essays commemorating the denomination's centenary.

Each of the above denominational histories was written from a pro-PAOC perspective, either because the PAOC published the volume, because the author or editor was a PAOC insider, or both. In 2020, Canadian sociologist Michael Wilkinson (Trinity Western University) and Canadian historian Linda Ambrose (Laurentian University) collaborated to co-author *After the Revival: Pentecostalism and the Making of a Canadian Church*, the signal scholarly and critical survey treatment of the denominational history of the PAOC. In its examination of the PAOC's organizational structure, the establishment of its identity, and its development of a flourishing "subculture," *After the Revival* chiefly argues that the administrative, business, and leadership abilities of the PAOC's founders, subsequent leaders, and ministers contributed to the movement's numeric success. Ambrose and Wilkinson portray a cautionary tale for the wary, however, in their conclusion that although the PAOC historically worked its way out of the religious periphery and into the mainstream of Canadian culture, a shifting Canadian socio-cultural landscape with values increasingly different from those of the PAOC presents considerable challenges as the denomination moves into its second century.

Among collections of essays, the most significant is *Canadian Pentecostalism: Transition and Transformation* (2009) edited by Michael Wilkinson. A chapter by Robert K. Burkinshaw outlines the history of Pentecostalism among Indigenous people on Vancouver Island. *A Liberating Spirit* (2010), co-edited by Wilkinson and Steven Studebaker (McMaster Divinity College), includes Clinton Westman's chapter on Nehiyawak Pentecostals in northern Alberta. Wilkinson has also co-edited *Winds from the North: Canadian Contributions to the Pentecostal Movement* (2010) with Peter Althouse (Oral Roberts). A final useful volume pertaining to the history of the AG USA is Gary McGee's *Miracles, Missions, and*

American Pentecostalism (2010), which includes sections about Native American Pentecostals.

Because this monograph addresses themes of both mission and intercultural encounter, an understanding of the PAOC's missiology is crucial. Enshrined within the periodically updated iterations of the PAOC's constitution are various missionary policies, which this monograph references. The most noteworthy single-volume treatment of the PAOC's missiology, however, is former Tyndale Seminary Missions Department Chair Irving Whitt's 1994 doctoral thesis, *Developing A Pentecostal Missiology in the Canadian Context (1867–1944)*. Whitt traces the history and evolution of the PAOC's missiology and argues that Canadian Pentecostal missionaries replicated the methods of their longer-established church predecessors. Still, Whitt found that the PAOC's eschatology and pneumatology cumulatively contribute to a unique missiology characterized by the at times complementary and at other times conflicting pressures of urgency and pragmatism.[62]

Two aforementioned monographs that influenced the early NLM missionaries' missiology and methods are also important for this study: 1) Roland Allen's *Missionary Methods* (1912), which, although not written from an expressly Pentecostal perspective, became influential among Pentecostals; George Upton, PAOC Executive of Missions from 1945 to 1966, personally signed and distributed the volume to PAOC missionaries.[63] 2) Melvin Hodges's *The Indigenous Church*, inspired by Allen's volume and written at the request of the AG USA. In his influential 1953 monograph, Hodges opined: "The successful missionary is one who has done his work so well that he is no longer needed in that area. He can leave that work to his converts."[64] Hodges had been a missionary in Central America for seventeen years by the time of his book's publication. His work reflected not only the ethos of Pentecostal mission as he practised it, but also the prominence within the PAOC of the indigenous principle.[65] Hodges interviewed Upton, whose observations and quotes feature prominently and extensively in *The Indigenous Church*.[66] NLM leaders vied to espouse the values pertaining to the indigenous principle contained within these volumes.

Over the course of its history, the NLM's sponsors included the Eastern Ontario and Quebec (EOQD) and Western Ontario districts of the PAOC, and several congregations and individuals therein. Geographically positioned within the WOD, a large and rich collection of primary source materials is located at the Mississauga, Ontario–based

PAOC archives. Michael A. Tapper, Chair of Religion at Southern Wesleyan University, approvingly noted of the archives:

> Researchers of the PAOC also benefit from an exceptional national archive collection at the ... denominational headquarters in Mississauga, Ontario. This well-organized research centre houses an extensive range of rare and historical documents, including many contemporary PAOC and Pentecostal resources.[67]

The archives contain large numbers of records specific to the NLM, comprising the following:

- Northland Mission written correspondence: letters, memorandums, and other general communiqués spanning the mid-1940s to the late 1990s.
- Northland Mission administration records from the same period, including but not limited to meeting minutes, financial records, employment records, aircraft maintenance records, building project schematics, and Northland Mission Bible College yearbooks.
- Northland Mission evangelistic records: newsletters, sermons, devotions, and testimonies (autobiographical, spiritual accounts). The testimonies included are from both missionaries and Indigenous people whom the NLM missionized.
- NLM missionary diaries, journals, and memoirs, including Spillenaar's two-part published autobiography.
- Records of the beginning and consolidation of Aboriginal Ministries.

Lastly, the archives made available all issues of *The Pentecostal Testimony* (abbreviated *Testimony*), the PAOC's flagship magazine first published in 1920. This collection contains several articles pertaining to PAOC missionization of Indigenous people, and many issues printed after 1943 contain articles about the NLM.

On this point it is worth noting that this monograph does not offer exhaustive coverage on the subject of Pentecostalism among Indigenous people in the whole of what is now Canada, but rather serves as a book-length treatment providing an historical examination of the PAOC's missional development among Indigenous adherents in parts of north-central Canada. This approach was feasible and favourable because the PAOC archives presented an incredible opportunity to write on this topic. With some exceptions, the PAOC archives' records in this area had not received substantial attention. Thus, on this subject, the archives proved to be a largely untapped resource. The approach taken in the monograph suits this line of inquiry as in large part it critiques the effectiveness of the PAOC in accomplishing (or not accomplishing) what it set out to do. An archive-based research method further proved to be indispensable in determining how the PAOC historically perceived itself throughout the process. This allowed for critique of missionary methods not simply by how those methods might be perceived at present, but more by examining how the PAOC's strategies and outcomes measured up to its own intentions. That is to say that while this monograph is critical in its methodology, it does not seek to be so unfairly. Certainly, this monograph will critique aspects of the PAOC's missionary effort. When such criticism appears, however, it is directed towards the outcomes flowing from the missionary methods the PAOC claimed to practise. It would not be fair for the twenty-first-century historian to criticize based on current cultural norms and standards. In its critical methodology, this monograph attempts to uncover assumptions, biases, and sentiments behind various parties' motivations.[68] Thus, this monograph critiques the PAOC by comparing its stated intentions with its success at implementing those intentions in actual practice.

Further, an archive-based methodology has not been undertaken at the expense of the Indigenous Voice, which this monograph seeks to amplify by reading primary sources critically, but also by reading them "against the grain." This requires two main steps. The first is reading the source "with the grain," to determine what the writer intended to communicate explicitly. The second and more critical step is reading "against the grain," uncovering hidden, even unintentional, elements and messages imbedded within the source. By taking both steps, historians can compare and contrast readings "with" and "against" the grain, thereby deducing what underlies and influences the primary source and its writer.[69] Submerged voices within the sources both reveal and veil attitudes and perspectives.

Several testimonies provided by Indigenous men and women are kept at the PAOC archives among NLM records. Reading them "against the grain" reveals Indigenous perceptions of the PAOC, the NLM, and its directors. Sermons and testimonies are particularly valuable for historical research, as through these mediums, Indigenous Pentecostals might be more candid and likely to express sentiments not typically shared in common parlance.[70] Still, within the missionary record, the indigenous principle can and does blur into inculturation. Several testimonies were recorded and curated by Euro-Canadian missionaries. While the testimonies do not provide evidence per se of PAOC-attempted assimilation, the ones contained within the archives appear to be written from a perspective partial to the PAOC.

Potentially as important as the testimonies' content is what is left unsaid.[71] Opinions excluded from the sources must also be considered. Essentially, this monograph attempts to "present and listen to voices commonly ignored."[72] The historian interrogates a document to ascertain the audience to which it is addressed, which issues seem intentionally ignored, and what is said without explicit articulation. Other issues to examine include the ways in which Pentecostalism, as adopted by Indigenous adherents, differed either from other expressions of Christianity they had previously encountered or from Pentecostalism as practised by other groups of people. Only rarely does Christian mission operate simply as traffic along a one-way street; there is always an exchange. This monograph examines both sides of that exchange, investigating potential reversal of roles, leading to PAOC personnel's alteration of Pentecostal practices because of interaction with Indigenous people's religious and cultural norms.[73] For instance, another missiological practice analyzed within this monograph is that of contextualization, which is the intentional integration of cultural expressions into Christian devotion for the purposes of making missionary efforts more accessible and engaging, and to encourage the autonomizing process.[74] This practice becomes increasingly interesting in instances where missionaries not only advocate such practices, but also integrate them into their personal devotional lives.

Related to this point, Tolly Bradford and Chelsea Horton observed:

> During recent decades, scholars ... have dissected the intricate and powerful roles played by Christianity in the colonization and transformation of Indigenous societies. Challenging established narratives of the missionary-as-hero and the missionary-as-villain, these critical reappraisals of religious encounter have hinged on such concepts as cultural imperialism, hybridity, and especially, Indigenous agency and action.[75]

In reference to Diné Neo-Pentecostalism, Kimberly Jenkins Marshall continued this methodological dialogue, aptly articulating as follows:

> By focusing on the ways that Christianity has been *practiced* by Native Christians, we can begin to see the ways in which Native Christians (both past and present) have used Christianity as a tool to assert and maintain cultural stability. Rather than taking the perspectives of the missionaries (typically the authors of archival accounts) at face value, historians and ethnographers alike have been attending to Native perspectives on the mission encounter, with the aim of discovering "what native people *made* of the Christian tradition." These accounts tend to emphasize how Native people have used Christian forms such as hymn singing, funerary practices, interactional symbols, and language to preserve long-held values, community identities, languages, and kinship structures ... Natives have used adaptable strategies of rearticulation to forge alliances with diverse Christian actors in order to advance Native causes.[76]

Although the PAOC archives' collection is composed primarily of documents written by Euro-Canadians, these missionaries recorded their observations of Indigenous participants' involvement in Pentecostal worship, funerals, integration of Indigenous cultural practices, language preferences, and familial exchanges. Through critical interaction and interpretation, historians can derive a picture of Indigenous people's involvement in and adoption of Pentecostalism through the communities' encounter with the missionaries and their methods. This is one of a few approaches available to the historian in instances when interviews are no longer possible, such as in cases where early generations of Indigenous Pentecostals have since passed away.

Finally, throughout this monograph, the Indigenous Voice is elevated and heightened by drawing from the existing literature of influential Indigenous figures on this subject area, and by researching otherwise unpublicized documentary materials. Nevertheless, the historian would be remiss to disregard the particular sensitivity required with respect to Indigenous people's history and the history of encounters between Euro-Canadian representatives of the Christian churches and Indigenous people. Accordingly, this volume depends upon conversations carefully, respectfully, and sensitively undertaken with and alongside of Indigenous Pentecostal spiritual leaders according to methodological best practices, crucially resulting in their indispensable involvement in the observations and conclusions emerging from this monograph. Although typical protocol encourages presenting a gift of tobacco to an Indigenous elder being interviewed, doing so in an Indigenous Pentecostal context is not always appropriate. Accordingly, a gift of the participants' preferred coffee was given instead.[77] Principally those Indigenous Pentecostal leaders are: George Gunner (Moose Cree First Nation; Moose Factory, Ontario), Dan Collado (Kanien'kehá:ka; Tyendinaga Mohawk Territory, Ontario), and Levi Samson Beardy (Anishinini, the exonym for which is Oji-Cree; Bearskin Lake, Ontario).

On the subject of terminology, for the purposes of this monograph, "Indigenous" will be used when referring to an Aboriginal population group such as the First Nations, Métis, or Inuit peoples in what is now Canada. The uncapitalized spelling "indigenous" will be used in the standard sense to refer to the original inhabitants of an area elsewhere in the world. Typically, the phrase "indigenous principle" will not be capitalized, whereas when referring to Indigenous people in Canada, capitals will be used, except when another writer's work is cited. When referring specifically to Indigenous people within what is now the United States, this monograph generally will employ the term "Native American" as that is the most prevalently used term within US-based literature and parlance. In order to avoid the typical error of using settler-colonial state possessives to describe Indigenous people, for example "Canada's Indigenous people," this monograph instead will generally use more appropriate wordings such as "Indigenous people in what is now Canada." The distinction is considerable, as Indigenous nations assert sovereignty, and while some Indigenous people identify as Canadian, many do not.[78]

Even within Canada the term "Indigenous" is still broadly applied; for instance, "First Nations" alone refers to hundreds of culturally and linguistically distinct groups.[79] Accordingly, and wherever possible, when referring to First Nations individuals, this monograph will strive to identify the nation with which the individual identifies and, if possible, his or her ancestral and/or territorial home. Furthermore, to the extent that it possible and suitable, this monograph will strive to do so in a way that refers to national, linguistic, and preferred endonyms. For example, the First Nations that have been referred to as Cree, Oji-Cree, and mainline Ojibway will instead be referred to by their endonyms of Nehiyaw, Anishinini, and Ojibwe Anishinaabe respectively. As Nehiyaw has subregional endonyms, likewise those will be employed.[80] When referring to First Nations communities or individuals with respect to whose nationality the documentary record is silent, this monograph will refer to them as just that, "First Nations."

Periodically throughout this monograph the term "non-Indigenous" will be used in reference to people who are not Indigenous. This term too has subcategories. The term most frequently used will be "Euro-Canadian," which refers to Canadians whose ancestry is predominantly European. Varyingly other and more generic terms such as "Westerner" and "settler" will be used when referring to similar or collective groups who might not be Canadian but whose ancestry is European and who are inhabitants of other countries with comparable settler-colonial legacies such as Australia, New Zealand, and the United States. The term "newcomer" will also be employed, typically in reference to citizens and inhabitants of Canada whose ancestors were not Indigenous, European, nor Euro-Canadian. Realistically these terms are imperfect and do not adequately capture the complexity of the subjects of ethnicity and nationality. However, they do serve to facilitate the necessary discussions contained within this monograph.[81]

Lastly, throughout this monograph, any references that might otherwise be in the first person will instead refer to the subject as "the historian." This practice, although contributing to a more graceful prose, may not always aptly reveal the perspective (or bias) of the author. For that reason, it is helpful, at this time, to deviate from the third person and say something of authorial positionality. I identify as a settler Canadian. My ancestry is predominantly Euro-Canadian, and I am an anglophone. I furthermore identify as a Christian, and related to that (as well as of particular significance to this monograph), I am a practising minister holding ordination with the Pentecostal Assemblies of Canada. The PAOC is my home. Faith and family have been two consistent threads throughout my life, but the PAOC comes in a close third place. To this extent I too may be considered a PAOC insider.

Still, and as has been thoroughly stated, the pages of this monograph employ a critical method and seek balance in their analysis and evaluation of the PAOC and its missionary methods. My interrogation of the documentary record requires "self-scrutiny" and interpretation. It is my hope that self-awareness of my positionality will at least reduce the potential for "ideological interference."[82] That being the case, it is safe to state that one motivation for this monograph is as an exercise in self-reflexivity. Although I do not intend to express any condescension toward the missionaries, ministers, and leaders who contributed to the formation of this denomination, this monograph does seek to take account of the way things have been done. Finally, I am interested in reconciliation and hope that a recovery of the historical record may contribute to the process of pursuing that ideal.

Writing this history was neither as chronological nor as straightforward as I might have hoped; after all, institutions (certainly religious ones) do not always progress in a predictable trajectory that can be easily told as a narrative. I am reminded of the words of author Thomas King (Anigiduwagi, the exonym for which is Cherokee; San Francisco, California), who said that "writing a novel is buttering warm toast, while writing a history is herding porcupines with your elbows."[83] The historian is required to gather scattered fragments, piece them together as best as possible, and analyze them along the way. But quite a story do those pieces cumulatively tell. While this monograph strives to highlight the opinions and perspectives of Indigenous Pentecostals, I am not so presumptuous as to assume that it speaks on their behalf. I wrote this book, but I do not own this story. Thus, any mistakes contained herein are entirely my own.

CHAPTER OVERVIEW

The process of analyzing the above-described materials constitutes a chronological progression divided into six chapters and a conclusion, laid out as below and addressing the following areas:

Chapter 1, "Pentecostalism's Place," outlines the PAOC's origins and then provides a very cursory account of the history of European and Euro-Canadian mission to Indigenous people. This approach draws out parallels with other denominations in their respective domestic missionary enterprises, thereby positioning the PAOC within the historical exchange between Euro-Canadian missionaries and Indigenous people.

Chapter 2, "The Heavens Have Become a Highway," introduces and features Northland Mission founder John Spillenaar. As the PAOC's first missionary pilot and the NLM's founding and longest-tenured director (1943–76), Spillenaar warrants special attention. This chapter also emphasizes that the NLM did not start as a mission to Indigenous people specifically. Rather the NLM began as a general evangelistic initiative based in north-central Canada, and only through the advent of aviation developed into a mission to Indigenous people. This chapter examines some of the reasons some

Indigenous people chose to become Pentecostal, assessing the areas of overlap between Pentecostalism and Indigenous traditional spiritualities. Not long after the PAOC adopted its mission to Indigenous people, the denomination realized the need to train Indigenous ministry leaders.

Chapter 3, "Leadership Qualities and the Call of God for the Ministry," describes the NLM's Bible college, which represents the Mission's best attempt to fulfill its claim of the indigenous principle. However, rather than providing accessible education for ministry trainees, the college ultimately faltered as it struggled to satisfy the PAOC's surprisingly stringent requirements for ministerial credentialling. In the end the college became less interested in empowering Indigenous ministry leaders and more concerned with its own survival.

Chapter 4, "Contention and Contextualization," examines the NLM's documentary record, lending special attention to the Indigenous Voice. NLM leaders and missionaries believed themselves to be proponents of Indigenous autonomy, but a thorough reading of the documentary record reveals that they ignored and opposed Indigenous culture and opinions for decades, promoting a Euro-Canadian brand of Evangelical Christianity. Simultaneously the NLM's Indigenous ministers vied to contribute to the mission's direction while mission leaders subtly undermined them.

Chapter 5, "Standing at the Shoreline," demonstrates that by the 1990s, financial and socio-political factors finally left the PAOC with little option but to empower Indigenous ministers to lead their own ministries. In 1996 the PAOC dissolved the NLM, replacing it with Aboriginal Pentecostal Ministries (APM). Although left without assets, in the subsequent decade the APM's Indigenous leaders more than doubled its number of churches.

Chapter 6, "Past, Present and Future," addresses the fruition of the indigenous principle during an era of apology and reconciliation within the PAOC's Aboriginal Ministries, demonstrating striking parallels to similar processes occurring nationally and in the longer-established churches. Finally, the chapter demonstrates that although Pentecostalism remains a prominent religious force among Indigenous people, these communities' allegiances are not always directed toward the PAOC. The now century-old denomination is currently one of several Pentecostal players attracting Indigenous adherents, a trend that may present challenges, but also opportunities, for the denomination's future.

The conclusion, "Breaking New Ground," provides a final analysis of this monograph's arguments and findings. The conclusion further points to opportunities for future research, identifying parallels between Indigenous Pentecostalism in Canada and the explosive growth of Pentecostalism in the Majority World. It also reflects on the PAOC's past mismanagement of its ministry to Indigenous people, pointing at the implications of this for the present as the PAOC becomes increasingly diverse along cultural, ethnic, linguistic, and gender lines.

CONCLUSION

Historian of Christianity and missiologist Dana Robert stated: "The story of how Pentecostalism has affected missionary activity and emerging indigenous Christianity is just beginning to be told."[84] Michael Wilkinson reiterated that Indigenous Pentecostalism in Canada is "a story yet to be told."[85] Given the movement's significance, a monograph addressing the history of Pentecostalism among Indigenous people is warranted.[86] Indeed, this monograph provides the first comprehensive, book-length treatment of the subject.

Still, the history of Pentecostalism's encounter with Indigenous people cannot properly be understood apart from the broader histories of Canadian Pentecostalism, as well as Pentecostalism's place among the longer-established denominations which the PAOC joined in their missions to Indigenous people. This context is one of complex dialogue and dynamic religious encounter, as well as one of cultural exchange between Indigenous people and predominantly Euro-Canadian missionaries. Furthermore, the history of Indigenous Pentecostalism in north-central Canada can be viewed as a story of Indigenous assertion, endurance, and persistence. As such, the NLM and its missionaries present some puzzles for the historian.

While the PAOC may not have been innocent of attempting to assimilate Indigenous mission participants, it did have an advantage over other, longer-established churches in that it did not represent as much of the pre-existing cultural assimilative history so frequently associated with those churches. While it is commonly assumed that conversion constitutes a one-way process of cultural loss, Pentecostalism proved that it can co-exist with Indigenous culture and in dialogue with the religious and spiritual traditions that preceded it. That is to say that conversion implies transition and transformation, but it simultaneously involves continuity.[87] Thus, although the fulfilment of the indigenous principle stalled, it appears that ultimately the PAOC attracted Indigenous adherents with some degree of success. It is to this seeming paradox that chapter 1 of this monograph now turns its attention.

1

Pentecostalism's Place

Positioning the Pentecostal Assemblies of Canada within the Encounter between Euro-Canadian Missionaries and Indigenous People

A new alliance of church and ... government ... promoted fundamental changes in those First Nations ... They tried to convert Natives in religious terms and to remake them culturally by the twin instruments of church and school ... In these new institutions, children were insulated from the influences of their own people and subjected to a program designed to lead them to forget who they were and adopt the ways and values of their teachers.

J.R. Miller, University of Saskatchewan[1]

The Pentecostal missionary impulse ... is part of the broader missionary activity of Protestantism ... shaped by Victorian sensibilities and ... is one of colonial encounter between Europeans and the rest of the world as they endeavoured to "unify the world through a twofold process involving modernization and Christianization."

Michael Wilkinson, Trinity Western University[2]

Back in the 17, 18, 1900s the priests didn't know that we were all worshipping the same God. They were greedy, they wanted all our souls. Look at the Pentecostals today, they come in, they storm the reserve. They get a few souls but they ain't going to get them all.

Michael W. Francis, Mi'kmaq[3]

Pentecostals intensively engaged in mission to Indigenous people in what is now Canada during the second half of the twentieth century. However, compared to the longer-established churches, the Pentecostal Assemblies of Canada (PAOC) proved a latecomer to this mission. When Pentecostals commenced in mission, they built upon a foundation already established by churches such as the Anglican, Catholic, Presbyterian, and United. While the PAOC came to view itself as espousing a mission and vision distinct from the longer-established churches' civilizing and missionizing efforts, in many ways the PAOC replicated their methods. This included the PAOC's inheritance of the longer-established churches' "Three-Self" or native church policy missiological model.

This chapter introduces the PAOC through a brief synopsis of the denomination's origins. Subsequently it discusses the Christian missionary background preceding the PAOC's prominence. Accordingly, this chapter endeavours to discuss early missionary activity for the purpose of identifying some of the reasons why the interests of many Indigenous people might have shifted toward Pentecostalism during the twentieth century.[4] Finally, this chapter positions the PAOC as a denominational entity built on top of a religious foundation that was established by the longer-established churches, and in many cases still remains.

CLASSICAL PENTECOSTAL ORIGINS

When referring to Pentecostals, it is necessary to define exactly what is meant. Pentecostalism's theories and practices, of course, are traceable to the Bible, particularly the New Testament books of the Acts of the Apostles and the Epistles to the Corinthians. The beginning of this twentieth-century religious movement, however, comprises a polygenesis that can be traced to a number of theological currents prevalent in North America and beyond during the century prior.[5]

Multiple influences such as Methodism and its descendant Holiness movements contributed to the spiritual fervour of the late nineteenth century and fertilized the ground from which Pentecostalism would sprout. Fledgling charismatic groups sprang up in the United States and beyond, prioritizing the distinctive doctrines of baptism in the Holy Spirit (described more fully below) and divine healing.[6] Important revivals had been taking place in Wales and India, with word of the revivals spreading through missionary networks and periodicals.[7] A similar revival commenced at Charles Parham's Holiness

Bible college, famous in Pentecostal lore for its corporate experience of speaking in tongues, in Topeka, Kansas, circa 1900. Related events occurred thereafter at the Azusa Street Revival, conducted by William Seymour in Los Angeles beginning in 1906.[8] For three years Seymour's Apostolic Faith Mission served as the American hub for the burgeoning classical Pentecostal movement.[9]

It is interesting to note that Indigenous leaders had been emerging within the Holiness movement before, during, and following the Azusa Street Revival, such as through the "Mohave Indian revival," which took place after 1903, conducted by George Mutcumalya (Aha Makhav; Needles, California). Furthermore, Native Americans, as well as Indigenous spiritual seekers from what is now Mexico, participated directly in the Azusa Street Revival and its derivatives, with records of adherents quickly joining the nascent movement in Oregon and Washington.[10]

Classical Pentecostalism is generally Evangelical Protestant in its theology; however, it maintains a unique stance on the doctrine of baptism in the Holy Spirit. Generally, Pentecostals interpret the book of Acts to imply that the baptism in the Holy Spirit – the defining Pentecostal position – occurs subsequent to salvation, is distinct from sanctification, is experiential, is evidenced by speaking in tongues and other associated charisms, and is for the purpose of empowering the believer to evangelize boldly.[11] Believing the aforementioned twentieth-century charismatic outpourings were replicas of the apostles' Upper Room experience described in Acts 2, Pentecostals also believe Christ's second coming to be imminent. Holy Spirit baptism's boldness to witness is instrumental for attracting as many adherents as possible in anticipation of Christ's awaited return. As such, in both its doctrine and missiology, Pentecostalism espouses eschatological and pneumatological emphases, with both contributing to a sense of evangelistic urgency.[12]

The nascent Canadian Pentecostal movement drew its adherents, and inherited its missionary impulse, in large part from Charles and Ellen Hebden's East End Mission and revival of 1906.[13] There is no historical evidence indicating the Hebdens had any interaction with William Seymour's Apostolic Faith Mission on Azusa Street, Los Angeles, during the same year. Further, historical evidence suggests the East End Mission originated independently from the Apostolic Faith Mission. Ellen Hebden became the first historically confirmed individual to undergo the Pentecostal baptism in the Holy Spirit in Canada.

For that matter, the Hebdens recorded a number of firsts. Not least of these was their role in establishing the first Pentecostal mission to Indigenous people not only in Canada, but likely in North America.[14]

Within five months of Ellen's Pentecostal event, eighty others had shared in the same experience. Reports of the East End Mission – located at 651 Queen Street East in Toronto – spread throughout Ontario and internationally. Toronto became referred to as a "Canadian Jerusalem," with Pentecostal pilgrims making the East End Mission an essential stopping point. In September 1908, the city became the location of the world's first Pentecostal Workers' Convention.[15] Finally, most of Canada's early Pentecostal evangelists originated from the East End Mission and were responsible for establishing many of the earliest Pentecostal churches in Canada, some of which are still in existence at the time of writing.[16]

Still, the Hebdens were opposed to denominational organization, believing it would quell the spontaneity of their revival. This view was not uncommon among some of the Hebdens' Canadian contemporaries.[17] Thus, in part, the denominational structures eventually adopted by the PAOC are generally attributable to the Pentecostal movement's American influences.[18] The first generation of Pentecostals in Canada developed strong relationships with their contemporaries in the United States.[19] By the twentieth century's second decade, American-based Pentecostal ministers and missionaries were networking through camp meetings, revival circuits, and newsletter and periodical publications. This fledgling circle felt the need to formalize their organization. Three hundred such like-minded ministers gathered in Hot Springs, Arkansas, in early April 1914. Their objectives were to: 1) forge connections between congregations; 2) continue the emphasis on evangelism at home and internationally; 3) provide better support for missionaries; 4) observe scriptural requirements for ecclesial oversight of churches; 5) unify under one name in order to apply for a federal charter; and 6) establish a ministerial training school. Howard Goss, pastor of the Pentecostal church in Hot Springs, began in 1913 to attract delegates by advertising in the aforementioned Pentecostal periodicals. In Hot Springs the delegates voted on core leadership, drafted and implemented a constitution, and chose the name "Assemblies of God," alluding to the New Testament scriptural passage of Hebrews 10:25.

More than just the PAOC's denominational older sibling, the Assemblies of God (AG USA) had a Canadian connection from the start.

J. Roswell Flower, although ultimately a United States resident, was born and raised in Belleville, Ontario. In 1914, aged twenty-five, Flower co-wrote the AG USA General Council Constitution.[20] Its "Preamble and Resolution" contained the following mandate:

> We recognize ourselves as a GENERAL COUNCIL of Pentecostal (Spirit Baptized) saints from local Churches of God in Christ, Assemblies of God, and various Apostolic Faith Missions and Churches, and Assemblies of like faith in the United States of America, Canada, and Foreign Lands, whose purpose is … to recognize Scriptural methods and orders for worship, unity, fellowship, work and business for God.[21]

The Hot Springs delegates elected Flower as the AG USA Presbytery's General Secretary. Following the AG USA's establishment, its ministers and churches began to form districts across North America and the world.[22]

In 1919, a network of twenty-seven Pentecostal churches in eastern Canada united to form the PAOC, to whom the Canadian federal government granted a charter under the *Companies Act*. The nascent PAOC adopted nearly word-for-word the AG USA's Constitution, effectively functioning as an international district of the denomination. In 1920 the PAOC partnered with another network of Pentecostal churches in western Canada, officially affiliating with the AG USA. The churches formed two districts: the Eastern and Western Canada District Councils of the AG USA.[23] The predominant motivation for officially integrating the Canadian districts into the AG USA was to train and deploy missionaries more effectively.[24] By the mid-1920s, however, the Canadian districts disagreed with some policies of AG USA's Missions Department. There were, of course, also geographic and diplomatic challenges to participating in a predominantly United States–based organization. In 1925 the Canadian districts withdrew from the AG USA, becoming again the autonomous PAOC, while maintaining cordial, ideological, and theological ties with their American counterpart. This included ultimately adopting the AG USA Statement of Fundamental Truths.[25]

Like the AG USA, quickly after its founding the PAOC established several districts. Throughout the twentieth century, the PAOC grew, becoming a nationwide denomination. In 1991, the PAOC claimed approximately 222,000 adherents, and in 2001, 232,000 adherents.

At the time of writing, the PAOC claims eight geographic districts, two linguistic branches, 250,839 adherents, 3,717 ministers, and 1,057 churches.[26] In Canada, the PAOC is both the largest Pentecostal organization and the largest Evangelical denomination.[27] While many Evangelical denominations are regionally concentrated, the PAOC is distributed evenly across the country, with churches in every province and territory except Newfoundland and Labrador (which has its own Assemblies of God–affiliated denomination, the Pentecostal Assemblies of Newfoundland and Labrador).[28] Further, the PAOC is the most ethnically and linguistically diverse Canadian Evangelical denomination.[29] Holding a high view of baptism in the Holy Spirit, the eschatological implications for such, and its related urgency for evangelism, a core PAOC distinctive element is emphasis on the necessity of mission.[30]

Obviously, mission is not exclusively the Pentecostals' domain. It is a core Christian concept, practised for nearly two millennia before classical Pentecostalism arose. PAOC missionaries were not the first to introduce Christianity to Indigenous people in what is now Canada, but rather proselytized a demographic that had already heard the message from earlier and even contemporaneous missionaries. To this end, the PAOC continued (perhaps at times unknowingly) many missionary methods inherited from its denominational predecessors.

A BRIEF SUMMARY OF CHRISTIAN MISSION AMONG INDIGENOUS PEOPLE IN WHAT IS NOW CANADA

The earliest recorded communication of Christianity to Indigenous people within what is now Canada occurred on the Gaspé Peninsula, on 20 July 1534. Jacques Cartier, sailing on behalf of France, landed and planted a cross, suggesting to the local Haudenosaunee (the exonym for which is Iroquois) that they should look to it for their salvation. Blair Stonechild (Anishinaabe, in this instance the exonym for which is Saulteaux; Muscowpetung, Saskatchewan), professor of Indigenous Studies at First Nations University of Canada, observed that through this action the colonizers furthermore "assumed ownership over the entirety of the land's inhabitants, animals, plants, and all other resources, the vast majority of which they had not even seen." Not surprisingly the Haudenosaunee were bewildered and resisted the incursion. Subsequently, Samuel de Champlain, a founder of the Acadia colony, maintained a vision of a new society that would be French in culture and Christian in religion. The population therein "would consist of converted Indians leavened with French colonists." Historians charge that Champlain's vision conflated Christian and colonial agendas, or perhaps more condemningly, co-opted Christianity for the purposes of colonization.[31]

Unimpressed by Indigenous culture and spirituality, European colonists perceived their Indigenous hosts "as people without cities, without roads or bridges, without governments or courts of law, without ... a written language, and, most seriously, without civilized manners."[32] Missionaries further were dismayed by the perceived absences of places of worship, ministerial ordination, liturgies, or any form of organized religion. Of course this perception did not reflect the reality of Indigenous traditional spiritualities, which were inseparable from any other dimension of Indigenous culture or feature of life. Indigenous people exercised deep spirituality, permeating all aspects of their experiences. Respect for Creator, a sense of shared relationship with creation, and a reverence for mystery all cumulatively served to fuse the natural with the supernatural.[33] Jack Forbes (Powhatan/Lenape/Saponi; Long Beach, California) wrote:

> "Religion" is, in reality, "living." Our "religion" is not what we profess, or what we say, or what we proclaim; our "religion" is what we do, what we desire, what we seek, what we dream about, what we fantasize, what we think – all of these things – twenty four hours a day. One's religion, then, is one's life, not merely the ideal life but life as it is actually lived.
>
> "Religion" is not prayer, it is not a church, it is not "theistic," it is not "atheistic," it has little to do with what white people call "religion." It is our every act ... All that we do, and are, is our religion.[34]

Terry LeBlanc likewise explains how

> Indigenous people ... say that the whole of our existence, in fact all that lies within the boundaries of existence, is of a spiritual nature. More than anything else, this is what differentiates Indigenous understandings from those of the majority in the Western Christian world.[35]

To this extent, and because spirituality was and typically remains so integrally practised among Indigenous people, there were no words for "religion" in Indigenous languages.[36] These facts might partially have influenced missionaries' misguided perceptions. In return, the Indigenous hosts saw missionaries as disrespectful toward Indigenous traditions and inept at living off the land. Generally, both the colonists (including the missionaries) and their Indigenous hosts tried to gauge how the other might meet their respective needs.[37]

For both colonists and missionaries, primary points of contact in early encounters were diplomacy, trade, war, and the communication of Christianity.[38] To be sure, geographic expansion and economic enterprise motivated European colonists. Still, Christianization maintained high priority. While Jesuits imported French culture, their key aim was "to save Indian souls." Accordingly, Jesuits effectively evangelized by communicating through Indigenous languages and adapting some cultural and traditional observances, adjusting them to Catholic purposes. In so doing, the Jesuits demonstrated a level of flexibility and pragmatism that other denominations' missionaries would not match for centuries.[39]

Of even greater consequence was the Jesuits' use of formal education as a device to retain and catechize Indigenous adherents. Indigenous boys went to Catholic schools, and later, acolyte men attended seminaries. The most promising of them transferred to France to continue their education. The Jesuits' use of education for missionary purposes established a standard since emulated by other denominations. Indigenous participants had long practised a measure of inculturation among themselves, viewing the varying religious beliefs of one nation as neither better nor worse than those of another.[40] Upon the arrival of Christianity, many carried this practice forward by adopting Catholicism and often blending it with their own Indigenous traditional spiritualities.[41] Religious studies scholar Solange Lefebvre (Université de Montréal) thus described the practice:

> The First Nations did not insist on spiritual exclusivity ... and so their "conversions" did not necessarily constitute a rejection of traditional ways. Europeans of the seventeenth and eighteenth centuries often idealized Native peoples as *bons sauvages* (noble savages, thought to represent humanity in its natural state of purity and innocence). Indeed many missionaries saw Aboriginal peoples as central figures in their utopian quest of recreating

the fervour of the primitive church and the simplicity of the apostolic church in New France.[42]

Throughout the Seven Years' War (1756–63) and following the 1763 Treaty of Paris, most North American colonies previously claimed by France came under British rule. Policies for relating to Indigenous people appeared in the 1763 Royal Proclamation. One policy sought friendship between Indigenous people and colonists. The Church of England adopted this approach. With "friendship" as the order of the day, British colonists were less fixated than the French on mission as a means of Europeanizing Indigenous converts. Although the British did make some efforts to this end, their larger interests remained mostly in matters of military strategy. Still, the Crown supported Anglican mission to Indigenous people, provided such efforts did not create controversy or social upheaval. Effectively the Crown wished for the Church's mission to complement the strategic goals of the state.[43]

During the years of peace following the Seven Years' War and later the American War of Independence (1775–83), Anglicans, Methodists, Congregationalists, and eventually Presbyterians all contributed varyingly to missionary efforts in the former colonies which now make up Canada. Thereafter some Indigenous Christian communities emigrated from the newly formed United States. Most Haudenosaunee (in particular Anglican Kanien'kehá:ka, the exonym for which is Mohawk) had fought on the side of the British, many relocating in the Canadian colonies. The Church Missionary Society (CMS), founded in 1799, existed as the Church of England's primary missionary arm, eventually operating throughout Canada's northwest. By the 1820s, CMS missionaries encountered Inuit with increasing frequency, and relied upon Inuktitut interpreters in their interactions with them. Other missionary agencies included the Church of Scotland's Glasgow Colonial Society and the Methodist Missionary Society of England.[44]

During the eighteenth century's closing decades, the American Episcopal Methodist Conference sent circuit preachers to the Canadian colonies. American Methodists such as William Case and Alvin Torrey were among the first Protestant missionaries to attempt to missionize members of the First Nations surrounding the Great Lakes. Among colonists, popular support for mission resulted from the series of revivals sweeping the British Isles and colonies.[45] Methodists launched their first formal mission to Indigenous people in what was then Upper

Canada among the Grand River Kanien'kehá:ka. In this region the Methodists competed with the Church of England for the loyalty of Indigenous adherents.[46]

By the mid-nineteenth century, Methodism's growth rendered it potentially the most popular brand of Christianity among Indigenous people. Indigenous Methodist clerics and evangelists – most notably Peter Jones, also known as Kahkewaquonaby or Sacred Feathers (Mississauga; Burlington Heights, Upper Canada) – accounted for Methodism's advances in such territories as the Credit River, Grape Island, Rice Lake, and Lake Simcoe.[47] Euro-Canadian Methodists took pride in this trend, believing their movement's success among Indigenous people indicated the effectiveness of civilizing through Christianization. These concepts became wedded, and missionaries assumed that "civilization" and "religion" formed the basic requirements for the establishment of an indigenized Christianity, with the only question being which would occur first.[48] These same Euro-Canadian Methodists expended great effort teaching trades, crafts, agriculture, and formal education to a frequently receptive Indigenous student base throughout the region. Teachers usually were Euro-Canadian, but Methodists also employed Indigenous evangelists. Described as a revival, this movement spread across Kanien'kehá:ka boundaries into Anishinàbemiwin-speaking (Algonquin) First Nations.[49]

Yet into the late nineteenth century, Methodist influence among First Nations declined. The atmosphere of the missions had become quite routine, the spontaneity of the movement's revivalist meetings waning. Subsequently, Indigenous initiative decreased as the first generation of leaders died off with few successors poised to replace them.[50] With an increasing Euro-Canadian population, subsequent loss of Indigenous lands through the settling and treaty processes, and the decreasing influence of Methodism among the region's nations, the missionary enterprise shifted attention from south to north. In these regions along the shorelines of Hudson Bay and James Bay, the populations predominantly were Nehiyawak, with some Anishininiwag, and Ojibweg Anishinaabeg further south. By going north, missionaries went to lands and peoples who later came under the influence of the PAOC's Northland Mission (NLM). The missionaries entered a region that was largely untouched by permanent colonial settlements.

The Jesuits had ventured through these regions during the previous century but had not maintained a lasting presence. In 1818 Catholic priests arrived to stay, marking a return and resurgence of Francophone

Catholic missionary work in the regions. Church of England missionaries followed. Through much of the nineteenth century, the rival Anglicans and Catholics competed for ecclesial hegemony in the north. In 1830 George Archbold, a missionary of the Anglican diocese of Quebec, went to Sault Ste Marie, Upper Canada. There, in 1832, the Church of England established a society for "converting and civilising the Indians." That same year, Upper Canada's Lieutenant-Governor Sir John Colborne sent William McMurray to Sault Ste Marie as well. Warmly welcomed, McMurray baptized 160 Ojibweg Anishinaabeg adherents in six years, and built a church and school there. The first Protestant worker to arrive in the James Bay region (a locale later frequented by NLM missionaries) was the Wesleyan George Barnley. The Wesleyan effort was not particularly successful, however; the subsequent Anglican mission to the region between Fort Severn and Little Whale, established in the summer of 1851, proved longer-lasting.[51]

In 1853 the Church of England ordained its first Indigenous priest, Henry Budd, in Manitoba.[52] In 1865 the Anglican Church named Robert Machray Bishop of the Northwest. Machray convened a conference of clergy and lay delegates, leading to the 1867 formation of a synod. Crucially, the bishop determined that the church in the region must be self-supporting, self-governing, and comprising a complement of Indigenous clergy were it to succeed. Thus Machray embarked on developing "indigenous churches."[53] In fact, this period was marked by significant Indigenous involvement in the propagation of church mission, with Christianity encountering many Indigenous communities independently from Euro-Canadian missionary effort. Testament to their effectiveness is the fact that First Nations as far west as present-day British Columbia had become aware of Christianity as early as the 1830s, long predating Euro-Canadian missionaries' permanent presence.[54]

In 1889 John Horden, the Anglican Bishop of Moosonee, visited Big Trout Lake and Fort Severn (later major NLM mission locales), baptizing and confirming two hundred Anishininiwag and Nehiyawak adherents. Meanwhile, Methodism's occasional appearance in the north paled in comparison to its prominence in the south, and to the magnitude of Anglicanism and Catholicism in the north.[55] The Presbyterian Church in Canada – although a relative latecomer – showed some early promise of autonomizing its ministry efforts among Indigenous people in northwestern Canada.[56] By 1887, four out of the ten ordained Presbyterian missionaries working among Indigenous people on the Prairies were themselves Indigenous.[57] Presbyterian missionaries and laity interacted, and the cultures and traditions of both were recognized. Yet when the churches shifted their attention toward residential schooling (described subsequently), this "middle ground" eroded.[58]

Even as the longer-established churches experienced success in attracting acolytes and in further training some Indigenous clergy, eventually these churches became less desirable for would-be adherents. Some Indigenous people began to resist the longer-established churches, perceiving participation in church leadership as increasingly unattainable. Fewer adherents were interested in lengthy seminary training or the celibate lifestyle of Catholic vocations. Additionally, Anglican and Catholic Church hierarchies were reluctant to alter ordination requirements. Further, the Canadian nation-building enterprise introduced new ideologies, threatening the established norms for Euro-Canadian and Indigenous relations, and infiltrating the churches' missionary policies. As the twentieth century approached, these factors combined and contributed to a regression from what had been a hopeful period for Indigenous ministry leadership.[59]

Canadian Confederation in 1867 marked a most significant turning point. Aiming to establish a Euro-Canadian national identity, the government redoubled assimilative policies, with churches becoming integral to the process. It had not been uncommon for governments to employ religion for colonial purposes. For instance, William Baldridge (Anigiduwagi) maintained that a "central agent in the colonization of this hemisphere has been the Christian church."[60] To this point the church-state relationship had been both implicit and symbiotic. The unofficial partnership involved the processes of missionization and acculturation, whereby "the kerygmatic content of the missionary's Christian faith became confused with the accoutrements of the missionary's cultural experience and behavior."[61] But by the late nineteenth century, Canadian churches had become complicit in these assimilative efforts, playing official and key roles in the establishment of and negotiations for the federal Indian Reserve system. Concerned by what they perceived to be nomadic lifestyles among Indigenous people, the churches found it difficult to adequately catechize a broadly dispersed population. The churches partnered with government in its negotiation with Indigenous people towards the establishment of reserves. The churches' embrace of reserves marked a missiological shift from encouraging Indigenous autonomy to practising paternalistic protectionism (or, perhaps more aptly, isolation) and attempted assimilation.[62]

Among other things, the reserves contributed to keeping populations concentrated, in an endeavour to ease their integration into church life, and allowing the churches to attempt "civilizing" Indigenous adherents to Western norms through missionary expression. By 1876 the partnership of Church and Crown received the full force of law through the first *Indian Act*, intended to separate Indigenous people from their traditions, and continue the assimilative effort.[63] Thus the reserves definitively affected Indigenous people's culture, economy, politics, and lives. The reserve system, today a mainstay of Indigenous life, still carries the unmistakeable fingerprints of the longer-established churches, who willfully partnered with the state in its negotiations thereof.[64]

In addition to the reserve system, during the late nineteenth and much of the twentieth centuries, the Canadian federal government established day, boarding, industrial, and later residential schools for Indigenous youths. The Final Report of the Truth and Reconciliation Commission of Canada (TRC, 2015) described the schools and their legacy as part of "the larger international context of colonial policies that predated the schools and have continued on after their closing."[65] The Riel Resistance of 1885 (historically referred to as the North-West Rebellion, a short and ill-fated uprising by the Métis people led by Louis Riel)[66] frightened the federal government. Blair Stonechild posits that First Nations people also contributed to the Resistance, the government's response to which was the mobilization of the greatest number of troops amassed to that point in Canada's history. Forty-two First Nations people were convicted, including eight who were sentenced to death by hanging. This constituted the largest mass hanging in Canadian history, witnessed by hundreds of people from nearby First Nations territories, who were "brought to witness the executions." The government furthermore responded to the resistance by sentencing Riel himself to death by hanging, and by funding "Indian schools."[67]

The schools' key goal was to contain and subdue Indigenous nationalism and spirituality through Canadianization and Christianization. The longer-established churches were instrumental in the schools' operations, which represented the "biggest single item in the budget" for the Anglican mission. For the Presbyterian Church in Canada, "the schools became the primary mission tool reaching Native peoples."[68] Although operated by the churches, these schools existed largely as instruments for the assimilation of Indigenous youths to Euro-Canadian cultural norms. Many clergy believed "conversion was not complete until the hair was cut, the blanket was shredded, and the new convert entirely torn from the evil influences of the Native environment."[69] For their part, proponents of assimilation considered their efforts to be humanitarian in nature, believing that

> Aborigines could hope to survive only by becoming like Europeans ... and it was the responsibilities of missionaries and administrators to give them all possible help ... to cope with European technology ... adapt[ing] to European economic patterns, and eventually ... adopt[ing] European manners and dress.[70]

Contrastingly, Canadian Presbyterian historian Peter Bush described the schools' agenda as "nothing less than the social and moral reconstruction of the Native people."[71]

The government apprehended many Indigenous youths from their homes, entrusting them to the churches' supposed care. Students had classes and chapel, but spent half of their time working in fields and kitchens, doing laundry, sewing, or doing other various chores. The churches rationalized this curriculum, claiming it instructed Indigenous youths in Euro-Canadian agricultural, marketplace, and domestic disciplines. More realistically these arduous tasks served to reduce overall expenses through the fruit of students' labours. Canadian historian of Christianity Alan Hayes assessed the system thus:

> The collaboration between "throne and altar" was an odd one. The Church saw Indians as souls to be saved and converts to be educated; the government saw Indians as a political problem to be solved, preferably without undue expense. For both Church and government, "civilizing" Indians (that is, europeanizing them) was part of the strategy.[72]

Unsurprisingly the schools contributed to the deterioration of churches' relations with Indigenous people, and signalled an even further departure from previous efforts to equip Indigenous clergy. Bush maintained that rather than "being places where Native church leaders were formed, the schools became institutional ministries and symbols of the church's partnership in the dominant culture's assimilation of Native peoples."[73] This missionary model continued for more than a century, with latent remnants persisting into the late twentieth century.[74] For instance, in 1963 the Anglican Church historian Philip Carrington wrote: "The 'Indian School Administration' ... has been carried on for many years ... with extraordinary vigour and ability, negotiating with the Department of Indian Affairs on the one hand and the Diocesan Bishops on the other."[75]

The churches' assimilative policies were not constrained to the schools. Common observances such as the potlatch and Sun Dance likewise drew missionaries' ire. While Indigenous people prioritized these practices as means of maintaining cultural observations and integration within and among communities, missionaries typically perceived them to be a distraction from industriousness, as well as involving the celebration of "'drinking, gambling, horse-racing, and changing of wives' ... contrary to the church's moral standards."[76] Likewise, politicians legislated bans on the former – sometimes going so far as to criminalize them, jailing participants – constituting an extensive attack on Indigenous cultural practices.[77]

It is worth pausing to note that denominations and missionaries were not homogeneous in their mindsets. Neither are these observations intended to suggest that as a rule, church leaders consciously made or even understood the significance of this assimilative shift. Certainly the churches' missions could still be advanced through education, medical work, and aid. However, when evangelism ceased to be the primary motivation for these tasks, the churches were no longer missional entities exclusively, rather becoming purveyors "of the social mores of the dominant culture."[78] The consequences of these changes were enormous. Not surprisingly, Indigenous participants resisted the education system, associating it with the attempted eradication of their culture, and with the decline of adolescent health owing to malnutrition, emotional abuse, and physical and sexual abuse and assault, among other factors.[79] In the popular, public memory, the churches' domestic mission legacies have become all but indistinguishable from the substantial stain of residential schooling. What is more, the governments', schools', and churches' actions in this regard increasingly have been labelled genocide.[80]

The longer-established churches continued to evangelize actively during the twentieth century. Salient is that the Indigenous revivalistic fervour of the nineteenth century had waned because of the process of institutionalization. Further, the priority of civilizing through Europeanization vis-à-vis the reserve and residential schooling systems became a major preoccupation for the longer-established churches. It may be argued that civilizing (forcibly attempting to make Indigenous people into Canadians) drew the longer-established churches' attention away from discipling (forming Christian acolytes) and the training of Indigenous clergy. Although some ordination of Indigenous ministerial candidates was ongoing throughout the assimilative period, it was not until the late 1940s that the longer-established churches began to realize the culturally damaging effect of their residential schooling system. Thereafter the churches gradually shifted their Indigenous mission policies from assimilation to recognition of their role in colonialism.[81] For their part, the longer-established churches have since apologized to Indigenous people for their assimilative policies, as well as for the wrongs of residential schooling, and have sought reconciliation. Chapter 6 will address these themes more fully.

The Anglican, Catholic, and Methodist churches' long history and tradition of mission among Indigenous people predated the Pentecostals' arrival by more than a century. Anglican missionaries in Canada's north were particularly prominent. The Church of England's primary missionary organization, the Society for the Propagation of the Gospel in Foreign Parts (SPG), was renowned for its efficiency and systematic organization. By 1900 the SPG had installed 389 missionaries in Ontario, who successfully won over local adherents.[82] Yet this success was not without interruption. 1893 marked the formal birth of the Church of England in Canada, signalling its autonomy from its founding church in England. While the Anglican Church continued to prioritize mission to Indigenous people through the twentieth century, in some ways the stage was being set for the Pentecostals' numeric success. Independent from its British antecedent denomination, Canadian Anglicanism's missionary efforts experienced financial burden. By 1905, the London-based CMS began to withdraw support from Canadian operations. Finally, from 1911 to 1922 the SPG began phasing out its grants to several Canadian dioceses, with all SPG subsidy to the Anglican Church ceasing in 1940. From then, the Domestic and Foreign Missionary Society – the primary missionary arm of the Church of England in Canada – felt its domestic missions bear the brunt of the fiscal shortfall.[83]

Into this socio-religious milieu, the PAOC inserted its evangelistic message, experiencing some success at winning over Indigenous adherents. Additional factors, such as Anglican clergy returning to England following the First World War, the Great Depression, and rapid immigration following the Second World War,[84] contributed to an environment that allowed newly arrived Pentecostal missionaries to fill gaps left by the atrophying Anglican effort.

THE PAOC'S MISSIONS TO INDIGENOUS PEOPLE AND INTERACTIONS WITH OTHER CHURCHES

Before the 1940s, what missionary effort the PAOC extended toward Indigenous people held no specific focus or significant organization. PAOC work among Indigenous populations in the Manitoba and Northwestern Ontario District (MNWOD) has the longest continuous history, although early efforts were neither formal nor coordinated. Canada's first Pentecostal congregation was in Winnipeg (by the 1930s named Calvary Temple, led by Canadian Pentecostal pioneer Watson Argue). Calvary commenced outreach to surrounding Indigenous populations as early as 1907, over a decade before the PAOC's formal organization. It should be noted that not only did the church reach out to these populations, but many Indigenous pilgrims also travelled by dogsled and train from northerly territories to visit Calvary Temple.[85] The early Canadian Pentecostal pioneer, statesman, and Winnipeg pastor A.H. Argue recorded at least one such episode:

> A company of Indians from Fisher River and other Indian reservations, about two hundred miles north of Winnipeg, hearing of this gracious outpouring, came to see for themselves. Soon they were down on their faces before God and a number of them received this wonderful Baptism. On the return of these Indians to their reservation a remarkable revival broke out in their midst, and God's Word truly was confirmed with signs and wonders and diverse miracles and gifts of the Holy Ghost.[86]

The Winnipeg-based pastor A.G. Ward, who would go on to become missionary secretary of the PAOC, followed the group back to Fisher River Cree Nation (Néhinaw), Manitoba, to participate in the revival. While preaching through an interpreter there, Ward began speaking in tongues. Apparently Ward's outburst was in Nêhinawêwin, as his interpreter replied, "Why, you are now speaking to us in our own language." British Pentecostal pioneer, pastor, and author Stanley Howard Frodsham recorded of the event: "It was a call for these Indians to advance. This remarkable manifestation had a marked effect on the hearers."[87]

Concurrent events took place, whereby messengers of Pentecostalism (both Indigenous and non-Indigenous) carried the movement to the northern Manitoba communities of Peguis First Nation (Anishinaabe), Lake St Martin First Nation (Ojibwe Anishinaabe), and Pinaymootang First Nation (historically referred to as Fairford River; Anishinaabe, in this instance the exonym for which is Saulteaux) by 1911. Néhinaw Pentecostal evangelist Jim McKay (Fisher River Cree Nation), spread the message to Pinaymootang, and later Norway House Cree Nation (Néhinaw), Cross Lake First Nation (Néhinaw), and other communities in the region. McKay characteristically would visit a home in the community, where he sang and played his accordion, following which he shared the Pentecostal message. Oftentimes McKay was able "to start a church in the host family's home, and eventually to establish the Pentecostal church in the community." McKay succeeded in so doing, notwithstanding the fact that he lacked formal theological training.[88] The PAOC church birthed in Fisher River, named "The House of Prayer," celebrated its sixtieth anniversary in 1977, claiming to be "the oldest Indian Pentecostal Church in Canada."[89]

While pastoring in Parkside, Saskatchewan, in 1925, PAOC pioneer Walter McAlister reached out to the Nehiyaw community in Mistawasis First Nation, Saskatchewan.[90] That same year in southeastern Ontario, Nehiyawak people participated in Pentecostal mission outreaches in Ottawa. Near Deseronto, Ontario, there was a church with entirely Kanien'kehá:ka membership, established during the early 1930s. Also founded in the 1930s was a church in Kanesatake (Kanien'kehá:ka; near Oka, Quebec). This congregation's origins traced to lay evangelists from a non-PAOC-affiliated, independent Italian Pentecostal congregation in Montreal.[91] In southern Ontario, *Testimony* recorded a small Kanien'kehá:ka Pentecostal chapel in Brant County in 1939.[92]

On another occasion, this time in British Columbia, the activity of Indigenous adherents predated that of Euro-Canadian Pentecostal evangelists and missionaries. In 1909 a First Nations Pentecostal man recounted that he had been crossing from the United States through the Salish Sea during a violent storm. The traveller prayed for deliverance and docked safely in Victoria, perhaps marking the earliest arrival of an Indigenous Pentecostal in BC. Later that evening he offered up a prayer of thanksgiving and "saw a tongue of fire descend" on his canoe.[93] Similarly, sixty representatives of First Nations communities in northern British Columbia travelled south by boat to Vancouver in 1923 to experience the ministry of healing evangelist and PAOC affiliate Charles S. Price.[94]

It would be another two decades before Euro-Canadian Pentecostal missionaries undertook working in these regions. When at first they began to do so, their efforts tended to be quite independent, with the limited mission work occurring in a highly localized or regional manner. Thus, it is helpful to review these regional PAOC domestic missionary efforts, which began in earnest in the 1940s.

British Columbian Pentecostals used "Gospel Boats," converted trawlers ferrying evangelists to First Nations territories in northwestern and coastal British Columbia.[95] Some early First Nations adherents were drawn over to Pentecostalism from the Indian Shaker Church through the work of one of the PAOC's collegial denominations, the classical Pentecostal Four-Square Church, in the region now called the Pacific Northwest.[96] The evangelistic fervour continued through the British Columbia and Yukon District (BCYD) and ultimately was carried on by Indigenous Pentecostals among their respective communities.[97] By the 1950s, coastal evangelism had contributed to the establishment of twelve Indigenous Pentecostal congregations, totalling three hundred members.[98] In 1967 Charles Whaley, of the Mission for Canadian Natives in Vancouver, established the West Coast Indian Pentecostal Bible School. Whaley sought to recruit First Nations commercial fishers to attend his college during the winter fishing offseason, attracting eight students to the first-year class.[99] Later Jack and Peggy Kennedy contributed to the leadership of the BCYD's Native Pentecostal Bible College in Vancouver into the 1990s.[100]

Across the country, evangelism began among Inuit, Métis, and First Nations.[101] In 1940 the PAOC enacted the Home Mission and Extension Department, "aimed at reaching the unevangelized in our country especially the non-English speaking people."[102] In 1958 the department became further formalized by means of a PAOC General Conference decision establishing the Department of Home Missions and Bible Colleges. Distinguishing Home Missions from International Missions meant the PAOC (particularly the geographic districts) began

Figure 1.1 PAOC Home Missions map

to concentrate attention on reaching Indigenous communities.[103] Still, ministry among Indigenous people occupied a somewhat exotic space in the Euro-Canadian, Pentecostal mind. In the late 1950s, PAOC historian Gloria Kulbeck lauded missionaries' efforts in the face of seemingly overwhelming economic, ecological, and infrastructural obstacles. She employed characteristically Pentecostal and Lucan terminology to explain:

> In spite of these hindrances, many … have carried the gospel into Canada's Northland. Some have gone to "Judea," that is, Northern Ontario and Quebec; others have gone to "Samaria," that is, the lake country of Northern Manitoba; still others have ventured into "the uttermost part of the earth," as a part of the Sub-Arctic Mission of the Pentecostal Assemblies of Canada.[104]

Said Sub-Arctic Mission in the Northwest Territories centred on the H.H. Williams Memorial Hospital in Hay River. Started as a postwar nursing station, the hospital became fully accredited in the late 1950s. It was the first and only hospital the PAOC operated within Canada and the only Pentecostal hospital in North America. PAOC General Superintendent W.E. McAlister, Executive Director of Home Missions Tom Johnstone, Edmonton Central Pentecostal Tabernacle's pastor

R. Taitinger, and PAOC Alberta and Northwest Territories (ABNWT) District Superintendent S. Tilton all were on hand for the dedication of the H.H. Williams Memorial Hospital on 13 October 1957. The hospital was named for the generous endowment from the estate of the late Toronto-based businessman and philanthropist H.H. Williams. Williams had served as the chair of the board of governors of Toronto's Hospital for Sick Children, and had been a long-time member of the Stone Church Pentecostal Assembly in Toronto, which supported Ken Gaetz's mission. Hailing originally from Edmonton, Ken Gaetz graduated from the PAOC's Western Bible College in Winnipeg, Manitoba, in April 1948. He arrived in Hay River in 1949 "to begin a Pentecostal ministry among Northerners." Ken and his wife Sarah coordinated the hospital while also itinerating among First Nations and Inuit territories by dogsled. One missionary described Sarah Gaetz as only "the tenth white woman to come to this northern outpost … [whose] population consisted of a few white fisherman … about 300 Indians … a Mounty, the Anglican nurse, and a few school teachers." The Gaetzes completed construction of a Pentecostal chapel in May of 1950, the first church to be built in the settlement of Hay River. As the Gaetzes simultaneously directed the Sub-Arctic Mission, evangelized, pastored, and operated the hospital, they filled the joint roles of missionaries, pastors, and paramedics. Under the ABNWT's purview, the mission maintained stations in about twelve NWT locales, reaching as far north as Fort Norman (present-day Tulita) and Coppermine (Inuit; present-day Kugluktuk, Nunavut).[105]

Ken Gaetz demonstrated considerable cognisance of Indigenous traditions and frequently ministered to Deh Cho Dene communities that allegedly had no prior knowledge of Christianity. Missionary literature described this early period of the Gaetzes' ministry thus:

> The Natives love to sing the Gospel songs … ceremonial chants and dances with drums. They … sing in Slavey or English until their throats are husky. Time means nothing to them, and the services last for hours. Each one has his say in a testimony or sermonette. Their worship is spontaneous, vigorous, and inspiring … [T]hey accept the Gospel, the Baptism of the Holy Sprit, and Divine healing … Naturally warm-hearted and emotional … they clap their hands, beat time with their feet, and sing or praise the Lord … At this time they were comparatively unspoiled by the evils of our civilization.[106]

Through the years, Ken Gaetz associated closely with the neighbouring Katl'odeeche First Nation chief John Lamalice (Deh Cho Dene). Lamalice became a devoted Pentecostal adherent, translating Gaetz's sermons as the duo visited "different Indian camps ... on board ... that long journey down the MacKenzie River to the Arctic Circle." Both Ken and Sarah Gaetz studied Dene vocabulary as they evangelized Dene settlements scattered along the banks of the Mackenzie River aboard their boats christened *Messenger* and *Messenger II*. While the lion's share of the ABNWT's missionary effort concentrated on the Northwest Territories, periodically Ken Gaetz ventured into Alberta to work among Dene First Nations there, with the assistance of local Dene translators.[107]

During the 1960s, Pentecostal revivals that had been occurring among Siksikaitsitapi in Montana, spread north into Káínawa and Siksika Nations in southern Alberta.[108] Emphatically Pentecostal revivalist camp meetings likewise gained cultural and spiritual significance, with First Nations evangelists Alex Anderson, John Sinclair, and "Northpeigan, from the Blackfoot Reserve at Brocket, Alberta" enjoying receptive audiences throughout the Sub-Arctic Mission.[109] The mission also launched the Sub-Arctic Leadership Training program (SALT), drawing enrolment from across the NWT. This program grew out of Ken Gaetz's and the Sub-Artic Mission's board of directors' 1980 decision to approve the development of a formal theological training program located in Fort Smith. "Health and wellness, economic development, and stability of leadership formed the platform" of Ken Gaetz's administration.[110] The ABNWT reported Indigenous Pentecostal congregations in the aforementioned Brockett, Alberta (Piikani First Nation), and among the Nehiyawak territories near Hobbema, Alberta.[111] Lastly there was a Native Pentecostal Church in Calgary, by the early 1990s pastored by Dean Shingoose (Anishinaabe, in this instance the exonym for which is Saulteaux; Coté First Nation Treaty Four Territory, Saskatchewan).[112] Throughout, the expansion of Pentecostalism among Indigenous people in northwestern Canada garnered the wider society's attention. John Webster Grant recorded:

> The late twentieth century has been the great period of Indian response to the gospel ... [B]y 1950 outriders of Pentecostalism were on their way down the Mackenzie ... into communities as familiar in the missionary story as Moosonee, Mistawasis and Ile-à-la-Crosse.[113]

In 1958, Carson Latimer and Jean Dennis met at the Sub-Arctic Mission's church in Hay River. Dennis had worked for the Sub-Artic Mission throughout the 1950s while Latimer had been employed by the Canadian federal Department of Fisheries before deciding to pursue church ministry vocationally. Following Latimer's completion of studies at the PAOC's Central Pentecostal Bible College in Saskatoon, Saskatchewan, that same year, the two married and entered mission together "among the Saskatchewan Indians on the Mistawasis Reserve near Mont Nebo." The couple expanded their work, opening another church in Sandy Lake First Nation, Saskatchewan. In 1961, the Latimers established a school there (later moving to Parkside, Saskatchewan) to train Indigenous candidates for church ministry leadership, where they continued to work into the late 1970s.[114]

It was during the 1960s that the Saskatchewan District named Sam Biro its director of Native Evangelism. From that decade through the 1980s, the Saskatchewan District's Native Ministries and the Parkside Bible school sought to direct Indigenous candidates into positions of ministry leadership.[115] By the 1980s, Saskatchewan was among the few PAOC districts to have a full-time director of its Native Ministries. Saskatoon's Native New Life Assembly named NLM associate Pat Linklater (Môsonîw Ililiw, the exonym for which is Moose Cree; Moosonee, Ontario) its resident evangelist. In 1980, Roger Ratt (Nīhithaw) was the first Indigenous student to graduate from Central Pentecostal Bible College (CPBC) in Saskatoon, Saskatchewan, before establishing a church in his hometown of La Ronge.[116]

Ratt commented:

> I believe God has allowed me and enabled me to take this course … so that I can teach our Indian people the deeper truths of the Bible. I believe Indian people are tired of running after every preacher and strange teaching that comes our way. God's Word is the only sure and stable foundation for our personal lives and our churches.[117]

The Parkside Bible school integrated into CPBC, offering a degree program tailored to Indigenous ministerial candidates. By the 1990s, various PAOC ministry leaders proposed making CPBC the denomination's designated Indigenous ministry candidate training institution; however, the plan never materialized.[118]

Delineating Indigenous people's initiative in the spread of Pentecostalism within the Province of Quebec, Joseph Jolly (Eeyou; Waskaganish, Quebec; raised in Moose Factory, Ontario) described how

> the Waskaganish Cree Pentecostal Church is one of the largest Native indigenous churches in Canada. The gospel which started in Waskaganish started to spread to the other Cree communities along the east coast of James Bay.[119]

Concurrently the Eastern Ontario and Quebec District (EOQD) established its Native Bible School in Senneterre, Quebec, in 1965,[120] and later operated the Native Pentecostal Bible College at Chibougamau.[121] Under the direction of Enoch Hall, the college served a constituency of seven Eeyouch churches in Quebec's James Bay region, offering on-campus and off-campus Bible training for ministry leadership candidates. Between three campuses, this college enrolled fifty students by the late 1980s.[122] Graduates Morley and Pauline Etapp planted churches at the Lac-Simon and Lac-Rapid First Nations (Omàmiwininì; the exonym for which is Algonquin, not to be confused with Algonquian).[123] Unfortunately little information is available pertaining to the history of the PAOC's Maritime District work with Indigenous people. However, Pentecostalism is a growing religious force in the Mi'kmaq nation, historically and contemporaneously associated with the region now called the Maritimes.[124]

PAOC historian Gordon Atter noted the success of Pentecostal outreach tailored to Indigenous people: "Indians have proved to be very receptive to the Pentecostal message, and are enjoying the outpouring of the Holy Spirit."[125] This generation of Indigenous Pentecostals developed into a significant contingent. As described above, every district missionizing Indigenous communities established Indigenous candidate-focussed training institutions, alleging to espouse the indigenous principle and intended to equip Indigenous ministers in a local context, with the goal of eventually replacing Euro-Canadian missionaries. Chapter 3 will address this subject more thoroughly.

The longer-established churches continued mission efforts to Indigenous people into the twentieth century, concurrent with Pentecostal work,[126] but historically expending more time and resources than did the PAOC, resulting in these denominations' numerical superiority historically. Canadian Pentecostal missiologist Irving Whitt claimed that over seventy-five per cent of the Indigenous population identified as Christian by the start of the twentieth century, implying that Pentecostal missionaries attracted many Indigenous adherents who already identified with a pre-existing denomination.[127]

When Pentecostal missionaries commenced in the mid-twentieth century, they sought in part to appeal to disillusioned Indigenous Christians, thinking the longer-established churches had become less relevant to them and believing their pre-existing brand of Christianity to be invalid when compared to Pentecostalism. The Pentecostals' approach in this matter provides a modern, Christian analogue to John Webster Grant's hypothesis that the longer-established churches supplanted Indigenous traditional spiritualities during the seventeenth through twentieth centuries. Pentecostalism won adherents in part because other denominations had shifted their focus away from prioritizing an autonomous, Indigenous clergy, appearing reluctant to facilitate such channels. In contrast, the PAOC appeared to enhance Indigenous people's influence. Pentecostalism succeeded in attracting a substantial number of adherents, to be sure. The result of this is that the reserves' ecclesial landscape today, long the domain of the Anglican, Catholic, and United churches, is often marked by the prominent display of a Pentecostal church. The PAOC gained significant ground particularly in north-central Canada. For instance, the James Bay region, where many Indigenous communities as recently as the mid-1970s were devotedly Anglican, by the 2010s had become about fifty per cent Pentecostal.[128]

Pentecostalism's ease of accessibility appears to render it further attractive to Indigenous spiritual seekers. Indigenous Pentecostalism only partially represents a new brand of Christianity, however, in that it is one that exists in interchange with its denominational forebears.[129] Many aspects of Indigenous Pentecostalism on an individual level, such as reasons for conversion and the expression of religious rituals, are best understood in relation to the well-established Christian traditions predating Indigenous Pentecostalism,[130] and from which many adherents transitioned to Pentecostalism.

Notwithstanding their inheritance of souls, Euro-Canadian Pentecostal missionaries often failed to correlate their work with that of their denominational predecessors. They tended to believe their Pentecostal message was the first true gospel presentation to Indigenous people, a trend that Grant summarized as follows:

> Around the end of the Second World War John Spillenaar began to cover areas east and west of the Hudson Bay from his plane *The Wings of the Gospel* ... Pentecostal[s] ... do not so much compete with established agencies as simply ignore their existence, reporting the first entry of the gospel into communities ... For the most part they offer a conventional message of salvation and emotional experience reminiscent of the older Methodism ... Confident in the truth of their message, however, few ... have sought to learn any lessons from the experience of earlier missions that began with equal enthusiasm and apparent success.[131]

The PAOC, interested in disseminating its Pentecostal message, was not concerned with matters of history or style, so long as the denomination saw steady numeric growth wherever it missionized.[132]

Still, the Pentecostals were not entirely ignorant of the longer-established churches' presence and efforts. The PAOC did in fact compete with the established agencies of those other churches, contrary to Grant's assertion. The denomination frequently criticized longer-established churches for what it perceived to be their insincerity, not so much in the longer-established churches' so-called civilizing efforts, but rather in their supposedly deficient grasp of the gospel. In short, the Pentecostal documentary record reveals an intense rivalry with longer-established churches (particularly the Catholic Church) and a contest for Indigenous people's allegiance.[133] Grant's claims of the PAOC's denominational obliviousness are true to the extent that the PAOC did not systematically analyze other churches' efforts and implement its findings into its own practices. Still, the PAOC was not oblivious to the prominence of these other denominations, rather willingly competing with them.

Nearly universally, Pentecostal missionaries perceived the Catholic Church not as an missional partner, but rather as a rival, and one whose adherents needed to be converted.[134] The PAOC did not criticize the Catholic Church for its residential school legacy; instead, it perceived the Catholic Church as ritualistic in its doctrine and ecclesiology, and thus creating an obstacle to evangelism.[135] The extent of the disdain may partially be a result of a number of Pentecostals (Indigenous and non-Indigenous) having formerly been Catholics. In many cases Indigenous Pentecostals claimed to have left Catholicism in favour of

Pentecostalism because of the former's perceived "excesses" in weakening traditional Indigenous life prior to the 1950s.[136]

Pentecostals were somewhat less vitriolic toward the Anglican Church. In the regions around Hudson Bay and James Bay, where the PAOC expended significant missionary resources, Anglicanism's long and continuing presence strongly influenced the religious landscape.[137] Frequently Pentecostal missionaries required the translation services of Anglican clergy. Further, many key Indigenous-language texts employed by PAOC missionaries were translations by Anglican clergy. Thus Pentecostals benefited from, and often relied upon, an established Anglican presence.[138] NLM missionaries occasionally employed Anglican parish halls for Pentecostal worship meetings within Indigenous territories. Sometimes the two groups worshipped together in the shared space. These periodic times of ecumenical cooperation and collegiality often provoked contemplation among Pentecostals.[139] While PAOC missionaries were more tolerant of Anglicanism than of Catholicism, there still was not a generous spirit of cooperation. PAOC records from the period indicate a pattern of PAOC missionaries' attempts to proselytize Anglicans.[140] However effective the Catholic and Anglican churches were in attracting Indigenous people to Christianity, to Pentecostals, said adherents generally seemed less than Christian.[141]

Yet this rivalry proved to be a two-way street. Anishinaabeg Pentecostals in the Pinaymootang region recalled that they were not simply opposed, but were even "ridiculed and called names like 'Shakers' and 'Holy Rollers.'" The derogatory term (when applied to a Pentecostal) "Shaker" purportedly was also used in correspondence between agents of the Department of Indian Affairs and appeared in the *Manitoba Free Press* in 1911 in reference to Néhinawak Pentecostals from Fisher River Cree Nation. Anishinini Pentecostal Pastor Jerry McKay reported that some Anglican clergy wrote letters to northern Ontario First Nations elders "telling them to oppose these Pentecostal interlopers." Some band councils went so far as to pass resolutions forbidding non-Anglican and non-Catholic missionaries from entering territories.[142] Likewise Euro-Canadian PAOC missionaries felt Anglican, Catholic, and United Church ministers opposed them, benefiting from government favour, which the PAOC's ministers and missionaries did not. One Pentecostal reflected that Anglicans seemed to believe they possessed exclusive rights to hold services in First Nations territories, and that government needed to acknowledge that others were labouring allegedly to "improve" Indigenous peoples' situation as well.[143]

For that matter, Euro-Canadian Pentecostals often believed their efforts contributed to the "improvement" of the "lot of Indians." This sentiment obviously parallels the assimilative, Christianizing, colonial, and educational ambitions of the longer-established churches. In many respects Pentecostals espoused similar sentiments, while at the same time denying the longer-established churches' devotional legitimacy. For instance, one missionary's record of the period exclaimed:

> The poor Indians were confused over too many religions. They had a mixture of Romanism, Protestantism, and their own heathen ideas. Not until they experience the new birth through a vital faith in Jesus Christ do they come out of this confusion and begin to live like Christians. But when the miracle does happen, their lives are transformed. They stop drinking, clean up their homes, and testify to real happiness in Jesus Christ.[144]

The same record went on to refer to a lapsed Catholic Métis man who "was a heavy drinker" but ultimately proved receptive to the PAOC missionaries' message. The record describes that subsequently he "receive[d] the Lord as his Saviour … and has consistently followed the Christ from that day. He attends church faithfully, holds a good job with the government, has a new car, a good home, and a fine family." This account suggests an idealization of certain Indigenous individuals who met denominationally desired outcomes, and implies the conflation of adherence to Pentecostalism with material, moral, and social improvement, demonstrated through a lifestyle consistent with Euro-Canadian ideals.[145] Although later Pentecostals were not as immediately concerned by Indigenous people's adoption of Euro-Canadian manners or patterns of dress, much like their longer-established ecclesial predecessors, Pentecostals did expect their mission participants to oppose Indigenous cultural norms.

Evidence of PAOC interaction with the United Church is limited and rarely positive. In Wiarton, Ontario, where the PAOC maintained a mission to Indigenous inhabitants, PAOC officials claimed the local United Church exhibited "no evangelical work."[146] Some maintained that both the Methodist Church and later the United Church had "long lost most of the revivalist fervour which had marked their earlier days." Pentecostals perceived themselves as sole carriers of the evangelistic flame. Indigenous PAOC minister James Kallappa (Kwih-dich-chuh-aht, the exonym for which is Makah; Neah Bay, Washington State) argued: "The gifts of the Spirit were so appealing to the Natives ... They wanted 'life,' not the 'deadness' of the mainline denominations ... They want and need 'the anointing.'"[147]

Still, the Methodists' historical evangelistic efforts, and the United Church's ongoing work with Indigenous populations, provided some foundation for Pentecostalism. It was not unusual within Indigenous territories for elders to step away from the United Church and join the Pentecostal Church, believing more leadership opportunities awaited. What is more, the United Church proved as capable of rivalry as the PAOC. Loraine MacKenzie Shepherd confirms:

> Pentecostals upset some United Church members of reserve missions by violating the "gentleman's agreement" concerning denominational territory and establishing their own churches on the same reserves, thereby competing for church members. However, [the Pentecostals'] church polity was more flexible, allowing them to honour and engage the traditional leadership of the elders.[148]

Stan McKay (Néhinaw; Fisher River Cree Nation, Manitoba),[149] a United Church minister and former United Church moderator, historically reflected that "Pentecostals are filling the gap because they allow the people some say in decisions. Our church doesn't."[150]

It is not surprising, then, that such outright denominational rivalry would prove detrimental to the religious common cause. Would-be Indigenous adherents grew tired of the religious competition, some as a result losing interest in Christianity altogether.[151] In recent years, relations between Pentecostals and their Anglican, Catholic, and United Church counterparts have thawed, and even improved in some quarters. In fact, in certain cases these groups join efforts to facilitate religious participation in northern Indigenous communities.[152] Canadian anthropologist Clinton Westman observed that Pentecostalism, as practised among Inuit, has influenced Anglican practice among the same population. Westman argued that Anglicanism, previously the primary denominational affiliation of Inuit, now encounters Pentecostalism as friendly competitor but also as partner in influencing the region's religious landscape.[153]

Comparatively little can be said about the Presbyterian Church in Canada. While Presbyterians engaged in mission to Indigenous people, the NLM's work concentrated in regions where Presbyterians were not involved. Region and place are crucial factors in determining the direction of Christian mission among Indigenous people. The PAOC's mission trajectories differed substantially, limiting contact with Presbyterian missionaries, and as such, few PAOC records address any interactions.

In its near-ubiquity within Indigenous communities, Pentecostalism differs from its contemporaneous Evangelical denominations. Pentecostalism alone is nearly universal in reaching Indigenous territories, having invested far more resources and personnel than its contemporaneous peer Evangelical denominations. The notable exception to this might be the Northern Canadian Evangelical Mission (NCEM), a denominationally unaffiliated, Evangelical missionary agency launched in 1946 in Meadow Lake, Saskatchewan. Tailored to an Indigenous audience, the NCEM possessed few associations with Pentecostals. At its peak in 1966, the NCEM boasted forty-six mission stations and one hundred and twenty-three missionaries, fourteen of whom were Indigenous. It is noteworthy that the NCEM, like the PAOC, perceived itself to be the only "evangelical mission in Canada taking the Gospel of Christ to the Natives."[154] There are only a handful of interactions between the NCEM and the PAOC accounted for in the documentary record.[155] Further, the NCEM does not present an exact parallel to the PAOC as it does not maintain affiliation with any particular Evangelical denomination, but rather exists as an independent agency, drawing its missionaries from an assortment of church networks. Thus, this monograph will not thoroughly analyze the NCEM. Still, in addition to work by the longer-established churches, a comparison between the PAOC and the missionizing efforts of its Evangelical peer denominations is warranted.[156]

The earliest Evangelical church to missionize Indigenous people in Upper Canada were Baptists, around the turn of the nineteenth century.[157] Many Baptist missionaries to the First Nations in Upper Canada came from the nascent United States. The War of 1812 meant that missionaries returned stateside, thus hampering Baptists' early missionary efforts. By 1835, Baptist missionary activity in Upper Canada resumed, and concentrated on the Six Nations of the Grand River territory (Haudenosaunee). By the 1840s, Baptist meetings were well-attended, and in 1842 the denomination established the Tuscarora

Baptist Church on the territory. Haudenosaunee Baptists experienced opposition from other Christian groups. As a result the Baptists petitioned the Governor General of Upper Canada for civil and religious liberty in May of 1842. Several Haudenosaunee adherents became ordained ministers and the Baptist message also spread among the Onyota'a:ka near London, Ontario. By the turn of the twentieth century, Indigenous ministers such as William Henry Prince, "the son of a Manitoba Indian chief," had carried the Baptist message to Néhinawak and Anishinaabeg in Manitoba.[158] Baptist churches generally avoided becoming embroiled in residential schooling because they refused on theological principle the acceptance of government funding.[159] As with other denominations, Baptist women contributed significantly to both the fundraising and execution of Baptist mission, most notably Phoebe Parsons, who worked as a medical missionary in Portage La Prairie, Manitoba.[160]

There are few accessible records of any Baptist missionary learning Indigenous languages, which typically required them to evangelize and preach through an interpreter.[161] The notable exception was Silas Tertius Rand, an ordained Baptist Minister who studied the Mi'kmaq language with the primary intention of missionizing Catholics. In 1851, Rand became Indian Commissioner in the colony of Prince Edward Island and assisted the Mi'kmaq in petitioning the Crown to uphold the First Nation's treaty rights. In 1853, Rand relocated from Charlottetown to Hantsport, Nova Scotia, where his mission purchased 450 acres for Mi'kmaq to farm and operate small businesses. Although Rand witnessed very few Mi'kmaq become Baptist, his efforts at Bible translation proved beneficial to those who remained Catholic. Baptists in the Maritimes did not continue Rand's vision for Indigenous ministry following his death in 1889, and in 1907 the Canadian federal government acquired the property, turning it into a reserve. Historian David R. Elliott concludes: "Baptist work … has continued into the twentieth century, but with less than enthusiastic support from the Baptist Convention."[162] Because the Baptist missionary effort among Indigenous people predates that of the Pentecostals, and as they are generally not concurrent, little more will be said on the subject.

Likewise little will be said about the Christian and Missionary Alliance (CMA), other than that it was influential in the spread of Evangelicalism among Indigenous people in Alberta. In 1958 the CMA's Western Canada District Conference initiated an "Indian mission program," which emphasized Indigenous language training for missionaries.[163] As the NLM did not itinerate in Alberta, and because there is little if any archival record of CMA and PAOC interactions in this area, the subject does not merit further comparison.

The PAOC shared the most collegiality and cooperation with the Mennonite Brethren, perhaps because the PAOC drew many early leaders and adherents from the Mennonite church.[164] A small amount of Mennonite work among First Nations territories in northern Ontario took place around the same time that PAOC missions began, with pacifist Mennonite conscientious objectors during the Second World War undertaking missionary work there.[165] Likewise the Mennonite Canada Inland Mission commenced work among First Nations communities in northern Manitoba in 1943, and in British Columbia in 1949. Mennonite missionaries continued to arrive for the next two decades. Unlike the Pentecostals, the Mennonites withdrew their mission stations from Indigenous territories in 1970. They had gleaned from anthropologist J.A. Loewen that their approach to mission among Indigenous people "was too Eurocentric" and they perceived their work to have been misguided. More recently Mennonites have sought to function as allies in pursuit of social justice for Indigenous people. At the time of writing, the Mennonite Church Canada has expended considerable effort and resource in the pursuit of reconciliation.[166]

Some might be surprised by the PAOC's relationship with non-PAOC Pentecostal groups involved in mission to Indigenous people, sometimes cooperating, but often competing rigorously.[167] PAOC missionaries generally remained disdainful and wary of non-PAOC Pentecostal networks. At times the PAOC criticized independent Pentecostal movements working among Indigenous populations nearly as much as they did the Catholics. In particular, the PAOC opposed "Jesus Only" or Oneness Pentecostalism, perceived to be "spiritually dangerous" and heretical by early classical Pentecostals.[168] In its interactions with and behaviour toward the independent Pentecostals, the PAOC demonstrated that although the denomination fundamentally advocated freedom in worship, affiliation with any Pentecostal organization other than the Assemblies – or even worse, no affiliation – took charismatic freedom too far. In this sense, the PAOC articulated a very exclusive position.[169]

In short, the PAOC's interaction with other denominations in their mission among Indigenous people was rarely cooperative. Nearly universally, the PAOC extended its greatest disdain toward Catholics and non-PAOC Pentecostals, presumably feeling threatened by both. In its ferocity, the PAOC established that in the marketplace of faiths, it was one of the many contenders competing for Indigenous people's allegiance.[170]

CONCLUSION

Pentecostal mission to Indigenous people was not as singular as the PAOC claimed; Pentecostals were one of many Christian agencies and denominations competing for Indigenous souls. If the PAOC's mission was unique, it was mostly because of its narrowness and anti-ecumenism. As they attested the effectiveness of Pentecostalism among Indigenous people, both Grant and Stackhouse maintained that the Pentecostal mission differed from those of the longer-established churches because Pentecostal mission: 1) did not aim to civilize in the way other churches did; 2) among Christian groups possessed unique parallels to Indigenous traditional spiritualities, due to a mutual emphasis on tangible spiritual experience; and 3) offered Indigenous ministry hopefuls access to positions of leadership and influence.

It is only partially accurate to say the Pentecostals did not seek to "civilize," as they did not partner with governments in negotiating for reserves and operating the residential schools. Nor did Pentecostals force Indigenous participants to cut their hair, dress in Western fashion, or fully forsake their first languages. The longer-established churches had largely attempted to establish these precedents, providing a foundation that allowed the PAOC mission to continue within the established colonial status quo.[171] Only exceptional Pentecostal missionaries bothered to learn Indigenous languages. Earlier "civilizing" efforts allowed them mostly to speak English or French to Indigenous participants who had facility in a European language. Indeed, an early PAOC mission policy acknowledged this benefit, noting that colonized countries had "advantages over other fields [because] … the people, although in heathen darkness, speak the English language. Consequently, the missionary can begin work immediately."[172] Hypothetically, had the Pentecostals arrived earlier, presumably their missionary efforts would have been similar to those of the longer-established churches. As other denominational missionaries continued teaching English and French to Indigenous youths, and with commerce and industry's encroachment into Canada's north reinforcing English and French as commercial languages, the PAOC faced fewer linguistic and infrastructural obstacles to communicating their message.[173] Thus to a great extent, to say that the Pentecostals did not seek to "civilize" in the way that the longer-established churches did makes an unfair comparison, casting Pentecostalism in an unmerited favourable light.

Second, although it is true that the Pentecostal experience's emphasis on spiritual matters periodically presents parallels to that of Indigenous traditional spiritualities, Pentecostalism is not unique among Christian denominations in this regard. Even before the Pentecostals arrived, mid-nineteenth-century Methodist missionaries such as James Evans advocated a spiritually intense Christian experience that included revival and speaking in tongues.[174] During that time Letitia Hargrave, the wife of the York Factory, Manitoba, Hudson's Bay Company factor, observed: "The Indians here are all labouring under a religious frenzy. They preach, perform miracles, speak unknown tongues, die & come to life again, won't hunt & it is extraordinary how many performances they have."[175] By the late nineteenth century, the Canadian northwest no longer represented a monopolized "religious frontier" but rather exhibited a "high level of religious pluralism."[176] To this end, Robert Penner recorded Indigenous Methodists of the period "weeping, roll[ing] ... in the aisles, and fall[ing] to the floor as if dead."[177]

In the early 1900s even the Presbyterians undertook Pentecostal-like evangelistic camps and crusades within First Nations communities. In Regina in 1908, long-time Presbyterian missionary Hugh McKay included an altar call in one such service, during which thirty-one First Nations young people accepted the invitation "to follow the Christ." At the end of the service, six of these stood to deliver their testimonies, and two young First Nations women extemporaneously concluded the meeting with prayer.[178] Likewise one should not assume that every Anglican and Catholic service was a rote, by-the-book, non-experiential affair. The other denominations' charismatic and revivalistic practices among Indigenous adherents provide precursors to the later Pentecostal expressions.

This is not to dismiss Pentecostalism's potential attractiveness to Indigenous spiritual seekers. Indeed it is possible (if not likely) that the pneumatological expression and fervour of the longer-established churches had waned by the time Pentecostal missionaries arrived in the mid-twentieth century. Still, Pentecostalism is not entirely distinctive among Christian denominations in its parallels to Indigenous traditional spiritualities. Although the PAOC claimed its missiology was unique, it did in fact have much in common with other denominations. Even the PAOC's leading missiologist Irving Whitt believed many "of the methods used by [Christian] missions in general and Pentecostal missions in particular were similar." Whitt further described that such similarities were apparent in leadership training, denominational structures, the employment of mission stations, and overall missionizing methods.[179]

While the PAOC believed its methods were exceptional, in many ways the Pentecostals were latecomers who replicated the efforts of their longer-established church predecessors. When one considers the sheer volume of Pentecostal contribution to the evangelization of Indigenous people, the PAOC more closely resembles the longer-established churches than it does other Evangelical denominations, who by comparison expended considerably fewer resources in missionizing Indigenous people. Still, the PAOC's missiology was uniquely and overwhelmingly characterized by its eschatological and pneumatological emphases. The urgency of evangelism, associated with the Pentecostal doctrines of baptism in the Holy Spirit and the anticipated second coming of Christ, allowed the PAOC to carve out a niche as a distinct competitor alongside the longer-established churches.[180] While not as numerically prominent nor affluent as the longer-established churches, the PAOC proved to be equally attractive to would-be Indigenous adherents, allowing it to punch above its weight. Thus to borrow R.J.B. Bosworth's phrase, compared to these churches, the PAOC can aptly be referred to as the "least of the great powers." After all, in ecclesiology as in geopolitics, it is in the process of becoming a great power that rising powers typically morph into the very thing they formerly resented or at least refused to be identified as. This theory gains further traction when one considers that the PAOC ultimately came to closely resemble the denominations that it most resisted.

Grant's and Stackhouse's third claim for the success of Pentecostalism among Indigenous people – that Pentecostalism offered Indigenous ministry hopefuls better access to leadership and influence than did the longer-established churches – will be addressed in chapter 3, and can only be evaluated following an examination of the NLM's origin and evolution. As such, it is to the NLM and its missionary founder, John Spillenaar, that chapter 2 now turns its attention.

2

The Heavens Have Become a Highway

How Aviation Indirectly Enabled a PAOC Mission to Indigenous People

The Assemblies of God has given wings to its missionary enterprise. The heavens have become a highway linking the mission fields of the world.

George Carmichael, Assemblies of God missionary[1]

Lord, show me the way – is it Indian religion or another?

Anonymous First Nations man[2]

Alvyn Austin and Jamie S. Scott have claimed that "today, unlike a century ago, it is no longer the Natives, but rather the missionary who needs to be explained."[3] John Webster Grant, also intrigued by missionaries' curious characters and attitudes, posited the following:

> Not many years ago one of the chief difficulties confronting the author of a book on Indian-Christian encounter would have been to make sense to the average reader of the religious practices of the Indians and to explain the strange inability of some of them to recognize the superiority of Christianity. Today, at least among the student generation, it is the missionary who has become the puzzle. Once almost universally acclaimed as a self-sacrificing benefactor, he or she is now more commonly dismissed as an interfering busybody and in all probability a misfit at home who could find only among the colonized a captive audience on whom to impose a narrow set of beliefs and moral taboos.[4]

More recent scholarship charts a middle ground, where the missionary represents neither the lionized hero nor the universal destroyer of culture. This third view recognizes the power disequilibrium between Euro-Canadian missionaries and Indigenous participants. However, it neither dismisses the latter as simply the "other," nor does it portray the former in polar opposition to their acolytes.[5] Pentecostal Assemblies of Canada (PAOC) missionary John Spillenaar is one example who intriguingly fits within this middle ground. Indeed he seemed a more comfortable match to the northern expanse than to the PAOC's ecclesial structures. Yet Spillenaar's path to missionizing Indigenous people was indirect, and was not his original goal. This renders apprehending the missionary's motivations a significant step in uncovering and understanding the Northland Mission's (NLM) history.

The background of the PAOC's mission to Indigenous people is worth explaining. The NLM did not start as a mission to Indigenous people specifically. However, it became one. Since Spillenaar founded the NLM, pioneered the PAOC's mission to the Indigenous people of the region, and served the longest tenure of any NLM director, more attention will be directed to his background than to those of his successors. Drawing principally from denominational periodicals such as the *Pentecostal Testimony* as well as John Spillenaar's autobiography, this chapter examines the missionary's motivations, as well as the NLM's early years. In so doing, this chapter argues that mission to Indigenous people was not the PAOC's original intention. Spillenaar initially was drawn to the geographic north more than to the Indigenous people there. His motivation was to get further from the south (and perhaps denominational governance there). Finally, it was only through the serendipitous realization of missionary aviation that Spillenaar and the PAOC became aware of opportunities for itineration among Indigenous communities in Canada's north. Once the NLM had identified its Indigenous audience, it sought in earnest to attract them to Pentecostalism. Although an aircraft was crucial for establishing the mission, its financing and operation created challenges that ultimately complicated the NLM's attempts to implement the indigenous principle.

JOHN SPILLENAAR'S EARLY YEARS

In 1911, Rienhardt and Cornelia (née Van Loow) Spillenaar immigrated to Toronto from the Netherlands.[6] Rienhardt and Cornelia embraced the Pentecostal message at Ellen and James Hebden's Toronto

East End Mission.[7] After their conversion, the couple demonstrated lifelong loyalty to Pentecostalism. It is interesting to note that Rienhardt himself inadvertently contributed to early Indigenous Pentecostalism. Andrew Maracle (Kanien'kehá:ka; Six Nations of the Grand River, Ontario) became a very influential minister within the Native American Pentecostal movement of the Assemblies of God (AG USA), in 1944 becoming the first Indigenous minister ordained by the denomination. In his memoirs, Maracle recalled his mother's conversion to Pentecostalism while Maracle was an infant in 1914. "My Long House Religion had seemingly been good enough for me." The word Christian was "foreign, but I recalled ... Spillenaar Sr ... visited mother's little store at Sixty Nine Corners on the Six Nation Reserve." During lunch, Rienhardt Spillenaar talked "about 'the Lord.'" Maracle's mother "accepted with joy, the message of salvation." She took Rienhardt Spillenaar to her mother, who "also accepted the Lord as her Savior. Mother, with her baby [Maracle] on her back ... walked many miles, telling of her new found joy and of the goodness of Jesus."[8]

John Spillenaar was born to Rienhardt and Cornelia on 7 October 1916. The Spillenaars worshipped at Elim Tabernacle, St. Catharines, Ontario, during John's youth. There, in 1929, John responded to an evangelistic message and experïenced a dramatic conversion.[9] At one point Rienhardt operated his own mission in Toronto.[10] In the 1930s Rienhardt Spillenaar was a leader at the PAOC church in Gooderham, Ontario, near Bancroft.[11] John went from the sawdust trail to the farmer's field, helping Rienhardt operate the homestead and church, as well as attending elementary school. Garnering experience of enduring value during these bi-vocational years, John Spillenaar felt pulled toward full-time ministry. He recounted seeing a vision while working a neighbour's field. The vision consisted of Psalm 32:8, which states: "I will instruct you and teach you in the way you should go; I will counsel you with my loving eye on you." Under the passage Spillenaar envisioned "a very large eye," which he believed instructed him to "go north."[12]

In his autobiography, Spillenaar recorded that in 1935, aged nineteen, he walked northward as far as he could, stopping at every Pentecostal church and home along the way, disseminating religious tracts and preaching. He had no exact plan other than to share his faith story and beliefs with as many as possible.[13] He characterized his openness to spiritual prompting for ministry in his oft-repeated phrase: "The only direction I can get from the Lord is to go north."[14]

So strong was his desire to travel northward that he applied to become a missionary to Greenland.[15] This did not materialize, the Danish Evangelical Lutheran Church advising him that they were "well able to care for the spiritual needs of Greenland's people."[16] Spillenaar proved content to remain in Canada. However, as he travelled north, he did not at first encounter Indigenous people.

In 1936, Spillenaar settled in Kirkland Lake, Ontario. He is commonly credited with establishing the PAOC church there that same year, but work on it had already begun a few years prior. Preceding Spillenaar's arrival, "several young ladies ministered to a small congregation of two or three families."[17] One of them was Tyyne Nykanen, a Finnish-Canadian who had pioneered that Pentecostal mission. Born in 1905 in the rural town of Virtasalmi, Finland, Tyyne emigrated to Canada as a young adult. In Kirkland Lake she bought a house and rented a room to Spillenaar.[18] The landlady and tenant fell in love and married on 15 January 1938. During this time Spillenaar took a mining job in order to pay for familial expenses, as well as to finance the burgeoning pastoral work in Kirkland Lake. For the remainder of the 1930s and into the early 1940s the couple itinerated through northern Ontario and Quebec mining towns, travelling mostly by train and in some places establishing churches.[19] The couple concluded their work in Kirkland Lake,[20] and launched a Sunday School in Matachewan, Ontario, in 1942.[21] Eventually John Spillenaar earned enough to resume full-time ministerial work.[22] Although much of the PAOC's literature attributes the couple's ministerial success to John, it is likely that Tyyne was an evangelistic force in her own right.

In 1943, the couple accepted pastorates of the PAOC churches in Timmins, Ontario, and nearby South Porcupine.[23] In July the PAOC Western Ontario District (WOD) named John Spillenaar the "PAOC Northland missionary," marking the Northland Mission's establishment.[24] Minutes of the 1943 District Conference decision made no mention of Indigenous people, noting only delegates' approval for "the missionary thrust into the North country."[25] In 1946 Spillenaar again relinquished local church pastoral duties, choosing South Porcupine as the nascent mission's headquarters. He visited surrounding industrial logging and mining settlements, and accompanied Euro-Canadian construction crews installing radar equipment across the north.[26]

Spillenaar wrote in the *Pentecostal Testimony* about a ministry pioneering project in Hearst, Ontario. Although there were established churches in Hearst, none were associated with the PAOC. Typical of the era's Pentecostal evangelists, the absence of a Pentecostal church caused Spillenaar to doubt the legitimacy of Hearst's Christian representation, the latter lacking the PAOC's eschatological and pneumatological urgency. Candidly he wrote: "I believe we have a great opportunity here for the Lord, as there are no Gospel works, only French Roman Catholics, United and Anglican churches."[27]

The Spillenaars launched the Hearst congregation in the mid-1940s, acquiring a church building in 1948.[28] The majority of parishioners were Finnish, allowing Tyyne to preach in her first language. Their description of the demographics of Hearst was again typical of the period: "Some ... are quite communistic, and others strict Catholic," and few were welcoming. The "further the home is back in the bush or backward place, the greater the urge we feel to visit them, because we know that they ... seldom have visitors and perhaps never have a missionary in their home."[29]

During the better part of the NLM's first decade, the Spillenaars concentrated their efforts on Euro-Canadians and recently arrived immigrants from Europe, predominantly Scandinavians.[30] One of the stations John and Tyyne oversaw was in Timmins, where the mission enjoyed steady growth, notwithstanding the ongoing trend of Euro-Canadians' relocation to southern Ontario for employment.[31] Throughout the 1940s, the couple conducted outreaches tailored to children in Timmins and neighbouring South Porcupine, resulting in many subscribing to Pentecostalism. Reliant on faith for material provision, John reported: "I haven't the slightest idea where the money will come from, but am confident that God will provide."[32] As they evangelized Euro-Canadian settlements, they petitioned denominational supporters for the necessary funding to do so, with PAOC laity willingly bankrolling these efforts.[33]

An ongoing feature of the NLM's operations was to provide conferences for its workers and volunteers, a practice continued into the mid-1990s. In 1946, the Northern Ontario Mission Workers' Convention at South Porcupine Assembly drew ministers from many nearby towns and settlements.[34] Further, Spillenaar enjoyed a wide audience through broadcasts of evangelistic sermons from regional radio stations. After three years, the NLM began to experience significant geographic dispersion. The mission steadily grew numerically, and new Pentecostal church buildings opened.[35] Yet the PAOC concentrated on these locations because they were northern population centres, and not particularly because of any Indigenous residents. Canadian

Pentecostal historian Gordon Atter noted: "New Assemblies are being constantly opened. Pioneer fields have been entered among the mining towns ... new towns, and ... immigrant settlements."[36] Vestiges of the NLM's orientation toward proselytizing non-Pentecostal Christians and ministering to non-Indigenous Pentecostals persisted even into the 1960s, as one radio listener described

> how much *Revivaltime* [the radio broadcast] means here in the French Catholic northland ... There are many small, isolated communities and farms up here, and it is so good to know the full gospel is beaming in. We are pioneering a work here in Cochrane. *Revivaltime* is our only contact with Pentecost in the winter, and it is such an inspiration to us.[37]

Legitimate challenges accompanying the establishment of mission stations in these remote regions delayed the NLM from reaching Indigenous people. For example, the proposed station in Baie Comeau, Quebec, faced logistical problems, the missionaries there requesting Spillenaar provide building supplies, which he did.[38] This project would have required considerable attention. For years to follow, the Baie Comeau church and its growing building expenses created ongoing tension between Spillenaar and the Belleville, Ontario–based PAOC Eastern Ontario and Quebec District (EOQD) superintendent, Wilbur B. Greenwood. In fact, Greenwood became suspicious of Spillenaar's use of funds, auditing the NLM with the assistance of the WOD. Spillenaar cooperated with the audit, and in the end it was determined that he had not misused any funds.[39]

Similarly, in 1949 Spillenaar established Silver Birches Camp, a WOD summer camp in Kirkland Lake, Ontario, where the NLM held meetings and revivals, popular with Euro-Canadians living in nearby towns.[40] Details of its founding confirm that Spillenaar's attention was not upon mission among Indigenous people during the NLM's first decade. Silver Birches Camp is illustrative of the NLM's philosophy then, an illustration borne out by other examples throughout the source material. Outreach was the goal, but the focus upon Indigenous people by which the NLM eventually identified itself was not a factor during the mission's early years. Without criticizing the NLM's concentration on northerly non-Indigenous communities, the point to be emphasized is that ministry to Indigenous people was not the primary intention of either the Spillenaars or the PAOC.

Concentrating on Baie Comeau, Silver Birches, and other places like these preoccupied missionaries, diverting them from reaching their ultimate audience: Indigenous people. Eventually, an infrastructural innovation made missionaries aware of the Indigenous populations they had yet to reach.

REALIZATION OF MISSION TO INDIGENOUS PEOPLE

Broadly speaking, and especially so within the NLM, PAOC leadership at first was attracted to those communities linked to the commercial, industrial, and natural resource sectors' expansion into Canada's north, the region's mining boom remaining central to many Pentecostals' thinking. These developments occurred contemporaneously with the ongoing popular realization of rich natural resources and their role in bolstering Canada's economy, thrusting the country into the forefront of international affairs. The PAOC expended many thousands of dollars supporting Spillenaar's missionary work to reach these northern mining settlements from the 1930s through the 1940s, populated by Euro-Canadian labourers representing a prime audience for the PAOC's evangelism.[41]

Spillenaar's passion to travel north equalled his passion for evangelism in general. It was as though the more cold, northerly, and remote, the more attractive the destination became for Spillenaar. His desire was not focused not on any particular group of people. Other than an occasional visit to Moosonee, Ontario, a James Bay town accessible by rail but not by road, Spillenaar had not demonstrated specific focus on any predominantly Indigenous communities.[42] At this time, his was a geographic vocation rather than a demographic one. Yet the era's limited transportation infrastructure allowed Spillenaar to travel only so far north by road. He believed these constraints interfered with his calling to "Go North," raising the question of how to reach people further north more effectively.[43]

By the 1940s and 1950s, missionary aviation was developing among Evangelical missions. Between 1948 and 1951, the AG USA employed two retired and retrofitted Second World War United States Air Force aircraft (a Curtiss-Wright C-46 Commando, and later a Boeing B-17 Flying Fortress) to shuttle missionaries internationally. Beginning in 1952, Jim Elliot and the Palm Beach Martyrs flew a Piper PA-14 Family Cruiser in their outreach among Huaorani people in what is now Ecuador, until their untimely deaths in 1956, a legacy feted and acknowledged across the denominational spectrum.[44]

For his part, Spillenaar investigated aviation beginning in 1948. He realized that since Ontario's far north was inaccessible by highway, he could only accomplish his northward ambition by learning to fly. After prayer, he believed "the Lord [was] opening the way … to take a six month's course in aviation, maintenance and repair" at Chicago's Moody Bible Institute. John and Tyyne claimed, "our aim is to take the gospel to the folk of our far North by plane."[45] Spillenaar commuted from northern Ontario, paying from his own savings, all while he and Tyyne maintained existing NLM engagements. He received his pilot's licence in 1950, and the following year purchased a Piper Super Cub with the financial assistance of his supporters, predominantly Toronto's Stone Church Pentecostal Assembly.[46]

While Spillenaar did not pioneer this particular missionary method, he numbered among the vanguard of its development. Spillenaar's aviation endeavours were unique among his peers, his status as the first missionary pilot within the PAOC affording him a broad denominational celebrity. The PAOC laity found the idea so exotic that even his acquisition of a pilot's licence and aircraft were attributed to divine intervention.[47] PAOC members popularly referred to his aircraft as "the Wings of the Gospel." Gleefully, the missionary itinerated throughout northern Ontario, as well as communities bordering Hudson Bay and James Bay in Manitoba, the Northwest Territories, and Quebec.[48]

Although aviation costs were great, the PAOC's investment paved the way for concerted missionary work among northern Indigenous territories. Fewer predominantly Euro-Canadian towns and settlements existed north of the roads' extent, introducing the missionary to another demographic. Simply put, the further north Spillenaar travelled, the more likely he was to encounter Indigenous people and their communities. Owing to their respective histories, and because of their geographic isolation, Indigenous territories in northern Ontario generally retained concentrated populations, thus forming an optimal locale for Pentecostal missionary outreach. Consequently, Spillenaar's route to the skies also proved to be the PAOC's path to Indigenous souls. Once PAOC leadership decided to concentrate the NLM on Indigenous people, the mission's northerly location proved strategic and beneficial. Even so, the PAOC's dramatic shift of mission-focus in the north from Euro-Canadians to Indigenous people went largely

Figure 2.1 Spillenaar family in Hearst with the NLM's first aircraft

unexplained. The period's missionary literature implied that nearly overnight the NLM had serendipitously reconcentrated its efforts.

Gordon Atter, after noting that Spillenaar was instrumental in planting churches "among the white settlers," abruptly and without explanation added: "Then, being burdened for the natives, he became a competent plane pilot … and flew further north."[49] Atter's description is not entirely accurate. The missionary was first burdened for the north, and his pivot was abrupt. Further still, his change in focus to Indigenous people was made only after he became a pilot. Freshly aware of the potential missionary opportunity, he shifted in the sudden fashion typical of the Pentecostal penchant for pragmatism.[50]

Several *Testimony* articles, while lacking explicit explanation, elucidate Spillenaar's ultimate interest in these Indigenous communities. He recounted a 1951 encounter with a chief near Sachigo Lake (Anishinini). The apparently chance meeting may have signalled Spillenaar's initial shift from a regionally based mission to a culturally and ethnically oriented one. The chief, upon reception of the Pentecostal message, insisted Spillenaar "must promise to take the gospel to all my people." The chief accompanied the missionary on a flight, pointing out neighbouring communities, requesting that Spillenaar conduct outreaches there. Spillenaar concluded by noting: "Even today the only white person living there is the teacher." The local First Nation maintained their own language, including a syllabic hymn-book with English on one side of the page and an unspecified First Nations language on the other side.[51] Presumably Spillenaar was referring to pre-existing Nêhiyawêwin Bibles, prayer books, and hymnals prepared from the 1830s and onwards.[52]

Of devotional trends, Spillenaar opined: "The Indians ... become eager and enthusiastic believers ... accept[ing] with simplicity the Bible as the Word of God and thus the power of God is manifested in their services and in their daily lives." The missionaries encouraged belief in healing; the "natives also encourage one another to believe."[53] Spillenaar did not explicitly state so, but it is plausible that the First Nations people in this account were receptive of Pentecostalism because they or their ancestors had already transitioned from Indigenous traditional spiritualities to a form of Christianity other than Pentecostalism, demonstrated by their possession of Nêhiyawêwin Christian literature.

At this juncture in the Northland Mission's story, it is worthwhile discussing why an Indigenous individual might become attracted to Pentecostalism. For analytical purposes, there are four main, documentary reasons, each typically working to some degree in tandem with the others. The first of those reasons is described as deprivation theory. This theory encompasses the idea that the world Indigenous people inhabited was changing. They were experiencing economic difficulties and scarcity during the mid-twentieth century unlike what they had experienced in their personal history, and the advent of Pentecostalism afforded them an outlet or release valve through which they could overcome that adversity. The second hypothesized reason for Pentecostalism's popularity was its personal connections. This rationale espouses the notion that non-Indigenous, Pentecostal evangelists cared about Indigenous adherents and loved them in a way that the missionaries of the longer-established churches did not. This expression was well-received by the Indigenous participants who in turn became even more attracted to Pentecostalism.[54] Where a missionary of a longer-established church or a representative of another institution (such as a Hudson's Bay Company store manager, military member, government official, or police officer) did maintain a positive or at least functional relationship with an Indigenous community, a

Pentecostal missionary could benefit from their relational networks if vouched for.

The third theory attests to Pentecostalism's appeal in that it permitted a greater degree of Indigenous autonomy than did the longer-established churches. This approach maintains that Pentecostalism's decentralized ecclesial polity and flexible liturgy allowed Indigenous adherents "a tremendous amount of self-governing autonomy within a religion that, to date, had been controlling."[55] Pentecostalism may prove additionally attractive to an Indigenous adherent due to its pragmatic penchant of recognizing spiritual authority due to ministerial capability rather than conventional training.

The fourth theory attributes Pentecostalism's popularity to the compatibility of its pneumatological emphases with Indigenous traditional cosmologies and spiritualities. It is important to clarify that any of the following references to Indigenous spiritual concepts are primarily for the sake of scholarly comparison and can neither be fully explained nor understood by one who is neither a practitioner of Indigenous traditional spiritualities, nor a speaker of Indigenous languages.[56] Still, comparisons of the practices and their perceived compatibility are useful. Perhaps by the mid-twentieth century these points of compatibility may even have been more prevalent within Pentecostalism than they were within the longer-established churches at that time.[57] Joseph Jolly (Eeyou; Waskaganish, Quebec; raised in Moose Factory, Ontario) described Pentecostalism's appeal thus: "Pentecostal and Charismatic movements are appealing to Native people because their theology and methodology relates to the way most Native people experience religious concepts."[58] Some Indigenous proponents of Pentecostalism perceive the movement as a natural progression from Indigenous traditional spiritualities, believing the God of the Bible to be the same deity their ancestors revered.[59]

Pentecostalism further maintains a similarly oral tradition, through which worldview and beliefs are relayed intergenerationally. Indigenous traditional spiritual rituals such as fasting and prayer, healing, vision questing, meditation, drumming, dancing, and sacred dreaming likewise find points of parallelism with Pentecostalism. These points become particularly pronounced where cultural and social aspects of Indigenous people's lives have become influential within traumatized communities. Accordingly, Pentecostalism allows a metaphysical experience that is available in the present, providing a "soul translation: a direct encounter with the divine that cannot be fully expressed in human terms." In other instances, Pentecostalism's emphasis on healing strikes a chord with Indigenous participants, including, for some, in the area of overcoming addiction. This penchant for healing holds the potential to render Pentecostalism attractive to Indigenous spiritual seekers, and may contribute to the movement's success in winning over adherents. The combination of these factors allows Pentecostalism to be particularly palatable to an Indigenous audience, where acts of healing often form an accompanying component for the traditional leadership role. In fact, an evangelist's legitimacy, prestige, and reception among an Indigenous community might at times be contingent upon his or her capacity to demonstrate the charismatic and spiritual gift of healing.[60] Put another way, the "power of prayer attracts people to the healings, at least partly because the experience of Pentecostal healing is dramatic and tangible."[61]

While these final hypotheses may appear obvious on the surface, the reality of said theories would be tested on the ground. These contentions apply both to the rigidity of PAOC denominational hierarchy impressed upon Indigenous adherents, and to the alleged compatibility between Pentecostalism and Indigenous traditional spiritualities. The expressions of the latter would be particularly scrutinized, as various non-Indigenous and Indigenous Pentecostals took varying positions on the integration of the two traditions. Said encounters often resulted in complex exchanges between Euro-Canadian missionaries and Indigenous Pentecostals. While these points of contention are not easily parsed out and may never be fully understood (not least by a non-Indigenous historian), chapter 4 seeks to analyze aspects of them.[62] The four major theories (deprivation, personal connections, autonomy, and spiritual compatibility), rationalizing the popularity of Pentecostalism among Indigenous people, by no means form an exhaustive list of reasons many Indigenous people became attracted to Pentecostalism. Indeed, every individual's spiritual story is unique. Put simply, those who chose Pentecostalism "did so on their own terms." Yet the above hypotheses do find supporting, and at times conflicting, evidence within the documentary record.[63]

For his part, Spillenaar attempted to explain the background of the new adherents to Pentecostalism. After noting that he relied on interpreters to translate testimonies offered at a revival meeting in Sachigo Lake, he recalled "that they had always considered themselves Christians," having "been taught that they were children of God," until they heard preaching "that all are sinners until they accept Jesus as Saviour." They spoke confidently of "going to Heaven" and no longer relying on written prayer, having learned to "pray from [their] hearts," joy radiating "from their faces as they told ... of their new found experience."[64]

While Spillenaar's accounts are filtered through several layers (that of missionary, Pentecostal, and anglophone Euro-Canadian), much may be deduced from these memoirs.[65] His reiteration of Indigenous Pentecostal testimony reinforces the aforementioned finding that in their competition for souls, PAOC missionaries did not attract adherents directly from Indigenous traditional spiritualities, but rather from rival Christian denominations. These were most obviously from the Anglican church, as indicated by the prayer book in this instance, but also from the Catholic and United churches. Additionally, he implied that upon receiving the Pentecostal message, Indigenous Pentecostal adherents came to believe that their previous devotion was lacking, hinting that association with other denominations was not sufficient for one to perceive oneself as Christian. While not diminishing the legitimacy of the individual's conversion experience, this critique does demonstrate the varied religious backgrounds of the NLM's adherents, as well as the PAOC's pneumatologically motivated insistence on conversion not just to Christianity, but specifically to Pentecostalism. Spillenaar never learned Nêhiyawêwin, Ojibwemowin Anishinaabemowin, or Anishininiimowin, instead closely relying on translators.[66] Additionally, he frequently relied on the local Hudson's Bay Company factor, Anglican priest, or Catholic priest to translate, as well as to help him gain the local Indigenous population's trust.[67] Nevertheless, Spillenaar encountered many previously unreached by Pentecostalism, who in turn became attracted to it.[68]

An anecdote about a longer-established church's missionary working contemporaneously to Spillenaar paints a vivid picture of early PAOC missionary efforts, as well as their reliance on already-established networks, thus providing a compelling example of the personal connections theory. Spillenaar began travelling to Big Trout Lake, a predominantly Anishinini settlement, around 1953. He recalled a "white missionary" had resided there but had never met him. Upon arrival, Spillenaar was surrounded by Indigenous people. He "noticed a white man in clerical garb among them," clearly the missionary, who was likely Anglican. The two shared a meal, and Spillenaar recorded the other missionary as lamenting: "The people now appear to be worse than when I first came." At first many came but now it was "hard [for the missionary] to get even a few to come to the service."[69] According to Spillenaar, during his visit, a local man came to the door, with whom the other missionary spoke in a language that was unfamiliar to Spillenaar, presumably Anishininiimowin. It is noteworthy that the other missionary had made the effort to learn the local language, a practice not unusual for Western missionaries opting to remain within Indigenous communities for protracted periods. In fact, facility in Indigenous language often became a metric by which to measure a missionary's success.[70] The Anishinini man – whom Spillenaar described as the chief – invited him to hold an evangelistic service for the community. Spillenaar recorded that he felt "really put … on the spot." A guest of a long-serving missionary who had related difficulties getting people to services, he hesitated to insult his contemporary, but soon resolved to fulfill his calling to preach in the north.

A meeting was set for early the next day. At breakfast, Spillenaar's "missionary friend expressed surprise at the chief's request," suggesting there would be just five or six present, only to find "that place packed full with people." Spillenaar asked the Anglican to translate for him. He recorded the interaction as follows: "We had a good song service and the Holy Spirit was present in a real way." As he concluded the sermon, Spillenaar invited people to come forward to "be saved." With few respondents, Spillenaar was concerned the people did not understand his message. Spillenaar asked the Anglican "if he was telling the people exactly what [he] was telling him. [The Anglican] replied, 'What do you mean to be saved? Do you mean they have to belong to your church?'" Spillenaar responded that "they could belong to all churches and still go to Hell. They must belong to the Lord Jesus Christ." Thus appeased, the Anglican relayed Spillenaar's call, with the result "that the whole congregation rose up" to come forward, "people on their knees calling upon the Lord to save them." The Anglican missionary was excited as he had "'never seen anything like this in all [his] life.' [Spillenaar] replied, 'That's the work of the Holy Spirit.'"[71]

The missionary with whom Spillenaar interacted was almost certainly Anglican priest Leslie Garrett, who had served continuously in Big Trout Lake from 1923 to 1955, thereafter working as a missionary with the Northern Canada Evangelical Mission (NCEM) in Trout Lake and a variety of other locales throughout north-central Canada. True to Spillenaar's account of his exchange with Garrett, the Anglican himself referred to his season in Big Trout Lake as having been characterized by "an evident decline of spiritual power," despite the great effort he had expended appealing to his audience. Without the luxury of aviation, Garrett did not itinerate as Spillenaar did, instead undertaking local language study from first arriving, then employing it throughout his tenure there, even producing print materials. The priest, believing "God wanted [him] to carry on at Big Trout Lake ... spent seven years learning their language and ways," even though "tremendous changes were coming all over the Northland." Bush flying, radio, and the formation of winter roads to serve new mines meant that "suddenly all Indian life was becoming engulfed in the white man's culture ... [causing] great repercussions to the economy and spiritual lives of the native people."[72]

As early as 1899, two decades before the PAOC's founding, more than 70,000 of the 100,000 Indigenous people counted by the federal government had some denominational affiliation. By 1967, of the 215,000 "treaty Indians" in Canada, twenty-five per cent identified as Anglican.[73] Churches and a network of other church-related institutions such as schools, hospitals, and the like dominated many territories, rendering missionary engagement feasible in nearly every part of Canada.[74] Yet even as the PAOC began to establish itself as a new player in the pre-existing ecclesial marketplace, it was not the only denomination to employ innovative missionary methods in Indigenous territories. Into the mid-twentieth century, the Anglican, Catholic, Presbyterian, and United churches, as well as the NCEM, likewise came to rely on aviation as well as radio broadcasts.[75] By the 1950s, Spillenaar was one of several missionary aviators enjoying Garrett's assistance and hospitality in Big Trout Lake.[76]

Pentecostalism rode the wave of industrial development to the north,[77] yet the longer-established churches were aware of the economic boom for some time. Phillip Carrington, historian of the Church of England in Canada and former Anglican Archbishop of Quebec, confirmed industry's role in "invading the territories of the Indian and Eskimo ... linked and supported by the aeroplane, the power-plant and the radar station." Churches followed, building new parishes, recruiting clergy, and learning new techniques. Carrington described how modern missionaries needed "to learn how to hitch-hike on a plane ... fraternise with construction engineers and cooperate with the company personnel," in addition to ministering to "Indians or Eskimos."[78] Comparison can only be drawn so far, however, as it appears the efforts of these longer-established church workers were more nuanced. Unlike the PAOC, other denominations' missionaries viewed northern commercial expansion only partially as an evangelistic opportunity, but also as an incursion into Indigenous people's lives that needed to be accounted for.[79]

For his part, Spillenaar believed the Pentecostal message uniquely interested Indigenous listeners because of "a hunger in these people's hearts for reality."[80] While not explaining what he meant by "reality," he implied that something about Pentecostalism offered gratification to Indigenous listeners. The missionary's recollection of a desire for experiential reality denotes an emphasis on provision that is more than material. For example, some Indigenous Pentecostals refer to the prospect of obtaining "a better life and help from above for their temporal struggles." To be sure, material needs may be met. But an emphasis on experience and "reality" implies an appeal to Pentecostalism's propensity to provide for material *and* spiritual needs, perhaps in a way that the missions of the longer-established churches may not have seemed to be doing. Through Pentecostalism, Indigenous adherents perceived "not just a handout, but a helping hand to a better way of life through Jesus Christ."[81]

The draw to the PAOC on the part of Indigenous adherents with pre-existing denominational affiliation warrants exploration. The other denominations certainly were active and seemingly successful in catechesis. Yet Indigenous people opted to participate in Pentecostalism's expansion, requiring some explanation. Pentecostalism may have appeared accessible and relevant, presumably in ways that other variations of Christianity were not. There may even have been a perception that Pentecostalism was a religion for the time – that is, the late modern era – with many Indigenous adherents perceiving it to be "the belief system appropriate for the contemporary world." Pentecostalism's pragmatism, as well as the fact that it is a brand of Christianity that came of age during the twentieth century (post–colonial encounter), rendered it particularly compatible with notions of modernity, and thus perhaps well-suited to varied cultural and ready regional adaptation into Indigenous people's lives. In short, Pentecostalism proved popular because its openness, flexibility, and adaptability to the local context allowed it to uniquely reflect as well as connect with certain normative Indigenous social structures.[82]

What is more, some Indigenous Pentecostals believe that Christianity is useful, but that Pentecostalism in particular is effective, practical, and powerful. Proponents uphold this view of Pentecostalism, maintaining that it is experiential, even more so than the style of Christianity associated with the longer-established churches.[83] Another reason Pentecostals recorded success in the second half of the twentieth century is that, despite many similarities, Pentecostalism is still visibly distinct from other denominations, its eschatological and pneumatological emphases potentially appearing unique to Indigenous spiritual seekers. Further, acceptance of Pentecostalism might be considered an act of Indigenous divergence from the longer-established churches' norm, and a vehicle to autonomy through a new religious alternative.[84] Finally, conversion is a complex phenomenon, and in the case of Pentecostalism it represents both conversion from and continuity with pre-existing Christian and Indigenous traditions.[85]

To be sure, Indigenous communities provided a culturally and spiritually "fertile ground" for Pentecostalism. On one occasion Spillenaar recorded seventy-five people coming forward at an NLM outreach altar call to receive the baptism in the Holy Spirit.[86] Pentecostal missionary work among Indigenous people during this period typically did not prioritize precise attendance records "since 'saving souls' was viewed as more desirable than promoting regular weekly attendance at services." Still, Spillenaar did recall the number of those responding to his invitations. While it is difficult to verify the accuracy of these numbers, several similar accounts suggest that well-attended events occurred regularly.[87] Spillenaar's infrequent quotation of Indigenous individuals' explanations illustrate these correlations and trends. As his autobiography focuses primarily on the aircraft, records of such instances as cited below are significant and rare enough to be considered at length.

Spillenaar routinely arrived at Indigenous territories in the early mornings. The missionary shook hands with the curious who had gathered while himself seeking an interpreter. An evangelistic pitch soon began, people listening "attentively to the Word of God as it was being interpreted by one of their own people." He told his listeners "that each one must voluntarily accept Jesus Christ as Saviour and Lord ... to become true 'born again' believers, in the family of God." The missionary provided an invitation at the end of his sermons for listeners to make a decision, reporting: "In most of the services ... men, women and young people come forward, many with tears running down their faces, to accept Jesus into their hearts and lives." Spillenaar was caught up in the joy upon hearing the typical testimony, which he summarized as follows:

"I have lived here in this village all my life. All of you people know me. I have always attended church services and took for granted that I was on my way to Heaven; but when Mr. Spillenaar came and explained to us from the Word of God that we were all sinners and that we all needed to be saved from our sins through the precious Blood of Jesus, I then realized that I too needed Jesus. Now I have prayed and asked Jesus to come into my heart. He has come in, and I just feel so wonderful. I know now for sure that I am a child of God."

They appreciated these services so very much and tried their best to thank me. They always wanted me to have a meal with them – no matter what time of day it was and I enjoyed many meals with these precious people. After a meal, I would bid them farewell as I climbed into the plane which was christened 'Wings of the Gospel'. And away to another settlement, another service and to another meal, then off again to reach other village before dark – on and on – day after day.[88]

These quotations remain useful and telling. They offer a degree of an Indigenous person's perspective, despite potential contamination of a purely authentic Indigenous Voice, since they are Spillenaar's recollection of an amalgamation of exchanges with assorted people, years prior to writing his autobiography. Recent ethnographic work undertaken by Kimberly Jenkins Marshall, Mark Clatterbuck, and Clinton Westman strives to provide a less contaminated, contemporary report of Indigenous people's perspectives on and motivations for subscribing to Pentecostalism. Furthermore, Indigenous Pentecostals from the communities outlined within this chapter can provide those accounts unhindered. These factors combined point to productive avenues for future study on this important subject. That being the case, in this brief and uncharacteristic synopsis, and for historical purposes, Spillenaar included much telling information.

Certainly, this is the definition of a fly-in, fly-out operation, without much on-ground follow-up – least of all from the mission director. Ironically the success of Spillenaar's maverick methods may have been one of the initial obstacles preventing the NLM from reaching Indigenous people earlier. Itinerating by air depended on the missionary pilot and delayed the formation of a local, permanent Pentecostal ministry presence. This style of evangelism periodically could be counter-productive as it contributed to gaps in leadership and community, proving detrimental to the continued and ongoing local participation necessary for the Pentecostal mission's viability.[89]

That the described Indigenous participants already attended church indicates yet again that the PAOC did not introduce Christianity, but rather won its adherents from other churches. Neither was it uncommon for Indigenous Pentecostals to have held multiple religious affiliations prior to Pentecostalism. One might observe that in some respects the Anglican, Catholic, and United churches served as a sort of halfway house somewhere along the path from Indigenous traditional spiritualities to Pentecostalism. While this may be true of the experience of some, it is furthermore useful to surmise that the trail may not end there. From an anthropological perspective, it is helpful to consider the process of religious association as a continuum rather than a destination. There is no reason to think that Pentecostalism is an endpoint. It may instead "be regarded as only one epoch in the continuing evolution of" Indigenous cultures. Cultures are often fluid, evolving, and ever-changing. As such, outsiders should be careful when it comes to creating definitions and categories for the various parties to fit within.[90] Still, there was something about the Pentecostal message that appealed to these Indigenous listeners.

This was a key period during which the PAOC uncovered its impulse to missionize Indigenous communities and individuals, much later than other denominations. Missionaries historically occupied multifaceted, unique, and privileged positions of influence and ability. But by the 1950s they were only one voice amid a chorus of individuals from multiple disciplines. The shifting nature of the missionaries' role was particularly felt by the longer-established churches.[91] In this context of diminished influence, perhaps it was Pentecostal missionaries' penchant for healing, experiential spirituality, and evangelistic urgency that distinguished them from their denominational peers. This in turn allowed them to gain prevalence within Indigenous communities.

It is also noteworthy that the missionary's invitation required local Indigenous interpretation. This trend presents an early element of mission indigenization, and implies translators' ability to present an appealing Pentecostal proclamation. Thus, factors such as these may have been influential in prompting Spillenaar's listeners to accept his invitation to become Pentecostal, and led to the movement's subsequent growth in the region.[92] Ministering to the growing number of Pentecostal adherents required commitment, dedication, perseverance, and sacrifice on the part of the Spillenaars. What is apparent is Spillenaar's determination to physically reach them. There is no indication that Indigenous laity felt slighted, nor that they perceived that the PAOC came to them only as an afterthought. They only expressed wonder as to why the NLM had not evangelized their communities sooner,[93] emphasizing the Indigenous Pentecostal laity's sincerity in their embrace of Pentecostalism and the elements thereof.

This chapter has described the PAOC's attraction to the north for economic and geographical reasons. By the 1960s, PAOC conversation shifted and better acknowledged the presence of Indigenous people within the region. It was not uncommon for the scope and nature of this missionary work to extend beyond evangelism into efforts considered to be humanitarian and philanthropic, including the extension of aid to Indigenous children and families.[94] PAOC executive Robert Argue described the PAOC's increasing concern for – and activity among – Indigenous people in terms of the vast and sparsely populated territories in north-central Canada. "Little settlements of 150 to 350 people are scattered 75 to 250 miles apart, and the men trap the waste land in between ... Each place has a little settlement of small, simple houses, the newer ones built by the government." A Hudson's Bay store that traded goods for furs, a government school, and the Anglican or Catholic church rounded out a typical community. As soon as basic greetings were over, a time and place were decided for the service and "the important people of the village" were consulted. Congregations ranged in size from fifteen to eighty-five, with most around twenty-five to thirty, often filling a room. Of the gatherings, Argue recounted: "The men sit on the chairs, the ladies and children squat on the floor. The singing is different ... the melody of the hymns is usually the same, but adjusted, particularly in time, to fit the Cree words." Usually there were testimonies to God's saving grace, healing, and presence.[95]

Although initially the concept of a mission to Indigenous people was novel, by the 1960s the NLM had embraced it, maintaining express interest in spiritual transformation.[96] Pentecostal missionaries spoke particularly favourably of Indigenous people's hospitality, outlining living arrangements to an extensive audience through the *Testimony*.[97] Thomas William Miller recalled that "the flying missionary" had "helped publicize the plight of Canada's Native peoples ... and the necessity of training them to evangelize their own races ... [A]lways the need for Native workers has been paramount."[98]

Yet Miller's glowing account of the NLM was not entirely accurate. Although the mission made strides in its missionization and won favour with Indigenous adherents, progress toward the indigenous principle was hampered by the PAOC's penchant for pulpits filled by familiar faces. When Spillenaar did recruit missionaries, most of them were Euro-Canadian. In so doing, the PAOC spoke of the indigenous principle, but its leaders did not always appear to prioritize it. PAOC missionary policy as stated in its General Constitution since 1932 had been: "Wherever on the foreign field it is workable and practical ... to establish a self-supporting native church ... from the beginning."[99] Perhaps the oversight here was not identifying mission to Indigenous people as intercultural because it occurred within domestic borders. Circumstances require an answer as to why the NLM slowed the process towards autonomy. Perhaps this was partly because of the means by which the NLM accidentally realized its Indigenous audience in the first place.

THE IRONY OF THE AIRCRAFT

In 1959, *Testimony* described the NLM and its churches as "endeavouring not only to become indigenous, but also to reach the moving population by every available means."[100] Of course the primary means was the aircraft. Aviation opened the previously difficult-to-access Canadian north to the PAOC's evangelistic endeavours. This proved a great advantage to the nascent PAOC mission, but it also carried some disadvantages created by a core issue. By and large Euro-Canadians, particularly Spillenaar, alone had access to the aircraft, rendering it a mixed blessing. Here is where the irony lies: although crucial for reaching northerly Indigenous territories, the aircraft became somewhat of an obstacle for the fullest achievement of the indigenous principle.

The first major challenge posed by the aircraft was its disruptive effect on administration and ecclesial polity. A 1962 *Testimony* article indicated the NLM's outreach ranged from the "Gulf of St. Lawrence to the Western border of Manitoba," encompassing geographic areas within three provinces and a Canadian territory, and covering three PAOC districts.[101] Spillenaar himself claimed his operational range extended even into Newfoundland and Labrador, a province within which Pentecostal ministry was overseen by a separate denomination altogether, the Pentecostal Assemblies of Newfoundland and Labrador.[102] One early long-distance flight into "the unknown north" included stops at "many Indian" and Inuit settlements. The flight log is unclear, as though Spillenaar himself was not always certain of his own location. This captivating land's intrigue continued. During an early visit, Spillenaar claims an Inuk tried to murder him by firing his rifle at – and narrowly missing – the missionary.[103]

Despite such encounters, Spillenaar continued to test the limits of his geographic boundaries, the operational range of his aircraft, and the patience of his denominational higher-ups. His northward vision was clear and at the forefront. He was happy to arrive in various host communities and spark revival. However, when the time came for Spillenaar to depart the faithful of one territory and go to the next, the PAOC's offices were left with the mandate of administering the church he had started. Periodically it was unclear which PAOC department or district was responsible for it. The missionary's widespread excursions generated much deliberation between district superintendents as he stepped on many clerical toes. At one point the WOD and EOQD formed a joint committee composed of the district superintendents, their assistants, and the Department of Home Missions and Bible Colleges (DHMBC) director, intending to ground Spillenaar and his aircraft. Finally, the missionary pushed too far with district and home missions executives, leading the DHMBC to persuade Spillenaar to respect district boundaries, entering the EOQD and the Manitoba and Northwestern Ontario District (MNWOD) only upon the invitation of the respective district executives.[104]

Fortunately for Spillenaar, heated tempers cooled. As his perceived evangelistic effectiveness increased, so too did the denomination's willingness to embrace his mission, and to overlook his disregard for district boundaries. The PAOC General Conference delegates acquiesced, opting instead to redefine district boundaries, allowing some of the NLM's territory to overlap into the MNWOD, thus partially reducing tensions caused by Spillenaar's sojourns. An article contained within a denominational periodical addressed the boundary extension, noting that the MNWOD would "have much closer fellowship with Rev. J. Spillenaar and the Northland work of which he is overseer."[105] Despite these allowances, in the decades following, the NLM's work increasingly focused on the regions geographically contained within the WOD.[106]

The second major challenge caused by the aircraft was its contribution to a form of cultural colonialism. Aviation suggested that the last frontier of the north could be conquered. Many NLM representatives' writings employed what Jamie S. Scott labels the "cultivation trope." Although not a new concept, since even the Bible employs agricultural metaphors, Scott refers to the use of agrarian terms to describe the "civilizing" of Indigenous people through Christian mission. Scott argues that "the discourse of 'cultivation' lubricates the slippage between the salvific and civilizing agendas of Christian colonialism."[107] In another essay, Jamie S. Scott and Alvyn Austin claim that metaphors "of the Bible and the plough assumed a particular resonance" in Canadian Protestant missionary parlance, "at once expressing and embodying church-state relations from the metropolitan centre to the far-flung outposts in the Canadian Arctic."[108] While not explicitly articulating a desire to "civilize" Indigenous participants, the PAOC sometimes implied evangelism preceded affluence and material comfort. NLM missionaries did not criticize other denominations' missiological practices of civilizing, and the PAOC itself employed cultivation vocabulary, implying a penchant for acculturation.

Certainly the aircraft became a vehicle, both physically and metaphorically, and agricultural vocabulary abounded, especially when linked to it. An NLM missionary expressed the analogy well:

> In recent years, aerial crop-spraying has become widely used throughout the country. Airplanes fly low and scatter their load over a wide area for varied reasons. We can think of our missionary plane in much the same way as we fly over the vast northland spreading the gospel message wherever we go.[109]

This missionary account details how the aircraft itself played a role in cultivating disciples like crops, emphasizing its "faithful year of 'aerial-spraying' the gospel message to needy multitudes." Missionaries also wrote of flying Indigenous youths into Moosonee, Ontario, noting their wonderment at seeing cars and railways for the first time. The aircraft's role in "civilizing" is highlighted through Indigenous youth's novel exposure to implements of Euro-Canadian technology and infrastructure.[110]

A third major challenge associated with the aircraft was its great fiscal costs, both routine as well as those resulting from Spillenaar's many mishaps.[111] The PAOC idealized his aviation, stating: "He carries

Figure 2.2 The Spillenaars with the NLM's Cessna C172, circa 1950s

the gospel to the isolated villages where the appearance of a new face is hailed with delight."[112] Yet this work was anything but glamorous, as itinerating in Canada's north presented challenges such as navigation and accessibility, owing to the harsh climate and lack of transportation infrastructure. Contributing to the danger and risk was the isolation where Spillenaar itinerated. He often served as an ad hoc emergency responder, since few others were available to assist.[113] The missionary's track record with aircraft safety, maintenance, and longevity was less than optimal. Over the course of his itineration with the PAOC, he went through five airplanes. Spillenaar gave great attention to these mishaps, many providing captivating tales. In addition to providing good reading, these anecdotes were essential to his ministry and fundraising efforts.

Even the pedestrian, non-catastrophic incidents reveal interesting dynamics in Spillenaar's tours. As previously noted, he pioneered new territory for Pentecostalism but found missionaries of other denominations and benefited from their assistance. In early 1952, Grace

Oates and Ruth Antonelli established an NLM church in Fort Severn, Ontario (Néhinaw), located along the shore of Hudson Bay. There, on 30 December 1952, Spillenaar damaged the aircraft's landing gear and propeller. The local Catholic priest, Rev. Morin, assisted the missionary, completing repairs at the Catholic mission's workshop. Spillenaar recalled: "We got the Indian women to make a canvas cover to fit over the end of the [damaged] wing ... We laced it down tight and it looked fairly strong." In what must have seemed like an ecumenical miracle, the combined efforts of local Néhinawak and a denominationally diverse clergy were successful in rendering the bush plane airworthy. Spillenaar concluded: "I was so grateful for the help of Rev. Morin. It took us three days to complete these emergency repairs and each night we held services." A decade later, in 1962, the evangelist attempted a flight from Fort Severn to Churchill, Manitoba. This time Spillenaar's aircraft failed to become airborne, its landing gear suffering a broken axle during takeoff. Again, Father Morin came to the rescue and assisted Spillenaar with his repairs. Absent in these accounts is the Pentecostals' otherwise typical bias against Catholics, apparently a luxury that necessity could not afford.[114]

On another occasion, Spillenaar recorded nearly landing on a group of inhabited igloos, mistaking them for barren ice. In 1959 his aircraft was totalled when it capsized in the river after a surge in the current unmoored it from its offshore anchorage. In 1963, the missionary recorded venturing near Churchill, Manitoba, into a no-fly zone accidentally. An air traffic controller radioed him, informing him that the armed forces were testing heat-seeking missiles in the area. Fortunately the previous missile they had tested had malfunctioned; otherwise Spillenaar's aircraft would have been destroyed and him with it.[115]

During a subsequent episode while flying his recently acquired six-passenger-capacity Cessna C-185, Spillenaar rescued two lost trappers. With two First Nations guides and cargo already on board, the heavily loaded floatplane struggled to take off. Then one of the aircraft's pontoons struck a boulder, puncturing it and causing it to fill with water, severely crippling the landing gear. All four passengers disembarked while Spillenaar temporarily took off with only himself aboard, but because of the added water weight, he was forced to make an emergency landing downriver. Stranded and now separated, all of them had to wait over three days in the wilderness, enduring elemental exposure before being rescued.[116] Spillenaar later recounted another near miss while landing in a narrow river. The missionary credited local First Nations people for his rescue "with their canoes" when his floatplane failed in the water.[117]

Throughout Spillenaar's travels, much of the damage to the aircraft was accidental or simply routine "wear and tear" from bush flying. Spillenaar did not deliberately cause damage. Rather, these cases illustrate the risks linked with such daring undertakings. Throughout twenty-six years of flying on behalf of the PAOC, Spillenaar crashed his aircraft fourteen times.[118] His recurring survival was seen as nothing short of miraculous. Once he recollected an exchange between himself and a rescuer: "'Man you are lucky.' 'No,' I said, 'we are not lucky, but it was the Lord who protected us.'"[119] Committed to sharing the Pentecostal message any time, he characteristically gave God credit.

Specific to the missionary's record, considering the literary attention Spillenaar afforded the aircraft and their accidents contrasted against the lesser focus assigned to the Indigenous people whom he missionized, it might seem he prioritized the former over the latter. Due to aviation's novelty, PAOC leadership also marvelled at the aircraft's fantastic capabilities, attention that might otherwise have been shown to the NLM's actual mission to Indigenous people.[120] Although the ends seemed to justify the means, one wonders why such literature gained prominence while many details of the actual mission, as well as Indigenous people's opinions and stories implied within the articles, often went overlooked.[121]

Edward Said, the literary theorist and pioneer of the academic discipline of Post-Colonial Studies, described the cultural form of the novel as having immensely influenced colonial attitudes, considering it "*the* aesthetic object whose connection to the expanding societies of Britain and France is particularly interesting to study." Labelling Daniel Defoe's venturesome *Robinson Crusoe* the "prototypical modern realistic novel," Said added that it is "certainly not accidental … [that] it is about a European who creates a fiefdom for himself on a distant, non-European island."[122] Analogous to Said's suggestion, John Stackhouse maintains that the genre of missionary literature is equally influential among "evangelicals[, who] apparently do read [it]. And what they have read over the past four decades tells us a lot about them."[123] Stackhouse claims, for instance, that Elisabeth Elliot's aforementioned *Through Gates of Splendor* "motivated many to join in the evangelistic enterprise."[124] Likewise, the dissemination of Spillenaar's harrowing tales of the adventurous, Euro-Canadian, northward-bound missionary of fortune proved appealing to the

Figure 2.3 The NLM's Cessna C172 callsign LGT ("Let God Through")

PAOC's primary constituency, motivating them to join (or at least contribute to) the cause. Thus a plausible explanation is that these literary accounts' focus on the missionary (as well as his giving credit to God) may have helped garner financial support.[125]

Owing to accidents and heavy usage, the aircraft's lifespans were exceedingly short, with replacement aircraft often needed suddenly. To reduce expenses, the PAOC often purchased previously owned aircraft, which were unfortunately more inclined to break down. Little was budgeted beforehand for such inevitabilities, as any available money was already committed to aircraft maintenance and upkeep. At one point, the PAOC General Executive even considered selling the aircraft so as to offload its high operational costs altogether – a conversation kept secret from Spillenaar. Thus, the financial burden of aircraft replacement fell on the shoulders of the mission supporters, who received funding requests in the form of compelling testimonies. *Testimony* was often the main vehicle to raise awareness of these needs. The PAOC and Spillenaar both realized this forum's significance and potential effect. Put another way, "missionaries often wrote strategically to promote their own work." Publishing stories about the aircraft's misadventures and redemption from disaster served both a spiritual and a pragmatic purpose; a *Testimony* reader might find his or her faith strengthened, but also might be inspired to donate. As a result, the PAOC always managed to come up with sufficient funding for aircraft expenses. Over the course of Spillenaar's tenure, the Stone Church Pentecostal Assembly in Toronto – a church that particularly prioritized mission to Indigenous people – purchased two aircraft outright for the NLM.[126]

By and large, missiological challenges related to aircraft matters stemmed from the simple fact that Spillenaar was the aircraft's primary operator. The aircraft initially proved necessary for spreading the Pentecostal message; however, the administrative, cultural, fiscal, and communication complications of aviation dependence proved a persistent obstacle to the NLM's accomplishment of the indigenous principle. While a necessary accessory for the advent of the mission, the aircraft itself did not provide avenues for Indigenous people to have direct ministry involvement. For instance, the NLM's laity had no access to nor knowledge of the resources required for the aircraft's operation. One Pentecostal First Nations elder later recounted how

> the missionaries came with the appearance of wealth, operating their own plane ... at virtually no cost to the Native churches or [ministerial] candidates, with no explanation given to these people of the financial structures which enabled them to do such 'magnanimous' deeds.[127]

Without access to flying lessons or resources required to pay for lessons, Indigenous people could not assume leadership of a PAOC mission so fixated on the novelty of Spillenaar's aircraft.

Lastly, the aircraft contributed to a missiological irony in that the newly acquired ease of transport meant Spillenaar did not remain in any one community long enough to learn the local language, nor to become familiar with the locals to whom he ministered. Unlike their denominational predecessors, access to flight meant Pentecostal missionaries (Spillenaar specifically) could come and go as they pleased. This was especially detrimental during an era of rapid change in the north. During the second half of the twentieth century, within the span of a generation, many northerly Indigenous communities underwent substantial changes in the areas of family life and subsistence, hunting, and labour practices.[128] During this time, an integrated

NLM that implemented the indigenous principle might otherwise have lent a supportive presence.[129] Although this "radical socio-economic dislocation" might initially have contributed to Pentecostalism's success vis-à-vis its appeal to the economically, politically, and socially disenfranchised Indigenous communities of north-central Canada,[130] the means by which the message was distributed ultimately would prove unsustainable. In an ironic twist, the very thing that permitted Pentecostals to reach an Indigenous audience also impeded missionaries' ability to accomplish their own indigenous principle ideal.

THE GENDERED PAST OF PENTECOSTAL MISSION

Aviation enabled evangelism, but delayed discipleship. As a result, it ultimately became apparent even to Spillenaar that the NLM needed its leaders to be indefinitely present on the ground to help foster growth within the local Pentecostal churches.[131] Thus the NLM began to attain and dispatch missionaries in earnest. Their goals were to establish local churches, and to train Indigenous Pentecostals to evangelize. Although Spillenaar received much public attention, among those missionary recruits were some tenacious workers, many of whom were women. As mentioned earlier in this chapter, starting in 1952 Grace Oates and Ruth Antonelli pioneered the NLM church in Fort Severn. By 1956, the NLM established churches in Manitouwadge and Hornepayne, pastored by Milda Rosenke, Shirley Wicks, and Gladys Prest into the 1960s. Later, PAOC International Missions veterans Erna Alma Peters and Annie Cressman likewise participated.[132] Of course, Tyyne Spillenaar herself was a powerful force behind much of the couple's ministry.

It is regrettable but unsurprising that the women mentioned above did not feature more prominently in PAOC lore. This was partially the result of a mission and support base so intensely focused on one man. Further, women's roles in the Pentecostal hierarchy were often determined by their marital status. Single women frequently served as evangelists and missionaries. Young married women might continue to travel with their itinerating husbands. However, following the birth of children, a married couple would settle into a local church where a husband would serve as the pastor, and a wife would function in a supporting role. Unfortunately, as the PAOC and NLM institutionalized, women's access to leadership roles became more restricted.[133]

Additionally, denominational documentation and literature from the period unfortunately paid more attention to men than to women. When women were acknowledged, it usually was a result of the conventional (albeit substantial) clothing, financial, and material donations from the prominent Women's Ministries of the WOD's southern Ontario churches,[134] rather than a recognition of women ministers' and missionaries' contributions to the NLM's functioning. This outcome might also have been a result of the fact that the PAOC maintained a conservative stance, opting not to ordain women until 1984.[135]

Michael Wilkinson and Linda Ambrose commented on the gendered dimensions of these processes, arguing "that PAOC women were encouraged to embrace the socially constructed gender roles that created a hierarchy in which men had work to do for God and women alongside them to assist" and "that as a movement becomes more institutionalized, women are often marginalized. The PAOC, with its expanding organizational structures and reinforcing cultural patterns, seems to be a case in point."[136] The NLM was no exception, demonstrating aspects of the above by assigning work that constrained female ministers once they married. However, it would not appear within the documentary record of the NLM's churches that the same applied to female laity (who were as involved as male laity in church services). Still, there may have been limitations placed on levels or degrees of female laity's roles in church governance (for instance, deacon board membership). Fortunately, some ground has been made up in this area. As of 2018, one-third of PAOC credential-holders were women. Still, disparity remains, as women serve as lead pastors within only five per cent of the PAOC's churches,[137] indicating the denomination's stained-glass ceiling has yet to be broken.

The concern of overlooking these realities is amplified when one considers the frequent omission of such significant figures from the historical record. Ambrose describes:

> [I]n the growing literature of women in the Christian church, the neglected area is women in Charismatic and Pentecostal churches ... [T]here is very little Canadian scholarship on Pentecostals in general, and even less on Canadian Pentecostal women in particular. While some reference to Canadian Pentecostalism can be found in broader studies of evangelicalism ... there is very little on the gendered aspects of Pentecostal experience.[138]

Hopefully volumes such as this one can in some small way help to mitigate the severity of this oversight. For it is these important gendered dimensions that point to the significance and intersectionality of gender studies, Indigenous studies, Pentecostal studies, and history within Canadian scholarship. Supremely, writing the history of the gendered aspects of Pentecostal mission must be more than merely "adding women" to the PAOC's and NLM's stories. Rather, it should serve to demonstrate that women ministers and missionaries strove (and continue to strive) to obtain their rightful place at the table of leadership.[139]

CONCLUSION

Despite administrative challenges, Spillenaar's work was revolutionary. He was not only a pioneer because he was the PAOC's first missionary pilot, but also because organized domestic mission was just coming into the denomination's focal point[140] – a publicity opportunity of which Spillenaar took full advantage. Moreover, Spillenaar transformed the NLM from a generic evangelistic ministry into a missionary enterprise specific to reaching Indigenous people (even if serendipitously). These factors, coupled with the region's relative remoteness, lead to the conclusion that Spillenaar was a pioneer in Pentecostal mission just as much as were his international forebears and contemporaries.

Although the denomination did not initially set out to do so, the PAOC had reasonably well established its mission to Indigenous people by the mid-to-late 1950s. There was a short-lived moment within the NLM's history when everything appeared to be getting along. Very quickly, though, it became apparent that NLM missionaries employed autonomizing vocabulary, but struggled to execute their own ideals on a practical level. In response to this apparent vacuum, the NLM established a ministry training school, which this monograph refers to as the Northland Mission Bible College. The NLM Bible College's objective was to train Indigenous acolytes to be the next generation of Pentecostal leaders and ministers, in keeping with the PAOC's indigenous principle. It is to the supposed attempt to develop and empower Indigenous leaders that the third chapter of this monograph turns its attention.

3

Leadership Qualities and the Call of God for the Ministry

The Northland Mission Bible College and PAOC Ministerial Credentials

Mission work and equipping personnel to be involved in mission are inseparable entities. Any church involved in mission needs to realize that theological education is the backbone of the church for it is through it that her leaders are prepared.

Dickson K. Nkonge, Senior Lecturer at Chuka University, Kenya[1]

We found that if a white man takes a pastorate in an Indian village, it takes six months or better for him to be accepted as a sincere friend. This suspicion has its roots deep in past conflicts. However, almost immediately, all are ready to hear an Indian preacher.

Charles Whaley, PAOC Minister[2]

Native people who are struggling with a call to the church's ministry … find a cold world in the church in terms of process … The church needs to … provide a candidate with nurture and encouragement. Maybe then we would have more Native Americans as clergy. It's a dream and a dilemma that we as Native American Christians face.

Tweedy Sombrero, Diné, Northern Arizona,
United Methodist Church Minister[3]

Although the Northland Mission's (NLM) focus on Indigenous people commenced somewhat serendipitously, within a few years of mission work among the population, the NLM had identified its ideal of the indigenous principle. The Northland Mission Bible College (NLMBC) became the primary conduit for attempting this objective, as Pentecostal Assemblies of Canada (PAOC) leaders intended the college to train Indigenous ministers. The earliest mention of the NLMBC was in a December 1953 NLM newsletter. John Spillenaar claimed the "next objective in the Northland" was to "open a short time BIBLE School for the natives, to give them basic training to enable them to preach the Gospel to their own people."[4]

Erna Alma Peters, an NLM missionary during the 1980s who began studying the PAOC's mission efforts even before working for the NLM, noted the prevalence of Euro-Canadian missionaries. Although "better than no pastor at all," Peters observed that missionaries faced "definite handicaps ... not knowing the languages of the Indians" or their culture, limiting "both the time and energy" for pastoral work. Peters recounted that many Indigenous laity wished to minister, but had "limited schooling." Peters continued, "when they preach to their own people they are accepted immediately for now it is their gospel, not just the white man's gospel."[5] Although Peters's observations came after the NLMBC's establishment, similar sentiments had prompted the PAOC to create the NLMBC in the first place. By 1965, PAOC Home Missions director Robert Argue said specifically of the NLM:

> A Bible school is held for the training of the Indians ... The Indian convert is being trained so that he may go back to his own people and "teach" them. Since the evangelist cannot stay in any one area for more than a short period, it is necessary to send [an Indigenous] teacher in to care for the spiritual growth of the new converts. The indigenous way is the best way.[6]

Denominational leadership thus determined that training Indigenous evangelists was the surest path to their desired outcome, believing Indigenous evangelists would be more successful at winning followers from among their own than Euro-Canadian missionaries could hope to be. NLM staff affirmed this conviction by founding a Bible school intended to train Indigenous laity for ministry and leadership. The NLMBC thus warrants significant attention, because it represents the PAOC's best attempt at implementing the ideals of the indigenous principle within the NLM. Much of the source material for this chapter is drawn from archived PAOC documents. While the documentary record employed here preserves aspects of the Indigenous Voice, these sources are primarily from a Euro-Canadian perspective. Still, the implications of what the NLM and PAOC said they would do, versus what they actually did during that era, come through very clearly, and it is through that lens that this chapter interprets said material.

In his 1976 autobiography, Spillenaar stated that the feted "Three-Self" missionary policy formed the rationale of the NLMBC: "As ... more native people became born again believers, I realized that in order for the Lord's work to be self-supporting, self-maintained and self-propagated, we must begin to teach and train these Indian people to become pastors and evangelists to their own people ... We began ... plans to open a Bible School." Peters recalled of the NLMBC's founding: "the need for Indian pastors was most apparent. The only way this could be done was to have a Bible School where the Indians themselves could study God's Word and learn to pastor their own people."[7] Peters continued:

> John [Spillenaar] realized that to have a self-supporting, self-propagated, self-maintained work they must train the Indians to become pastors and evangelists to their own people. Plans were laid to open a Bible School in the Mission ... and the search was on for potential students.[8]

In addition to recruiting and educating local clergy, the NLMBC's goal was to "meet the needs" of Indigenous ministerial candidates.[9]

Periodically the NLMBC experienced some success, reaching peak enrolment in the 1980s and enticing prospective students with the offer of ministerial credentialling.[10] That process for graduates was complicated in the extreme, eventually becoming a disincentive to would-be students. As the PAOC's expectations of the NLMBC grew, its focus shifted away from Indigenous people's needs. Rather than emphasizing the "Three-Self," in later iterations the NLMBC emphasized its own self, becoming self-serving. In the college's twilight years, its leadership was interested in generating enrolment primarily to secure the school's survival. Notwithstanding this, geographic and property transition and institutional and management turnover rendered enrolment nearly nil by the early 1990s, leading to the college's closure. This monograph gives an entire chapter to describing the Bible school because the NLMBC existed as a brainchild of the NLM's Euro-Canadian leaders, who only listened to Indigenous ministers decades later – a fact to be highlighted in chapter 5. As the Bible college's sporadically shifting location affected the institution's trajectory, it is helpful to outline events in terms of where the school was situated.

NLMBC BEGINNINGS IN MOOSONEE

On 6 July 1955, the NLM launched the NLMBC at its Moosonee mission station.[11] While the college had various names throughout its lifetime, it remained the NLM's sole ministry training institution. Spillenaar's description of the early student recruitment process included some students' three-hundred-mile travel by canoe, as well as his own flights into the north to collect students. Indigenous individuals and communities both were interested in the college, with even a chief asking that his daughter attend.[12] In its inaugural year, the NLMBC enrolled a modest five students, Spillenaar flying them in two at a time. He recalled that none of the first cohort of students were Christians. Presumably this means they had not been converted in the pneumatological and Pentecostal sense. After all, had the students no association with Christianity, then presumably they would not have been interested in attending a ministerial training institution.[13] The missionary's approach proved effective, and by year's end several students identified as Pentecostal. Following a later term, the missionary explained that some students had been "filled with the Holy Spirit,"[14] and that fourteen in all had experienced a Pentecostal conversion.[15]

Students varied in age; some were as young as fifteen. NLM missionary Elizabeth Fraser wrote to PAOC Eastern Ontario and Quebec District Superintendent (EOQD) Wilbur B. Greenwood, providing her perception of the students and their Bible School lifestyle:

> They were all earnest students but neither of them were the most brilliant … The girls were expected to do household duties – dishes, beds, and all general care of house, school and church … The boys were made responsible for all water carrying and this was carried quite a distance.[16]

Students were required to assist with much of the food preparation.[17] Additionally, Spillenaar recruited students to travel up the Moose River, where they caught pike and pickerel as a supplement to donated food.[18] The rationale from the period was to have Indigenous students

Figure 3.1 Northland Mission Church in Moosonee

cultivate, gather, and prepare their own food, presumably presenting a parallel to typical First Nations subsistence practices. It was further thought to reduce potential culture shock from adjustment to a monetary, transactional economy and lifestyle. This was an approach commonly employed by church-run schools, and was motivated by efforts to reduce overall costs.[19]

In its early years, both the college's living arrangements and its academic offerings were modest. In order to graduate, a student needed to attend three successive summer sessions, each two months long. The NLMBC offered Bible courses, gradually expanding to teach doctrinal theology, with a distinctly Pentecostal emphasis. The NLMBC's informal nature meant that it was not accredited. Rather, it was an introductory catechetical program intended to prepare Indigenous Pentecostals for lay evangelism.[20] Although the NLMBC did not offer the same level of education as the PAOC's accredited, conventional Bible schools, it nevertheless strove to be reputable, attracting prospective students by offering them the PAOC's entry-level ministerial credential of Lay-Preacher's Certificate upon graduation.[21]

The college produced yearbooks with records of students and graduates. Citations from yearbooks are useful as they capture an aspect of the Indigenous Voice. Methodologically, however, it is important to acknowledge these accounts have been preserved by and maintained within the missionary (Euro-Canadian) documentary record from the period and as such should be analyzed with some degree of scrutiny, requiring thorough interrogation.

Generally, the student body was composed of comparable numbers of male and female students from First Nations territories in northern and northwestern Ontario, home to the NLM's nascent congregations. While many ultimately went on to become evangelists, most students at least held lay ministry roles during and after their study period.[22] Even before graduating, students engaged in regular evangelism, and were invited to participate in weekly evangelistic outreaches.[23]

Reportedly there was a rich sense of community among students, and a genuine belief in God's provision whatever the circumstance. For example, in 1962 Eddie Gilles, an Anishinini student from Pagwa River, Ontario, fell off his bicycle while riding across a railway bridge, plummeting eighty-five feet to a riverbank below and narrowly avoiding a plunge into the frigid river water. Gilles broke his back and lost movement in his legs. After much prayer, Gilles received healing, regaining mobility in his legs.[24] Following the incident Gilles cited Psalm 91:4, declaring: "Truly the Lord is wonderful, for He brought me back to full recovery after the serious accident I had last fall … Also the Lord baptized me with the Holy Spirit while at Bible School this year."[25] Testimonies emphasizing Pentecostal experience and physical healing were common in these yearbooks.[26]

The yearbooks also encouraged some propagation of Indigenous culture, allowing students to make their mark with Indigenous language.[27] James Barkman, a Néhiyaw student in the class of 1962, contributed an article titled "What the Bible Means to Me." Barkman wrote the assignment entirely in Nêhiyawêwin.[28] That same year he shared his joy at being able to attend the NLMBC: "My prayer is that God will bless all of us here in a wonderful way. I praise Him continually for the strength He gives me. Jesus never fails!" He finished by citing John 3:36 from the Bible.[29] A closer analysis reveals that the NLM indeed was an intercultural mission, although missionaries did not always realize it. Most students comprehended English (particularly the younger ones),[30] yet many continued to use mostly Indigenous languages. One might argue that by using these languages, and by compiling translations of scripture and hymns, the NLMBC's yearbooks inadvertently contributed to the preservation of this aspect of Indigenous culture.

Spillenaar was the creative force behind the NLMBC's Moosonee campus, but mission administration and aircraft itineration proved demanding of his time. As such, Spillenaar could not operate both the mission and the NLMBC alone. The missionary realized he required a generous volunteer base to instruct students. These teachers were Euro-Canadian, mainly high school teachers, Bible college students, or pastors, and almost exclusively from southern Ontario.[31] Volunteer cooks were Euro-Canadian,[32] with NLMBC operation requiring great effort from NLM staff.[33]

In addition to that support, it also became clear that Spillenaar needed administrative and organizational help. Typically this responsibility fell to whoever happened to be pastoring the NLM church in Moosonee at the time.[34] However, it became necessary for the NLM to acquire an official Bible college director. The PAOC looked to Harold Howarth.[35] Born in Yorkshire, England, Howarth moved to Canada as a teenager, and as a young man volunteered teaching Sunday school. In 1941 he graduated from Two Rivers Bible Institute in Saskatchewan. Two years later Howarth "experienced Pentecost in his own soul at Shadeland Pentecostal Camp," the Manitoba and Northwestern Ontario District's (MNWOD) camp in Devlin, Ontario. In 1945 the PAOC ordained Howarth while he and his wife Lillian pastored in Manitoba.[36] In 1946 they moved to northern Ontario, in the mid-1950s to British Columbia, then in the early 1960s to New Brunswick. By April 1965 the PAOC placed Howarth "in charge of the work at Moosonee," Ontario, where he served most resolutely as director of the NLMBC.[37]

As the NLM's awareness of its mission to Indigenous people grew, so too the PAOC's literature attempted to pay attention to Indigenous adherents' perspectives. The denomination eventually expressed a position more sympathetic to the realities of reserve life. For instance, in 1968 Howarth related how a young Indigenous man accidentally discharged his shotgun on a hunting and fishing trip, the close-range shot killing his brother. Howarth declared: "Those who say the Indian is lacking in emotion may not have visited an Indian home when death has taken a loved one. The people of Moosonee show a tremendous depth of compassion for one another in times of trouble."[38]

Howarth described the funeral as barren and basic in comparison to typical Euro-Canadian funerals. The family ferried the deceased by canoe partway across the Moose River to nearby Moose Factory and conducted the interment in a Protestant cemetery, as there was then only a Catholic cemetery in Moosonee. "These are the people we love – for whom we are giving our years. God loved them."[39] Despite the cultural and linguistic challenges that accompanied teaching and sharing, Howarth's later record demonstrates a positive shift in PAOC literature of the time. The upstart NLMBC further attracted attention within the PAOC, as documentation and literature of the period credited the college with a degree of success and uniqueness.[40] Even beyond typical denominational communications, the PAOC made great claims of its NLMBC. *Testimony* editor Earl N.O. Kulbeck highlighted the college in a 1968 presentation to the Canadian federal government, crediting it "for the development of lay leadership amongst the Indians."[41] Although the NLM was slow to realize its mission to Indigenous people, accounts by Howarth and others illustrated that missionaries were intent upon providing holistic ministry instruction to Indigenous acolytes.[42]

A general sense of pride in the NLMBC's accomplishments is well illustrated by PAOC General Secretary-Treasurer C.H. Stiller's comment: "This school is dedicated to the principle of the indigenous church." Mission staff in Moosonee were supplemented by volunteers who gave "their time and talents to spread the gospel among the Indian population through the ministry of the students whom they have taught." Although the PAOC did not publish detailed enrolment or financial figures at the time, NLMBC leadership emphasized that students paid no tuition fees. Still, poverty impacted some students' ability to attend. Stiller stated: "Some have never seen flush toilets and are not accustomed to eating at a table with a knife, fork and spoon … Christ died for them. Pray with us that light will shine in the darkness."[43] Although Stiller's comments were intended to highlight certain students' limited financial means, they also give insight into the era's Pentecostal missionary perspective. The association of Christianity and Euro-Canadian domestic etiquette echoes the longer-established churches' civilizing axiom, "cleanliness is next to godliness." This hints at an assimilative educational agenda by mission leaders,[44] while NLMBC instructors ostensibly trained Indigenous students to minister to their own people.

In response to Stiller's comments, it should be clarified that students were impoverished because many Indigenous young people from economically underdeveloped northern territories had modest monetary underpinnings. Additionally, the considerable demands of their dormitory chores meant that students often did not have sufficient time for paid work while also studying. Nevertheless, the Euro-Canadian missionaries countered such limitations by emphasizing supernatural provision for tangible needs, never missing an opportunity to request financial support from Euro-Canadian sponsors, praising the generous, and thanking God for providing.

PAOC lay sponsors often directed funds to Euro-Canadian instructors rather than to Indigenous students and evangelists.[45] This trend can be traced partly to the PAOC periodicals' glowing portrayals of Euro-Canadian missionaries.[46] Neither did this direction of funds fully acknowledge that Euro-Canadian missionary efforts closely relied on Indigenous participation.[47] For instance, Wallace (Wally) McKay (Anishinini; Sachigo Lake, Ontario) began his studies at the NLMBC in 1965.[48] McKay went on to study at the PAOC's accredited Eastern Pentecostal Bible College (EPBC) in Peterborough, Ontario. In 1967, McKay returned to the NLMBC to translate English lecture notes into Nêhiyawêwin. Howarth celebrated the enthusiasm shown for McKay's work, proving "that the time, money and effort to produce them was well spent." Howarth continued, "we plan to produce all the course in Cree." The arduous task was essential to effective training.[49] McKay eventually translated into Cree notes for sixteen different courses.[50] While PAOC constituents read mostly of Euro-Canadian missionaries and instructors, as evidenced by this episode, those Euro-Canadians relied on the insight and contributions of Indigenous individuals, many of them students. McKay's vital role as an Indigenous minister within the PAOC continued for decades. In the NLM's final years, McKay's contribution to long-awaited autonomy (described in chapter 5) proved indispensable.

NLMBC students represented ethnic and linguistic diversity. In its early years the NLMBC enrolled Nīhithawak, Nehiyawak, Môsoniyi Iliniwak, and Néhinawak students, as well as Ojibweg Anishinaabeg and Anishininiwag students, and eventually expanded to draw students from as far away as Saskatchewan as well as Kanien'kehá:ka students from Quebec. This diversity presented pedagogical challenges due to Euro-Canadian instructors' inability to speak Indigenous language. Howarth attempted to rectify matters, relying even more on volunteer translators.[51] Throughout his NLMBC tenure, Howarth generally embraced the integration of Indigenous language more readily than did his contemporaries, and to his credit undertook some study of Nêhiyawêwin.[52] He concluded: "God said his word would not return to Him barren nor unfruitful. There is bound to be a reaping in return for all the seed sown in Moosonee over the years."[53] Still, on the exceptional occasions when Indigenous language was used, it was predominantly Nêhiyawêwin. The NLM rarely provided significant attention to Ojibwemowin Anishinaabemowin or Anishininiimowin.

The NLMBC displayed some early signs of success. After only six years of operation, twelve students had graduated and went on to minister to some of the NLM's congregations. By the mid-1960s the NLMBC had increased in popularity, graduating close to ten students annually.[54] By the late 1960s, the NLM claimed 10,000 Indigenous constituents in twenty-five Indigenous territories accessible only by air. Presumably this figure referred to the total populations in all of the communities in which the NLM was located, rather than actual adherents. By 1967, eight NLMBC graduates worked in these communities alongside ten Euro-Canadian missionaries.[55]

Yet not all was as well as it might otherwise have appeared. Students seemingly demonstrated great ministry ability and willingness, and certainly there was space within the NLM for Indigenous evangelists. But graduates wishing to pastor churches encountered challenges, as it would appear that Euro-Canadian missionaries proved reluctant to vacate their pulpits to make room for Indigenous preachers. An additional struggle was the NLMBC's recurring financial challenges, necessitating substantial sponsorship, with the college attempting to provide tuition relief on a per-student basis.[56] The realization of such difficulty stood in stark contrast to the NLMBC's self-promotion, requiring some reflection and analysis. Yearbooks and other records indicate that by the 1960s, the NLMBC averaged ten or more students per term, a respectable level of enrolment for an institution of its type. Even so, it is unlikely that everything went as well as PAOC literature implied. Kervan Chalmers, NLMBC principal in the 1990s, later noted that through the 1960s the NLM experienced "less than encouraging results," without providing full analysis of why the results were poor.[57]

Another of the NLMBC's early challenges was its location, which often proved as influential and significant as its principal. The Moosonee campus's remoteness and associated transportation costs led PAOC leadership to discuss closing it altogether.[58] As early as 1968, Spillenaar wrote of potentially moving the NLMBC to Nakina, which he perceived to be more geographically central. The move would save "endless flying miles on every round trip."[59] The decision seems to have been the administration's alone, as throughout this process the NLM did not publicly consult Indigenous representatives. While there was no apparent resistance, neither was there any obvious expression of Indigenous Pentecostals' desire for the NLMBC to move. Possibly mission leadership anticipated the move might help to bolster enrolment, and they officially relocated the college to Nakina in 1969.[60]

THE WILDERNESS YEARS: THE NLMBC IN NAKINA AND ITINERANT

Harold and Lillian Howarth left the NLMBC in 1971, and their successors, Dale and Alberta Cummins, had previously served as missionaries in Kenya from 1959 to 1969; thereafter Dale taught at EPBC. Dale perceived an "almost total lack of Christian education among the Indian churches in Northern Ontario," describing this as what "led Alberta and [him] to become involved with the Northland Mission."[61] The couple taught at the NLMBC in Nakina during the summers of 1971 through 1973 while Dale also served as principal.[62] Cummins likened the perceived laid-back pace of northern Ontario to his previous experiences as a missionary in the Majority World.[63] More than once his international and intercultural mission experience provided him opinions more astute than those of his contemporaries. He appreciated and understood that although the NLM existed inside Canada, it was essentially an intercultural mission. Cummins's ability to apply his insights practically, however, was another matter. At the very least, with Cummins present to shore up the NLMBC, the PAOC continued its positive reporting, stating in 1971 that the college performed a "vital service to ... Home Missions work among the Cree."[64]

Another development in Nakina was the NLM's official articulation of its intention to train NLMBC students to become ministers. In the past there was some ambiguity as to whether students were training for lay or full-time, vocational ministry. On this point it is worthwhile pausing to evaluate the PAOC's desired outcome for the NLMBC. If not intended to train students for full-time ministry, then what purpose did the college serve? It was not a lucrative enterprise, and as such the PAOC cannot be accused of operating the NLMBC with an eye to profit. Further, graduates probably could not be considered any worse off for having attended. After all, the college at the very least served to offer some level of Pentecostal ministry training to Indigenous students where previously there had been none.

Still, the NLMBC must be analyzed both for what it was and what it was not. Although Cummins and other NLM leaders portrayed the college as a vehicle for Indigenous ministers' autonomy, truthfully it was a vehicle for denominational goals. However well intentioned, at its core, the PAOC established the NLMBC to meet its own needs, contrary to its claim of existing to meet Indigenous students' needs. The ideal of a "Three-Self" church ultimately would require the PAOC to encourage indigenization and allow autonomy. While the PAOC wanted to evangelize Indigenous people, training Indigenous evangelists to accomplish this goal more rapidly, the denomination did not intend to contribute to a distinct, independent, Indigenous Pentecostal movement. It is true that students wanted to receive a theological education. But to that point, where autonomy was present, it was so only through Indigenous people's insistence and not through denominational empowerment. This failure revealed a fundamental flaw in the NLMBC's underpinning philosophy – that is, exclusively seeking the results-based outcome of producing graduates who would run more churches.[65]

Further, the NLMBC did not train Indigenous Pentecostals for ordained ministry. This raises the pertinent conversation of ministerial credentialling, which proved to be crucially important, significantly affecting the NLMBC's trajectory. For that reason, this conversation resurfaces at multiple points throughout this monograph. Within the PAOC there are various levels of credentialling available to clergy, conveying commensurate levels of rights, privileges, and responsibilities. The standard credential is the Licence to Minister, a prerequisite to ordination, itself the highest ministerial credential. Yet to this point in the NLMBC's development, the college had been unable to qualify its graduates for anything more than the entry-level Lay-Preacher's Certificate. Ironically, according to the PAOC's Constitution, this same credential could be granted even in the absence of any formal education. This meant that Indigenous ministry hopefuls could qualify for this credential even without training from the NLMBC, rendering theological qualification somewhat vocationally moot.

Motivated by the scarcity of credentialling options available to Indigenous trainees, and aware that the NLMBC was not a professionally qualifying institution, in 1971 the PAOC financed an experimental program to offer advanced courses in Bible, doctrine, and practical theology. John Spillenaar and Dale Cummins operated these summer seminars, with then–Department of Home Missions and Bible Colleges (DHMBC) director Robert Argue reporting on the successful training of "ten Indian pastors from Northern Ontario ... [for] four weeks ... in the Indian Bible school in Nakina." Argue continued, "this summer's post graduate school will have far reaching effects on our Indian work in Northern Ontario."[66] Upon the course's conclusion, the PAOC presented diplomas to all students, officially recognizing the following newly minted credentials: Letter of Privilege to Preach and Special Ministerial Certificate, which Spillenaar described as "our highest Indian Worker Credentials."[67]

This of course was precedent-setting. Although the PAOC did not present to these candidates full Licences to Minister, this episode at least is an early example of the PAOC General Executive granting more than a token qualification to the graduates of a training institution tailored to Indigenous students. Further, in granting this recognition, the PAOC demonstrated at least a symbolic honouring of the indigenous principle. The college's strategic shift may have resulted from a denominational realization that equipping laity alone would not secure the mission's longevity. Indigenous clergy would be necessary. Notwithstanding this acknowledgment, the issue of ministerial credentialling for NLBMC graduates continued to be a significant challenge throughout subsequent decades.[68]

This initiative to train Indigenous clergy suffered an otherwise unlikely setback in 1973. Somewhat counterintuitively, after only four years of operation in Nakina, the NLM decided to close its college. Spillenaar in all probability influenced this decision, which he claimed to have made under "the leading of God." The missionary recounted the decision's substance in the first person plural: "We were not entirely satisfied with our Bible School program and after much prayer and consultation decided to sell the Nakina property."[69] Presumably Spillenaar was not dissatisfied with a lack of students or graduates, as most denominational documentation indicated the college's moderate success. Spillenaar himself spoke very highly of the college, praising its graduates.[70] One reality is that even with Cummins on board (and Howarth before him), the college still required

Spillenaar to function in an administrative capacity, drawing him away from his beloved itineration.

At any rate, the DHMBC, and in particular Robert Argue, were not content with the complete closure of the college. In its place, Argue recommended an itinerant school, of which Spillenaar recorded: "Instead of flying the students out we decided to fly the teachers in to spend two weeks in one settlement. With two teams on the go we could reach six settlements each year."[71] For his part, Argue allegedly drew inspiration for the idea from "a method that had been used in Africa."[72] The itinerant college was a joint venture between the DHMBC, the PAOC Western Ontario District (WOD), and the NLM. Cummins remained principal, and most instructors were EPBC senior students or recent graduates. The travelling college continued for "a number of summers," but did not produce a strong rate of graduation.[73] Additionally ironic is the fact that while the NLM justified the college's move from Moosonee to Nakina on the basis of reducing air travel, the new itineration system of flying instructors to individual First Nations territories surely must have required significant resources.

One conceivable motivation for the transition was that changing the NLMBC from a stationary institution to an itinerating one allowed more opportunities for Euro-Canadian Bible college students and graduates. As the DHMBC oversaw both the PAOC's domestic missions and its Bible colleges, the department was uniquely positioned to create domestic missionary and teaching placements for its own Bible college graduates. This would explain closing the Nakina NLMBC, justify the expense of college itineration, and all the while increase EPBC's graduate placement rates. In denominational leaders' and mission supporters' hearts and minds, this would justify the NLM's abrupt action, as well as reflecting well upon the DHMBC.[74]

The PAOC branded the initiative "Theological Education by Extension" (TEE). TEE employed an all-Euro-Canadian, all-male faculty. Similar to the early incarnation of the NLMBC, TEE's "objective was to teach the assigned subject material, then allow opportunity for the students to accept Christ as Saviour." Again, as TEE served as a Bible college, presumably its students would have had some form of Christian association prior to enrolment. Thus, emphasized here once more was the requirement that non-Pentecostal students transition to a pneumatologically and eschatologically emphatic, charismatic form of Christianity during their studies. TEE instructor E.S. Hunter recounted:

> The Second Coming of Christ ... was taught in the last class each day, lending opportunity for an invitation to receive the Lord ... The result of all of this was that many were saved. In one community over thirty were saved ... While the emphasis was on teaching the Christians, often in the evenings non-Christians were present and responded to the invitation.[75]

Presumably Hunter described many and not "all" as being saved because many already had subscribed to Pentecostalism prior to this encounter. Hunter's observation about evening sessions implies that TEE blurred lines between Bible college and tent revival.

The travelling college had its share of critics among NLM missionaries, including Cummins, whose enduring impression was that TEE was inadequate and, owing to its transience, unable to overcome intercultural obstacles. It became apparent that Indigenous ministry hopefuls deserved a more comprehensive means of acquiring ministry training. Aware of TEE's limited capacity, the General Executive allowed Indigenous ministry hopefuls to receive yet another form of ministerial credentialling. In 1974 the PAOC General Conference standardized the aforementioned Letter of Privilege to Preach credential. Although similar to the former Lay-Preacher's Certificate, the new Letter of Privilege to Preach was specifically tailored to Indigenous applicants. Essentially, an aspiring Indigenous minister could be eligible for the Letter of Privilege to Preach without any theological training. Simultaneously the General Conference also standardized the Special Ministerial Certificate, which typically did require Indigenous ministry hopefuls to be educated through a training institution such as TEE or one of the other districts' Bible schools for Indigenous students.[76]

Again, creating these levels of ministerial credentialling was significant, as it affected the NLMBC in subsequent decades. The General Executive intended to make ministerial qualification for Indigenous ministers more accessible, but in so doing inadvertently created a two-tier credentialling system. While one track (the Special Ministerial Certificate) required education, the other (the Letter of Privilege to Preach) did not. Further, any differences in the rights, privileges, and responsibilities of each credential were largely arbitrary and would not majorly affect an Indigenous minister's vocational trajectory. As a result, many would-be students opted for the Letter of Privilege to Preach that did not require formal education. As it relates to the

NLMBC, certainly one can see the disincentive to attending an institution that offered no higher level of professional qualification than could be had without even attending.

The would-be trainees' decision not to attend the NLMBC typically was not a case of students' wishing to avoid the hard work that theological education required. Rather, many began to perceive the NLMBC as a Euro-Canadian-dominated institution. Effectively TEE served as little more than an opportunity for recent EPBC graduates to dabble in practical ministry. Remote First Nations territories provided instructors a testing ground far from the coveted pulpits of settler regions (where youthful inexperience might prove detrimental). In what could be described as cultural resistance,[77] many would-be students likely opted not to attend the NLMBC for this reason, negatively affecting the college's appeal and enrolment figures and contributing to its decline.[78]

While it is to the NLM's credit that it founded the college only ten years after the establishment of the mission itself, the NLMBC's trajectory implies that it was not a high priority for the mission director, Spillenaar. He started the Bible college intending to equip Indigenous evangelists, yet abruptly moved the college to Nakina and shortly thereafter sold all its material assets. No sooner had Spillenaar dispossessed the college of brick and mortar than he converted it into a travelling operation. With TEE's conducting of lectures and revivals simultaneously, it was unclear whether the travelling college's intended audience was ministry trainees or new spiritual seekers who might be won over to Pentecostalism. Unable to find its footing, the college's security suffered. These changes all took place fewer than twenty years after its founding, not likely sufficient time to evaluate its long-term chances of success. It is possible that the director saw the travelling college as a cost-saving measure, but again, extensive operation and usage of the aircraft still would have been very expensive.

Additionally, Spillenaar implemented these abrupt changes fewer than two years before his own resignation from the NLM, denoting a degree of arbitrariness and perhaps correlating to his foreseeing his own tenure with the NLM coming to a close. In the final analysis, it is hard to assess exactly how Spillenaar felt about the NLMBC.[79] His many articles for PAOC periodicals praised the NLMBC's effectiveness, but the volumes of his autobiography suggest his priority may have lain elsewhere. In his first memoir, *Wings of the Gospel*, Spillenaar committed only a few pages to describing the NLMBC. In his second volume, *To the Regions Beyond*, he wrote of his departure from the NLM: In "January 1976 ... I ... announced a 'New Challenge'. Instead of retirement, the Lord led me to go further north than ever before."[80] For a man whose driving ambition was always to go further north, perhaps the institutionalization of the NLM and NLMBC moored Spillenaar too far south. Or perhaps his perceived vision of a "Three-Self" Indigenous church proved out of reach, so he settled for what Angela Tarango termed the "halfway indigenous principle."[81]

John Spillenaar resigned from the NLM on 14 January 1976, citing a desire to itinerate further north, among Inuit.[82] His subsequent resignation of his PAOC credentials was not without controversy, as he parted with the PAOC on less-than-amiable terms.[83] In 1976, WOD superintendent Howard Honsinger reluctantly wrote:

> John Spillenaar ... given the option of abiding [by] the reasonable directives of the Western Ontario District or turning in his credentials ... sent his credentials to the District Office ... [Thus] he is no longer recognized by our District and should be dropped from our listings ... I deeply regret this whole unsavoury process has had to be negotiated to the conclusion it has reached ... Insofar as Mrs. Spillenaar is concerned ... I have reason to believe that she has not been in agreement with many of her husband's decisions. She has the right to stand on her own merit.[84]

Honsinger's comment regarding Tyyne Spillenaar implies that her influence was more than a behind-the-scenes force, and that her opinion was loud and clear enough to be acknowledged and recognized by denominational executive leadership. Yet it is unclear what decisions Honsinger referred to that landed John in hot water. Archival records indicate his ongoing frustration with denominationally imposed geographic restrictions.[85] His departure from the NLM and subsequent resignation of his ministerial credentials may have been a result of his insatiable desire to itinerate further north, particularly while the NLM was institutionalizing and developing fixed infrastructure. Following Spillenaar's departure, one member of the WOD executive hinted at this possibility: "He was a daring individualist with an unusual evangelistic gift. His visits resulted in many salvations and some churches being established. However, the work of consolidation and training was weak."[86] Erna Alma Peters described Spillenaar's decision thus: "Now on his own, John flew up to Quebec to carry on there, without the burden of the NLM."[87] Although the missionary's evangelistic enthusiasm was undeniable, these comments hint that Spillenaar was not the universally celebrated son he appeared to be in earlier literature. Or at the very least, Spillenaar found himself in a scenario where the PAOC sought to institutionalize the NLM while he preferred to itinerate unencumbered by administrative accountability.

Spillenaar spent the years following his 1976 resignation from the PAOC itinerating throughout the Arctic. In Nunavik, Quebec, the Spillenaars founded the Arctic Mission Outreach Trust Fund. It was financed by multiple churches, denominations (other than the PAOC), and individual contributors. Through this new ministry, John and Tyyne Spillenaar established five churches in Inuit territories. John Spillenaar continued full-time itineration by air until at least 1991. The couple retired from active ministry in 1992, settling in Kitchener, Ontario.[88] In 1995 John sent fifty dollars to the PAOC General Executive, enclosing a handwritten note stating, "this donation [is] to ... defray the cost of producing credentials."[89] The PAOC obliged, reactivating his credentials to the highest status of ordained minister.[90] That same year he made one final northern tour, now as a passenger on chartered flights, visiting seven different Arctic communities. In the public memory, Spillenaar ended an illustrious half-century evangelistic career where it all began, with the PAOC.[91]

Following Spillenaar's 1976 resignation, that same year the WOD executive promoted Cummins from NLMBC principal to NLM director. In his new role Cummins moved the NLM headquarters from South Porcupine to Pickle Lake, Ontario, where one of his first acts was to reopen a brick-and-mortar college.[92] Simultaneously the NLM named Ian Winter, a licensed pilot originally from British Columbia, to the role of NLMBC principal. Since 1969, Winter had assisted in operating the NLM's aircraft while pastoring the NLM's Moosonee church.[93] He had "a heart burdened for the Northland Mission, the native people, and a vision of what [could] be accomplished for God in this area."[94]

"A MONUMENTAL DECISION": THE NLMBC IN PICKLE LAKE

NLM leadership chose Pickle Lake for its headquarters' new site, perceiving the town to be a hub of northern commercial activity, as it was Ontario's northernmost settlement accessible by road at the time. Pickle Lake proved to be the NLM's most enduring location. Future college principal Kervan Chalmers recalled it was "a monumental decision in the history of Native Ministry in Northern Ontario ... Over the next 15 years much effort was expended to make this facility and the program productive for Native ministries."[95] In the years following, the NLMBC sought to implement ambitious program and course offerings.

NLM literature described the NLMBC's Pickle Lake relocation as a decision taken at the request of Indigenous pastors. Still, other sources point to an overwhelming absence of denominational consultation with Indigenous ministers, countering that the "setting was chosen by non-Natives ... [who] thought this would be the sort of setting northern Native peoples would choose." In any case, NLM leadership promoted "a Bible School to train native leadership for the Indian churches: pastors, evangelists, [and] workers."[96] Cummins was pleased to revive the NLMBC, expanding from the course offerings in Moosonee and Nakina. The re-establishment of a brick-and-mortar campus improved students' prospects that had been tarnished during the wilderness years of the Nakina campus and the itinerant TEE.[97] The NLMBC's first graduates in Pickle Lake were John and Lydia Mekenak (Anishininiwag; Sachigo Lake, Ontario).[98] Cummins recalled:

> We've come at last to the time of first fruits in our Bible school ministry. John and Lydia Mekanak and their two children moved from Sachigo Lake to Fort Severn this week, the first fruits, the gracious promise of an entire harvest to come from the Bible school, of many like John to launch into true pastoral ministry, a whole new era for the churches here.[99]

Indeed PAOC leaders held the Mekenaks and their leadership abilities in high regard.[100]

In 1980 Cummins positively reported that the NLMBC had resumed a six-week course offering. Although the Moosonee and Nakina colleges had offered longer, two-month terms, six weeks in Pickle Lake certainly was an improvement over the whistle-stop courses the itinerant TEE had offered. Indigenous Pentecostals also demonstrated their commitment to the NLMBC's successful redevelopment. Following terms of study, students and graduates alike departed Pickle Lake, eagerly returning to their home territories to assist in their local NLM congregations' ministries. As the duration of courses continued to expand, in an unprecedented turn, entire communities released labourers from their subsistence duties, enabling them to attend the NLMBC year-round. Churches and students also increased their contributions toward offsetting college costs.[101]

Yet with new opportunities came new challenges, particularly funding shortfalls, a recurring test to the college during its redevelopment and eventual decline.[102] Indigenous Pentecostals donated, but the NLM relied more heavily on the contributions of the PAOC's southern Ontario–based settler churches and their parishioners.[103] Even here, money proved difficult to raise, as canvassing for the newly revived NLMBC competed with the PAOC's international missionary enterprises. Cummins protested the trend of the PAOC and its laity supporting international missions more readily than domestic ones, as did other pastors and mission leaders, often with little success.[104]

The NLMBC tried hard to weather financial shortfalls but suffered yet another setback from personnel transitions.[105] Although a capable writer, rarely did Cummins produce the solutions Indigenous communities required and even requested. In many cases, portrayals of Indigenous people's lives were intended to drum up funds and portray his leadership of the NLM positively. Cummins mostly portrayed perceived spiritual depravity, rarely describing the specifics of legitimate material needs. Presumably mission supporters and PAOC leadership would have benefited from descriptions of resources that communities, churches, and the NLMBC actually required in order to ameliorate potentially difficult situations.

Oversight was one factor among others causing PAOC leadership's disillusionment with Cummins's effectiveness. In March 1980, WOD superintendent Homer Cantelon noted: "Rev. Dale Cummins has been the Director of the Northland Mission for several years ... we have not experienced rapid progress in this field."[106] Ironically Cummins signalled his own demise from the position, indicating to PAOC leadership that the NLM was drifting from its appropriate mission context and falling out of touch with the realities of reserve life.[107] On 30 October 1980 the director submitted his resignation, citing the NLM's alleged need of a pilot. Cummins had already spoken with then–NLMBC principal Ian Winter about taking over the mission. The WOD executive requested that Cummins remain in his role another year while they considered alternatives.

In a 28 January 1981 meeting, the WOD executive decided Cummins's leadership of the NLM had become problematic. Cummins had already indicated more than once his desire to resign, citing issues related to funding shortfalls and differences of opinion regarding mission philosophy. This time the WOD executive accepted Cummins's resignation, asking that he remain another six months while they sought his replacement. The executive concluded Cummins's involvement with the NLM on 31 October 1981.[108] Thereafter residing in Saskatoon, Saskatchewan, Cummins maintained ministerial credentials with the WOD.[109]

Cummins's lacklustre departure from the NLM demonstrated that autonomy was required at both a ministerial and leadership level. The decision to appoint Cummins rather than an Indigenous director is telling and troubling. Thirty years into its mission to Indigenous people, operating a Bible college to train Indigenous leaders and planting Indigenous churches, the PAOC still did not view any Indigenous candidate as capable of directing the NLM. This gap demonstrates that the PAOC verbally supported the indigenous principle while its action (or inaction) undermined it. Instead, the PAOC again opted to employ the halfway indigenous principle, maintaining the status quo, appointing Ian Winter, yet another Euro-Canadian, as Cummins's successor.

PAOC records credited Winter with contributing to a season of productivity and expansion not seen since the early days of Spillenaar's leadership.[110] What is more, the NLM's Indigenous ministers admired him.[111] Nevertheless, Winter's appointment as director was problematic were one to consider the indigenous principle. It might have been forgivable that the PAOC had not named an Indigenous successor to Spillenaar. It is disappointing the denomination did not do so following Cummins's resignation. Certainly by then several NLM churches had active and successful Indigenous pastors capable of leading:[112] Moses Anderson, pastor of Kasabanica; Isaac Tait, worker from Sachigo Lake; Geordie Thomas, pastor of Fort Severn; Joseph McKay, pastor of Sachigo Lake; and Eli Mickenack, pastor of Big Trout; not to mention the celebrated John and Lydia Mekenak. All of these had secured at least Letters of Privilege to Preach, and some had earned the Special Ministerial Certificate.

While many acknowledged Ian Winter's dedication, Indigenous ministers still desired an Indigenous director for the NLM. George Gunner (Moose Cree First Nation; Moose Factory, Ontario), who would gain prominence within the NLM during the late 1980s and into the 1990s, reflected thus:

Figure 3.2 Northland Mission Bible College Chapel

> The goal was for the director of the Northland Mission to train an Indigenous person to take over, and that never happened. I often wondered why didn't it happen? It could have happened. There were some good people that could have taken over … Why did they not train that person, empower him, and let him take over? Because I think we did need an Aboriginal person in that position of director of the ministry … There has to be Aboriginal leadership if it's going to go anywhere.[113]

Gunner did not doubt PAOC leadership's interest in the missionization of Indigenous communities, nor did he question the sacrifice of many Euro-Canadian missionaries, expressing appreciation for both. Still, there was an expectation that the PAOC could at least have offered a better demonstration of their intention to transition the NLM to Indigenous leadership.[114]

This shortcoming, unfortunately, was at least partially bureaucratic. The PAOC's stringent requirements for directorship were inaccessible for most Indigenous ministry leaders at that time. Prospective directors not only needed to be experienced, but also required significant ministerial qualification, including ordination. As the Indigenous ministers could not earn ordination through the NLMBC, it was very difficult for them to access leadership positions requiring it.[115] All of this suggests that inasmuch as it was individual missionaries or NLM leaders who failed to implement the indigenous principle, so too did the systems of the PAOC's governance structures through their rigid requirements for clerical qualifications.

During the early 1980s, Winter concurrently filled the roles of NLM director and NLMBC principal. He was charged with remoulding the college curriculum, schedule, and vision.[116] This development included the introduction of English-language courses, marking a curious linguistic shift. Now, rather than relying on Indigenous volunteers to translate lectures into local languages, the NLMBC opted to teach students English. To be clear, these were not merely theology courses taught in English, but rather English-language courses specifically aimed at teaching Indigenous students to communicate in English rather than Nêhiyawêwin, Ojibwemowin Anishinaabemowin, or Anishininiimowin.[117] These courses also spared Euro-Canadian instructors the effort of learning Indigenous languages. While this was pragmatic, mandating language courses that required Indigenous students to learn English indicated an increasingly marked shift away from the college's intended indigenous principle. Still, it is possible that NLMBC leadership felt this instruction would provide Indigenous ministry trainees with a wider range of vocational prospects. To this end, the college offered travelling internships to students and young people in NLM churches. On occasion, students itinerated during their summers throughout the PAOC's settler churches of southern Ontario. These tours became popular, and something of a novelty among the host churches.[118]

Winter served as principal until 1985 when Guy Campeau replaced him, Winter thereafter concentrating on full-time direction of the NLM.[119] Before graduating from EPBC in 1981, Campeau earned a BA in Native Studies from Laurentian University. While serving as NLMBC principal, he also pastored the NLM church in Pickle Lake. Campeau additionally established the NLM church in the neighbouring Mishkeegogamang First Nation (Ojibwe Anishinaabe) in 1984.

Campeau resigned in the autumn of 1986 and returned to his home in Sudbury, citing personal reasons. Despite Campeau's brief tenure, he attracted monetary support for the NLMBC from francophone Pentecostals.[120]

Following Campeau's resignation, the NLM named Graham Gibson principal in 1987. Graham and Linda Gibson, originally from southern Ontario, graduated from EPBC in 1981. The Gibsons began as short-term NLMBC instructors in December 1986. As the two-week course ended, Winter invited Graham to remain as college principal. Linda Gibson recollected the unexpected move to the isolated Pickle Lake, which shared "a single radio phone with everyone on the Mission grounds." Her first lunch at "a student's home involved going into the bush and seeing dinner knocked out of a tree." These were just the obvious differences for a southern Ontarian.[121] Graham reflected: "I went, having absolutely no training in Native religions or cultures other than what I had gleaned from some brief works put out by the Anishnawbe centre in Sudbury, ON."[122] As principal, Graham revised the NLMBC's curriculum, also implementing a faculty rotation. Instructors came to Pickle Lake for two-week courses while students were also flown in and out, taking up residence at the NLM Mission Centre while enrolled.[123]

The college experienced a modest increase in enrolment throughout the 1980s under Gibson's direction, peaking at thirty-five. The college provided four dormitories, reportedly occupied to capacity. Occasionally quarters were so crowded that some students were housed in the NLM's offices. Many students brought their families with them, resettling from northerly towns into college residences. College staff described students as diligent and desiring to learn. In fact, the college's unprecedented success spurred expansion into a third semester in autumn. Effectively the NLMBC was becoming an efficient and somewhat reputable, even if Euro-Canadian-led, full-time training institution.[124]

Under Gibson's principalship, students became favourably engaged. Enrolment records reflect a "who's who" of students and families from a variety of stages of life, ranging from "Eli Mekinak to his grandson Caleb McKay, John Beardy, Samson and Ruth Beardy, Allan and Josephine Etapp, Rudy Turtle and others." PAOC leadership recounted: "They represent the future of our work in the North, eager to learn and improve themselves, open to change, and hungry for God."[125] Rudy Turtle went on to pastor the church in Fort Severn, where he

Figure 3.3 Northland Mission Bible College and Mission Headquarters in Pickle Lake

enjoyed success and church growth.[126] Samson Beardy (Anishinini; Bearskin Lake, Ontario) was the newly expanded program's first graduate in 1985.[127] Samson's brother, Ziggy (Anishinini; Bearskin Lake), pastored the church in Bearskin Lake,[128] alongside John Beardy (Anishinini; Bearskin Lake) following his 1988 graduation.[129]

The NLM described the student base as coming from all over Canada to study the Bible "and develop their own Christian character and ministry." NLM leadership continued: "This distinctive Pentecostal Bible School is committed to meeting the needs of Christian Native people."[130] Generally, students expressed enjoyment of and satisfaction with their Bible college experience. Several gave sacrificially out of their own earnings in order to attend. One, Mary Jane Cavanaugh (Ojibwe Anishinaabe; Sioux Lookout, Ontario), was a grandmother and also the 1993 NLMBC valedictorian. Her student profile described her desire to be known as "someone after God's own heart."[131] Her daughter Pamela graduated from the college the same year. Mary Jane went on to minister in Mishkeegogamang, expressing "a deep desire to see the establishment of a locally-led group of Native Christians" there.[132] Another graduate, Maggie Minister (Eeyou; Nemaska, Quebec), served as interim pastor at Weagamow Lake, Ontario, returning after a month to Nemaska, wishing to pastor her home church. Such accounts demonstrate a positive aspect of the NLMBC in its prioritization of gender equality in education and ministry. At the same time, it presented Indigenous Pentecostalism as a vehicle through which female leadership could be acquired, fulfilled, and executed. These trends simultaneously mirrored Indigenous communities' practices, where women were not marginalized from leadership in the way they might have been within Euro-Canadian structures.[133] Although these women would fare no better than their male counterparts in obtaining mission leadership, their passion for study and commitment to their calling were unmistakeable.

It is essential to emphasize that it was the NLM's Euro-Canadian leadership that preserved records of students' sentiments. Not surprisingly they portray the college positively.[134] Such favourable descriptions of the NLMBC served the college's ability to appeal to prospective Indigenous students. One may only wonder to what degree Euro-Canadians might have attempted to influence these testimonies. Thus, it is difficult to determine from documentary sources alone what exactly the prospect of Pentecostal ministry meant to Indigenous students. There is a general perception that Indigenous persons with a penchant for ministry were attracted to Pentecostalism because of its accessible avenues for leadership. Whereas the longer-established churches were perceived as requiring ministers to undertake lengthy education, the PAOC granted entry-level qualifications to ministry hopefuls, regardless of education.[135] Nevertheless, as the NLM developed and evolved, so too did expectations of higher qualification for Indigenous ministers. Certainly this was the case if an Indigenous minister wished to serve beyond the local church context and participate in mission leadership. When this shift in expectations occurred, early positive perceptions of the NLMBC morphed, and became more critical.

Again, the conversation must return to ministerial credentialling, as the issue intensified during the 1980s. To be clear, Indigenous men were never restricted from ordination (and women across the PAOC received ordination by 1984); they just could not earn it or, until this time, obtain the requisite Licence to Minister through the NLMBC. Instead, they had to graduate from an accredited PAOC Bible college such as EPBC in order to be eligible, which some students did. For instance, Central Pentecostal Bible College (CPBC) in Saskatoon, Saskatchewan, recorded in 1980 the "first Treaty Indian" to graduate from the school, Roger Ratt (Nīhithaw, the exonym for which is Woods Cree; La Ronge, Saskatchewan).[136]

Although the PAOC did not prevent Indigenous students from attending conventional Bible colleges, some college administrators did not make integration into those colleges easy. NLM leadership preferred that Indigenous students attend the NLMBC, recommending that only "brighter students" be encouraged to enroll at one of the PAOC's conventional, accredited colleges.[137] An administrator from one of the PAOC's accredited colleges stated that they "actually would discourage a Native Canadian from attending [there] because the [Native training institute] would do a better job" and that "sending northern Christians to southern Canada to train for ministry in the north is not educationally helpful." The college's administration revealed vestiges of settler colonialism when its representative concluded: "For those Native candidates who have not been significantly assimilated into broader Canadian culture, there would be culture barriers."[138] On the other hand, since a Letter of Privilege to Preach did not require formal education, one might argue that Indigenous students for their part attended the NLMBC not solely for ministerial credentials, but because they were genuinely interested in learning, and in receiving training for ministry leadership.[139]

Still, no credential tailored specifically to Indigenous ministerial candidates was equivalent to the highest level: ordination. By contrast, by 1984 anyone graduating from the three-year diploma program offered by a conventional PAOC Bible college was eligible for its Licence to Minister, and after two years of ministering full-time could be ordained. Following this track, within five years, a student at an accredited college could go from no theological education or qualification, to ordination. For an NLMBC graduate, full credentialling required nearly double the time.[140]

In its early decades, as the NLMBC operated with only introductory and catechetical sessions lasting a few weeks, graduates generally were satisfied with the basic Lay-Preacher's Certificate. While there were occasional critics of this credentialling track, Indigenous students and leadership alike largely seemed content with the status quo throughout the NLMBC's first three decades (1950s through 1970s). The WOD's expectations changed, however, when the district named Ian Winter mission director. Winter was charged with further developing course offerings. He obliged; under his direction the curriculum expanded to a three-year, full-time program of study. As previously outlined, all PAOC districts engaged in missionizing Indigenous communities established Bible colleges tailored to Indigenous ministerial candidates, five schools by this time, mostly independent of the PAOC's conventional, accredited Bible colleges. Winter's eventual expansion of the NLMBC's offerings to a full-orbed program made it exceptional among the PAOC's training institutions tailored to Indigenous students, whose ministry training programs ran for only two years.[141] Still, approaching the late 1980s, the NLMBC remained officially unaccredited and thus incapable of qualifying its graduates for the Licence to Minister credential.

Increased course offerings stirred greater expectations. The WOD envisaged Winter's securing of more outside funding. Several Indigenous Pentecostals awaited ministerial credentialling equivalent to that of conventional Bible college graduates; however, actual outcomes frequently disappointed. Many Indigenous students decided investment in a program offering no straightforward track to ordination, making it "virtually impossible for a native person to be ordained," was too costly.[142] Many students withdrew, applying for entry-level credentials not requiring formal education.[143]

Conscious of this discrepancy's potential for further loss of enrolment, Winter asked the DHMBC to allow the NLMBC to seek accreditation with the North American Association of Bible Colleges (NAABC) as well as the General Executive's permission to qualify graduates for a full Licence to Minister, just like the PAOC's conventional Bible colleges. DHMBC Director Gordon Upton admitted that existing credentialling of Indigenous ministers was inadequate and replied that the PAOC sought to standardize the PAOC's five training institutions tailored to Indigenous ministerial candidates. He recommended the General Executive change its constitutional requirements, hoping standardization of training programs would be met with approval from the NAABC. It was believed that accreditation in turn could make possible the funding of the NLMBC by Indigenous bands and councils, as well as the Department of Indian Affairs and Northern Development (DIAND).[144]

Upton sympathized with Indigenous trainees seeking a Licence to Minister, proposing that the General Executive grant licences to graduates of the five institutions, with ordination conferred upon completion of adequate ministry experience. The motion carried at the PAOC's 1986 General Conference, a decision reflected in its subsequently amended Constitution. For the first time in PAOC history, the denomination made provision as follows: "Native students who graduate from the authorized two-year native training program and ... enter ... definite ministry may be granted a Licensed Minister's Certificate and, following four years of proven ministry, may be eligible for ordination."[145] While this represented a great step forward for Indigenous ministers, ironically it proved less than ideal for the NLMBC. Indigenous ministers still faced the NLM's distinctive three-year program and then pastoral duty for four more years, meaning seven years of education and ministry before being eligible for ordination.

The amended constitution also maintained a two-tiered credentialling process that exempted Indigenous ministers not seeking ordination from formal education. The Constitution offered ministerial hopefuls a means to side-step the NLMBC via the newly minted (but less than Licence to Minister) "Recognition of Ministry Certificate."[146] The latter credential was granted to a "native applicant of proven character, having indication of leadership qualities and the call of God, who is active in the ministry, and who has not completed the prescribed two-year native training program."[147]

Many would-be Bible college students, discouraged by the cost and length of formal education at the NLMBC for a Licence to Minister and ordination, opted instead for a more-accessible Recognition of Ministry Certificate. As anticipated, this undercut the college's enrolment.[148] Presumably provoked by this decline and desiring to increase enrolment at its Bible colleges for Indigenous ministerial candidates, in 1990 the PAOC General Conference again altered the denomination's entry-level credential: "Native credential holders must [take] one of the various theological training programs available through the districts ... [and] those presently holding the Recognition of Ministry credential [will] be given eight years from this date in order to meet the education requirements.[149] Effectively, the PAOC was grandfathering out its two-tier credentialling system and requiring active Indigenous ministers to re-enter theological training. Yet the effort offered little in the way of actual consolation for the NLMBC, as the lengthy time frame permitting acceptance of Recognition of Ministry allowed the two-tier system to persist. Constitutional changes, perpetuation of a two-tier system, and the resulting decline in NLMBC enrolment likely did not please principal Graham Gibson.[150]

THE BEGINNING OF THE END: THE NLMBC IN SIOUX LOOKOUT

NLM leadership became aware of the necessity to at least change something about the NLMBC. Pickle Lake, once a bustling northern centre of industry, by the late 1980s had been reduced to a commercial trickle, with many viewing it as undesirably remote.[151] As a result, the NLMBC moved to Sioux Lookout in 1991, hopeful of increased enrolment in what was perceived to be a more viable northern town.[152] The WOD executive thus described the rationale behind the move:

> The School's isolation from town, once thought an asset for native training, became one of its biggest hindrances to growth. So, after … listening very carefully to Native input and a lot of prayer, we discovered there was legitimate need [to] change … to see future growth and … more workers for the betterment of the whole northern work … [A]fter looking at all the options, the decision was made to move to SIOUX LOOKOUT – a thriving northern white/native community, the new HUB of services for the Indian north.[153]

Among the reasons for specifically selecting Sioux Lookout was its successful and ethnically blended PAOC congregation, the only local Pentecostal church in Pickle Lake having been composed primarily of Euro-Canadian congregants.[154] Mission headquarters followed the college's lead, moving all NLM operations from Pickle Lake to Sioux Lookout shortly thereafter.[155]

During the nearly fifteen years that the NLM and NLMBC were situated in Pickle Lake, the PAOC invested extensive time, energy, finances, and other resources to develop and maintain facilities.[156] Thus PAOC leadership would not have been eager for the NLMBC to leave that location, doing so only under immense pressure. Indeed, other, less publicized problems motivated the move. Although having students reside on campus was necessary given the college's remote locale, that reality also brought unfortunate challenges. The combination of religious education provided by Euro-Canadians for Indigenous youths, coupled with compound-style and space-limited living arrangements, made for unfortunate optics and evoked some negative associations that proved detrimental to the Pickle Lake college's viability. Gibson recounted the facility as having significant structural and practical inadequacies. The buildings' construction and insulation were insufficient for the harsh northern Ontario winters. Further, the facilities relied on firewood for warmth, requiring approximately 2,000 softwood trees to be felled and burned annually. Students were responsible for much of the harvesting, stacking, and stoking of firewood. Accordingly, the move from Pickle Lake to Sioux Lookout was prompted in part by Bible college students' concerns.[157]

Undoubtedly, Gibson was aware of students' dissatisfaction with Pickle Lake's insufficient and compound-style accommodations, with one student reporting that living on campus reminded her of time served in prison. Others raised concerns about drafty and poorly insulated accommodations, and having to carry water and use outhouses during the depths of winter.[158] Complaints also likely arose from strict and invasive management of students' lifestyles. Instructors opposed students' desire to leave campus, even for recreation, and kept close tabs on classroom attendance and students' general whereabouts. Students could travel into town only once a week, and then only with chaperones. Teenage and even adult students were treated as if they were children, subjected to constant and close supervision. Understandably this influenced students' desire for more independence, as well as Gibson's forthcoming decision to resign.[159] Gibson announced his resignation in February 1991, citing a return to southern Ontario for further studies. Yet other factors potentially also prompted this decision, possibly indicating a desire to dissociate from an institution that had deviated from its originally identified objective. Gibson's parting words advised PAOC leadership to no longer offer student accommodations, and urging, "it is increasingly important to avoid the stigma of church run residential schools." Now that the college was located in the more populous Sioux Lookout, on-campus residence was no longer necessary.[160]

The prevalence of Indigenous ministry hopefuls who relinquished formal education implies the NLMBC was perceived as an undesirable, stigmatized, Euro-Canadian-dominated institution. It is also plausible that declining enrolment and the public's emerging awareness of the residential schooling legacy might have influenced DIAND's and various Indigenous bands' and councils' perception of the NLMBC.[161] Although the NLMBC continued seeking public funding and official accreditation, ultimately neither was attained, save isolated exceptions of some bands and councils subsidizing on a per-student basis.[162] The latter faced tightened budgets themselves, and closely scrutinized programs for credibility before providing funds.[163]

The NLMBC's request for public funding evidently differed from the longer-established churches' adjusted mission policy, which entailed relinquishing residential schools to the Canadian government. A mutual decision by both Church and Crown, the Church had rethought assimilative missiological practices while simultaneously the Crown adapted its approach to Indigenous relations. Already, the number of residential schools had declined from seventy-two to fifty-two between 1948 and 1969.[164] Although the longer-established churches' involvement with the residential schools effectively had ceased by this time, concerns about them persisted, the final residential schools remaining in operation until as recently as 1996.[165] The NLMBC's funding request came when residential schools' historical abuses were becoming increasingly apparent to the public, and when the government and churches had finally begun to acknowledge the schools' legacy.[166] Certainly, the government would not be interested in funding such an institution when collaboration between Church and State had become anachronistic, especially as it related to Euro-Canadian religious education for Indigenous students.[167]

Still, the NLM and its Bible college soldiered on. Upon arrival in Sioux Lookout, the NLMBC began classes at the local PAOC church. Students enjoyed being located in the town's centre, experiencing an independence not possible in Pickle Lake's isolated and enclosed facility. In its inaugural year in Sioux Lookout, the NLMBC celebrated enrolling fifteen students. Faculty, coming from as far away as Washington State, British Columbia, Quebec, and Ontario, included some Indigenous instructors. The optimism surrounding this new cohort led PAOC leadership to proclaim a goal for faculty composed primarily of Indigenous teachers, even hinting at appointing an Indigenous principal.[168] This likely would have been beneficial in the face of decreasing funding and popular support, and presumably would have been welcomed by Indigenous ministers and laity.[169]

In 1990, NLM leadership named John Beardy as the NLMBC's dean of students to "assist Principal Gibson." The WOD executive described Beardy as "a graduate of our NLM College, a fine, intelligent, spiritual young man who is fitting in well, developing every month, doing a fine job and providing an excellent role model for the native students."[170] Partially pressured by Indigenous ministers, NLM leadership reported that "as of the academic year 1991, the college president will be a native person, thus turning the training and direction of the daily affairs over to native control."[171] Although Beardy had been named dean of students and not principal, it was expected that eventually he would rise to this role. Upon Beardy's appointment to the position of dean, PAOC records reported the NLM had appointed its first Indigenous president to the college. While presumably a slip of the pen, the insinuation was that denominational opinion shifted toward favouring Indigenous leadership of the NLMBC.[172] The WOD executive doubled down on this position:

> The long range goal in the Western Ontario District is and has always been to have qualified Native leadership in our Bible College in line with the goal of indigenization and the provision of culturally appropriate training ... As conclusions are reached, we can move toward agreement on Native involvement in the Northern Bible College.[173]

Yet ironically and without explanation, within only a few months of these reports, the NLM appointed Kervan Chalmers, a Euro-Canadian, as principal.[174]

Originally from Sarnia, Ontario, Chalmers graduated from EPBC in 1964. Initially he pastored PAOC churches in Quebec and Saskatchewan. From 1977 to 1980 Chalmers and his family worked as missionaries in Bungoma, Webuye, and Kapsabet, Kenya. Upon returning to Canada during the 1980s, Chalmers pastored the PAOC church in Thorold, Ontario.[175] Thus Chalmers brought a wealth of pastoral and international missionary experience to his new role as NLMBC principal in 1991. Professionally qualified though he may have been, Chalmers lacked a crucial qualification. He was not Indigenous. Unperturbed, the newly minted principal started his role with great enthusiasm, receiving the WOD executive's overwhelming moral support.[176]

The next year Beardy resigned from his position as dean. Chalmers later intimated that Beardy did so because Chalmers's being principal led Beardy to realize he would not ascend to that role as had previously been implied.[177] In 1993 the NLM named Alex Gunner (Môsonîw Ililiw; Moose Factory, Ontario) dean of students.[178] Gunner had graduated from the NLMBC in 1992 and had been his graduating class's valedictory speaker.[179] NLM leadership asked the WOD executive to make an exception and grant Gunner the elusive Licence to Minister even before graduation.[180] The WOD executive agreed, but required Gunner to pursue further studies at EPBC concurrent to his work at the NLMBC.[181]

The newly installed dean's salary was a modest two hundred dollars per week.[182] The NLM reported Gunner's success as he balanced his roles of dean of students, course instructor, and EPBC student: "He is proving to be a very fine addition to our Native College. He has the potential to be the first Native Principle [*sic*] of the Native Bible College."[183] However, this was not to be. In 1994 Alex Gunner resigned from the NLMBC, becoming principal of a new primary and secondary Christian school in Lac Seul First Nation (Ojibwe Anishinaabe, Ontario), and thereafter joining his brother George Gunner at the church and Christian school in Moose Factory.[184] It is possible that, like Beardy, Gunner perceived the principal's position to be unattainable and so sought out a more stable position. At the very least, two Indigenous faculty members' departure in short order could not represent the college well to prospective students.

Suspicions were confirmed as Chalmers noted that NLM leadership's rapport with Indigenous ministers was deteriorating: "There is a growing desire for native leadership and an unwillingness to be pushed by white leadership."[185] It is highly probable that this so-called push from Euro-Canadian leadership frustrated Gunner to the point of departure. Jeff McGregor was named Gunner's successor. Although reportedly a good instructor, the Euro-Canadian McGregor's appointment represented a step backwards from the indigenous principle.[186] While claiming to prioritize autonomy, denominational and mission leadership maintained the state of affairs, making it difficult for NLMBC graduates to ascend the ministerial hierarchy. Effectively, NLM leadership failed to realize that it could not achieve the indigenous principle without naming an Indigenous principal.

The NLMBC encountered even further problems as the honeymoon in Sioux Lookout drew to a close. The college faced a shortage of affordable housing for students and experienced deepening fiscal troubles. Hoping to generate funds, the WOD executive attempted to sell the otherwise abandoned Pickle Lake facility to another recently incorporated ministry also tailored to Indigenous people.[187] The executive reported: "It will be a great relief and much cause for praise to God when this property is finally disposed of and in use again in a constructive way for our native peoples."[188] Nevertheless, three years after the move, the PAOC ultimately sold the Pickle Lake facility to a private developer.[189] NLMBC leadership believed that moving to Sioux Lookout would boost enrolment prospects. Yet a housing shortage, lack of funding for students, a prevailingly Euro-Canadian ethos, and declining enrolment all contributed to its gradual demise through the first half of the 1990s.[190]

Chalmers corresponded with the new DHMBC director Kenneth Birch regarding the NLMBC's fiscal deficit, concluding: "Certainly, unless we attract new students in the immediate future the writing is on the wall ... I'm sure the Lord isn't finished with us yet, so we are hopeful the right things can be put in place to see this decision reversed."[191] Both Birch and the DHMBC were unable or unwilling to further support the NLMBC.[192] Again the college shifted focus away from Indigenous students' needs, becoming preoccupied with institutional survival.

The situation Chalmers inherited initially appeared healthy but ultimately disappointed. The NLMBC was reputable insofar as it offered a reasonable level of education: at one point a three-year diploma,[193] and at another, the option for students to extend their course of study to four years.[194] Yet the NLMBC encountered complications because: 1) DIAND and the First Nations bands and councils lacked confidence in the level or kind of education offered and thus withheld funding;[195] 2) many students lacked secondary school education;[196] 3) it remained unaccredited; 4) it could not adequately qualify graduates for ordination; and 5) it could neither retain nor attract sufficient enrolment.

The NLMBC's decline was the product of outcomes that did not match expectations. The PAOC expected a financially viable college, with academic qualifications comparable to those of its conventional Bible schools. NLM leadership expected the PAOC and the bands and councils to contribute to the college's funding, and its students to excel. Students expected the college and PAOC to grant them opportunities within NLM leadership. There appeared to be a sufficient pool of prospective students from which to recruit. Yet without the college offering any real credentialling advantage, without affordable housing, and facing the NLMBC's high-cost tuition, these students sought alternatives.

An attractive alternative to many would-be NLMBC students was the non-PAOC National Native Bible College (NNBC) near Deseronto, Ontario. EPBC graduate Ross Maracle (Kanien'kehá:ka; Tyendinaga Mohawk Territory, Ontario), although at one time affiliated with the PAOC, independently founded the NNBC in 1978. Its mission was to train "First Nations people to become effective communicators of the Gospel."[197] The NNBC was equipped with buildings for classrooms

Figure 3.4 Northland Ministries Bible College in Sioux Lookout

and dormitories. At its peak, the NNBC boasted eight instructors (five of whom were Indigenous) and an enrolment of thirty students.[198] For some time, Maracle and the NNBC remained somewhat at odds with the PAOC. Erna Peters wrote disparagingly, "Some prospective students were lured away from our PAOC school to an independent school down south with the promise of 'free' tuition and 'easy-to-get' credentials. It seems that integrity is not always a mark of those who profess concern for the native people." In 1992, Chalmers reported that eight students had transferred from the NLMBC to the NNBC.[199] The NNBC could not qualify its students for the PAOC's Licence to Minister, but it was more affordable and more thoroughly indigenized. The NNBC's Indigenous origins, leadership, and instructors created a more Indigenous student-focused educational option, as well as a segue for trainees into Indigenous ministry networks.[200] Maracle himself proved integral to creating an environment at NNBC that was attractive and inspiring to these students.[201]

Many within the PAOC were sympathetic to the students' desire for relevant ministry education. Offering the perspective of an Indigenous minister, Wally McKay stated: "We are not against the [NLM] Bible College, but as things stand right now, many cannot afford to go yet they feel called to ministry."[202] Evidently would-be students possessed the desire, but the PAOC fell short in financing and equipping them during their pursuit of a theological education and formation for ministry. The NNBC in the end proved more attractive, drawing students away from the NLMBC.[203]

The correspondence and records from this period point to an exchange of blame taking place between various parties over the NLMBC's failure to satisfy expectations, as may be expected from any organization undergoing decline. Even the students themselves were not off-limits. Chalmers candidly wrote to the WOD superintendent:

> Aboriginal people (generally speaking) do not avail themselves of Bible College possibilities ... because they feel so threatened by our way of doing things, and by the system we have in place. Most Aboriginals average grade six or seven in education. High School graduation is still quite rare among the Aboriginal peoples of Canada ... [T]heir ways are so opposite to our own way of thinking, or doing things.

The principal proceeded to lay out the financial situation:

> The bottom line is, the way we would like things to go will not actually work without a large input of funds. Even then, the results at the end of the day don't always seem to bring the anticipated results within this culture.[204]

Evidently at this late stage in the NLMBC's life, with declining enrolment and financial instability, Chalmers was disappointed. Nevertheless, his words hint at a latent preconception, and a denominational reluctance to implement changes that would work with, engage, and exchange dynamic ideas with Indigenous ministry leadership candidates. Generally, Indigenous Pentecostals felt that programs and initiatives had failed to realize the movement's true indigenization. Rather than addressing inadequate denominational efforts to aid students, review committees on occasion blamed Indigenous students with excuses such as: "Probably many of them are not called into ministry in the first place."[205] According to Erna Peters, most students "needed encouragement to go to Bible

School ... not used to being away from their homes for such long periods of time."[206]

Much can be said about the personal motivation of those choosing the NLMBC over alternative post-secondary options. Ministry hopefuls were aware that pursuing education did not guarantee easy credentialling. If anything, these courses lengthened the time required for ministry qualification, adding expense and other challenges. Nevertheless, they pursued education to improve their grasp on the Pentecostal message they sought to disseminate. When graduates did earn ministry credentials and obtain key leadership positions, such accomplishments were well-deserved. These accolades truly were a testament to their desire to realize the indigenous principle for themselves, becoming leaders in their communities and the NLM's churches, the latter of which through their efforts they sought to indigenize.[207] Notwithstanding their sometimes surprising receptivity to the theological training that was offered by non-Indigenous instructors, NLMBC students did recognize that the system was flawed and in need of deconstruction. One NLMBC graduate "spoke of how he felt he benefitted from his [NLM]BC training, yet he also suggested that without some re-evaluation, 'the Native Bible college as we know it today will be ushered into Jurassic Park.'"[208]

With only three students registered for the autumn 1994 semester, the college was forced to suspend programming for yet another season.[209] As the college's closure loomed, Chalmers lamented in a letter dated early 1995 what seemed to him the NLMBC's inevitable demise, claiming it had graduated its final student.[210] Thus the NLM closed the college's doors, deciding to sell the recently acquired and renovated Sioux Lookout facility.[211] The NLMBC's winding tale warrants some reflection. As chapter 2 demonstrated, initially Spillenaar did not aim for Indigenous mission. However, once the NLM's mission to Indigenous people was defined and in play, the NLMBC positively claimed to practise the indigenous principle, articulating its desire to meet Indigenous Pentecostals' needs.[212]

CONCLUSION

In its early years, the NLMBC offered unique training options for Indigenous ministerial candidates, but eventual outcomes disappointed. Although the PAOC viewed the NLMBC as a tool to make Indigenous people Pentecostal, Indigenous people did not view the college as a means of making Pentecostalism Indigenous. Neither PAOC nor NLM leadership had the patience to see the NLM become autonomous and achieve the "Three-Self" ideal. Perhaps here lies the crux of the NLM's challenge in making good on its indigenous principle. Pentecostal missiology maintains a pneumatological character, but it is motivated by a sense of eschatological urgency.[213] So long as PAOC leadership believed the NLMBC trained Indigenous converts to be highly effective evangelists, then the school fulfilled denominational expectations. However, if said evangelists did not attract adherents at the rate, at the speed, or in the manner that the PAOC desired, then the college was deemed redundant. If not in their words then at least in their actions, PAOC leaders demonstrated their belief that Euro-Canadian missionaries could win converts just as quickly. But realistically they could not effectively indigenize the NLM. Only Indigenous ministers could do that. Still, doing so would require the PAOC to allow autonomy, something that could only come about through significant investment and trust on the part of PAOC leadership. When the goal is urgent evangelization, a lengthy autonomizing process became a luxury that the PAOC and ultimately the NLMBC apparently believed they could not afford.

The NLMBC, and potentially the PAOC's understanding of the indigenous principle altogether, was more about pragmatism than about indigenization, a reality that renders the central concept itself very complicated. As such, the NLMBC's core character remained thoroughly Euro-Canadian. Some principals attempted to engage Indigenous culture better than others, but ultimately the NLMBC became known as a Euro-Canadian acculturating institution, making alternative avenues for ministerial training (such as Ross Maracle's NNBC) appear more attractive. Contrary to its oft-repeated claims, the NLMBC did not meet Indigenous students' needs. If indeed the NLMBC's goal was to meet those needs, then a resulting administrative and moral obligation would have been the provision of accessible, affordable, effective, practical, and applicable ministerial education, which the NLMBC did not or could not offer. With respect to the NLMBC, the PAOC did not make ministry leadership easily accessible to would-be Indigenous ministers. Consequently, aspiring students sought alternatives, which meant a downturn in enrolment and revenue and the college's eventual discontinuation.[214]

Despite promises to support Indigenous Pentecostal leadership, the PAOC instead maintained the Euro-Canadian-led pattern at the

NLMBC, altogether reluctant to relinquish leadership to Indigenous ministerial candidates. While graduates eventually did occupy ministry roles in local churches, they were rarely chosen for the mission leadership positions necessary to influence decisions and policy-making. The PAOC perceived itself to be a proponent of autonomy, yet always managed to keep this objective just out of reach. Again, credit must be given to NLMBC graduates, who proved time and again their loyalty both to the PAOC and to their own Indigenous Pentecostal movement. These students' perseverance undoubtedly contributed to the prevalence of Indigenous Pentecostalism in Canada. Yet however much Indigenous Pentecostals expressed their views on ministerial matters, PAOC leadership remained resistant to Indigenous cultural norms. It is to that dialogue between Indigenous ministers and Euro-Canadian Pentecostal mission leaders that chapter 4 now turns its attention.

4

Contention and Contextualization

Tensions between Euro-Canadian Missionaries and Indigenous Ministers

The usual missionary perspective ... defined positions in terms of stark dichotomies: whatever was most opposed by the missionaries was deemed un-Christian and vice versa (so that Christianity, for example, became synonymous with anti-potlatching).

Susan Neylan, Wilfrid Laurier University[1]

The word "missionary" is not very popular with the secular Indian leaders because of the negative connotations associated with it from the past ... [They] do not overlook the mistakes the early white missionaries made in cross-cultural ministries ... Today's missionaries, by learning from past mistakes, have a better understanding of the need to preserve the culture of the native people.

Joseph Jolly, Eeyou; Waskaganish, Quebec;
raised in Moose Factory, Ontario[2]

Pressing issues ... must be resolved and overcome in order for ministry to First Nations to be accurate in its presentation and thereby effective. The Native people must own the gospel. This has never really happened in the life of the indigenous church of North America; they have never been fully trusted.

Cheryl Bear, Dakelh; Nadleh Whut'en First Nation, British Columbia[3]

The intentional integration of cultural expressions into Christian devotion for the purposes of making missionary efforts more accessible and engaging, and to encourage the autonomizing process, is a practice partially described through the term "contextualization." Richard Twiss (Sicangu Lakota; Rosebud Indian Reservation, South Dakota), cofounder of the North American Institute for Indigenous Theological Studies (NAIITS), defined contextualization as the "process of framing the gospel message culturally as either a sacred story or a myth of divine proportions so that it makes sense to people 'on the ground' where they live every day."[4]

Although there were a variety of sentiments and positions with respect to the efforts of Euro-Canadian missionaries and educators, generally, the Northland Mission's (NLM) records imply that Indigenous Pentecostals wanted the NLM to reduce its association with Euro-Canadian culture and become more accessible and relevant to Indigenous culture.[5] Rather than accommodate by contextualizing the message, Euro-Canadian NLM leadership instead opposed Indigenous cultural norms, the integration of which they believed could lead to something they called syncretism (the fusion of religious markers resulting from missionization and cultural interchange, further explained below).[6] What is more, they enforced their own cultural practices.

Drawing primarily from denominational documents and literature, this chapter critically analyzes the exchanges and interactions of Indigenous participants and the NLM's Euro-Canadian leadership between the early 1950s and the late 1990s. A thorough examination of these period materials demonstrates that the former practised a measure of resistance to the latter, while the NLM's leaders opposed Indigenous culture. While this chapter draws from fewer exclusively Indigenous sources, it does strive to interrogate Euro-Canadian denominational sources so as to listen to the Indigenous Voice as it comes through the documents. This remains an effective method, as it goes without saying that Indigenous people existed within the PAOC as their authentic selves. Accordingly, their Pentecostal identity did not detract from their Indigenous identity, and this is apparent throughout the documentary materials examined herein.

By investigating NLM records, this chapter demonstrates that the NLM's Euro-Canadian leadership claimed to support the indigenous principle, yet subtly undermined it by not fully trusting Indigenous ministers. While this chapter makes many references to Euro-Canadians in NLM leadership, its overarching intention is to shift focus away from the PAOC's goals, and to highlight the Indigenous laity's and ministers' engagement with the Pentecostal message so as to set the stage for the NLM's transition to Aboriginal Pentecostal Ministries (APM, described more fully in chapter 5).

An ongoing point of major contention between Euro-Canadian missionaries and Indigenous adherents was the significance of Indigenous culture for ministry leadership. On this point, it is important to address that the term "syncretism" alone does not provide an accurate description for the sort of spiritual exchange highlighted within this chapter and indeed demonstrated in the religious and spiritual expressions of many Indigenous Pentecostals. Furthermore, syncretism as a term often is employed in a pejorative fashion by its detractors; at least, such was the case within the documentary record of the PAOC's missionaries, examined for the purposes of this monograph.

This is not to suggest that syncretism does not take place in both its simple and complex forms, but rather to propose two anthropological phrases that more aptly describe said processes. The first phrase, coined by anthropologist and scholar of religion Joseph Epes Brown, is "nonexclusive cumulative adhesion," and it describes the overall religious fluidity that occasionally exists among Indigenous Pentecostals as well as practitioners of Indigenous traditional spiritualities. Jace Weaver (Anigiduwagi), Professor of Native American Studies and Religion at Franklin College in the University of Georgia, and author of *The Red Atlantic: American Indigenes and the Making of the Modern World, 1000–1927*, proposes the second phrase, termed

> religious dimorphism ... [which] is the practice of two forms of religion. It is distinguished from syncretism, which occurs when two different religions are blended to form a third. Rather, religious dimorphism occurs when a person participates in two different religions. There is no mixing other than within the practitioner.

Weaver continues: "As I have heard Natives say, it is as simple as 'This is what I do when I go to church. And this is what I do when I go to ceremony.'"[7]

As the definitions of the above terms imply, the concepts they seek to describe are fluid and varied. Cultural exchange is a complex process, with conversion not simply being a matter of exchanging one lifestyle for another. For instance, Indigenous lifestyles, cosmologies, and spiritual traditions continued to be observed within Indigenous Christian communities, giving rise to new local church structures, relationships, and expressions of worship.[8] Further, for many Indigenous people, Christianity is not viewed as a monolithic unit to be accepted or rejected wholesale. Rather it is frequently perceived as any other spiritual system or worldview: that is, composed of a multiplicity of aspects, with some being accepted and others being ignored. Neither is it the place for non-Indigenous observers to propose rigid definitions of processes to which they are not privy. These descriptions simply provide guidelines, assisting in the desire to understand. Finally, many Indigenous Pentecostals identify as Christian, while at the same time demonstrating "a great deal of knowledge of, and respect for, traditional ways."[9] At times the same can be said of the analogous examples illustrated in the NLM's documentary record, and contained within this chapter.

TENSIONS UNDER SPILLENAAR: 1950–76

In PAOC literature from this period, the NLM's founding and longest-tenured director John Spillenaar was a celebrated, favoured, and heroic son. Further, owing to his trailblazing methods, Spillenaar's position within the Pentecostal popular memory was one of great repute. Although his directorship generally was marked by Euro-Canadian prominence, an early exception is found in Spillenaar's recruitment of Rodger Cree (Kanien'kehá:ka; Kanesatake, Quebec). Cree's involvement within the NLM establishes an early pattern for contention over contextualization.

In 1928 Cree's parents responded to an evangelistic message from a young protégé of Aimee Semple McPherson (a famous Canadian-American, female, Pentecostal evangelist from the early twentieth century). While Cree was born into what could be described as a Pentecostal home on 21 November 1931, he did not immediately identify with the faith, wrestling with the racial tension characteristic of the period. Angela Tarango described how Cree's "hatred of French-Canadians was fed by their own colonialist and racist attitude toward him – until his conversion to Pentecostal Christianity."[10] In his late teens, Cree had a vision: "I saw a ball of fire that was lodged in the ceiling – when that ball of fire touched my head, I began to speak in a different language altogether, Supernatural." Following his charismatic experience, Cree enrolled in the PAOC's French-speaking Bible

College, Institut Biblique Bérée. Cree, conscious of social and racial unrest within the Institut, asserted: "The French and Indian Wars never really ended." Although Cree described the Institut as maintaining a racist environment, he credited the Holy Spirit for helping him to "overcome his own racial prejudice." Cree recounted: "I remember going to school and walking and I heard someone say (in French) 'the savage has come.' The Holy Spirit kept me from turning around ... I learned how to deal with those people."[11] During his second year of study in 1951, Cree experienced a second vision, this time of an Indigenous woman ill in bed with a candle on her table, crying out in hunger and pain. As a result of the second vision, Cree dedicated his life's work to mission among Indigenous people. Cree was the NLM's first Indigenous minister, and among the PAOC's vanguard of Indigenous ministers at a national level.[12]

Cree was Kanien'kehá:ka, but the congregants of his first pastorate in Pagwa River, Ontario, were mostly Anishininiwag. Cree did not view this as an obstacle to prevent him from accomplishing his goal.[13] In 1953 Cree oversaw construction of Pagwa Pentecostal Chapel's first building, inaugurated by Spillenaar the same year. Cree was successful, the congregation quickly growing to fifty parishioners.[14] While in Pagwa River, Cree recounted entering a tent and seeing the ill woman from his vision, confirming his vocational placement.[15] Cree viewed the NLM as a vehicle for his ministry vocation to Indigenous people, and he experienced early success in that role.[16] Spillenaar reported: "Bro. Rodger Cree has a full mission at Pagwa River even on an off night ... Souls are being saved, and the Sunday School is on the increase."[17]

Regarding Indigenous culture and contextualization, Cree maintained that being Indigenous and being Pentecostal were not mutually exclusive. From his perspective, Indigenous culture was not solely the domain of Indigenous traditional spiritualities. He claimed: "When you're a Native, you don't have to do cartwheels, or play the drums, or put on regalia. You know who you are, your identity. You cannot dress it up."[18] Cree's words are reminiscent of Bonnie Sue Lewis's conclusions that "in becoming a Christian, they did not have to sacrifice being an Indian. Christian Indians may have transferred their 'primary religious identity,' but they did not relinquish who they were."[19] Cree embraced language as the key element of Indigenous culture, allowing him to evangelize and forge an identity that was both Indigenous and Pentecostal.

Still, Rodger Cree's religious observance likely did not fit within either Brown's nonexclusive cumulative adhesion or Weaver's religious dimorphism. Rather, for Cree, Pentecostalism in part was a vehicle through which individuals and communities could overcome difficulty. Cree attested:

> Spreading the pentecostal [*sic*] message throughout the Indian communities is our highest priority. It not only provides power to save souls, but it also is the power of deliverance for our people from alcoholism, drug abuse, suicide, broken homes, child abuse, teenage pregnancy and a myriad of social problems that plague Indian tribes and communities …
>
> We believe that the pentecostal message has the power to set our people free. Further, we believe it is only through an out pouring [*sic*] of the Holy Spirit that there will be real healing throughout our reservations and communities.[20]

Cree's reflections above point to his belief in the unique suitability of Pentecostalism (even more so than other variations of Christianity or Indigenous traditional spiritualities) to address the challenges he described as frequently endured by Indigenous people and communities.

Cree married Esther in 1955 and in 1958 they left Pagwa River for Kanawake, Quebec, a predominantly Kanien'kehá:ka town near Cree's ancestral territory, to build and pastor a Pentecostal church.[21] That same year Cree recalled his meeting with "Anglo" Assemblies of God (AG USA) missionary Alta Washburn at the Fifth World Conference of Pentecostal Churches in Toronto:[22]

> She had started an Indian Bible school in Phoenix, Arizona, just a year earlier … [H]er 'frail' appearance failed to suppress an irrepressible call and indomitable spirit to serve the Lord as a missionary among the Indians … Esther and I both sensed that she was indeed a visionary pioneer in uncharted and even controversial territory – that of 'raising up' indigenous Native pastors.
>
> It was so touching and yet hard to believe that anyone else cared about Native people like we did – but her call to Native ministry was clearly confirmed in our spirits. It was also clear to Esther and me that she saw great value in the people she

> was called to minister to. Her vision was not only to reach Native Americans with the gospel, but also to equip them to reach their own people – an integral component of the indigenous principle.[23]

This recollection is quite telling, implying that Washburn's enthusiasm and calling to mission appealed to Cree, and that they were unrivalled, not least among non-Indigenous people. Angela Tarango described,

> Cree's advocacy for Native leadership came from his life-long suspicion of white missionaries. The Holy Spirit may have cured him of his hatred of French-Canadians, but he also understood that indigenous [*sic*] leadership was crucial to making Pentecostalism a form of *indigenous* Christianity outside of white structures of power.[24]

Undoubtedly Spillenaar did care about ministry to Indigenous people, otherwise he would not have dedicated decades of his life ministering to them. Although the documentary record does not demonstrate Cree's suspicion being directed toward Spillenaar specifically, Cree's recollection nevertheless suggests that Spillenaar did not possess a passion equal to Washburn's to train and empower Indigenous ministers to lead Indigenous churches.

Were it not for illness forcing him to move to a more favourable climate, Cree would likely have remained full-time in Canada. Rodger and Esther took up a pastorate first in Phoenix, Arizona, and shortly thereafter at a Tohono O'odham church in Sells, Arizona, "taking charge of [local] Indian work … under missionary appointment by the Assemblies of God."[25] Following his move stateside, Cree continued as a major influencer among early waves of Indigenous ministers within the AG USA, serving on the Board of the American Indian College started by Washburn. It was within the context of the AG USA that Andrew Maracle (Kanien'kehá:ka; Six Nations of the Grand River, Ontario) mentored Cree, an investment upon which Cree gratefully opined as follows:

> Native pastors are uniquely qualified to mentor other Native leaders because in many cases, they understand the language and cultural differences that differ from the dominant society … It's good for Native leaders to have role models who can "flesh out"

> Native ministry in a culturally relevant fashion – people they can relate to socially, culturally, and even linguistically.[26]

Cree himself espoused that priority to mentor subsequent generations. Accordingly from 1977 to 1982, Cree served as the first Indigenous president of the AG USA's Eastern Indian Bible Institute in Shannon, North Carolina (also known as Native American Bible College, and at the time of writing called Lumbee River Christian College). He maintained ties with the PAOC, itinerating throughout Canada during the subsequent decades. Cree was the first of several Indigenous Pentecostal leaders who pressured the PAOC to fulfill its own claims of the indigenous principle.[27] Cree died on 22 July 2020.[28] With the early exception of Cree's ministry, Euro-Canadian predominance within the NLM remained the norm.

With respect to Spillenaar, few records from his tenure portray him negatively. Indeed, several Indigenous people's testimonies reflected Spillenaar quite positively.[29] Nevertheless, the missionary and his methods were not perfect and at times betrayed cultural insensitivity. Spillenaar employed stereotypes to describe those to whom he ministered, referring to "the Indians'" war bonnets and tipis. Typically these are cultural expressions associated with Plains Nations, somewhat out of place for a mission aimed predominantly to Nehiyawak, Anishininiwag, and Ojibweg Anishinaabeg in what is now northern Ontario. This is a general observation and not always the case, as individuals from those nations may observe those expressions. Additionally, Nakawēg, Nehiyawak, and some Anishinaabeg from what are now the western Canadian provinces (where Spillenaar did not itinerate) generally observe Plains culture.[30]

The Stone Church Pentecostal Assembly in Toronto invited Spillenaar to their frequent mission conferences. He once arrived wearing "Eskimo garb."[31] While at the time of writing such a presentation may seem culturally insensitive, Spillenaar received a warm reception nonetheless.[32] The general acceptance of these sort of descriptions and appropriated displays like it are reflected in the words of Thomas King (Anigiduwagi; Sacramento, California):

> Whatever cultural significance they may have for Native peoples, full feather headdresses and beaded buckskins are, first and foremost, White North America's signifiers of Indian authenticity. Their visual value … is … priceless.[33]

Spillenaar's displays proved popular among the NLM's Euro-Canadian support base, and PAOC periodicals continued to report Spillenaar's successes.[34]

At a later conference, when Stone Church requested he "bring a native couple along," Spillenaar invited the Mickenacks (Anishininiwag; Sachigo Lake, Ontario), who were "surprised to see such large apartment buildings and the thousands of cars."[35] NLM leadership wanted newsletter readers to appreciate how enthralled the Mickenacks were by settler culture's advances. But the Mickenacks' account was not necessarily praise. It was a potential critique of settler culture's preoccupation with economic advancement at the expense of acknowledging and realizing other priorities. Reminiscent of J.R. Miller's seminal work, the Mickenacks' conclusion may have echoed that the *Skyscrapers Hide the Heavens*. Having Indigenous people accompany Spillenaar was by itself positive, and consistent with the desired outcome of the indigenous principle. The issue, however, was a sort of surveillance, presenting the Mickenacks to conference delegates wishing to observe and idealize an Indigenous couple subscribing to Pentecostalism. That a Euro-Canadian minister would request Spillenaar bring an Indigenous couple, like "show and tell," suggests paternalism and ethnocentrism engrained in the PAOC's mentality at the time.[36]

Similarly, missionaries intimated they were happier watching than listening to Indigenous Pentecostals. A missionary recalling: "Those people love strumming ... guitars ... and even if a building does not really need a mike for the music to be well heard, they are not really happy until there is a mike to bring up the volume."[37] Requesting amplification may simply display a preference for loud music, but perhaps it also indicates the musicians' desire to be heard. Literally, wrote Keith D. Smith, the "whispers, and even the shouts, of Indigenous people can still be heard through the written documents left behind." Even if Spillenaar did not attempt to contextualize Pentecostalism's message to Indigenous culture, Indigenous Pentecostals expressed a strong desire that the message be made relevant to their own contexts.[38]

The historian should be careful not to portray NLM missionaries too negatively. After all, without Spillenaar's efforts there would not have been an NLM to speak of. Further, these missionaries were a product of their time. Notwithstanding, some missionaries from this period were culturally astute, practising the indigenous principle and embracing contextualization. Grace Oates, for example, a 1952 graduate of

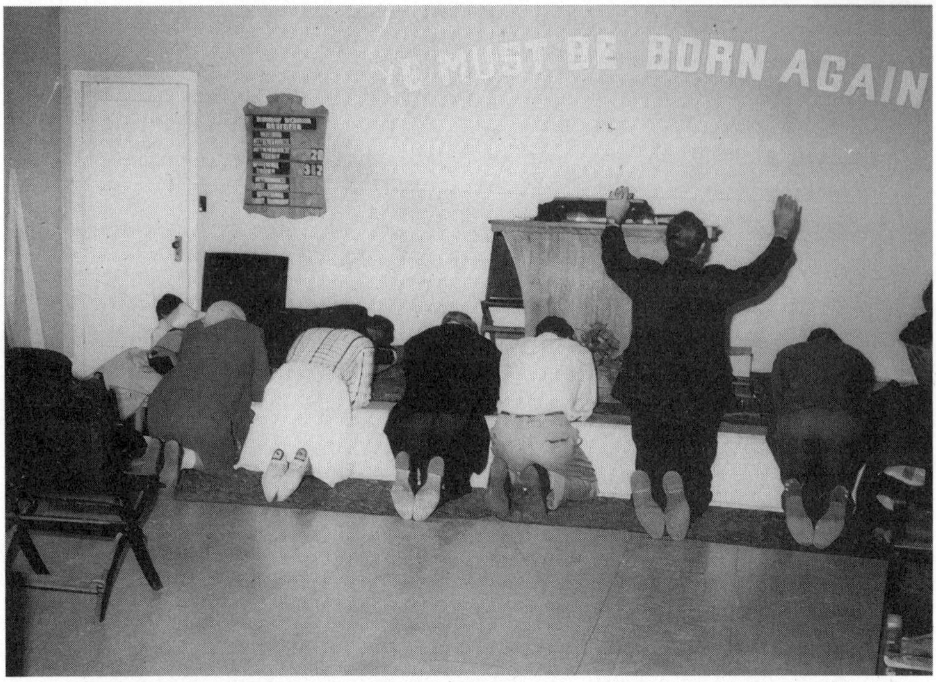

Figure 4.1 Worship service in Moosonee

Eastern Pentecostal Bible College (EPBC), accepted soon-to-be PAOC General Superintendent Walter McAlister's invitation to pastor the NLM church in Fort Severn First Nation (Néhinaw; Ontario). Oates wrote that "hearing the call, 'Go ye into all the world and preach the gospel ... ' [I turned] my face and heart ... to the Indians." When Spillenaar flew Oates into the Hudson Bay coast territory "about 160 Indians met the 'pimanagan' when it landed. Everyone shook hands and seemed glad to see them." A local Néhinawak man, Jeremiah Albany, billeted Oates and her missionary companion Ruth Antonelli.[39]

Oates and Antonelli immediately incorporated Néhinawak laity into their ministry practice, an act well-received by their hosts. Discouraged by the challenging living environment, the pair considered returning to southern Ontario, but the local Anglican priest "together with a delegation of local Indians" asked them to stay. The priest reported: "My Catechists tell me that the women are crying because you are leaving. They want you to stay and have asked me to tell you not to go away. You have done good to everyone: men, women, and children." The pair stayed, but Antonelli ultimately departed the following year.[40] Thereafter, Oates married Dan Priest, who joined her in Fort Severn after briefly ministering with the United Church in First Nations territories in Manitoba. The newlyweds co-pastored, training and empowering Indigenous leaders for ministry.[41] The couple always seemed to be well-received.[42]

Spillenaar reflected on a 1955 visit to minister alongside the Priests to "Indians in their winter trapping camps" at Kaska, York Factory, and Churchill, Manitoba: "The response to the Gospel was very good with quite a number of decisions for Christ. Many … asked so many questions pertaining to the Word of God … and also of some of their religious traditions … surprised to learn that most of these traditions were foreign to the Word of God."[43] The Priests' perceptions of Indigenous culture were more moderate than Spillenaar's. Further, their work at Fort Severn had gone well, having recruited "two fine Indian[s]" as Sunday school teachers. Even here the Néhinawak participants' desire for or interest in the implications of contextualization is evident. Also unmistakable was the Priests' commitment to the indigenous principle, notably being aware of and accommodating toward the Néhinaw winter, hunting-based subsistence calendar. Grace Priest wrote:

> During the winter months the Indians go out to trap. A few families stay home and the men all come in from time to time for more supplies. At Christmas and Easter most of them come in for church services. Then they go out again for trapping. After breakup we take a trip up the river … to visit the camps, and have services … The women write letters in asking us to come and see them soon. We send papers and books out … They asked us to stay here and build a church … We praise God for those who have taken God as their Saviour, and for those who can pray aloud and close in prayer, also for those who … read the portion of scripture in Cree for the service. Also we have a young man who helps play the organ.[44]

The couple told stories in their ministry, a didactic method familiar to their hosts. For example, Stan McKay (Néhinaw; Fisher River Cree Nation, Manitoba),[45] a United Church minister and former United Church Moderator, reflected on separate experiences from his ministry in Swan Lake First Nation (Anishinaabe, in this instance the exonym for which is Saulteaux), Manitoba:

> I was struck by their wonderful story-telling styles. The elders expressed their faith in the stories of the people. They loved the Bible, the biblical story. We had it in our own language, so they could hear it in Cree. Their faith was grounded in the biblical story ... This was a biblical people, more so than almost any other part of the church in terms of their familiarity with the biblical record, including some of the fairly exotic or strange imagery from the Judaeo-Christian heritage.[46]

Like McKay, Dan and Grace Priest also recognized Néhinawak acolytes' interest in scripture and thus communicated the gospel message in accessible ways, "so that the Children can understand too." The missionary couple recalled that they "like[d] the stories of Jesus best" and wanted them repeated. Children also quickly learned songs, the Priests reporting there had been "no Sunday School before we came. Now we have almost every child in the village coming" as well as some mothers and "grown young men ... [M]any a little Indian has come out and knelt down, giving their heart to Jesus." Sunday mornings they visited shut-ins, and would sing "the praises of the Lamb of God and read God's precious Word and pray ending up with Ma Me Chemick Way Oh ta Week."[47]

On the subject of autonomy, Grace opined, "you cannot tell the Indian what to do, he will do it if he wants to."[48] While ministering with the United Church, Dan learned to speak, read, and write in Nêhiyawêwin, with his facility in language enhancing his own ministry. "Indians were self-reliant," he reported. They "liked to keep independent of government financial assistance and were quite capable of running their own church and community affairs."[49] The Priests fundraised their own support, not requesting payment from Néhinawak laity.[50]

In 1958, the Priests accepted an invitation to join Ken Gaetz, director of the PAOC's H.H. Williams Memorial Hospital and Sub-Arctic Mission based in Hay River, Northwest Territories, thus leaving behind a thriving Indigenous church in Fort Severn. Through the Sub-Arctic mission, beginning in 1959, the Priests pioneered a Pentecostal church in Fort Norman, Northwest Territories (present-day Tulita), where Grace prayed "that God will call and use the Indians to witness to their own people."[51] In a similar fashion the Priests were well-received there, with one of Grace's students journalling:

> Mrs. Grace Priest is a Pentecostal missionary sent from the outside to teach us about Jesus … She is a very kind lady … she loves Jesus very much, and she loves us as well … She … somehow managed to have "tea" for us, which included homemade cookies. Her spirit was that of water, soft to the touch and unstoppable by force. She simply kept flowing around obstacles until she found another route on the way to her destination.[52]

The Priests continued to receive a warm welcome among their Dene hosts in the Northwest Territories, particularly through their ministry, which concentrated on acts of healing.[53] In 1967, the couple again relocated to establish a church in Coppermine, Northwest Territories (known today as Kugluktuk, Nunavut; Inuit). There, the Priests established "the first P.A.O.C. Inuit church," and denominational literature recorded that "the Eskimos liked Grace and Dan and came to their services." The Priests' roles in Kugluktuk expanded from those of missionaries, as Dan became Justice of the Peace, coroner, and fire chief, and "Grace organized the Girl Guides and Brownies." The Priests continued to lead the church in Kugluktuk until the mid-1970s.[54]

The Priests' success demonstrates that not all missionaries were possessive of their work among Indigenous people, as they proved the indigenous principle can work. Not only were the Priests adaptable when required, they also encouraged subscription to Indigenous culture, and trained and empowered Indigenous leaders. Finally, they recognized when it was time to exit, allowing Indigenous ministers to continue the work. When they did depart the NLM in Fort Severn, Erna Peters recorded, "the Indians brought them beautiful gifts; beaded belts, bands for their hair, and slippers." They declared, "You brought the Gospel of Jesus to us."[55] The Priests provided a true success story of missionaries entering an Indigenous territory, encouraging the indigenous principle, and leaving a healthy, self-sufficient church. Even into the new millennium this congregation continued to prioritize the indigenous principle, as demonstrated by "the little band of Indigenous grandmothers and great-grandmothers who teamed up in the early 2000s to pastor their church in Fort Severn near the shores of Hudson Bay."[56]

Yet unfortunately the Priests likewise proved somewhat of an exception within the NLM, with Euro-Canadian-led ministry remaining the rule. To be sure, relying solely on Spillenaar as frontrunner of a mission to Indigenous people was not ideal. Some individual churches could succeed, but the NLM collectively was aviation-dependent and entrenched in the PAOC's prevailingly Euro-Canadian cultural ethos. It would remain a mission rather than a ministry, thus not lending itself to a quick takeover by Indigenous ministers.

John Spillenaar died in December 2003 and Tyyne in October 2006, aged eighty-seven and one hundred and one respectively.[57] John Spillenaar is credited with having started forty-six churches throughout his ministry, the most recent of which was dedicated in Cape Dorset, Nunavut, during the month preceding his death.[58] Prior to his death, PAOC leadership acknowledged his contribution and sacrifice, noting his legacy of teaching, preaching, praying, and constructing churches: "There is scarcely a Reserve John did not touch with the gospel and even today … people of the North are still asking: 'How is John Spillenaar'?"[59]

Spillenaar was an imposing figure, unquestionably committed, talented, and indispensable in the NLM's creation. It is further noteworthy that Rodger Cree's and Grace and Dan Priest's dynamic and enabling ministries both occurred under Spillenaar's leadership, accomplishments that are to his credit. However, several of his practices contributed to the PAOC's inability to autonomize the NLM properly, and hand it over to its rightful heirs. They were: 1) a shortage of delegating and administrative interest; 2) insistence upon itinerating himself rather than coordinating efforts from mission headquarters and entrusting ministry to local Indigenous leaders; and 3) his unfamiliarity with the importance of sensitively integrating Indigenous cultural values into Pentecostal practice. Again it is important not to be too critical here, as Spillenaar cannot be held accountable to the standards of the present period. However, while Spillenaar was essential for the NLM's founding, he presents somewhat of a dilemma, as the historian is left to wonder whether the missionary actually contributed to the formation of an Indigenous church, or hindered that development in spite of himself.

CHRISTIANITY AND CULTURE

Many Indigenous Pentecostals often employ the term "culture" when referring to Indigenous traditional spiritualities.[60] Before continuing, and in order to bring some definition to the terms employed throughout the subsequent sections of this chapter, five points need to be clarified.

Figure 4.2 Worship service in Moosonee

1) There is not one cohesive Indigenous religion, but rather many spiritual experiences and expressions. The term "Indigenous traditional spiritualities" is helpful, and refers generally to a broad group of religious practices and spiritual observances, which are established and historical but also exist within a state of ongoing evolution and flux.
2) By that same logic, it is reasonable to state that there is not one cohesive Indigenous Pentecostalism. Variation is a reality for all cultures in general and Indigenous Pentecostals are no exception. They are not all alike.[61]

3) Accordingly, Indigenous Pentecostals themselves did not universally favour contextualization. The term "struggle" in this monograph's title points to internal differences of opinion regarding what constitutes Indigenous Pentecostalism. Some Indigenous Pentecostals communicated wariness of what was perceived to be syncretism, and others additionally disagreed with integrating Indigenous traditional spiritual practices with Pentecostalism altogether (in opposition to both Brown's nonexclusive cumulative adhesion and Weaver's religious dimorphism). In some instances, anti-syncretism (elsewhere referred to as "antitraditional theology" and "syncretophobia") was not directly introduced to Indigenous Pentecostalism by Western missionaries, and thus does not exclusively constitute a colonialist action. Rather it occasionally was devised by Indigenous Pentecostals themselves, and as a result championed by its proponents as a characteristic and definitive component of Indigenous Pentecostalism.[62] Moreover, some Indigenous Pentecostals were cautious not because they were dismissive of Indigenous traditional spiritualities, but rather because they associated them with what they perceived to be at best "false prophecy" or at worst occultist power. This is what Kimberly Jenkins Marshall terms "a reinterpretation of the very efficacy of that system" and what José Casanova describes as "uprooted local culture engaged in spiritual warfare with its own roots." It is likely that aspects such as region, nationality, language, age,[63] and personal experience (among other factors) influence respective Indigenous Pentecostals' relationship with and response to Indigenous traditional spiritualities.[64]

Heather D. Martin, who conducted her doctoral research primarily among Indigenous PAOC adherents in the Northwest Territories, concluded:

> There are varying opinions when people think of culture and spirituality. Some respondents include spirituality as part of the definition of culture while others do not. Some define culture as good except for the traditional rituals and define those rituals as anything related to traditional native spirituality. Twenty-five percent of participants define spirituality according to the church they attend, emphasizing liturgy and affiliation

to an organization. One person did not define any of the terms and simply comments that the separation of culture and spirituality must be done prayerfully.[65]

Martin's findings further demonstrate the practice through which many Indigenous Pentecostals distinguish "culture" and "spiritual beliefs."[66] As traditional expressions appear in a variety of forms (including in some Pentecostal practices), it is helpful to consider an Indigenous Pentecostal practice as somewhat distinct from both contextualization with and opposition to Indigenous traditional spiritualities. This alternative approach can be referred to as "compartmentalization," a tendency whereby traditions are perceived as distinct, and practised separately and in varying degrees and forms.[67]

4) Consequently, and for all of their points of comparison and perceived compatibility, it is important to note there are also substantial and significant differences between Pentecostalism and Indigenous traditional spiritualities. The former often occur extemporaneously, and the latter typically are "highly elaborate ritually with complicated procedures and an emphasis on correct practice."[68] Thus,
5) the historian is careful in light of these insights that the following sections should not come across as prescribing contextualization (least of all for Indigenous Pentecostals who oppose it), as this in itself could be perceived as a colonizing expression. Neither do the following sections suggest that NLM missionaries' hypothetical attempts at contextualization would have been universally well-received. Settler missionaries' attempts to this end have on occasion backfired when met by resistance from Indigenous adherents.[69] Rather, the purpose of the following sections is to amplify the Indigenous Voice in the historical record and to demonstrate the contention over contextualization within the NLM.

Finally, the following sections serve to hypothesize that on those occasions when contextualization came at the invitation of Indigenous Pentecostals, engaging with that process might have served to enhance the PAOC's credibility, as well as improve its ability to accomplish its indigenous principle. The challenge for the PAOC in so doing became increasingly pronounced as the NLM encountered its first major leadership change following Spillenaar's resignation and the naming of Dale Cummins as director in 1976.

CONTENTION AND CONTEXTUALIZATION DURING THE TENURE OF DALE CUMMINS: 1976–81

Cummins was not a pilot, and his extensive background as an international missionary and educator meant his directorship marked a shift from Spillenaar's entrepreneurial leadership.[70] Indeed Cummins's contemplative style of reflection and writing suggest he was highly intellectual. Relying on his writer's craft to connect with people much as Spillenaar relied on practical trade skills, Cummins demonstrated a grasp of intercultural relations, initially lending more consideration to the realities affecting Indigenous people. He did not view those to whom he ministered as simply mission subjects, but rather showed genuine interest in knowing them and studying their ways of life. Although far from perfect, he demonstrated a desire to develop Indigenous leaders.[71] This good will yielded some early results.

During the second year of his directorship, Cummins positively reported on the denomination's and the mission's progress, stating: "Indian pastors and church leaders have met here with the District Superintendent … to share in solving mutual problems and to establish a methodology that will be culturally relevant and effective."[72] Although previous NLM meetings with PAOC representatives had often turned out to be token gatherings with only Euro-Canadian missionaries present, this summer 1977 meeting in Pickle Lake held promise. At this meeting, WOD superintendent Howard Honsinger met with Indigenous ministers. Cummins described the meeting as an evaluation and planning conference with the potential for great importance, future work, and growth of the NLM.[73] Cummins continued: "Men left with a new assurance of God's blessing on the Mission, of unity with brethren in the South of being part of God's larger program. We came away with a mind to work."[74] This meeting broke expectations of being routine and was significant both for Indigenous ministers and for Howard Honsinger. As a member of the PAOC executive, Honsinger intentionally invited Indigenous ministers' initiative within the NLM, winning the affection of many Indigenous representatives within the WOD. At one district meeting, Indigenous representatives named him an honorary Kanien'kehá:ka nation member, with the name Desagaswateda, meaning "Enlightener." Later Cummins reported successful meetings between Honsinger and eight Indigenous ministry leaders, representing five First Nations territories.[75]

Noting the uniqueness of northern Ontario's spiritual needs, as well as what he believed to be urgency regarding its inhabitants' missionization, Cummins described what he encountered in his travels: "Tiny widely scattered settlements, accessible only by airplane ... isolated by vast bushlands, lakes and muskegs. The people are Salteaux (northern Ojibway), gradually grading into almost pure Cree right along the coastlands of the Bay."[76] In contrasting Indigenous and Euro-Canadian cultures, Cummins sought to draw a correlation between the NLM and his intercultural and international mission experience. Cummins's words demonstrate an awareness of realities affecting Indigenous people, as well as cultural and national variation. It would seem here that the NLM's Indigenous participants appreciated (or at least acknowledged) Cummins's sentiment; a *Pentecostal Testimony* writer reported: "The love he and his wife shared for this important ministry was appreciated."[77]

What is more, Indigenous people's integration of Pentecostalism into the traditional subsistence calendar was also becoming apparent. Cummins wrote about NLM Bible College students John Mekenak and Caleb McKay, for whom

> [t]he difficult verse in Ephesians 4 surfaced: 'He led captivity captive and gave gifts unto men.' Immediately John and his brother-in-law, Caleb McKay, wanted an explanation and to my perplexed surprise they burst into laughter as I concluded. Querying their amusement, I learned these two men, out on their trapline in the dead of winter, travelling by skidoo, camping in a tent, with a kerosene lantern their sole source of light, 100 miles from home, were accustomed to have an evening Bible study together after the day's work. There they tried to come up with some logical explanation. Had I agreed with their conclusion? I asked. John laughed heartily, frankly open and honest. They'd been 1000 miles off course in their guesses, he said ... Just pause and picture these two young Indians in that context. How many of their age from our culture would even think of including a Bible among the meagre list of essentials on a skidoo trip in the frozen bush of northern winter?[78]

It would have been beneficial to have recorded exactly what Mekenak and McKay's interpretation of the passage was. While Cummins had been surprised by their scriptural intrigue while on the hunt, it is not uncommon for Indigenous Pentecostals to integrate their devotional and traditional lives without eliminating aspects of either.[79] In some instances Pentecostal devotion has developed spiritual significance for its role in assisting Nehiyawak subsistence gatherers during their hunt, a potential example of Brown's nonexclusive cumulative adhesion.[80] Further, many First Nations elders learned syllabics in the bush. There they also developed the spiritual disciplines of Bible reading and hymn singing. Clinton Westman describes: "Today, many elders' cabins and pickup trucks feature a Cree bible at easy reach."[81]

Divergent cosmologies typically spawn culturally relevant and specific interpretations of the biblical text. This can be seen in Mekenak and McKay's scriptural exegesis, the application of which is reminiscent of Jace Weaver's conclusions:

> Native Christians give authority to scripture specifically because it resonates with their experience ... they locate themselves and their perceptual experience in the story ... This is not the hermeneutics of professional exegetes. Rather, it is the folk theology upon which Christianity at the ground level has always thrived as a living faith. This process of appropriation of the text is no different than that which goes on in the lives of ordinary Christians anywhere in the world. Native Christians give authority to the biblical witness because ... there is something that "finds them" where they live their lives.[82]

Considering the above, the aforementioned episode features among some of the most compelling evidence contained within the PAOC documentary record pointing to the indigenization of Pentecostalism through the NLM.

Cummins also generally extolled the virtues of the Pentecostal message in reaching the Indigenous population as he specifically reported on the Néhinaw territory at Fort Severn:

> The Chief ... gave ringing testimony to the white officials and government representatives from the south, that neither legal system nor penal codes, as well intended as they may be, solve the sin problem man has. Only Christ can give a man a new

> heart with new desires. Only the Gospel can transform a derelict into a saint. The North accepts this truth more readily than the South generally.[83]

Conceivably the chief's specific wording indicated dissatisfaction with the Canadian government's approach to realities affecting Indigenous people, rather than articulating the problem of sin exclusively. It is possible he wished to gain the PAOC as an ally in expressing his dissatisfaction with the prevailing government system. Alternatively, Cummins may have adapted this exchange to suit more closely his own intended purposes. Potentially the reality rests somewhere between the two.

Unfortunately, the honeymoon period for Cummins's directorship was short-lived. While he had experienced international mission in Kenya, his new location was unique. The shift to northern Ontario had its challenges. Denominational accounts of the period indicated the PAOC laity's perception of the task. One *Pentecostal Testimony* writer asked: "With such a vast territory, how could this couple carry such a load on lonely shoulders? It is like having a half dozen congregations which are hundreds of miles apart."[84] Although more culturally conscientious than his predecessor, Cummins struggled to appreciate distinct Indigenous ministry methods. Almost as though a switch was flipped, his tone went from sympathetic to polemic. As the 1970s closed, he described Indigenous ministers' means of communication as inadequate: "The 'teachers' simply exercised the Indian story teller's expertise ... using Bible stories and inaccurately told at that ... The teachers didn't know English."[85]

Cummins interpreted Indigenous Pentecostals' instruction as incorrect and became troubled by teachers' inability to speak English. Not only does this response negate the centrality of Indigenous oral tradition in the conveying of doctrine,[86] it also stands in complete opposition to Indigenous culture, contrasting Stan McKay's more positive assessment:

> Time and again I was amazed at how their imagination and spiritual depth enabled them to understand something from so different a part of the world and make it relevant to their own context. The women and men I met had a capacity for doing theology far beyond what anyone might have imagined. And so it made me angry that the institutional church was not

> acknowledging the tremendous spiritual depth of biblical Christian understanding these people had.[87]

When spoken and heard by Indigenous people, the Bible conveyed accessible and relatable stories of diverse nations, tangible encounters with a higher power, families connected across generations by expansive kinship, and a God who delivers the oppressed.[88] Similarly Mark Clatterbuck deduced from his fieldwork among Apsáalooke in Montana that "discussion of Bible stories is punctuated with descriptions of dreams and visions that are, in turn, filled with Christian images … [demonstrating] the complementarity of … [Christianity and] traditionalism."[89] Perchance for Cummins, an action better suited to the accomplishment of the indigenous principle might have been recognizing that storytelling is not antithetical to spiritual depth, and allowing the Bible's integration into the instructors' cultural milieu.[90]

Cummins's apparent frustration continued:

> Much more than in our white culture Indian parents have abdicated all responsibility for educating their children, a terrible trap of satanic strategy working now in both cultures. So when the government began sending in white school teachers with the announced responsibility of educating their children, Indian society totally abandoned any idea of the next generation … Also they soon had good reason to fear this new education which was alienating their children from them and their life style [*sic*]. The white man's education has remained very suspect and on the whole is little valued in the North.[91]

To Cummins's credit, his final remarks on Indigenous families' apprehension of Euro-Canadian education provides a rarely documented record from the period of PAOC criticism of residential schooling. That aside, the accuracy of Cummins's claims of voluntary parental abdication is questionable. PAOC records from many NLM churches indicate Indigenous Pentecostals valued and upheld communal and familial practices. Cummins proposed: "The wonderful alternative to this bleak picture of hopelessness is the Gospel of Jesus Christ. There is a great spiritual vacuum eager to be filled whenever our Pentecostal churches make Christian education available."[92]

Cummins cannot be blamed for presenting Christianity as a solution to perceived social ills. After all, the NLM's foremost purpose was to missionize. Nor is this a uniquely Euro-Canadian proposition. Cheryl Bear (Dakelh; Nadleh Whut'en First Nation, British Columbia), associate faculty member of Regent College (a graduate school of theology affiliated with the University of British Columbia), Four-Square Church minister, and founding board member of NAIITS, wrote: "Jesus is the only medicine that can heal the Ancient Wounds."[93] However, despite an opening to acknowledge settler culture's participation in Indigenous communities' challenges, Cummins instead blatantly asserted PAOC churches and their missionization as the solution to right historical wrongs. There was no reason to believe that the PAOC would behave or be received any differently from the Christian mission enterprises that preceded it, nor that the PAOC's message could be communicated without association to the settler culture from which it originated. To be clear, the intention is not to make blanket generalizations of the longer-established churches' missionary methods,[94] but rather to underline that the NLM's Indigenous participants' desired solutions might have been for something more or other than simply the suggested insertion of yet another variation of Christianity.

Even with missionary experience, leading a north-central Canadian mission came with a learning curve, and Cummins missed a precious opportunity. He opposed Indigenous adherents' "strong beliefs in dreams, visions and mystical experiences." This was potentially detrimental to the accomplishment of the indigenous principle, as these elements bear some resemblance to Indigenous traditional concepts and practices, and "make Pentecostalism a good fit with subarctic or Aboriginal cultures."[95] Additionally, there is indigenizing precedent for continuity with said practices, whereby certain Indigenous people's "adherence to Christianity ... only truly occurred after visions of Christian entities began to be reported." Furthermore, many Indigenous Pentecostal adherents' "public declarations of personal salvation ... include dream revelations, a basic component of the Algonkian ... religion."[96] However, rather than grasping these beliefs' compatibility with Pentecostal practices, Cummins instead described Indigenous participants as tending "to be taken in by anyone who relates such experiences."[97] Here he referred to Euro-Canadian missionaries' disdainful perception of Indigenous adherents' periodic tendency to adopt the teachings of non-PAOC charismatic itinerant evangelists, as well as the practices associated with Indigenous traditional spiritualities.

Cummins continued critiquing Indigenous traditional spiritualities in a 1979 letter to NLM supporters: "Perhaps, like me, you hadn't realized how traditional spirits completely permeated all of life for them. Although outwardly broken, the ancient system still exerts amazing strength." Cummins criticized Indigenous participants' increasing desire for contextualization. "Old ideals and beliefs have often been adapted and adopted, even within the Christian church," he cautioned, and "unless we replace [them] with the ideals, goals and purpose of true Christianity, and we demonstrate the Holy Spirit as a beautiful and effective inner control, we leave our Indian brethren in dire circumstances."[98] The situation might not have been as "dire" as Cummins supposed, however; contrastingly, it is not uncommon for Indigenous Pentecostals to maintain "elements of practice which are explicitly borrowed ... explicitly rejected, quietly brought in the back, or claimed as having been always around,"[99] such as in cases demonstrative of Weaver's religious dimorphism.

Cummins's critique of the Pentecostal-traditionalist continuum provides a critical and contrasting parallel to Clatterbuck's more impartial assessment. Clatterbuck observed that in its ascendency, Indigenous Pentecostalism is increasingly influenced by aspects of Indigenous traditional spiritualities, while also simultaneously influencing those same spiritual observances.[100] On the other hand, for Cummins, both Indigenous traditional spiritualities and the longer-established churches' theologies stood in the way of what he believed to be "true Christianity," as he subsequently took aim at other denominations:

> Infant baptism and childhood confirmation, a religion accepted for children by parents, became a protective family insurance plan without need for renunciation of animism or repentance or regenerate Christian living. Semi-informed Indian fur-traders returning from posts on the coast carried early Christianity to inland villages. With outward forms accepted and observed, the church assumed wrongly in many cases that Biblical Christianity was understood.[101]

While Cummins's concerns about the comprehensiveness of other denominations' efforts at Christian education may have been sincere, it appears he missed the point. Perhaps owing to the PAOC's Evangelical requirement for a demonstrable conversion experience, Cummins did not view the longer-established churches' Indigenous adherents' conversion to Christianity as genuine – and certainly not biblical. It was also around this time that Evangelical missionary enterprises broadly were assuming a position against what they decried as syncretism. This sentiment most visibly materialized in *The Lausanne Covenant*'s 1975 declaration to "reject as derogatory to Christ and the Gospel every kind of syncretism and dialogue which implies that Christ speaks equally through all religions and ideologies."[102]

Yet it was probable that what Cummins described as syncretism was instead other denominations' efforts at contextualization, evidently resulting in some success at achieving Indigenous adherents' subscription to Christianity. Further, by Cummins's own admission, the longer-established churches' Indigenous acolytes proceeded to propagate the message. Even so, Cummins feared the same purported demise could occur to the PAOC's mission,[103] cautioning that

> Indian animistic spiritism lends itself well to Syncretism. Pentecostalism particularly, with its emphasis on spirit infilling and manifestation of spiritual power, has a strong appeal to the Indian mind ... [T]he Indian religion of fear of spirit power and superstitious seeking of greater power to ... protect from evil spirits make Pentecostalism especially hazardous. Our popularity is not all good.[104]

This demonstrates awareness by the NLM and its director of Indigenous laity's desire for contextualization. Pentecostalism's penchant for spiritual experience seems an obvious parallel to Indigenous spiritual observances. Its orality, dance, healing practices, ecstasy, testimony, tongues, and unique prayer style all combine to render it conducive to contextualization with Indigenous spiritual observances.[105] For their part (and consistent with Brown's nonexclusive cumulative adhesion), many Indigenous Pentecostals within the NLM observed and celebrated the parallels between Pentecostalism and Indigenous traditions. One First Nations NLM minister described it thus:

> We've had a lot of people that have been in Indian religion and have come to the knowledge of Jesus Christ, and they dance in the Spirit, and dancing in the Spirit is, for them, the joy of the Lord. Having the joy of the Lord just for you.

When asked to describe "the difference between dancing in a pow-wow and dancing in the Spirit," the minister replied: "When you dance in the pow-wow, you dance around the fire. But when you dance in the Spirit, you're in the fire."[106]

Despite the parallels and "complementarity" between Pentecostalism and Indigenous traditional spiritualities,[107] NLM leadership failed with contextual execution.[108] They continued to oppose Indigenous cultural practices, separating Pentecostalism from them.[109] Considering the PAOC's articulated desire to accomplish the indigenous principle, it is ironic that Cummins did not see Pentecostalism's appeal to Indigenous spiritual seekers as positive. Instead, he resisted contextualization, equating it with syncretism and believing "true Christianity" was the only solution. Realistically, his cultural brand of Christianity could not directly replace contextualized Christianity, as in truly intercultural mission there will always be some cultural interchange. For example, for many Eeyouch, adoption of Christian ideas and their contextualization to communication beyond the material world has become an integral part of life.[110] Thus a response better-suited to the NLM's indigenous principle might have been Cummins's acceptance of this reality by making provision for Indigenous participants' spiritual preferences.

An illustrative example of the shortcomings surrounding such outcomes is provided by NLM records of the territory of Weagamow Lake (Anishinini), which Cummins described as thoroughly Christianized. The director claimed that circa 1953 nearly all residents had been "born again." He observed that "tobacco sat [unsold] on store shelves" and could say that "nearly all the adults are solidly Christian (tho' not many go to the PAOC church)."[111] Weagamow Lake's residents likely attended other churches, whether longer-established, Evangelical, or independent Pentecostal ones – all were locally prominent.[112] For instance, the Northern Canada Evangelical Mission (NCEM) had been sending missionaries to the locale from as early as 1952.[113] Spillenaar had coordinated the efforts of Indigenous, Euro-Canadian, and Euro-American volunteers to construct a Pentecostal church in Weagamow Lake during the summer of 1972. By 1976, the itinerant Northland Mission Bible College (NLMBC) offered courses in the community, notwithstanding the low attendance at the PAOC church there.[114]

Presumably denominational allegiance in Weagamow Lake was strong, yet it was allegiance to non-PAOC churches. Although the NLM church in Weagamow Lake had an Indigenous minister, the locals were not confident in the Euro-Canadian-led PAOC. While other denominations granted Indigenous-led parishes increasing autonomy, the PAOC appeared to promise the same, yet in practice maintained a forbidding hierarchy. Ultimately the PAOC failed to retain its Weagamow Lake minister's allegiance, Cummins recording:

> Our month there in 1976 demonstrated that the pastor did not want teaching. His people have been led into an unhealthy emphasis on undisciplined fleshy experience not balanced or corrected by the Word. In October he submitted his credentials and is now with another denomination. [Now] there is no PAOC church at Weagamow.[115]

The pastor evidently found reason to leave both the NLM and PAOC. The claim that he "did not want teaching" could mean simply that he wished to exercise an independence to which he and his congregation were entitled. He may even have felt apprehensive of close NLM oversight. Cummins's quip about "undisciplined, fleshly experience" may be a pejorative reference to another denomination that made the minister a better offer, or to the Weagamow Lake church's efforts toward contextualization. Cummins may not have been personally responsible for the minister's departure, but this indicates that PAOC practices did not sit well with him, his church, and possibly other Indigenous ministers.

Neither did Cummins appreciate and understand the cultural shift First Nations faced in the late twentieth century, perceiving their reactions as wistful. For example, the Indigenous minister of the nearby Sandy Lake First Nation (Anishinini) NLM church resigned in 1979, moving thirty miles to found a new settlement "away from the encroaching influence our culture keeps introducing to attract young people to indolence, dependence on welfare, alcohol and accompanying evils." Cummins noted that the minister "resigned and withdrew to his trapline."[116] While initially this may have seemed detrimental to the PAOC's cause, missing from Cummins's critique was an appreciation of the fact that the minister's decision did not reflect an abandonment of ministry. For example, Hans M. Carlson wrote of a similar practice among Eeyouch, where one might

> retreat into the bush to find solace and space from the world of the mission. The bush still offered not only an environment in which to escape the tension ... but also an environment

> in which a different set of conceptual relationships held sway and whose power continued to move people's behaviour. The bush did not mean the abandonment of Christianity, but it was a place apart both materially and symbolically, and the reality of this was evident to the Cree, though for the most part missionaries seemed to have missed the power of Christianity to adapt to this hunting world.[117]

Mishkeegogamang First Nation (Ojibwe Anishinaabe), only forty kilometres from NLM headquarters in Pickle Lake, also caused Cummins concern. He lamented, "The small band of Christians have meetings but at irregular intervals, called or cancelled at a moment's notice according to whim ... The Nyyssonens are patiently building confidence."[118] Calling or cancelling meetings "according to whim" may not indicate poor planning or a lack of foresight but rather the exercise of independence. Their methods may well have been perfectly acceptable within their own circles.[119] These Indigenous Pentecostals likely communicated with one another more closely than with the Euro-Canadian missionaries, whose struggle for acceptance fits with Indigenous Christians' prior control of their church and confident refusal of outside influence.

Describing the liturgy of an NLM church service in Mishkeegogamang in February 1978, Cummins mentioned that lay participation predominated and "the whole thing is Ojibway or Cree of which we understand perhaps half a dozen words. Interpreters are rare ... Praying that the Holy Spirit has moved upon the people in some way, we ... start back home to Pickle Lake."[120] There is much to analyze in this account. To begin with, here is an NLM church that maintained a liturgy that was both lay-led and Ojibwemowin Anishinaabemowin and Nêhinawêwin in its language, evidence of the indigenization of Pentecostalism and seemingly a good realization of the indigenous principle. To some extent, Cummins understood elements of the languages, but additionally interesting is Cummins's conclusion of them offering a prayer, then heading home to Pickle Lake. That is to say that in Mishkeegogamang, Cummins and others from the NLM headquarters (situated some distance from Mishkeegogamang or any other First Nations territories)[121] were very much observers and not participants.

Unintentionally, Cummins indicated a degree of removal from action in the field. Even here, he unwittingly revealed a sense of "us and them," having made his observations and then retreating to the

Pickle Lake compound's safety. He literally shuttled in and out from Pickle Lake, without much meaningful on-the-ground connection with the Mishkeegogamang congregation. It was Cummins's decision to establish the Pickle Lake compound. As described in the previous chapter, the Pickle Lake compound's architecture and design (walled off from the surrounding forest) removed and isolated it from reserve realities. Although billed as accessible to First Nations territories, in many ways the NLM's Pickle Lake headquarters served as a remote outpost for the PAOC, standing in for the denomination's southern Ontario–based offices.[122]

Further, Cummins frequently wrote of the Mishkeegogamang church as notably unruly: "Accessibility to Pickle Lake's liquor store causes this reservation suffering beyond that of any other we visit," adding that "with liquor available at Pickle Lake, [Mishkeegogamang] needs much help." Erna Peters reported that Mishkeegogamang had "been a particularly difficult area for the Full Gospel [with] much opposition." She warned that "alcoholism is rampant; demon power was evident. The Long house [*sic*] religion is returning."[123] Michael J. Frost observed and recorded a similar trend among other Pentecostal missionaries to indigenous peoples globally: "While the spiritual worldview of pentecostalism [*sic*] has at times proved attractive, it often does so by characterizing indigenous religious and cultural traditions as subject to demonic influences that can be blamed for the social challenges faced in indigenous communities."[124] Thus in many ways Mishkeegogamang functioned as the literary foil or "worst case scenario" in PAOC missionary depictions of north-central Canada.

As much as the NLM functioned institutionally as a Euro-Canadian organization, there is evidence of Indigenous people's local ownership and leadership. Indigenous Pentecostals conducted their worship and the Euro-Canadian missionaries were welcome to join. Indigenous Pentecostals remained in the territory, but Euro-Canadian missionaries returned home to NLM headquarters. It is also apparent that Mishkeegogamang First Nation's parishioners were perfectly content with this pact, happy to have missionaries visit and happy to have their independence from them when they left.

Cummins grieved that Mishkeegogamang's youth had no memory "of revival 23 years ago ... and ... seemed confused as to whether it was expected that they should be friendly to ... whites." A few even "flaunted cigarettes and [a] hostile swagger."[125] Although it is true that many Indigenous Pentecostals do not use tobacco, Cummins's

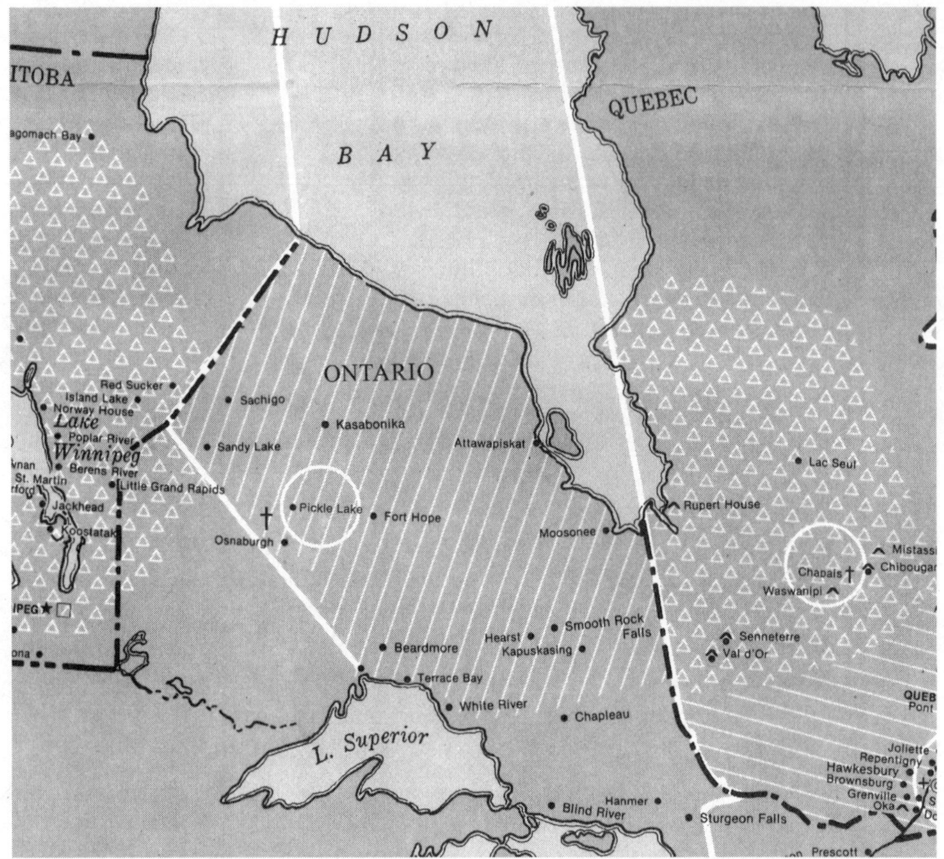

Figure 4.3 Map showing the extent of Northland Mission operations in 1982

emphasis on holiness codes potentially prevented him from appreciating that tobacco use among those not affiliated with the PAOC was not necessarily rebellion, overlooking tobacco's important role in most Indigenous cultures.[126] Even if the youth were not using the tobacco for traditional purposes, it should not have created so noticeable an obstacle to engagement. Indigenous traditional spiritualities contain nuances and contradictions not neatly aligned with definitive Western categorization. Foreign to Western outlooks, such contradictions are normal for practitioners of Indigenous traditional observances.[127] Indigenous audiences and the missionaries were in cultural confrontation, a tension occurring even when sharing Pentecostalism with Indigenous recipients who were already Christian but not Pentecostal.

This fundamental failure to communicate sparked the clash of Pentecostal holiness codes and Indigenous culture that persisted throughout the NLM's existence.

Such discrepancies contributed to the ongoing tension between NLM leadership and Indigenous Pentecostals. To Cummins's credit, he was the only NLM director to study Indigenous traditional spiritualities and to attempt the study of Nêhiyawêwin and Ojibwemowin Anishinaabemowin. Although not a pilot like Spillenaar or his successor Ian Winter, Cummins had the advantage of being genuinely intrigued by Indigenous cultures. However critical he was, he demonstrated the best attempt at effective missiology, at least in theory. Realistically he could only interact with Indigenous culture as an observer, not a participant, merely skimming the culture's surface and neither willing nor able to embrace it.[128]

Cummins's level of reflection for a time held him in good stead in the PAOC's written record, yet he later fell out of favour for not converting observations into the PAOC's desired outcomes.[129] While he seemed somewhat knowledgeable about Indigenous spiritual practices, he was not able to translate Pentecostalism into Indigenous idiom, or at the very least align himself with those who could and did.[130] As time passed, his once-glowing reviews soured, describing those he encountered as "obsessed with the idea of supernatural power, and see[ing] the Holy Spirit as a complete-coverage insurance policy against sickness and other fearful powers ... [D]enominational loyalty is rare indeed."[131]

Cummins certainly believed in the ideal of the indigenous principle, to the extent that he emphasized the need for "native evangelists, pastors, teachers, well-trained and able to teach their own people."[132] However, he did not successfully position the NLM to be contextual, not partnering with those who were translating Pentecostalism effectively into their own cultures. A period document thus summarized Cummins's leadership: "Very obvious lack of communication or poor communication over past couple of years between Dale Cummins, Superintendent and District. Dale Cummins ... [is] disappointed at this point ... [and presenting] many inconsistencies."[133] Given Cummins's strong presentation skills, this comment would not have been provoked by lack of ability to communicate. More likely, the reference to inconsistencies implies that his ornate communiqués did not accurately reflect the NLM churches' growing and diverse needs. This document might furthermore betray the bias of denominational leaders who had become dissatisfied with Cummins's work. Increasingly discouraged, he believed he lacked "complete control of the situation up there."[134]

Some time later, when asked by Erna Peters to reflect on his time with the NLM, Cummins responded:

> Some [information] should never be told!! We made a lot of mistakes. Having made the decisions we made, all we can do is live with the results and maybe more is being accomplished than I'll ever be aware of ... I know it is discouraging work. Likely if we had prayed more and done less ... we'd have been better off.[135]

It is hard to imagine what Cummins meant by his comment about doing less, although this may reflect his realization that Euro-Canadian missionaries had a responsibility to hand over the mission's operations to Indigenous ministers at that stage, or at least to better engage and enable Indigenous Pentecostals through the process of contextualization.

Cummins's leadership showcased his ability to identify and articulate the NLM's challenges in a nuanced manner. Still he struggled to turn words into meaningful action.[136] Following his resignation from the NLM, Cummins wrote several articles for PAOC publications before his death in October 2007.[137] Other than these, no records explicitly describe his later ministry. Perhaps his greatest shortcoming amidst trying not to discriminate was overlooking the reality that mission to a population subjected to aggressive settler colonialism required awareness, sensitivity, and intentionality. It is ironic, given that Cummins's international missionary experience and intellectualism should have made him the best-positioned NLM director to draw this correlation.

DIFFERENCES BETWEEN PAOC DOMESTIC AND INTERNATIONAL MISSIONS

On this point it is worth taking a short detour to examine the NLM's position on the indigenous principle by comparing the PAOC's international and domestic missionary enterprises. The PAOC's missionary policy (dating as far back as the PAOC's 1932 Constitution) required PAOC workers to train, equip, and empower indigenous ministers to replace the PAOC's predominantly Euro-Canadian missionaries.

PAOC missionaries typically achieved this task in international settings. While domestic mission workers also articulated the indigenous principle's tenets, they generally (but not universally) failed to execute their ideals in practice. This trend is consistent with Canadian historian Susan Neylan's and British church historian Eugene Stock's findings of CMS missionaries' struggle to implement the indigenous principle in Canada a century earlier. Yet NLM missionaries especially faltered through their inability to entrust church leadership to Indigenous ministers.

To be sure, there were domestic Indigenous ministry leadership candidates, with an exceptional few even promoted to leadership positions, such as in the Manitoba and Northwestern Ontario District (MNWOD). By and large, though, the PAOC's domestic missions departments (particularly within the NLM) routinely installed Euro-Canadian missionaries in leadership roles that rightly should have been filled by Indigenous ministers. Presumably this reluctance arose because the PAOC's 1932 policy specified "foreign fields," the omission leaving room for evident bias in domestic missions. By actions and words, the PAOC implied that the overseas church was good enough for, and worthy of, autonomy, but the Indigenous church at home was not ready, nor would it be for some time.

Generally (but not universally), NLM missionaries showed little regard for Indigenous cultures and languages, nor for their integration with the NLM's ministerial methods. This oversight proved detrimental to the cause. After all, a missionary's measure of success was contingent upon their ability to communicate Christianity without the baggage of Western cultural trappings.[138] This discrepancy furthermore was odd, considering these missiological concepts were practised by the PAOC's international missionaries. Perhaps many NLM missionaries neglected language-learning because of a lack of regard for Indigenous culture. Added to this was the prevailing opinion that Indigenous people, as residents of Canada, ought to learn either English or French. By way of comparison, many non-Pentecostal, non-Indigenous missionaries associated with the NLM's contemporaneous NCEM prioritized the learning of Indigenous languages, often with beneficial results such as more rapid missionary integration into Indigenous host communities.[139] Failure to recognize and then execute the NLM as an enculturated mission cost the PAOC's domestic missionaries dearly, revealing the NLM's ethnocentrism, paternalism, and settler colonialism.

Canadian Pentecostal missiologist Irving Whitt observed, "The growth of PAOC churches overseas has exceeded the growth of the PAOC in Canada. Some of this success can be explained by national and local institutional factors."[140] He added that Canadian Pentecostal work overseas grew disproportionately considering the number of missionaries, attributing its success "to the willingness of these missionaries to quickly turn the leadership over to nationals."[141] Similar institutional factors occurred in Canada, but within the NLM, Euro-Canadian missionaries frequently outnumbered Indigenous ministers (although documentary records would suggest they did not outnumber Indigenous ministerial candidates). The NLM failed to implement the indigenous principle effectively, pursuing that ideal but maintaining Euro-Canadian leadership for decades.

Perhaps the PAOC more readily allowed indigenous leadership overseas than in domestic missions because the geographic distance and separation of the former clarified that international PAOC missionaries were strangers in a foreign land.[142] Yet NLM missionaries in Canada often failed to appreciate their mission's intercultural nature. Cummins attempted to articulate this challenge but struggled to connect meaningful actions to his words.

TENSIONS DURING THE TENURE OF IAN WINTER: 1981–96

Alongside naming Ian Winter director in 1981, the WOD executive appointed southern Ontario–based pastor and district executive member Jack Ozard as NLM "officer and district liaison."[143] Ozard, who maintained an office in southern Ontario and periodically travelled to Pickle Lake, primarily wrote newsletters and other official communications and reports recounting to PAOC supporters the NLM's updates and developments. Winter handled the practical affairs in Pickle Lake.[144]

One of Winter's first initiatives was hosting a conference of Indigenous ministers at the Pickle Lake Centre during late autumn 1981. WOD executive members, including WOD superintendent Homer Cantelon, attended and were well received. Ozard described Winter's "good rapport with the natives." In the March 1982 NLM newsletter, Ozard reported that Winter had led the winter college term well, with his transition into directorship going smoothly.[145]

Ozard and Winter as a tag team earned some early credibility with the NLM's Indigenous adherents, consistent with preceding perceptions of NLM directors starting well. Ozard noted of a 1983 request from the Weagamow Lake chief for a worker that the site "had a Pentecostal church once but for whatever reason it was given away a few years ago." The chief wanted a resident pastor, but also listed some potential trade skills that would be helpful.[146] It seems the NLM had poor institutional memory, not recalling (or perhaps not caring to recount publicly) that Weagamow Lake's Indigenous minister had become so frustrated with PAOC leadership that he had led his church out of the denomination (an episode described in the previous section). Also apparent in this exchange is that the chief wanted his reserve to benefit from individuals who would help bolster the reserve's economy. The chief's gesture was an expression of trust, and of a legitimate need. Somewhat opportunistically the NLM leadership perceived the reserve's economic requirements as an entry point, regardless of the chief's actual objective. The NLM would have been wise not to dismiss this display of trust, considering the mission's unfortunate history in Weagamow Lake.[147]

Again in 1983, the chief and Council of the Mishkeegogamang First Nation requested that the NLM re-establish a church and install a minister. The chief offered to search for a suitable building.[148] In 1984, the NLM began ministry to the First Nation through NLMBC student Ruth Skunk (Ojibwe Anishinaabe), herself from Mishkeegogamang.[149] In September 1984, Jack Ozard, Guy Campeau, and Ian Winter met with the Band Council Chief Morris Loon.[150] Like Cummins before him, Ozard described Mishkeegogamang as crime-ridden and crippled by vice, "reminiscent of New York's Harlem in 'The Cross and The Switchblade.'" In another demonstration of good faith, the band council allowed Skunk free radio and television broadcasting airtime.[151]

While the realities of reserve life can periodically be stark, this particular account goes beyond the descriptions of scarcity, and provokes images of perdition. That the Mishkeegogamang First Nation radio and television stations gave airtime free of charge to the NLM minister illustrates that the territory's leaders were not totally opposed to the PAOC's activity. Even here the local chief wanted to establish that his reserve was more than a crime-ridden backwater. An invitation for the Pentecostal message was matched with an offer of cooperation in its dissemination.

The NLM continued to receive such requests. Sandy Lake Band Council backed an NLM church construction and expansion project, as by 1991 the Sandy Lake church had outgrown its venue. In 1989, the Sandy Lake church had reached out to neighbouring Deer Lake

First Nation (Anishinini). They too requested an NLM worker and church. In Fort Severn, the band council purchased a building, donating it to the Pentecostal church there.[152] Presumably, the bands, councils, chiefs, and reserves requesting ministers did not seek another Euro-Canadian missionary. Fortunately in the case of Ruth Skunk, the Mishkeegogamang church instead received an Indigenous minister. These instances demonstrate local support of and preference for organically run and Indigenous-led mission, independent of PAOC and Euro-Canadian control.

Indigenous ministers' involvement created a noticeable difference compared to when only Euro-Canadian missionaries were present.[153] Winter recorded an outreach to "the troubled reserve of Pikangekum" (Ojibwe Anishinaabe) that integrated the ministry of Indigenous evangelists and counselors. Their services, assemblies, and televised broadcasts addressed the challenging issues endured by Indigenous communities. These mediums successfully reached "adults who would not normally talk of such problems publicly." As a result, the Pikangikum chief requested the NLM "start up a church that will make a difference and breathe hope into the people."[154] The evident success of involving Indigenous evangelists and counselors drew the reserve chief's attention, and the PAOC leadership's praise.

As with previous directors, so under Winter: many NLM personnel struggled to appreciate the significance of Indigenous languages. Erna Peters arrived in Fort Severn in 1984, where she claimed the church had been stagnant in the months prior to her arrival. In short order, however, Peters won four adherents with the potential for more.[155] She recalled the congregation singing in Nêhinawêwin at worship services.[156] But Peters discerned a problem: she did not understand Nêhinawêwin and her mission participants did not speak English. To her credit, Peters did attempt to engage the women of her congregation, lamenting that while lack of language compatibility prevented deeper connections, they did understand some English even if they could not speak it. Peters noted one woman's traditional practices: "There is a lot of work involved in tanning a hide from start to finish, and fewer and fewer of the young girls were willing to learn how to do the job. Emily said, 'too much high school.'"[157] Apparently Emily referred to the government-run schools, and the Euro-Canadian cultural values they imposed upon students.[158] Yet, oddly, the NLM overlooked such critiques and their implied requirement for more contextual awareness of Indigenous cultures and lifestyles.[159]

Peters was reluctant to relinquish her leadership role, monitoring who the congregation invited as guest speakers and ignoring services not in English, instead absenting herself from them, stating: "I did not oppose them having meetings but for some reason they were rather reluctant to tell me about it ... [I rarely went] because it was all in Cree and quite long [and] ... did little for me except tire me."[160] To be sure, in an ecclesial environment where the majority of the service is conducted in Nêhinawêwin, the indigenous principle thrives as the local adherents actually direct the service, rather than the missionary.[161] Additionally, Indigenous ministers' bilingual abilities, the localized nature of their congregations, and the ease of access to membership all were advantageous to the growth of Pentecostalism. Where Indigenous communities might have been divided along linguistic lines (English, French, or Indigenous languages), bilingual Indigenous Pentecostals potentially contributed to community unity by becoming a sort of language bridge.[162] Specific to the episode Peters recounted, an extended length of worship service would have been well within the norm for Indigenous Pentecostals. Graham Gibson quoted one First Nations minister who recounted: "'I find that in Native churches they sing long,' ... and that it is not unusual for such services to go for three to four hours at a time."[163]

Again, Indigenous Pentecostals exerted autonomy over liturgical scheduling, keeping meetings secret from Peters. The very nature of Pentecostal worship in this context allowed for ritual moments free from Euro-Canadian control and observation.[164] Conversely the missionaries' imposing Euro-Canadian leadership style caused tension. While cooperative with and dependent upon Indigenous evangelists to operate meetings, Peters and other NLM missionaries were reluctant to hand over influence and leadership.

Peters's response is consistent with Leanne Betasamosake Simpson's (Michi Saagiig Nishnaabeg; Alderville First Nation, Ontario) analysis, as she described that Euro-Canadians

> have mistakenly characterized Nishnaabeg governance as less complex and less developed than western forms, primarily because it was localized instead of centralized ... [G]overnance was localized within an individual's self-determination, the self-determination of families, clans and communities, as well as being localized within a given geographical region.[165]

When Néhinawak Pentecostals asserted themselves, Peters withdrew, not a negative choice. Although withdrawal denoted lack of solidarity with her hosts, her periodic absence may have unwittingly facilitated an environment where Indigenous influence flourished. What emerges within Indigenous territories with churches led by Indigenous pastors is neither an imitation of a settler church nor an exclusivist entity. Instead what arises is a unique environment where the needs of Indigenous people are responded to in a manner relevant to each individual location.[166] To be sure, this pattern is observable within Fort Severn, and with some success.

To that end, when Indigenous ministers enjoyed visible success, the NLM eagerly celebrated. Ozard highlighted the work of Dan Doolittle (Kanien'kehá:ka; Six Nations of the Grand River, Ontario), well-liked and sought after by Euro-Canadian and Indigenous Pentecostals alike. A woman from Six Nations Pentecostal Church related: "I believe the scripture where the Lord said that he would give us pastors according to his own heart. I look at Pastor Dan and … see that in him."[167]

Doolittle described himself as a "Native Christian," believing the term to say much about his self-identity. In the first place, Doolittle identified as a Pentecostal. While distinguishing his beliefs from those of the "Long-House" tradition, Doolittle simultaneously considered his Pentecostal beliefs to be strongly tied to Indigenous traditional cultural observances, such as concepts of the nature of life; the spiritual realities of an Indigenous traditional cosmology; and the way human beings are to "interact with the spirit world." Doolittle saw no tension between Indigenous traditional concepts of spirit beings and Pentecostal notions of spirituality, demonology, and theology; but he did maintain that Christianity "clarifies who these beings are and how one might better relate with them." In sum, Doolittle considered "himself very much Native and yet also completely Christian."[168]

In 1983, Doolittle and his family moved to Big Trout Lake, a predominantly Anishinini territory, taking up the NLM church pastorate. Ozard stated of him: "Dan moved into a needy area with a firsthand knowledge of customs, culture, etc., and has proved a real blessing … This was quite a sacrificial move, far from their comfortable southern Ontario home."[169] Doolittle provided the following perspective:

> As God poured out His Holy Spirit on Big Trout, old and young came to Jesus and a mighty revival started … people are crying for Pastors … Since moving to Big Trout, we have started having

> Sunday School ... now up to 48 or 50 young people ... [W]e have approximately 15 adults attending regularly.[170]

While the success of Indigenous ministers such as Doolittle was touted by the NLM and many churches within Indigenous territories requested more like them, old Euro-Canadian attitudes persisted. In his 1986 WOD Conference report, Ozard made this condescending claim: "Training native workers is a slow process; the Indian doesn't take easily to moving off his home reserve ... nor is he received too well on a new one." He counterintuitively proposed "White workers – conscientious, caring, consecrated, committed people with a call of God, a love for the north and a willingness to sacrifice!"[171]

Presumably intended as an encouragement to the WOD's then predominantly Euro-Canadian clergy to serve within the NLM, Ozard's exhortation casts doubt on the executive's commitment to the indigenous principle. To realize it, the NLM needed to train and install Indigenous leaders early and often. Instead, Ozard implied that it was more feasible for Euro-Canadian missionaries to leave Canadian cities and integrate into Indigenous communities than for a veteran Indigenous minister to transition to a different territory.

Beyond highlighting discrepancies in the application of their own alleged indigenous principle, PAOC leadership's ignorance of and attitudes of arrogance toward Indigenous practices also point to the dismissal of the alternative possibility that Indigenous people learn and do things differently than Euro-Canadians do, and may even subscribe to entirely different ontologies altogether.[172] In her seminal volume *Dancing on Our Turtle's Back: Stories of Nishnaabeg Re-Creation, Resurgence and a New Emergence*, Leanne Betasamosake Simpson provides readers with a framework for Indigenous cosmologies. Simpson speaks to her readers about Indigenous ways of knowing and learning as she writes:

> Our Elders tell us that everything we need to know is encoded in the structure, content and context of these stories and the relationships, ethics and responsibilities required to *be* our own Creation story.[173]

Many Indigenous people believe that acquisition incorporates emotional, intellectual, physical, and spiritual processes. Spirituality frequently forms the foundation for all of these aspects, with a particular emphasis on mentoring subsequent generations for the realities of life.[174] This cosmology presents some parallels to Indigenous Pentecostals' expression and acquisition. For instance, one NLMBC graduate described, "it is not man's responsibility to teach spiritual truths from the Bible but that's the Holy Spirit's job." Another First Nations minister reported:

> I haven't been taught a white man's way, if you want to put it that way, but I know what the Bible says ... People [say that] ... you're going to at least start to depend on knowledge rather than the Spirit of the Lord leading you ... You'll start thinking man's way instead of God's way, you know.[175]

For that matter, it is commonly maintained by many Indigenous "Pentecostals that the minister will learn from the Holy Ghost and does not need other teachers."[176] While these methods of acquisition may seem improbable from a non-Indigenous perspective, they are commonplace to those with an Indigenous worldview. To be clear, these methods are more substantive than simply being a form of "instinct," but rather comprise metaphysical as well as intergenerational processes.[177] For instance, Lori Lambert (Nulhegan Abenaki and Mi'kmaq/Huron Wendot; Vermont), professor of pedagogy at Salish Kootenai College on the Flathead Indian Reservation, Montana, explained:

> Most Indian people try to make meaning of what they learn by linking new learning to old skills, to life's experiences, and to make meaning out of what is learned. Learning theorists call this the constructivist model of education. For Indian people we call it the way we learn things.[178]

Thus all of the above is to say that it is perfectly acceptable within Indigenous cosmologies for learning to be a process that takes place on both personal and spiritual planes, and within the context of Indigenous traditions. The application of that knowledge can also be carried out according to Indigenous norms. Or as Simpson continued to describe it:

> One of the most crucial tasks presently facing Indigenous nations is the continued creation of individuals and assemblages of people who can think in culturally inherent ways. By this I mean

> ways that reflect the diversity of thought within our broader cosmologies, those very ancient ways that are inherently counter to the influences of colonial hegemony.[179]

In a fashion similar to that proposed by Simpson, Doolittle subscribed to a form of acquisition which stands in contrast to that of the PAOC's leadership, who typically relied upon a structural, colonial, and institutional model in their interactions with Indigenous ministers. For his part, Dan Doolittle described learning as a deeply spiritual process, contending that the Holy Spirit provided him the knowledge to repair vehicles for the Big Trout Lake Band, to butcher meat for his job at a grocery store, and to minister to his congregations. Doolittle claimed no formal instruction from any human sources for these areas of his life. The approach to knowledge acquisition that Indigenous ministers proposed is consistent with that described by Simpson and Doolittle. It is furthermore compatible with Indigenous traditional notions about the transmission of knowledge through spiritual encounters.[180] Although Indigenous ways of knowing may never be fully understood by settler Canadians, the latter should at least convey respect for the former,[181] a point that NLM leadership – had they been serious about their indigenous principle – might otherwise have heeded.

In large part, Indigenous ministers' and congregations' resistance to these denominational norms have enabled Indigenous Christianity to serve as a vital contributor to Indigenous spirituality and vice versa, with Christianity being most successful when it enters Indigenous worlds through Indigenous means.[182] Supremely, Doolittle's experience points to the unique offering that Indigenous cosmologies bring to the practice of Pentecostalism. Citing this example, it would appear that Indigenous traditional cultural expressions are contextualized into Pentecostalism in the practice of an individual minister, akin to Weaver's notion of religious dimorphism. This takes place partially through a process that Derek Brothers Milne describes as "an ambivalent dialogue," whereby elements of Indigenous traditional spiritualities are experienced and filtered, then incorporated into Pentecostal beliefs and practices. This method in turn has bearing upon the congregation the minister leads. That is to say that a Kanien'kehá:ka Pentecostal preacher brings his culture to bear, and then that expression of Pentecostalism is contextualized as Kanien'kehá:ka and demonstrates ecclesial applicability, notwithstanding the fact that the congregation in conversation is Anishinini. Indeed this constitutes a process which might aptly be referred to as the "'traditionalization' of Pentecostalism."[183] Thus Ozard's dismissal of Indigenous ministers, his preference for Euro-Canadian missionaries, as well as his suggestion that said missionaries were better received on First Nations territories (even after praising Doolittle's transition), all stand in stark contrast to Doolittle's contextualized reality. The executive's failure to recognize the necessity of an enculturated Christianity was countered by Indigenous ministers' contextual work, establishing a foundation for Christian expression within the Indigenous community, notwithstanding denominational opposition to that culture.[184]

Unfortunately the sting of Ozard's words endured, with NLM minister George Gunner (Moose Cree First Nation; Moose Factory, Ontario) recalling them much later: "I remember … when Jack Ozard and Western Ontario District sent a letter to native leaders saying it's time for the native leaders to step up." Gunner remembered the "put-downs of how we were never involved; our attitudes (not understanding that as aboriginals [*sic*] we have different ways of doing things) … We were not included."[185] Gunner's words underlined how frequently Indigenous ministers' input to mission leadership were ignored, overlooked, or dismissed. Top leadership roles were all but inaccessible. Even into the 1990s, at least half of NLM churches' staffs were composed of Euro-Canadians.[186] This drew the Indigenous bands' and councils' ire. When the NLM sought to deploy a Euro-Canadian missionary recently graduated from EPBC, the mission required the Sandy Lake First Nation (Anishinini) chief's official permission. NLM leadership warned: "It will be a tremendous challenge and cultural adjustment. There is no guarantee from the District of regular support … We are hoping to challenge the natives to support their Pastor."[187] Remarkably, the denomination claimed not to be able to support its own staff, requesting instead that Sandy Lake's residents support a non-Indigenous missionary. All the while, unemployed Indigenous graduates were willing to minister voluntarily.[188]

Although the missionary couple received the chief's permission, the situation still presented challenges. NLM leadership reported in a newsletter: "They are the first white pastors to be resident there – perhaps really the first pastors. The natives have strange expectations: they find it extremely difficult to understand the principle of pastoral support and loyalty. There is a great cultural difference."[189] Obviously the Sandy Lake congregation was not interested in receiving a

Euro-Canadian missionary couple. What the NLM deemed as "strange expectations" was nothing more than Anishininiwag Pentecostals expressing their autonomy and exercising the indigenous principle. This was not a refusal of Pentecostalism, demonstrated by other towns' acceptance of Indigenous ministers and their message, but simply an expression of the desire for Indigenous ministers on reserves. Rather than install an Indigenous minister, the mission hoped that the residents of Sandy Lake would accept and financially support yet another Euro-Canadian missionary couple.[190]

Ironically, the same newsletter reported Winter's recent return from the Sachigo Lake church, pleased to learn that members were tithing. The newsletter continued: "For the first time the native believers have grasped this principle and are obeying the Lord. I am sure we folk in the south do not appreciate the enormity of this victory." Of course there was an enormity of difference between situations in Sandy Lake and Sachigo Lake. The Sachigo Lake pastors (the Mekenaks) were Indigenous.[191] Thus the concept of pastoral support was not lost on Indigenous congregations. It was the NLM's leadership that did not recognize (or wilfully ignored) the Sandy Lake congregants' signalling of their preference for Indigenous ministers.

Regarding the local, congregational level, Indigenous Pentecostals contributed to the NLM's longevity by establishing an infrastructure whereby churches could sustain themselves. An NLM Workers Conference's meeting minutes stated: "A note of victory is, that some ... have begun to tithe on a regular basis."[192] This was significant as tithing became indicative of individual and local engagement. In 1992, the NLM Board of Directors issued a statement to all NLM-affiliated congregations emphasizing the need to tithe.[193] With tithing in place, churches could become self-sustaining. Winter reported the following to the 1994 WOD Conference:

> I can see that there has been a slow but definite Spiritual growth in our Native Churches. Growth that has cost in time, effort and dollars but it has been worth it. It is exciting to see people grasp the spiritual truths of tithing.[194]

While this quotation seems to attribute this successful breakthrough to NLM missionaries and supporters (those contributing to defray the "cost in time, effort and dollars"), Indigenous Pentecostals themselves carried much of the burden. Indigenous people's tithing meant that the NLM could move toward autonomy; accordingly, Indigenous Pentecostals gave generously.[195]

In such a fashion it appeared that Indigenous culture could accept Pentecostalism, and could even fund it. But the governance structure of the PAOC did not reciprocate, with Ozard commenting:

> Did you know that Canadian tax dollars are being spent to help Canada's native people rediscover their ancient Indian culture and pagan religion? Indian young people and children are being trained ... in the old Longhouse religion of their fathers; taken by bus loads to Indian pow wows where they are exposed to the ancient ways ... This nationalistic trend away from the white man's religion and back to that of the medicine man with its demonism and superstition, can only be reversed by a mighty move of God's supernatural power by His Holy Spirit.[196]

While government prescription of Indigenous traditional spiritualities is not without its detractors, the above opinion's essence may leave some uneasy, not least because Indigenous people's adherence to a brand of Christianity dubbed "white man's religion" was deemed desirable by the district executive.

Additionally, rather than seeing Indigenous traditional spiritualities as lifestyle systems to be understood, NLM leaders attacked the beliefs. Instead of seeking contextual ways to communicate Pentecostalism, the NLM opposed Indigenous culture.[197] One might theorize, based on the NLMBC's applications for government funding around the same time, that had tax dollars been spent on the propagation of Pentecostalism, Ozard might have approved. The executive's words were carefully crafted, appealing to his southern-Ontario–centred, Euro-Canadian, Pentecostal funding-support base. The NLM portrayal of Indigenous people as unconverted and at risk of being swayed by publicly funded "demonism and superstition" prompted supporters to give even more generously. Finally, the PAOC's rigid control over Indigenous ministers' management of resources, notably finances, underscores this monograph's core argument that Euro-Canadian leadership lacked confidence in the emerging Indigenous leaders.[198]

Euro-Canadian missionaries spent most of the NLM's funding. Indigenous ministers and laity expressed discontent with a model that failed to deliver promised autonomy.[199] While influential members of the recently established, mostly Indigenous NLM Northern Board (essentially a subcommittee of the NLM Board of Directors) voiced concern in 1995,[200] NLM leaders simultaneously cast a situation they perceived early in the ministry of another Euro-Canadian missionary couple in Deer Lake as dire: "If you could see a picture of it you wouldn't believe your eyes."[201] Ozard urged supporters to "please pray … as they deal with the frustration of working with the slowness of the Band council and Church members."[202]

The Northern Board viewed the missionary couple differently, believing the problem lay with the missionaries, not the band council or church members. One board member reported: "The people of that community are not accepting this couple. They are only averaging 3 to 4 out to services." Another confirmed the decline in attendance. A final member added the suggestion: "maybe we should be pulling these people out."[203]

Winter opposed removing the couple. Wally McKay (Anishinini; Sachigo Lake, Ontario) responded that the decision was the Northern Board's, not Winter's. Ultimately the Northern Board voted to remove the couple.[204] This assertion of autonomy is striking, but it is crucial to note that the couple continued in ministry at Deer Lake, raising several issues. The part-Indigenous board may have been window dressing, feigning denominational recognition of the Indigenous Voice. Further, latitude was granted to unsuccessful Euro-Canadian missionaries where Indigenous ministers' efforts frequently went unrecognized and periodically were criticized. Consequently one is left to wonder who would be blamed if an Indigenous minister appeared to fail.[205]

NLM leaders' criticism and distrust of Indigenous ministers intimates at least two things. 1) Mission leadership's actions contradicted articulated intentions, effectively undermining the indigenous principle. Even where and when relationships between Indigenous ministers and Euro-Canadian missionaries were mutually (or at least superficially) amicable, brokering the boundaries between Indigenous and Euro-Canadian spheres regularly and routinely distracted from the NLM's intended work. 2) Indigenous ministers embraced the indigenous principle, carrying out ministry as they saw fit. It is at this point of tension that the indigenous principle succeeds or struggles. If NLM Euro-Canadian leaders handed over leadership and if Indigenous ministers remained loyal to the NLM, then the indigenous principle would accomplish its intended outcome. If either party did not cooperate, then the indigenous principle would falter. On balance, Indigenous ministers' willingness to remain loyal to the PAOC exceeded the Euro-Canadian missionaries' willingness to hand over the mission. When Indigenous churches with Indigenous ministers prevailed, they did so because Indigenous people wanted them.[206] If the indigenous principle were to succeed, it would rest largely on the Indigenous ministers' success, despite resistance from the NLM's Euro-Canadian leadership.

Speaking on behalf of NLM leadership in autumn 1995, Ozard wrote: "Our aim has always been to see an indigenous work throughout the Native community. It is now in the process of happening. However, the District is committed to continue supporting this ministry."[207] Ozard admitted that there were disproportionate numbers of Euro-Canadian missionaries within PAOC Indigenous churches across Canada, with "only some 58 Native Pastors serving approximately 100 PAOC Native congregations ... Solid, steady, consistent, balanced, loyal local leadership has been difficult to find and maintain."[208]

Perhaps the "difficulty" was more systemic than Ozard and others acknowledged. Euro-Canadian ministers' leadership of roughly half of the NLM churches potentially reflected nearly total Euro-Canadian denominational governance. Further, the NLM demonstrated an institutional preference for Euro-Canadian staff over Indigenous ministers. Ozard was ambivalent, sometimes speaking poorly of Indigenous leaders and requesting "white workers," yet sometimes requesting greater investment in Indigenous leadership development. Even the NLM Northern Board, intended to install Indigenous pastors and leaders, remained partially composed of Euro-Canadian members, including its chair. For the NLM to autonomize would require that a majority of leaders be Indigenous. Yet repeatedly Euro-Canadian leadership questioned Indigenous ministers' legitimacy and confirmed its reluctance to hand over leadership roles.

Perhaps the NLM's greatest shortcoming with Indigenous Pentecostalism was that Euro-Canadians rarely seemed to ask what the movement meant to Indigenous adherents. When Indigenous Pentecostals spoke, Euro-Canadian leaders did not appear to listen. This impeded the long-awaited transition to Indigenous leadership. Euro-Canadian leaders only listened to Indigenous people's interests when all other options had been exhausted and the extant organizational structures of the NLM neared potential obsolescence.

CONCLUSION

Unsurprisingly, an organization such as the PAOC, with its exclusivist model for conversion to Christianity, opposed what it suspected to be syncretism with Indigenous traditional spiritualities. It bears repeating that this chapter does not propose that Indigenous Pentecostals universally wished for contextualization, as they have at times held varying views on the issue of integrating Indigenous traditional observances into Pentecostalism. All but absent from missionaries' efforts, however, is an attempt to acknowledge Indigenous traditions' cultural significance, the rare exception being some of Cummins's writings. Yet even then, the mission failed to turn theory into practice. The patterns missionaries demonstrated resonate with Canadian Pentecostal theologian Van Johnson's critique of a dichotomy perpetuated by PAOC evangelism:

> Herein lies the dilemma: we may have unconsciously anointed a way of life that is more culturally formed than biblically shaped. Our context may have contextualized us. We may be preaching a "Christianized" version of Western individualism and materialism rather than the great narrative of God's saving work in the world.[209]

For PAOC missionaries to have wholly opposed other spiritual traditions without first engaging in dialogue with them was detrimental to the accomplishment of its so-called indigenous principle. Coupled with NLM and PAOC leadership's general opposition to the cultural input of Indigenous ministers, the effect was extraordinarily harmful.

By comparison, one may reflect upon the practices of one of the PAOC's historical rivals in this area, the United Church. By the time PAOC missionary efforts peaked, some churches, particularly the United Church, had become more accommodating of Indigenous cultural, spiritual, and traditional observances. As the twentieth century closed, the United Church introduced Indigenous traditional spiritualities at its "Sounding the Bamboo" conference. The United Church also developed a series of talking circles to encourage respectful dialogue between Indigenous people and settler Canadians. Among other things, the conversations revealed that Indigenous Christians also wrestled with the seeming contradictions and complementary wisdom within both Indigenous traditional spiritualities and

Christianity. Yet these dialogues led both settler Canadian and Indigenous United Church members to see the possibility of honouring both traditions.[210]

In 1994, late in the NLM's life, Ozard again articulated the indigenous principle. The WOD executive member stated that he was looking at "the Northland Ministries in general and how [to] best facilitate the indigenousness of the Native work and to create a climate conducive to the development, maintenance and propagation of ... Native Church institutions."[211] Winter also continued to emphasize theological training for Indigenous students and leadership candidates.[212] Unfortunately, in both cases, these initiatives were effectively too little too late.

It is interesting that NLM leadership ramped up discussions of autonomizing as they ultimately transitioned into what would be called the Aboriginal Pentecostal Ministries (APM). Unfortunately, as it relates to the NLM's Euro-Canadian leadership and their commitments, the transition to the APM corresponded with the NLM's financial and structural decline. The subsequent conversation about autonomizing the NLM in the mid-1990s supports the notion that NLM leadership could not secure sufficient funding for the mission's maintenance. Only after its near collapse did they hand it over to Indigenous ministers' leadership.

Throughout most of the NLM's existence, its Euro-Canadian leadership claimed to support the indigenous principle yet subtly undermined it, doubting and ignoring Indigenous ministers, and opposing the integration of Indigenous culture with Pentecostalism. Yet when the NLM transitioned to the APM, and as the NLM's Euro-Canadian leadership at last committed to handing over the mission to Indigenous ministers, the process was straightforward, quick, and efficient, effectively requiring just a year to implement.

This of course prompts the observation that in fifty years, the NLM had not made good on its autonomizing promises. To address this observation, this monograph now turns its attention to the enactment of that autonomy. While chapter 4 has expressed Indigenous people's effort for acceptance within Pentecostalism, chapter 5 highlights its greatest realization: the transition from NLM to APM.

5

Standing at the Shoreline

The Dissolution of the Northland Mission and the Birth of Aboriginal Pentecostal Ministries

I asked him how long the[y] ... intended to conduct mission activities among a tribe that had lived as Christians for over three hundred and fifty years. His answer to my question was representative of Christian attitudes toward Indian people today: "Until the job is done."

Vine Deloria, Jr, Íŋyaŋ Woslál Háŋ; Standing Rock Indian Reservation, South Dakota[1]

It is time we stopped reaching out our hands to government and to our white brothers saying, "help me"; rather, it is time that we stretched out hands of love and ministered to those around us.

George Kallappa, Kwih-dich-chuh-aht; Neah Bay, Washington, PAOC Native Leadership Council[2]

Most of the old people in the past had no training. People like my father just put themselves in the place where God could use them, and God did ... What they did was no easier for them, than it will be for us. There have been many godly people in our past. Old Eli Mackinac once went to a reserve where he was refused entry. He stood on the shoreline for hours, waiting, until night came. Someone crept out of the darkness to invite him to their home. He ministered to them, and so a work would begin. Many prayers and sacrifices went before us ... [R]emember, this is not an Indian/ White issue – this is a ministry issue.

Wally McKay, Anishinini; Sachigo Lake, Ontario, NLM Minister[3]

While the Northland Mission's (NLM) Euro-Canadian leaders believed that they had been proponents of Indigenous Pentecostals' autonomy, it became apparent that the mission had failed to properly fulfill its indigenous principle. To this point, the Pentecostal Assemblies of Canada (PAOC) had spoken the language of indigenization, but profoundly failed to enact it. Perhaps here is where the greatest source of difficulty lay. That is to say, it was the PAOC's executive and the NLM's leadership (both overwhelmingly Euro-Canadian) who were attempting to "indigenize," the fundamental flaw being that indigenization is the work of Indigenous people and really not something that non-Indigenous people are capable of. What the PAOC executive and NLM leadership likely meant by "indigenization" was instead decolonization. Decolonization is something that anyone – whether Indigenous or non-Indigenous – can capably participate in.[4] Still, indigenization would prove all but impossible without the necessary and prerequisite step of decolonization, and to this point in the NLM's trajectory, there had been little effort to that end. Fortunately, dialogue between NLM leaders and Indigenous ministers forced the former finally to listen; indeed, they claimed they had always intended to. But they also listened largely because by this time they had few other options, having nearly exhausted the NLM's resources. Meanwhile Indigenous ministers' desire for and interest in autonomy and indigenization mirrored socio-political events in Canada during the 1980s and 1990s.

The discussion of autonomizing within the NLM originated during John Spillenaar's tenure, evidently not producing the desired result. Indigenous ministers renewed the conversation on indigenization in earnest at the PAOC Department of Home Missions and Bible Colleges' (DHMBC) Second Annual Native Leadership Conference in Vancouver, British Columbia, in March 1985. The conference theme was "Making our Native churches across Canada indigenous." Further, both Ian Winter and Guy Campeau, at that time principal of the Northland Mission Bible College (NLMBC), attended the conference and contributed to the conversation.[5]

It is worth noting that the PAOC's ministries tailored to Indigenous people beyond the NLM and Western Ontario District (WOD) periodically fared better at autonomizing. For instance, by 1986 the PAOC Sub-Artic Mission (Alberta and Northwest Territories District; Hay River, Northwest Territories) attested to providing Indigenous ministers with training rooted "in the value structure of indigenous northerners."[6] This stood in contrast to the NLM and its Bible college, which heretofore had opposed Indigenous cultural expressions. Another exceptional example is the markedly successful Manitoba and Northwestern Ontario District's (MNWOD) engagement with Indigenous adherents. The MNWOD's initiatives provide a helpful counterpoint to the NLM, demonstrating that decolonization of ministry leadership was feasible provided appropriate steps were taken.

The PAOC recorded twenty Indigenous congregations in the MNWOD by the late 1950s, operating independently and without fiscal support from PAOC offices.[7] By the late 1960s, the MNWOD Native Ministries Department mobilized a team of seventeen Indigenous ministers.[8] Absalom Beardy (Anishinini; Bearskin Lake, Ontario) was one such minister, crucial in promulgating the Pentecostal message throughout northwestern Ontario. Beardy was instrumental in the planting of ten Indigenous congregations among the reserves of the region. Several members of these congregations went on to become ministers themselves.[9] The MNWOD's autonomizing of Indigenous ministries was further assisted by the 1970 district appointment of an assistant director of "Indian Ministries," Ralph Sanderson (Anishinaabe, in this instance the exonym for which is Saulteaux; Pinaymootang First Nation, Manitoba),[10] the first Indigenous person within the PAOC to occupy such a position.[11]

While the above initiatives yielded some early results at the district level, it would still be another fifteen years before the PAOC would establish the National Native Leadership Council (NNLC). Essentially this was a national-level committee of leaders from the PAOC's various Indigenous-focused ministries. At the 1987 NNLC conference, Indigenous Pentecostal leaders communicated their desire for more influence on the NLM's direction.[12] At the same meeting, James Kallappa (Kwih-dich-chuh-aht; Neah Bay, Washington State), brother of Assemblies of God USA (AG USA) minister George Kallappa (Kwih-dich-chuh-aht; Neah Bay, Washington State) and future director of PAOC Native Ministries, presented a workshop: "Hearing from the Native Lay Person."[13] Although the NNLC at first existed as the brainchild of then–DHMBC director Ken Birch, who envisioned that the committee would evolve "into a Branch Conference with native control,"[14] perhaps not coincidentally, the outcome was an NNLC board composed of both Euro-Canadians and Indigenous representatives.[15] During the 1990s, distinctions between national-level PAOC Indigenous ministries and district-level ministries lessened. This trend

Figure 5.1 Map showing the extent of PAOC Home Missions in 1982

positively influenced the NLM, as it reflected practices from the PAOC's better-autonomized ministries (such as that of the MNWOD).

While this chapter draws upon archival sources, it is unique compared to earlier chapters. The documentary record referred to here includes substantial testament from the Indigenous Pentecostal leaders who pressured the PAOC to make good on its promises of NLM autonomy, and thus influenced that eventual outcome. While this chapter still interrogates those sources critically, it also seeks to highlight that aspect of the documentary record that preserves the Indigenous Voice. Furthermore, compared to previous chapters, this one addresses a relatively short timeframe. This fact alone suggests that with the right combination of actions and factors, autonomizing without delay was feasible. Although Kallappa had urged PAOC leaders to listen to Indigenous ministers as early as the late 1980s, the NLM did not seriously act on the "Hearing from the Native Lay

Person" workshop's recommendations until the mid-1990s. All of this raises the question of why the process took so long. The chapter demonstrates that a combination of fiscal, socio-political, ecclesial, and temporal matters finally pressured the PAOC to execute its indigenous principle, and ultimately empower the NLM's Indigenous ministers to lead.

MONETARY MATTERS AND SOCIO-POLITICAL PROCESSES

The 1976 political thriller film *All the President's Men* popularized the phrase "follow the money" for finding hidden answers to glaring questions. The axiom holds true regarding the NLM rapidly autonomizing in the 1990s. The NLM acted on the PAOC's indigenous principle ideal a full fifty years after the mission's founding, and it only happened then, largely because its resources had grown sparse. So long as Euro-Canadian mission leadership and its support base could finance operations, Euro-Canadian missionaries were commonplace, and the status quo remained. Only when funding proved a great challenge did NLM leadership finally hand over a much-reduced mission to its rightful Indigenous heirs.

Notwithstanding repeated pleas to their settler support base, in 1996 the PAOC Western Ontario District (WOD) executive reported that with funding nearly exhausted, the NLMBC was officially defunct, with plans to sell its Sioux Lookout building and the NLM's aircraft.[16] The proposition of the sale of all holdings in Sioux Lookout seems somewhat hasty and short-sighted considering that Indigenous elders had approvingly supported the NLM's relocation to Sioux Lookout, in contrast to the earlier relocation to Pickle Lake, which did not have Indigenous support.[17] Speaking for the WOD executive, Ozard cited the prevalence of commercial airlines, plus the overwhelming operating and maintenance expenses of the aircraft highlighted in chapter 2. Ozard implied that the need to sell assets provided a timely opportunity to transition.

The WOD directed proceeds from asset sales to what became Aboriginal Pentecostal Ministries (APM, rebranded from NLM). However, encountering financial constraints, the WOD sold assets hastily, accepting sales prices accordingly.[18] Yet without significant assets and infrastructure – such as a mission centre, Bible college, and aircraft – and with liquid capital insufficient to repurchase said assets,

NLM shortfalls left the nascent APM at a considerable disadvantage. This reality proved reminiscent of Rodger Cree's (Kanien'kehá:ka; Kanesatake, Quebec) observations throughout his ministry of similar trends: "The missionary takes all the resources with him/her upon his/her departure ... Thus, the Indian pastor is left with very little material resources to begin his ministry."[19] Put another way, although the WOD had intended the APM to become autonomous, the district's decision to offload assets and dissolve the NLM meant the emerging APM had little infrastructure by which to exercise and enjoy that autonomy.[20] Monetary matters partially contributed to the PAOC's accelerated autonomizing, but ecclesial and theological developments do not occur in a vacuum. External socio-political pressures also factored into the PAOC leadership's decision. Ozard was thus aware of the ongoing national developments: "From Oka to Davis Inlet, the plight of our aboriginal people has been paraded before us ... The Native leaders clamor for 'self-government or self-sufficiency.'"[21]

Socio-political developments and events such as the ill-fated Meech Lake Accord and the Oka Crisis (both occurring during the spring and summer of 1990) helped to shift national public attention toward realities affecting Indigenous people (including the matter that Ozard referred to as self-government). The phrase "self-government" has since fallen out of use except when referring to the policy of the Department of Indian Affairs and Northern Development (at the time of writing the Department of Crown-Indigenous Relations and Northern Affairs). Given the ambiguous character of the term "self-government," "self-determination" has become the more appropriate and preferred term and is used in the United Nations Declaration on the Rights of Indigenous People (UNDRIP).[22] In national developments, self-determination in part means constitutionally recognized Indigenous sovereignty. Likewise, Canadian Evangelicals (both Indigenous and non-Indigenous) responded to Indigenous people's desire for self-determination and wished to see Indigenous ministry leaders gain more influence in church matters.[23]

The Meech Lake Accord was Progressive Conservative Prime Minister Brian Mulroney's attempt at constitutional reform. Partly motivated by the perceived under-representation and under-prioritization of Quebec in Canada's previous constitutional amendments of 1982, the Accord proposed to re-evaluate provinces' constitutional rights, aiming at recognition of English Canada and French Canada as the country's two distinct founding nations. Indigenous people largely opposed Meech

Lake for three related reasons: disagreement with the mythology of Canada as a country of two founding European peoples, the extension of "special status" to the province of Quebec when the same had been denied to Indigenous people, and the absence of acknowledgment of Indigenous title.[24]

Ultimately the Meech Lake Accord legislatively failed because the provinces of Manitoba and Newfoundland and Labrador rejected it. Elijah Harper (Anishinini chief; Red Sucker Lake, Manitoba), then New Democratic Party Member of the Manitoba Legislative Assembly, and the first "Treaty Indian" to be elected to his province's legislature, was instrumental in Manitoba's opposition. While the Manitoba Legislative Assembly was in session, Harper famously stood holding an eagle feather and simply said "no" on the grounds that legislative procedural rules had not been followed,[25] marking a turning point for Indigenous affairs in Canada. Canadian constitutional lawyer Ian Peach noted: "For many Canadians, the first time they ever understood some of the struggles of the First Nations peoples in Canada was when Elijah Harper said 'no' to the Meech Lake Accord." Harper's opposition ultimately resulted in the Accord's failure to come to a vote in the federal House of Commons prior to the 23 June 1990 deadline.[26]

The Oka Crisis, running from March to September 1990, was a standoff between the Kanien'kehá:ka of the Kanesatake First Nation (near Oka, Quebec), the Sûreté du Québec provincial police force, and eventually the Royal Canadian Mounted Police (RCMP) and the Canadian Armed Forces. The Town of Oka desired to build a golf course on land for which the Kanesatake Kanien'kehá:ka maintained a two-centuries-old claim of Indigenous title.[27] Asserting their rights, the Kanesatake Kanien'kehá:ka blockaded roads to the site. Law enforcement exchanged gunfire with the Kanesatake Kanien'kehá:ka blockade, and a Sûreté du Québec officer, Corporal Marcel Lemay, was killed. It was not clear who fired the fatal shot, many believing it was friendly fire. Kanien'kehá:ka elder Joe Armstrong also died, suffering a fatal heart attack attempting escape from an angry mob. The Sûreté du Québec, RCMP, and eventually the Canadian Armed Forces used aircraft, tanks, and armoured personnel carriers to restrict the movement of food and medical supplies across the blockade, drawing the ire of Canada's Human Rights Commission and the United Nations.[28] On 26 September 1990, the Kanesatake Kanien'kehá:ka blockade finally surrendered to the Armed Forces. Thirty-nine Kanien'kehá:ka were tried and two were convicted. Yet all was not lost. The Kanien'kehá:ka response became a rallying cry for Indigenous people.

Peach outlined the implications of Indigenous resistance to Oka and Meech Lake:

> The standoff at Kanesatake can be viewed as a logical outcome of the failure to reach agreement on the Meech Lake Accord; the empowerment that Indigenous peoples felt at the rejection of the Accord and that one Indigenous legislator did what several premiers could not do[:] emboldened Indigenous peoples and strengthened their resolve to demand that their constitutional concerns and aspirations be addressed ... [It] enormously increased the visibility of Indigenous issues in Canada ... The unusual display of militancy by Indigenous peoples ... drove home ... that Indigenous peoples were serious about, and impatient with, the normal political processes, and were determined to resist colonialism.[29]

Further, while the standoff at Oka predominantly involved Kanien'kehá:ka, the event became a watershed moment, galvanizing Indigenous activists across North America.[30] A dramatized re-imagining of Oka by Drew Hayden Taylor (Ojibwe Anishinaabe; Curve Lake First Nation, Ontario) interpreted the crisis thus:

> I was captivated by this standoff, proud of my Aboriginal brothers taking a stand ... [I]n the midst of socio-political upheaval, some emotions remain simple and highly recognizable, regardless of race or cultural background ... First Nations people from all over the country have pledged support for the actions of the Kanesatake Mohawks ... Native communities across the nation have vowed to send community members and supplies to aid the besieged Mohawk village ... [W]hen a single digit was threatened, all the fingers came together as a fist. Men and women from all over the country, from a dozen different Nations, and dozens more from the States, were flooding into Quebec to aid the Mohawks.[31]

Prominent Indigenous Pentecostals also became involved in the conversations and activities surrounding Meech Lake and Oka. Not only were these leaders influential, but they additionally solicited public sympathy and support. Ross Maracle (Kanien'kehá:ka; Tyendinaga Mohawk Territory, Ontario) served as a negotiator during the Oka Crisis. Maracle eloquently expressed the Kanesatake Kanien'kehá:ka's distress, decrying the governments' "colonial practices," and moved between lines occupied both by the Kanesatake Kanien'kehá:ka blockade and by law enforcement.[32] Also engaged was Matthew Coon Come (Eeyou; Mistissini, Quebec), a well-known PAOC adherent. Ian Peach recalled Coon Come's observations surrounding the lasting impact of the period's events:

> As Matthew Coon Come commented ... Canadians and their governments began to behave as though they genuinely wanted and intended to make space for Indigenous peoples to share the country; it quickly became clear ... that the nation's business could occur without difficulty when Indigenous peoples were fully involved and honourably treated.[33]

In addition, later in his career Elijah Harper forged ties with the PAOC, and found a sympathetic audience among its Indigenous ministers.[34]

The Meech Lake Accord's failure is directly attributable to Indigenous leaders' resistance to Euro-Canadian governance models. It thus offers a contemporaneous and societal parallel to PAOC developments. It is likely that the popular shift in sentiment toward realities affecting Indigenous people influenced similar trends within the PAOC. There can be no doubt that Meech Lake was on the denomination's radar. Pierre Bergeron, the Quebec-based assistant superintendent for the PAOC Eastern Ontario and Quebec District (EOQD), advocated resistance to "the Meech Lake discussions [for the purpose of] ... creating a sense of unity." Bergeron continued:

> Becoming a Christian does not eliminate our particular ethnic identity. However, as Christians we now belong to each other in such a way that distinctions that formerly divided us should lose their significance. This principle must be extended to deny ... all racial barriers. In Christ there must be neither black nor white ... nor Native or any other distinction.[35]

Likewise these episodes influenced denominational dialogue, elevating the sense of urgency toward autonomizing the Northland Mission. NLM minister Ernie Linklater (Môsonîw Ililiw; Moosonee, Ontario), communicated his observation of Indigenous cultural resistance to perceived Christian "colonialism" to then–WOD superintendent William Morrow:

> I am writing to express my concern that the transference of leadership into native hands must be carried out to the full extent originally envisioned … [T]he political climate in native communities impacts upon every aspect of life … In recent years there has been a strong push by many of the native politicians to … view Native Ministries under the control of 'non-native' leadership as another process of "colonialism". As aboriginal Christians we are best suited to reach our people for Christ because of our ties to our communities historically and culturally. We are not … "outsiders" because we are part of the community … I am … convinced that now is the time for this transference of leadership into native hands.[36]

The combined effect of Indigenous people's roles in Meech Lake's demise, coupled with the Oka Crisis, cumulatively placed "Indigenous claims squarely in the eye of the Canadian public [and] directly onto Canada's constitutional agenda."[37] As settler Canadians' awareness of realities endured by Indigenous communities grew, so did popular sentiment in support of Indigenous claims. Indeed, it seems Indigenous people's increasingly apparent desire for socio-political autonomy so affected sentiment within the PAOC that denominational leadership could not ignore it. Observations by ministry executives, such as EOQD Assistant Superintendent Bergeron, Department of Home Missions (DHMBC) director Gordon Upton and WOD executive member Jack Ozard, led to better awareness of these legitimate concerns, influencing subsequent PAOC decisions. This contributed toward the dissolution of the NLM and the birth of the autonomized APM in ways that mirrored developments in Indigenous people's civic self-determination.

DENOMINATIONAL DEVELOPMENTS

While the external political climate began to warm up the PAOC's inner chambers, it is likely that contemporaneous changes within other denominations also influenced Pentecostals to think differently. During a time of increasing corporate and governmental pressure for the economic and commercial exploitation of Indigenous communities and their lands, the longer-established churches (which historically had upheld government policy, typically enacted without Indigenous communities' agreement) began to question the price of their complicity. For example, the Anglicans supported Pentecostal Billy Diamond's (Eeyou; Waskaganish, Quebec, and at that time chief of the Waskaganish band of Eeyouch) coordination of the 1974 task force, opposing Hydro-Quebec's plan to flood the territory through the James Bay Hydro development. The Quebec government had initiated the project in the absence of consultation with the First Nations and Inuit whom it would affect. Diamond stated of the event, "The ... Church ... was never intended to be ... passive ... [or] to accept the status quo. The New Testament Church that turned the world upside down ... was supposed to be a militant church." Ultimately the Eeyouch reached an agreement with the Province of Quebec, of which Diamond stated: "It has been a tough fight, and our people are still very much opposed to the project, but they realize that they must share their resources." During the 1970s the Anglican Church furthermore developed special programs in Northern Canada intended to train Indigenous leaders to become clergy. The "Train an Indian Priest" program and the Arthur Turner Training School in Pangnirtung, Northwest Territories, formed the backbone of these initiatives. The latter by 1986 boasted fifteen graduates, thirteen of them working within the diocese. Then in 1988, the first Anglican National Native Convocation took place, following which Indigenous Anglicans increasingly asserted their right to contribute input. A nearly universal wave of support followed, and in 1989 the Diocese of Saskatchewan elected the first Indigenous Anglican bishop, Charles Arthurson (Néhinaw; Norway House Cree Nation, Manitoba). More Indigenous bishops were elected in 1993 and 1996.[38]

Likewise the United Church increasingly recognized it was imperative to autonomize its ministries to Indigenous people. As early as the mid-twentieth century, the United Church gave matters affecting Indigenous people more attention. The United Church examined its own Indigenous polices, held Indigenous Work conferences, and released the "Commission to Study the Indian Work," highlighting that churches should withdraw from the operation of the residential schools.[39] In 1973 the church proposed the development of the "Indian Ministry Training Program," which sought to graduate Indigenous ministers fluent in English and Indigenous languages. The United

Church subsequently developed a non-residential Indigenous ministers training model in 1984. The latter program allowed Indigenous trainees to minister in Indigenous communities while concurrently participating in instructional sessions at the Dr Jessie Saulteaux Resource Centre in Fort Qu'Appelle, Saskatchewan.[40] Finally, the United Church made progress toward the integration of Indigenous leadership at the national level by first naming Stan McKay (Néhinaw; Fisher River Cree Nation, Manitoba) Coordinator of Native Concerns in 1982, and then electing him to the position of Church Moderator in 1992.[41] Thus long-awaited and necessary changes were beginning to be made at the political level as well as across denominations. The time had come for the PAOC to do the same.

The 1989 NLM Leadership Conference in Sachigo Lake, Ontario, emphasized the "long term goal" to install more Indigenous leaders.[42] By then passing its forty-five-year mark, the NLM's long-term goals, one might have hoped, would already have been near to accomplishment. Late though it was, the timing of this renewed commitment to autonomize coincided with Indigenous nationalist sentiment broadly, and with the popular move toward political self-determination.[43] Upton supported self-determination primarily because he believed it could enhance evangelistic goals, serving as an effective vehicle for the indigenous principle.[44] In a later *Testimony* article, he asserted that Canada had been "torn apart by strife and discord between native peoples and the rest of Canada. But through Jesus Christ true peace and accord [could be] found."[45] Citing the Oka Crisis, Upton blamed "industrialized society" and "impersonal government" for Indigenous people's plight. Particularly critical of the use of armed force in Oka, he also lamented the shortage of Christian ministry and support as a means of resolution.[46]

As discussion of autonomizing continued, PAOC leadership broadly accepted self-determination, provided freedom of religion was guaranteed.[47] The PAOC's path toward the APM's autonomy affected local churches in ways that mirrored public appeals for self-determination. NLM leadership maintained that the "call for 'self-government' from the secular Native sources across Canada [found] its counterpart in many sectors of the Native Church," and believed it was "time to respond to this call."[48] Simply put, the increasing prevalence in the 1990s of popular sentiment within the PAOC supportive of Indigenous rights, particularly among Indigenous ministers, meant the denomination could no longer procrastinate in dissolving the NLM.

Finally, by this time PAOC leaders recognized the shortcomings of their previous claims of making good on the indigenous principle. In a 1990 letter to Billy Diamond, Upton admitted that only half of the over one hundred Indigenous PAOC congregations had Indigenous pastors. Conceding this PAOC shortcoming, Upton sought solutions.[49] Anishinini NLM minister Wally McKay believed such deficiencies occurred in local churches where denominational structures denied sufficient autonomy. McKay proposed allowing Indigenous ministers to create a new NLM "constitution the way they want[ed] it to be, ensuring that the essentials [would be] included."[50] In response, the NLM's leadership permitted member congregations to draft their own local church constitutions in Indigenous languages.[51]

Simultaneously, a notable group of Indigenous ministers began to emerge from within the PAOC. Not only were they successful pastors, they had become significant figures within the Indigenous Pentecostal community. These included John Saakanee, Dan Doolittle, Eli Mickenack, Gilbert Thunder, Myles Sturgeon, Samson Beardy, Ziggy Beardy, John Mekenak, Stephen Winnet, Rudy Turtle, and Chief Billy Diamond.[52] While the PAOC's Euro-Canadian leadership was late to involve Indigenous ministers in decision-making matters, clearly a well-prepared cadre was positioned to lead.

An additional group of Indigenous PAOC pastors from across the country organized in 1991 by forming an Indigenous executive. They aimed specifically to: 1) unite formally all PAOC Indigenous ministers; 2) organize leadership councils; 3) address issues affecting Indigenous people at a national level; and 4) bring Indigenous people's needs to the country's attention. This executive sought to mirror the format of a traditional Indigenous council of elders and to engage with the leaders of Indigenous communities. Again, this surge of denominational, Indigenous-driven leadership largely mirrored developments within the national Indigenous movement. Although financial woes impeded the accomplishment of their goals, this was a significant step toward actual indigenization.[53]

Another precipitous event occurred in late 1992, when at the request of several Indigenous ministers, the Western Ontario District demarcated the mission into two subgroups. One subgroup comprised James Bay Ministries in the east (made up of five primarily Néhinawak and Môsoniyi Iliwak churches along the James Bay coast). The second comprised the remaining churches (primarily Ojibweg Anishinaabeg and Anishininiwag congregations throughout northwestern Ontario), and retained the Northland Mission moniker. Originally the WOD executive appointed Robert Linklater (Môsonîw Ililiw; Moosonee, Ontario) as James Bay Ministries director, to work in cooperation with Ian Winter. Shortly thereafter, Linklater left to complete his education at Central Pentecostal Bible College in Saskatoon, Saskatchewan. In late 1993, the executive appointed Linklater's brother, Ernie Linklater (Môsonîw Ililiw; Moosonee, Ontario), as his replacement. The executive reiterated their intention that "in due time an aboriginal director will be appointed for the Western side of the region."[54]

Even with such changes, only in the mid-1990s did the PAOC address the disproportionate number of Euro-Canadian missionaries in positions that otherwise would have gone to Indigenous ministers had the indigenous principle been fully implemented. Finally in 1994, the WOD executive offered the following *nostra culpa* and apology:

> Although indigenization has been the stated goal of the Northland Mission, we recognize that this objective has not been achieved … It is with profound regret that we acknowledge that ethnocentric and paternalistic attitudes of the past have contributed somewhat to dependency training amongst Native peoples. We have, thus, failed to facilitate the indigenization of the maintenance and propagation of their own native Church institutions, and for this we must extend them our humblest apologies.[55]

While a confession of responsibility was necessary and positive, as an apology it was feeble. Even as they admitted errors, the PAOC leaders blamed NLM shortcomings on Indigenous people's "dependency" rather than admitting Euro-Canadian leaders' unpreparedness to stand back as promised.

Ozard's proposed solution was "a Committee of Native Leaders, with whom we can meet, share our heart, present our plan, and ask for their response and let them return with a counter plan … [working] to fine tune the plan and draw up a timetable for transfer of leadership." This new body, named the Native Leadership Committee, was similar to the existing Northern Board described in the previous chapter, but with the express goal of dissolving the NLM so as to bring about the autonomous APM.[56] This committee's work forever altered the trajectory of the ministry.

As meetings started, Ozard reported in the October 1994 *Northland Ministries Newsletter*:

> A momentous meeting was held with a special group of key native leaders in Sioux Lookout … This group was co-ordinated by respected Native leader Wally McKay and was made up of representatives of the Native Community, north and south: Dan Doolittle (Six Nations, Ohsweken), Ernie Linklater (Moosonee), George Gunner (Moose Factory), Pharaoh Thomas (Fort Severn), John Beardy, Ivan Iserhoff (Thunder Bay), Bart Meekus (Sandy Lake), [and] Alex Gunner (LacSeul [*sic*]). NLM Director Ian Winter, and NBC Principal Kervan Chalmers joined our District Superintendent and myself, to interact with these fine Native brethren. I must say a very productive dialogue ensued which resulted in some far-reaching recommendations being made.[57]

The Native Leadership Committee repeatedly expressed its desire to "have a say in appointing pastors and leaders." This was crucial considering the prevalence of Euro-Canadian ministers receiving appointments while Indigenous ministers went without positions.[58] Finally, this newly founded committee hastened to promulgate all of its outcomes to the NLM churches.[59]

THE WAY FORWARD

Western Ontario District Superintendent William Morrow and Jack Ozard jointly consulted the committee's coordinator, Wally McKay, seeking his direct input into transferring the NLM to Indigenous leadership. McKay's recommendations included installing Indigenous ministers in place of Euro-Canadian missionaries and addressing the discrepancy in wages between the Euro-Canadian missionaries paid by the NLM and the many Indigenous ministers who fundraised. Even so, McKay proposed PAOC support for Indigenous ministers only as a stopgap measure, suggesting that "native churches need to be taught to care for their own financial needs and future."[60]

Ministerial credentialling indeed was one of the primary motivations contributing to the proposed restructuring of the NLM. On this point, McKay stated: "We need to recommend a plan to make our northern ministries a native run organization ... Credentials need to be easier ... Native leaders need to be given more say in credential matters."[61] He later observed:

> Our people feel helpless without proper information about what is really going on. For instance, many of our people do not have a formal education yet they have 20 years of successful Pastoral experience, and a call from God. We must be looking at our Native ministries and determine who are called, then give out credentials and ordination based upon our own Native need and criteria. Self determination means we will make the decisions then learn to live with them. We need a criteria that will work right now, but will also change as time passes, and situations change.[62]

McKay was evidently frustrated with the PAOC's convoluted educational and credentialling requirements. He and others wanted a self-determining ministry to allow Indigenous Pentecostals to influence such matters. For instance, George Gunner seconded McKay's perspective while at the same time confirming the PAOC's challenges associated with professionally qualifying ministers who had not achieved the prerequisite educational requirements:

> There were pastors under us, a lot of them didn't even have a grade two education. Bible School for them was something that would be totally strange. And yet they knew the Bible. God would show them things, and they would teach. They were excellent pastors, but we couldn't credential them.[63]

Other Indigenous ministers pointed to "the need for more concentration on Native social issues and on Native ways of doing things in the training of a Native clergy."[64] The Native Leadership Committee responded by arranging for Indigenous leaders to form a credentialling board to examine Indigenous ministers' applications, facilitating a more straightforward track to ordination.[65] As chapter 3 noted, the PAOC's problematic credentialling of Indigenous ministers was not rectified until the late 1990s. Yet by then the APM no longer operated a ministry training college.

McKay and others believed denominational bureaucracy was counterproductive to disseminating the Pentecostal message. Established district boundaries and the PAOC's penchant for Euro-Canadian leadership formed recurring grievances for the NLM's Indigenous stockholders. Levi Beardy (Anishinini; Bearskin Lake, Ontario, and member of the NLM Northern Board) warned of the following preconceived notion: "Native people must comply with a white constitution, with no voice towards the administration and the 'whiteness' of the structure. If we can begin to show Native people that things are changing, they will come back."[66] McKay sided with Beardy and proposed a new model for Indigenous ministry within the PAOC.[67] He also observed that PAOC district boundaries divided and split Indigenous families without consideration of traditional territorial boundaries, which also affected ministry. Ernie Linklater cited similar difficulties. Certain Eeyouch and Môsoniyi Ililiwak churches were culturally linked to the NLM, yet they were ineligible to benefit from its ministry resources because they were located geographically within the EOQD. Desiring more cohesive ministry connections between these churches, some opted to "go with this new group headed up by Ross Maracle."[68] Linklater concluded: "They need someone to take an interest in their situation however it seems as if no one is willing to help them. District boundaries prevent me from intervening on their behalf."[69]

The WOD executive was, at the very least, sympathetic. One outcome of the consultation with McKay were "negotiations" between the NLM's Native Leadership Committee and the WOD executive. They discussed, according to Ozard, "the transfer of leadership responsibilities into the hands of ... Native leaders."[70] Ozard's interest in the prospect of autonomy appeared genuine. He acknowledged that the NLM had operated "from a missions perspective." Reviewing the NLM's track record as a Euro-Canadian-dominant, aviation-dependent mission, he noted attempts to develop and train a "self-sustaining, self-propagating, indigenous Native Pentecostal Church." Believing evangelism by Indigenous ministers to be more desirable, he hoped for "competent thinking committed Native leaders." To these the NLM would "transfer the reins of leadership."[71]

McKay provided this critical perspective in counterpoint to Ozard's conclusions:

> The P.A.O.C. came more than 40 years ago, with an airplane and missionaries. Here we are 40 years later and things are pretty well the same. The P.A.O.C. continues to send missionaries, and they still use their airplane, but overall there has been very

> little growth. Today, our people and the Churches throughout the north are still standing at the shoreline, looking at the ministry taking place.[72]

McKay offered a multidimensional solution to the perceived problem. While acknowledging the shortcomings of the NLM's historical methods, he shifted the weight of responsibility back to Indigenous Pentecostals, urging them to be accountable for their own ministry's future. He intimated that even as Indigenous ministers were poised for mission takeover, for whatever reason they were "standing at the shoreline," waiting for and watching what might transpire. His critical assessment lent some credibility to the WOD executive's claims of "dependency."[73] When questioned about the leadership transfer of the NLM, McKay replied, "It will be difficult for the community people to accept what is taking place today. Everything has been done for them for years. They will be reluctant and will fear failure for we will be taking this dependency away from them."[74]

Responding to tensions, the Native Leadership Committee wrestled with the significance of Indigenous identity and culture in what would become the autonomous APM. McKay suggested the strong position of moving "all white and non-Indian people out." He continued: "We have the need and capacity to take over this ministry, but does that mean it must now become totally Indian?" Linklater replied that the current arrangement was "unfair to Indian people for all money [went] to Ian Winter," adding that "we are part of the ministry … [yet a]ll the dollars go [to Sioux Lookout,] and it is unfair."[75] Interestingly, at this point Dan Doolittle countered: "In setting up this Native board we are out of line with the P.A.O.C. constitution for we are not ordained, and the constitution says we must be ordained to sit on a board of directors."[76] Indeed, even in establishing the board and seeking autonomy, the PAOC's established structures and ministerial norms contributed to internal differences in that struggle.

James MacDonald, pastor of the Fort Albany NLM church, affirmed the Indigenous ministers' preparedness to lead the APM, stating: "I believe there is a Pastor on every reserve who can rise up and do the work of God … Colour doesn't matter. But, God is raising up Native leadership as well. We have people here today that can fill these places of leadership."[77] Indigenous ministers were willing to lead, but hesitated because of PAOC-instituted bureaucratic obstacles. Unable to satisfy PAOC ministerial credentialling prerequisites, the committee was forced to maintain the status quo, even to the point of retaining and involving Euro-Canadian denominational executives on the board throughout the dissolution process in order to meet the PAOC's constitutional requirements.[78]

In a 1995 meeting of the Native Leadership Committee, McKay compared the PAOC's Indigenous ministries' attempts at autonomy to the reluctance exhibited by the PAOC leadership's old guard. The following quotation is given at length as it illustrates several previously undocumented dynamics:

> I could use the example of the dismantling of Indian affairs and what the chiefs are going through. The old colonial system of Indian affairs is something we never wanted, never liked. It was something we fought against every chance we would get. Yet when it was dismantled many of the people still held onto the past, still complained about it instead of letting it go. It reminds me of the Children of Israel when they came out of Egypt. Every time they had a need they referred back to their days in Egypt instead of concentrating on the future. This is a similar situation we find ourselves in today. The past is not going to change and people must find the courage to move forward. There are brighter things out there for them.
>
> The whole thing about moving towards autonomous mission work with the people in the north is the fact that we do have Aboriginal pastors out there, but they are content to let other people do it for them ... It is me they want to do these things for them. If this is the attitude I don't see how this is going to work. When I look at it I can easily become very frustrated over the whole thing. Not so much at Bill[Morrow]'s heart, and Jack[Ozard]'s heart in wanting to turn this whole thing over to us. But I'm disappointed in our part of this. That's the part I'm really getting frustrated with. We have to be willing to move together in a certain direction.[79]

McKay's quotation speaks to a number of issues. First, he critiqued what he perceived to be some Indigenous ministers' attitudes toward adopting responsibility for the mission. Throughout this monograph, responsibility for mismanaging the NLM has been primarily assigned to the Euro-Canadian leadership. Yet Indigenous Pentecostals, apparently not a cohesive bloc (as evidenced by their expressed differences of opinion), also contributed to the NLM's fate. McKay expressed frustration with the lack of cooperation among Indigenous Pentecostals, indicating that would-be Indigenous leaders themselves were reluctant to take on responsibility for the NLM's future leadership, thus slowing down the indigenization process.

For example, John Wong offered this perspective on what he had observed:

> Many people in Sachigo Lake are quite concerned about the process taking place and they feel we should be going slowly – over a period of 5 to 10 years. It is felt that if Native Pastors are going to take over these responsibilities, they need better training. Perhaps they should go south for a period of time and work within one of our southern Churches to learn from the Pastors who are involved there.[80]

As a newcomer Canadian minister, Wong's view offers a unique, valuable, and rare perspective. Perhaps Wong was voicing concerns about his own position in ministry, for Morrow reassured him, "we want you to know we will continue our involvement with you."[81] However, if Wong's concerns about ministerial accreditation accurately represented his congregation, then his comments add weight to McKay's argument that even Indigenous Pentecostals did not speak as a singular unit. As even some Indigenous laity were hesitant about autonomy, they may be considered in some small way party to the slowing of the dissolution process. There was a chorus of conflicting voices within the autonomizing contingent – and likely internal resistance that persisted even when autonomy finally was realized.

Although McKay critiqued Indigenous attitudes, he still felt the PAOC's Euro-Canadian leadership was largely responsible for the NLM's shortcomings. Further, he drew attention to the discrepancy between the funding of Euro-Canadian leaders and Indigenous ministers:

> Your Churches are looking after your travel expenses to come to these meetings. All the expenses of the Western Ontario Officers [are] covered by the District. There has to be some balance brought into this. We need to transfer some of the resources so we can cover the cost of the reorganization as it takes place. I've been looking after my own expenses … I don't complain about this, but this is indicative of the way it has

> always been. Whenever our people want to do something, the District has the resources to cover their own expenses but the Indian people have to muster up whatever they can to do it. We've been struggling to get this thing going but it isn't going to happen unless we settle some clear direction as to how it is to happen. In order to accomplish reorganization we must identify money which is going to be used for that.[82]

In response to the question of Indigenous ministries billing the WOD for expenses, Morrow answered that while the PAOC did not reimburse all expenses, it did offer some support to their ministry not available to the PAOC's ethnic minority ministry departments (with which the PAOC anachronistically linked ministries tailored to Indigenous people). Pointing to what he perceived as the NLM's preferential treatment (because it was permitted to keep its congregations' tithes), Morrow replied:

> We do not allow the Spanish to do that. There are more Spanish Churches than there are Native Churches. We don't allow the Romanian Churches to do that. There are over twenty language dialects within our fellowship. We don't allow any of them to do that. The only people we allow to do that is Native Ministry ... Now in terms of finances, all the other churches tithe to us ... we use those funds in any way we feel we should ... [G]et your Churches to tithe and use the funds in any way you feel ... You can continue to do so, and we will continue to work with you to raise new dollars for Northland Ministries ... Eventually our goal would be that you would become self supporting so these funds could go to some other ministry.[83]

It had become obvious by this time that the NLM's assets, capital, and fundraising were not in the best shape. This was partially because some NLM churches did not contribute funds to mission headquarters. Morrow was correct to highlight the amount the NLM had received from the WOD. The Indigenous Board's grievance, however, was the WOD's distribution of the NLM's diminishing resources in the mid-1990s, most of which were spent by Euro-Canadian missionaries and not Indigenous ministers.

Linklater countered, "so little comes down our way. Only $400.00."[84] Speaking for all five James Bay Ministries churches,

Linklater implied that the WOD had directed the NLM's budget, which during the early 1990s averaged between $100,000 and $200,000 annually, to areas other than local churches and their Indigenous ministers.[85] Later Gunner also objected to this perceived imbalance: "It is better to spend the dollars on the pastors rather than administrative salaries. We need to begin to treat all pastors equally, then we will begin to see things happen." Gunner felt that Indigenous ministers were kept in the dark about NLM finances, not knowing what amount of funding was available for various projects. He compared Indigenous ministers' request for PAOC funds to that of a child asking his or her parents for an allowance.[86] Backing the Euro-Canadian administrators rather than Indigenous ministers and churches undermined the purported goal of autonomizing, once again demonstrating the PAOC's mistrust of Indigenous ministers' resource management. Further, the alleged preferential treatment of Indigenous churches (compared to the PAOC's cultural, ethnic, and linguistic minority churches) is noteworthy. In its management of the NLM's finances, the WOD executive demonstrated colonial and paternalistic actions and attitudes. If the PAOC had embraced the indigenous principle, NLM funds would have instead been spent equipping and empowering Indigenous leadership, thereby allowing Indigenous ministers to manage resources as they saw fit.

Morrow challenged the board, reminding them of what he perceived to be their agency in the distribution of funds:

> As soon as this board decides how the money will be spent, as soon as you decide on a process to elect a chairman … [to] serve as the liaison person to the district, who will work with the district, it can change if the board wants it to … [T]he whole process here … is not us … slowing this down. It needs to be done right. If you will do it right we will work with you and give you authority so that this board can make the decisions as to how the money will be spent. I can't go back and undo the past. I can only tell you we are waiting for you to make this work.[87]

To their credit, Morrow and the PAOC expressed only interest in and support for forming the APM from the NLM. Morrow stated: "This process is something we've wanted for a long time, and we are very open to this. We are delighted." He added, "the only thing we ask is, that you stay connected with us."[88] By this request, Morrow did not so much express a desire to control, as a request that the soon-to-be-established APM remain associated with the PAOC, potentially concerned that the APM might join Ross Maracle or another rival denomination. McKay responded to Morrow's gesture of good faith with reassuring words: "There still needs to be accountability. Whatever government structure we arrange has to have freedom to lead and make decisions, but the native pastors will need to be in relationship with the P.A.O.C."[89]

At last the wheels were turning, the handover of leadership appearing to be on the horizon. Ozard referred to Indigenous ministry hopefuls in a 1996 newsletter, pleading with readers, "much trust and patience is needed; many challenges face this group."[90] For their part, Indigenous leaders also felt the burden to assume the mission's leadership. As McKay put it:

> Now, the time has come to pull up our tent pegs and move on to becoming a mission organization of our own ... We are part of a larger group, the P.A.O.C., still it is time for the Lord to guide us as Native people. If we make mistakes along the way ... God will forgive us. We will learn and go on from there.[91]

The February 1996 newsletter – the first to display the title "Aboriginal Pentecostal Ministries," wherein the APM identified itself as the rebranded NLM – stated: "This name reflects the vision and scope of this ministry to Ontario's aboriginal peoples, whether they be in the far north or south." Restructuring meant that in addition to reuniting all NLM and James Bay Ministries churches, the APM extended its work to all PAOC ministries in the WOD tailored to Indigenous people, not only those in the north. Historically the NLM had ministered among Nehiyawak, Ojibweg Anishinaabeg, and Anishininiwag in northern Ontario, but Pentecostalism had concurrently (and in some cases precedingly) spread among Kanien'kehá:ka in southern Canada. The APM integrated WOD ministries as far south as the Hamilton-Wentworth Region, Brant County, Haldimand County, and the Six Nations of the Grand River. Former NLMBC Principal Kervan Chalmers noted that "the board is seeking to tie Native work together across the broad expanse of our district ... working at fostering closer ties with our southern ... churches."[92] The APM opted to include both urban missions and those in northern territories.[93] Subsequent newsletters spelled out the APM's mission statement:

> Our purpose is to evangelize, disciple and equip Aboriginal people for Christian ministry, to minister to the spiritual and practical needs of the aboriginal peoples, to provide a forum for fellowship in the Body of Christ, and to model the Kingdom of God in the Church and in the world in the power of the Holy Spirit.[94]

When the NLM became the APM in 1996, its new constitution delineated an Indigenous governance model. Membership on the APM Board of Elders required that inductees "be of significant native descent."[95] Ongoing Euro-Canadian involvement within the APM would be the exception, existing only as a stopgap measure, in stark contrast to earlier Euro-Canadian dominance of the NLM and the predominance of Euro-Canadians during the transition. The constitution applied this standard to general ministerial membership in the APM as well.[96]

Ozard and Morrow remained on the newly minted board while the APM worked to establish a board composed exclusively of Indigenous members. The WOD executive also required former NLMBC principal Chalmers to remain as secretary-treasurer for a maximum of one year to complete his NLM tenure. While Winter also remained, the new board sought an Indigenous representative to replace him.[97] Anticipating this move, Winter shared administrative responsibilities with Linklater, informing a group of supporters that the PAOC would be replacing him with an Indigenous director.[98]

By late 1996, both Winter and Chalmers had resigned. Quickly the APM's executive named Ernie Linklater as director and George Gunner as associate director. Offices relocated to Timmins, bringing the ministry full circle, as under Spillenaar the NLM was first headquartered in the adjacent community of South Porcupine. The newly branded APM was responsible for fundraising for staff compensation.[99] Why McKay, in so many ways the spiritual father of the NLM/APM's autonomizing course correction, did not assume the role of director is unclear. It is possible that while willing to serve as chair of the transitional board, he declined the directorship, or was not selected. As Linklater himself was a graduate of the NLMBC and had successfully pastored NLM churches, he certainly was well suited. At the time of writing, Winter is retired, and Ozard and Chalmers have died.[100]

Also in 1996, the PAOC's General Executive named James Kallappa its first nationwide Indigenous director of Aboriginal Ministries.[101] He had pastored the Vancouver Native Pentecostal Church and served as principal of the Canadian Native Bible College before directing Native Ministries for the British Columbia and Yukon District.[102] Kallappa worked for stronger unity between Indigenous ministries across the PAOC's districts. Naming Linklater and Gunner as the APM's first Indigenous executives and Kallappa to the national Aboriginal Ministries bolstered the cause of Indigenous ministry leadership within the PAOC.

A final "Annual Northland Ministries Workers Conference" took place during the summer of 1996 with Canadian Evangelical broadcasting mogul David Mainse as keynote speaker.[103] The WOD executive officially renamed the NLM and unveiled the Aboriginal Pentecostal Ministries, at last handing over the organization to Indigenous leadership. The symbolic act came fifty-three years after Spillenaar's endorsement as the first missionary to "the North country."[104]

It is unfair and incorrect to criticize Euro-Canadian PAOC leadership as solely responsible for the APM's delayed realization of autonomy. Predictably, even with leadership changes, many of the former challenges persisted. Indigenous leaders still had to jostle for their place at the table. Even with an Indigenous director, the APM was perceived as an outlier to the Indigenous communities in north-central Canada, where some Indigenous Pentecostals were "accused of being colonized" by their detractors.[105] In order for the APM to earn credibility in those circles, the ministry needed to be perceived as a conduit for Indigenous autonomy. Anything short of this would be regarded as failure.

McKay believed it was possible for the APM to be fully indigenized and Pentecostal, but difficulties remained.[106] In a December 1997 APM board meeting, Linklater noted that Indigenous Pentecostals felt they were "going backwards," still not having "a Native Chairman." Linklater's criticism here was directed at the continuing presence and influence of Euro-Canadians on the APM board.[107] Of further concern were wages. When the WOD executive named Linklater as director, they promised him the same salary as Winter, but in his first year, Linklater earned less.[108] To the PAOC's credit, the WOD subsidized the APM with four per cent of the district's total annual church tithe for the initial five years, reduced thereafter to one per cent annually, ultimately covering the salary shortfall.[109]

INTO THE NEXT MILLENNIUM

In 2000, Linklater resigned from APM leadership. The WOD executive promoted Gunner to the position of APM director, and appointed him to the district executive. Gunner relocated the APM's headquarters to North Bay, Ontario, and in his new position noted fragmentation among the APM's churches, while inter-church contact had diminished. He observed that only sixteen congregations held affiliation with the APM, fourteen of them having Indigenous pastors. This was not to criticize Linklater, who had contributed to the increase in the number of churches after the APM succeeded the NLM and had ensured a high level of Indigenous ministry leadership during his tenure. In his next annual report, Gunner outlined that the APM had grown from ten churches in 1999 to twenty-two churches in 2001, all of them having Indigenous pastors. The APM churches increased their tithing to the WOD from $75,000 in 2000 to $90,000 in 2010. Direct district monetary support was no longer necessary, thus allowing the department to interact more readily with other national-level ministries.[110]

That the APM and its churches turned around financially in such short order under Linklater and Gunner bolsters the argument that the indigenous principle can work if Indigenous ministers are empowered to lead. Indigenization of clergy undoubtedly assisted Pentecostalism's growth, contributing to a "less exclusionary form than it had at the outset."[111] Both Linklater and Gunner proved to be highly effective leaders.

In 2001 Kallappa resigned from his position as national Aboriginal Ministries director, returning to his home state of Washington to pastor. The PAOC General Executive chose Gunner to fill the vacancy.[112] Gunner obliged, coordinating national-level Aboriginal Ministries work concurrent with his ongoing direction of the WOD-based APM, while also pastoring a congregation in North Bay.[113] His move to national leadership further blurred distinctions between district ministries and national-level ministries. This was not the end of the APM, but its congregations' associations with Indigenous congregations across the PAOC became more regular. Gunner attested to the fact that Indigenous churches situated outside of the WOD expressed interest in affiliating with the APM. Constitutionally unable to accept these proposals, Gunner instead directed inquirers to the analogous departments within their respective districts.[114] By 2007 the APM claimed twenty-three churches, and had reopened a ministry training institution, the First

Nations Satellite Bible College. This venture, however, was short-lived, and at the time of writing the college no longer exists. This presents some ongoing challenges to the movement with respect to training candidates for ministry and leadership in the twenty-first century. Meanwhile the DHMBC had shed its college responsibilities, and had been rebranded Mission Canada. This new entity continues to prioritize evangelism to and among Indigenous people.[115]

CONCLUSION

This chapter does not challenge the NLM's evangelistic achievement. Certainly the mission enjoyed success insofar as it attracted adherents, started churches, and operated a mission centre and the NLMBC. Mission supporters of the NLM gave money and time with incredible generosity. This chapter's purpose, rather, is to demonstrate that while the NLM's promise of autonomy was slow in its delivery, it was ultimately realized owing to the diligence, perseverance, and strong efforts of several committed Indigenous individuals. In many ways this development mirrored national-level trends toward Indigenous self-determination evident in events such as the Meech Lake Accord and the Oka Crisis. These socio-political developments, combined with the NLM's declining resources and Indigenous ministers' increasing assertion of autonomy, all contributed to the toppling of the NLM's decades-long Euro-Canadian predominance.

Even so, the autonomizing process had faltered before the effective dissolution of the NLM, and the transition to an Indigenous-led APM in 1996 did not eliminate all of the old and ongoing challenges associated with the antecedent organization. Yet this was a victory worth celebrating. Moreover, the growth associated with autonomy was unmistakable. Indigenous Pentecostals, having fought for the indigenous principle in the twentieth century, had by the twenty-first century established for themselves a distinct Indigenous Pentecostal identity. Still, the struggle to articulate a unique place and priority for Indigenous Pentecostalism within the PAOC was not just a matter for the past, but also for the present and future.

6

Past, Present, and Future

The Fruition of the Indigenous Principle in the Age of Apology, Truth, and Reconciliation

Sincere apology must be accompanied by acts that demonstrate contrition if restoration is to occur. The problem … is that aboriginal people view time differently than those with a Western worldview. The idea of forgetting the past is foreign to aboriginal peoples. Looking back and reconciling with the past is necessary. Further, reconciliation is not an event. It must be understood as a reality that includes the past, present and future … We look back to the beginning to move forward … Reconciliation involves people acting like God in relationship.

Terry LeBlanc, Mi'kmaq-Acadian, Executive Director of Indigenous Pathways, and Founding Chair and Director of the North American Institute for Indigenous Theological Studies[1]

I think the Church has been a part of the problem in the past, but now it is going to continue to be a vital part of the solution.

Ray Aldred, Néhiyaw; Swan River Band, Treaty 8, Alberta, Director of Indigenous Studies at Vancouver School of Theology, and Evangelical Fellowship of Canada Aboriginal Ministries Council Chair[2]

This COVID-19 pandemic has surely presented many of us with personal walls … for which … an entirely new approach … may be needed … to gain more context for understanding a biblical response to difficult issues like … racism within the church, and matters of injustice affecting vulnerable sectors of our society … We have been shaken by a series of devastating news in recent times – events that have either highlighted or introduced new "walls." … The revelation of unmarked graves of Indigenous children under several former Canadian residential schools underscores that there is something to be said for studying history intentionally and discerning current events through the lens of what has already been recorded.

Stacey McKenzie, PAOC *Testimony and Enrich* editor[3]

Throughout their many years of alleging to champion the ideal of the indigenous principle, the PAOC and NLM faltered in many respects because they did not consider that indigenization could not be accomplished in the absence of decolonization. In all probability, the PAOC's tendency to acquit itself of any vestiges, links, ties, or associations to or with colonial legacies obscured this necessary prerequisite. While PAOC leaders of the past probably would not have used the verbiage of decolonization, effectively they came to initiate this approach (or at least attempt to do so) through a series of events and encounters occurring during the opening decades of the twenty-first century. These steps further served to autonomize Indigenous Pentecostal ministry leadership. They also likely brought the PAOC closer to the fulfilment of its indigenous principle ideal. Indeed, Indigenous Pentecostals themselves furthered the application of the indigenous principle, bringing it into practice in spite of and not because of the NLM's methods, notwithstanding the missionaries' actions otherwise. One such example is APM director George Gunner (Moose Cree First Nation; Moose Factory, Ontario), who articulated how Indigenous Pentecostals kept the indigenous principle alive in the face of certain obstacles. Gunner expressed a sense of duty in so doing; as he stated, "we would hear around the table that we need to be the ones that step up and start to take over … We knew what we were facing. We knew what we needed to do. Out of that was a desire to … govern ourselves."[4]

The PAOC Western Ontario District's (WOD) APM ultimately represented the largest of the PAOC's ministries to Indigenous people. In this expanding capacity, the APM served as a harbinger of emerging trends among Indigenous Pentecostals nationwide. While it took some time for the PAOC's leadership to come to terms with its own role in delaying autonomy for Indigenous ministers and churches, the denomination ultimately did seek to make amends. During a period of apology, truth, and reconciliation, the PAOC's activities were of increased significance not simply within the organization, but also as they related to the PAOC's capacity to engage with social issues taking place contemporaneously to its own. Drawing primarily from more recently disseminated denominational and broadcast materials, as well as interviews conducted by the author, this chapter considers the implications of that finding. In so doing, this chapter further comments on the present state of Indigenous Pentecostalism in Canada, and points to literature and academics currently contributing to this field of study.

APOLOGY AND RECONCILIATION

By the turn of the millennium, Indigenous Pentecostalism in Canada had developed into a significant religious force, contributing to the ongoing dialogue on realities affecting Indigenous people in Canada. Of course this monograph's introduction drew attention to the notable election of Matthew Coon Come (Eeyou; Mistissini, Quebec), a Pentecostal, to the position of National Chief of the Assembly of First Nations (AFN) in 2000.[5] In this role, Coon Come advocated for Indigenous rights, opposing what he described as "terrible, violent, oppressive and disrespectful behavior [*sic*] toward our people," and decrying Canada's "repressive government that has finally shown its true face to the world."[6] Coon Come further pledged to elevate issues affecting Indigenous people to an international stage, and to bring disputes with the Canadian government to the attention of the United Nations (UN), should the Supreme Court of Canada make unfavourable decisions.[7] By 2007 the UN adopted the Declaration of the Rights of Indigenous People (UNDRIP), which in part outlines the importance of Indigenous traditional spiritualities. Although it was not formally adopted by the Canadian government until 2016, Indigenous people have frequently drawn on UNDRIP, advocating, among other things, their rights, civil and religious liberties, and Indigenous title.[8] Coon Come furthermore requested the formation of a national Truth and Reconciliation Commission "to act as a national forum for ... working out problems that have resulted from the residential school experience."[9]

In 2008, then–Prime Minister of Canada Stephen Harper offered a ground-breaking Statement of Apology to former students of Indian Residential Schools.[10] George Gunner responded to Harper's apology, stating:

> Our First Nations people ... waited for this. I was very glad our Prime Minister took that initiative ... that was huge in the eyes of the Native people, and they received that very openly. And

> many of them wept ... I would not say there has been a real shift [as a result]. I think more people are aware of what has happened now than ever before ... I think it has opened a lot of eyes.[11]

Canadian sociologist Michael Wilkinson observed an interesting feature of Harper's apology in remarking that while Pentecostals did not operate residential schools, "a message of spirit empowerment, healing, and restoration was well received among those in the aboriginal communities."[12]

By the second decade of the twenty-first century, Indigenous Pentecostals' story culminated in another ground-breaking moment, when in that same spirit of empowerment, healing, and restoration, the PAOC finally issued an apology all its own. In late 2010, the PAOC's Mission Canada department began the process of consulting its Aboriginal Ministries Guiding Group (representatives of Indigenous Pentecostal ministries across Canada) in preparation of the apology.[13] Based on the group's contributions, at the 2012 PAOC General Conference in Ottawa, the denomination issued the following statement:

> We, as the leadership of The Pentecostal Assemblies of Canada (PAOC), have a deep desire to be in right relationship with our Aboriginal ministries leadership and Aboriginal community serving the Lord together with mutual love and respect ... We acknowledge that there have been times when we were insensitive to the pain and suffering of the Aboriginal community. We are sorry and regret this insensitivity.
>
> For the purpose of reconciliation and to strengthen our mutual relationship, PAOC leadership apologizes and asks forgiveness of our Aboriginal leadership:
>
> - For attitudes and actions that have demonstrated discrimination and insensitivity
> - For not entrusting with responsibility when appropriate
> - For derogatory words that have been spoken
> - For sins of silence and omission when our voice should have been raised and ministry and healing offered
> - For our failure to address the hurt and harmful practices within residential schools.

> Our desire as a Pentecostal leadership is to be in right relationship with our Aboriginal community and demonstrate a mutual commitment:
>
> - To prepare a next generation of leaders who will fulfill the Great Command, the Great Requirement and Great Commission together
> - To honour our diversity
> - To share in vision and ministry development together
> - To promote equality in our relationship as we move forward.[14]

This was a powerful event, and a remarkable admission considering that generally the PAOC heretofore had not perceived itself as limiting Indigenous Pentecostals' autonomy.

Indigenous representatives at the 2012 General Conference responded: "For the purposes of reconciliation and a healthy unified relationship, the Aboriginal Ministries Guiding Group of the PAOC accepts the apology and extends forgiveness." The Guiding group continued:

> We also recognize that at times we have fallen short and apologize and ask forgiveness:
>
> - For attitudes and actions that have demonstrated discrimination and insensitivity
> - For derogatory words that have been spoken
> - For avoiding our responsibility in sharing our voice.
>
> Our desire for a healthy unified relationship with the PAOC and Aboriginal community is demonstrated by a commitment:
>
> - To bring healing to the Aboriginal community through the Gospel of Jesus Christ
> - To prepare a next generation of leaders who will fulfill the Great Command, the Great Requirement and Great Commission together
> - To honour our diversity
> - To share in vision and ministry development together
> - To promote equality in our relationship as we move forward.

"All this is from God, who reconciled us to himself through Christ and gave us the ministry of reconciliation: that God was reconciling the world to himself in Christ, not counting people's sins against them. And he has committed to us the message of reconciliation." 2 Corinthians 5:18, 19.
For God's glory we mutually make these commitments to one another,
David Wells, General Superintendent
George Gunner, Aboriginal Guiding Group[15]

To be sure, this was an historic moment within the PAOC. Gunner had ministered within the NLM, served as APM associate director and later director (a position he still held when the apology occurred), was coordinator of national PAOC Aboriginal Ministries, and chaired the Aboriginal Ministries Guiding Group which contributed to and participated in the statement of reconciliation. PAOC General Superintendent David Wells admirably apologized on behalf of the PAOC. Thus, this apology serves as the natural culmination of the NLM's and APM's historical trajectories from the Eurocentric mission founded by John Spillenaar in 1943 through to the autonomous movement of the twenty-first century. The apology represents the PAOC's clearest acknowledgment of the poor leadership decisions that contributed to the incomplete transfer of ministry to and lack of confidence in the emerging Indigenous leadership. The PAOC's leadership apologized for failing to keep the promise of the indigenous principle and sought reconciliation. The historian cannot overstate the significance of the denomination itself acknowledging its past failures.

Analysis of this exchange not only reveals the implications of the NLM's past for the present, but also provides insight into possibilities for future historical research, such as further study of the PAOC's doctrinal position during the ecumenical twentieth century. For example, other churches' apologies for historical wrongs committed toward Indigenous people predate this event. Thus it is useful to compare and contrast the PAOC's apology to those of the longer-established churches, discerning similarities and crucial differences, in order to provide an effective means of recalling how the PAOC mission to Indigenous people bears some similarity to the other denominations' mission efforts.

Immediately noticeable is the time gap between the other denominations' apologies and the PAOC's, some longer-established churches' apologies to Indigenous people coming more than twenty-five years earlier. Between 1986 and 1998, the United, Anglican, and Presbyterian churches, and at first only segments of the Catholic Church, issued apologies or confessions for their missionary involvement in colonization and residential schools.[16] While the PAOC entered the conversation on apology later, it also initiated its mission to Indigenous people much later than did the other churches. Another reason for the PAOC's later apology is the denomination's non-involvement in residential schools.[17] Still, the PAOC's apology for its failure to address the residential schooling legacy was necessary. For instance, around the time of the apology, PAOC minister Kyle Mason (Ojibwe Anishinaabe; Winnipeg, Manitoba) called upon the PAOC and its ministers to acknowledge that legacy's implications for Indigenous Pentecostal ministry, stating:

> We must remember that we represent a faith that may have done great harm to ... families and communities. This does not mean that we should withdraw from attempts to minister to Aboriginal people, but we must never do it without putting the encounter in context and recognizing the possible implications. Perhaps we feel that our Fellowship does not play a role in the healing of past wrongs committed by ... other denominations. But, while our denomination was not directly implicated in the problems of the residential school system, we are commanded to reach out to all who are hurting and broken hearted.[18]

Mason's bidding further cements the necessity and the requirement for all to engage in reconciliation, irrespective of perceived denominational inculpability.

What is more, even the longer-established churches' apologies were not motivated solely by the residential schooling legacy. The Anglican Church led the longer-established churches in addressing mistreatment of Indigenous adherents. At its 1969 General Synod, it accepted "responsibility for its history of paternalism and racism towards Aboriginal people." The church responded by supporting Indigenous rights through monetary assistance and placing political pressure on the government regarding realities affecting Indigenous people. At its 1977 Synod, the church sided with Indigenous people, resisting property developments until Indigenous title had been settled.[19]

Likewise, the apology by the United Church was not initially motivated specifically by residential schooling. Rather, the United Church's apology sought to make amends for "the denial of the value of Native Spirituality." At the United Church's Thirty-First General Council in 1986, moderator Robert Smith read the apology, which in part stated:

> Long before my people journeyed to this land your people were here, and you received from your Elders an understanding of creation and of the Mystery that surrounds us ... We did not hear you when you shared your vision. In our zeal to tell you the good news of Jesus Christ we were closed to the value of your spirituality.[20]

In October 1998 the United Church issued a second apology, this time addressing their role in the residential schooling system.[21]

For its failure to extend autonomy, as well as for its earlier attempts at assimilation, the Presbyterian Church offered the Confession of 1994 and its associated statement of reconciliation, requesting "forgiveness from Aboriginal peoples."[22] Canadian Presbyterian historian Peter Bush reports that in "the wake of the confession, Canadian Presbyterian ministry to Native peoples focused on finding healing and reconciliation."[23] Throughout the 1990s and onward, the Presbyterian Church's National Native Ministries Council brought together representatives from Indigenous ministries to discuss issues of common concern.[24]

Initially two organizations within the Catholic Church apologized. The Oblates of Mary Immaculate were the first. In 1991 the Oblates claimed responsibility for their role "'in the cultural, ethnic, linguistic and religious imperialism' that missionaries had inflicted on Indigenous peoples after contact." Also in 1991, a delegation of sixteen bishops, representatives of other Catholic agencies, as well as a cadre of Indigenous Catholics, expressed the Church's regret.[25] A comprehensive papal apology would not take place until 2022, an event to be addressed in a subsequent section of this chapter.[26]

Although the PAOC did not apologize for its longstanding opposition to contextualization as the United Church had, by 2000 the PAOC had changed its position on contextualization, a development also to be more closely examined later in this chapter. Another point of comparison is that the PAOC's 2012 apology, like the United

Church's 1986 apology, was issued in-house. Because the United Church issued the apology to its own assembly, the apology was extended primarily to Indigenous United Church adherents (including Indigenous clergy). Similarly, because the PAOC issued its apology at its own General Conference, the denomination did not directly apologize to Indigenous people beyond the PAOC's immediate sphere of influence. A further-reaching PAOC apology might have taken place on a grander scale. Throughout the 1990s, the Anglican, Presbyterian, and United Churches, and segments of the Catholic Church, each apologized for residential schooling abuses. The churches issued these apologies publicly, as the residential schools' legacy extends beyond those within the respective churches' immediate spheres of influence. Perhaps these apologies' public nature is owed to the wider media coverage the longer-established churches received, something to which the PAOC was not treated.

In many ways all churches' missions began similarly, with the intention to missionize Indigenous people and attract them to a European or Euro-Canadian brand of Christianity. While the longer-established churches' associated policies during the first half of the twentieth century generally were characterized by assimilative intentions, they had attempted the formation of Indigenous clergy during the nineteenth century, and re-emphasized it by the late twentieth century, during and after the time of the apologies.[27] The longer-established churches did not articulate an indigenous principle to the extent the Pentecostals did, partially because their nineteenth-century "Three-Self" and native church policies were already theologically embedded. Rather, the longer-established churches' late-twentieth-century initiatives to incorporate Indigenous clergy provide a sort of parallel to the Pentecostals' indigenous principle.[28] While the PAOC claimed a unique evangelistic exercise, ironically the results of the churches' missiological practices were eerily more similar than different; the denominations eventually offered comparable apologies. Two consistent strands in the apologies have been: 1) preparation of the apologies involving settler Canadian churches' consultation with Indigenous leaders and parties; and 2) the premise of reconciliation. The intent of apologizing was more than simply to say sorry, but also to "redress injustices." Apologizing was intended as a step to reframe relationships between Indigenous denominational members and the Euro-Canadian/settler churches that had behaved unjustly. Experiences taking place between when the apologies were issued and the present have demonstrated that meaningful reconciliation requires ongoing effort, being more than simply a one-time apology. What is more, before there can be reconciliation, there needs to be truth, which depends upon "really listening to what Indigenous peoples are saying."[29]

Regarding the PAOC's 2012 apology, it is to the credit of the denomination's leadership (General Superintendent David Wells in particular) that they engaged in the process of seeking reconciliation. It was all the more commendable for the Aboriginal Ministries Guiding Group to accept the apology, graciously agreeing to reconciliation. Still, in recent years academics and PAOC adherents alike have begun to question the rationale for having Indigenous ministers themselves offer an apology, considering it was the PAOC that acknowledged the wrongs committed against them. While the historian cannot overstate the PAOC's willingness to acknowledge its own past wrongs, some analysis on this point is merited. The order through which the apology came about may partially point to the reasons for this process. George Gunner recalled that the Aboriginal Guiding Group had initiated the process, seeking an apology from the PAOC at least in part because of the PAOC's silence on and historical denial of responsibility for the residential schooling legacy. This process again identifies residential schools as the signal motivation for church and state apologies to Indigenous people. Still, Gunner's sentiment was that an apology is something that should be offered, rather than something that should be sought.[30]

Dan Collado (Kanien'kehá:ka; Tyendinaga Mohawk Territory, Ontario), former NLM minister, member of the PAOC Aboriginal Guiding Group, and participant in the 2012 apology ceremony, likewise attested to Indigenous Pentecostals' desire for the PAOC to acknowledge the residential schooling legacy as having been a factor motivating the apology. Yet Collado continued to explain the Indigenous ministers' counter-apology thus:

> We weren't interested in simply heaping on guilt for the sake of getting a confession ... The PAOC event was really not about the residential school history. That might have been the catalyst ... but the impetus for us was always reconciliation. That was the driving force.
>
> Reconciliation requires – demands – both sides to walk the journey. As Indigenous people, we too recognize we have a

> burden to uphold our end of the reconciliation wampum belt … It's a case of if someone wrongs you, you're not automatically justified to wrong them. The Indigenous leadership wanted to publicly acknowledge that reality.[31]

The Aboriginal Guiding Group's commitment to reconciliation is admirable and commendable. Still, the requirement must be for the PAOC – who issued the apology – likewise to uphold its end of the process. As was demonstrated by other denominations' apologies, an agreement to reconciliation requires ongoing commitment. Spoken apology can occur frequently and relatively easily, but following through with reconciliation requires continued effort.[32]

Terry LeBlanc (Mi'kmaq and Acadian, with family roots in the Listuguj First Nation) is an ordained minister. He serves as Executive Director of My People International; Executive Director of Indigenous Pathways; Founding Chair and Director of the North American Institute for Indigenous Theological Studies (NAIITS); and has been in full-time ministry since 1979.[33] LeBlanc's comments on the process of apology and reconciliation cited in this chapter's opening epigraph pointed out that apology and reconciliation are not only an ongoing process, but perhaps even a series of processes. Two parties are required for reconciliation, yet the bulk of responsibility for apology rests upon those who inflicted the challenges in the first place.[34] The Anglican Church's 1992 Residential Schools Working Group, for instance, provided this appropriate reminder:

> It would be unfair to ask native people to take responsibility for cleaning up a mess they had no part in making. The [wrongdoings] were imposed on native people by the dominant society, and the main issue is for the church to come to understand that the system was wrong. That's not the native people's job.[35]

This advice should extend to those maintaining a Western worldview who offer apologies and seek reconciliation. Those who admit wrongs committed must also be aware of how Indigenous recipients hear those apologies and how they are conducted. The Aboriginal Ministries Guiding Group's willingness not only to receive the apology, but also to contribute to the process was highly admirable. The PAOC's apology marks an acknowledgment of the shortcomings of the past, but the work of reconciliation must be ongoing.

CHANGES AND DIFFERENCES FROM WITHIN

The 2012 PAOC General Conference Joint Apology and Statement on Reconciliation was highly significant, but an unexpected event followed. After serving in district and national roles from 1996 to 2013, Gunner resigned from them, relinquishing his PAOC ministerial credentials, in order to pursue "a vision for the creation of a national Aboriginal-led ministry."[36] Only a few years prior, while conducting APM itinerant ministry, Gunner and his wife Pauline had experienced a life-threatening aircraft crash-landing in Pickle Lake. The couple believed God had spared them for a specific purpose.[37] It is possible this near-death experience caused Gunner to take stock of his work and ministry, potentially prompting him to consider ministering in another capacity.

Another potential rationale for Gunner's move was his reluctance to embrace the PAOC's evolving missiological notions of contextualization, specifically the national-level Aboriginal Ministries' 2000 Statement of Affirmations. Created while James Kallappa was director, the Statement addressed the use of Indigenous drums, regalia, music, dance, spirit names, oral liturgy, narrative theology, and dreams and visions, and decided that PAOC Aboriginal Ministries should find ways to integrate some of them into Pentecostal worship.[38] Effectively the statement stipulated that certain Indigenous spiritual and cultural observances were now deemed permissible to be integrated into Pentecostal devotion. Chapter 4 of this monograph argued that Euro-Canadian missionaries failed to acknowledge Indigenous culture in their communication of Pentecostalism, with some opposing it entirely. Contributing to the NLM's challenges during that era was a near-total rejection of contextualization. The Statement of Affirmations thus reversed decades of PAOC opposition to such traditional practices, and encouraged their contemplative contextualization into Pentecostal expression.[39]

For their part, Indigenous Pentecostals maintain various positions on the subject of contextualization, and for a variety of different reasons. Reggie Neeposh (Eeyou and former Chief of Oujé-Bougoumou First Nation, Quebec), Senior Pastor of the Oujé-Bougoumou Cree Pentecostal Church, explained his embrace of contextualization as follows:

> Native spirituality was banned in our community by our previous Chief and Council ... Many people from all over were

very critical, saying we had been colonized – we are like the white people …

When I was Chief … I rescinded the resolutions and explained to the people that we cannot infringe on people's rights according to the constitution, and that there was a better way to explain to the younger generation. We could demonstrate to them that Jesus was real in our lives by loving them …

It's something the Cree people and other First Nations across the country understand. They have love in their culture. They love people; they love the animals; they love the land. They have compassion … People are not looking for a definition of Christianity but a demonstration of His power and love …

And that is what I do. I will attend powwows and share the love of God with them. I do participate in the group dances they do, but never in the shaking tent ceremony – there is a fine line that needs to be respected, and I respect these people. They are very loving and caring, more than those who claim to be Christians …

We have to be careful not to demonize everything. I believe God created each of us in a certain way, and we can worship Him within our culture – we should embrace that. We have used the drum as part of our culture from the beginning. My late grandfather David used to be a powerful shaman and when he got saved, he didn't touch the drum for a long time (about 40 years). But before he passed away, he picked up the drum again. When he was with our Grand Council and our Chiefs, they would ask him to sing. He explained to them that the words he was going to sing were words that would praise God. He said, "This is the only instrument I know. I used to use it in a bad way, but since being born again I rededicated my life and I have rededicated my drum. I will use it to praise Him." That was his testimony. Every culture has their own way of expressing who they are, and they can use that to praise God.[40]

Levi Samson Beardy (Anishinini; Bearskin Lake, Ontario), who serves as lead pastor of Aboriginal Believers' Church (WOD) in Toronto, likewise reflected on his embrace of contextualization stating: "Everything is redeemable … a drum cannot make decisions … a Christian can take that same drum and use it for the glory of God."[41] The title of this monograph itself draws inspiration from Beardy's reflection:

> When I first … became a Christian, there was … very much a fear that the spirit within the eagle feather would destroy a Christian's walk completely. But I believe that … the eagle feather is … an emblem. And even in Isaiah 40:31 it talks about that. But they who trust in the Lord will soar on wings as Eagles, and run and not be weary. And that whole aspect of the eagle being used as a representative of strength and courage as God directs them. I think sometimes when we talk about First Nations belief systems we take it to the extreme[, believing] that it's destructive, when at many times I believe it's in the same way as Christianity.[42]

Within Indigenous traditional spiritualities, the eagle is often "regarded as the most favoured of the Creator's animals," and thus holds considerable cultural and spiritual significance.[43] Accordingly Beardy encouraged Pentecostals "not to fear the eagle feather, but rather to redeem it."[44] Beardy further described an interpretation of smudging that can be observed "as unto the Lord." Reflecting on a passage of scripture found in Psalm 51, he recited: "Cleanse me with hyssop and I shall be made as white as snow." Recalling the experience, Beardy concluded: "As the sweetgrass started to flow, it was as … God's word [which] says … 'the prayers of His people are like incense unto His nostrils,' and so I felt strongly that this was as unto the Lord and that the cleansing of my body, soul, and spirit … was the true cleansing of Christ in my life."[45]

Yet as previously stated, not all Indigenous Pentecostals embrace contextualization wholeheartedly, and the dialogue continues into the present. Dean Shingoose (Anishinaabe, in this instance the exonym for which is Saulteaux; Coté First Nation Treaty Four Territory, Saskatchewan), former pastor of Native Pentecostal Church in Calgary, took a moderate position arguing, "There's a fine line between culture and religion, and there were qualities of our native culture that … could have been turned to the glorification of God …" Shingoose continued to critique Euro-Canadian opposition to Indigenous culture, highlighting, "but instead it was all crushed." Shingoose believed that had Pentecostals presented the gospel as something that could work in unison with Indigenous culture instead of rejecting it, then the message might be more attractive.[46]

George Gunner strongly opposed the integration of Indigenous traditions into Pentecostal expression, noting that it had become difficult even for those seated at the Aboriginal Ministries table to find consensus on this topic. Gunner recalled:

> It was always something that we were divided on amongst ourselves. I remember asking … David Wells … "I think we need to make a statement on where we stand regarding our culture." But we could never get there, because half the leaders were for it and half were against it, and that's the division that's in the midst of us today.[47]

Even while some APM ministers and congregations affirmed contextualization,[48] for Gunner and others, it represented syncretism and the embrace of Indigenous traditional spiritualities, which he believed could pose significant spiritual consequences. The minister commented:

> Aboriginal people all know there is a God. We all believe in a Creator. No matter where we are in life. Because we believe in a Creator, we are trying to reach that God. We are trying to do it through traditionalism, through our own way, through smudging and all these various ways. Jesus made a claim 2000 years ago … "I am the way, I am the truth, I am the life. That no man gets to the Father, God, the Creator, except through me." When the Spirit of God comes, the Holy Spirit, He brings peace into your life, and it is totally different from our traditional way of trying to engage with God. There is a danger that when we go into some of these places where the Spirit of God is not there that we can open ourselves up to a spirit that is not a godly spirit, but rather can be a demonic spirit.[49]

In reference to the counter opinion of adherents of Indigenous traditional spiritualities toward Pentecostalism, Gunner offered this perspective:

> I think that they … see it as a threat. They perceive us as a threat to who they are. And I heard about this as well, [they] try to cast spells and try to hit the church with their, what you call, "medicine."[50]

Evidently Gunner neither feared nor dismissed Indigenous traditional spiritualities, but rather attested to their significance. Or, put another way,

> When Pentecostals refuse to participate in ceremonial forms of communication with the spirit world, it is not because they do not believe in the existence or the powers of these entities. On the contrary, they affirm them to be powerful forces but ones that are of such potential danger that they must be avoided.[51]

For these reasons Gunner and others at times have been described as maintaining a sort of "anti-syncretism."[52]

Even so, the diversity of views regarding the integration of Indigenous cultural and traditional observances into Pentecostal expression serves to demonstrate the complexity of the subject. Much like Indigenous traditional spiritualities themselves, this is a subject which likely will never be fully understood by settler Canadian observers. It is an oversimplification to state that Indigenous Pentecostals either oppose or embrace the process, as though it were a binary. The decision to be Pentecostal is not based on a desire to be less Indigenous or less traditional. It may, in fact, be the opposite. Mark Clatterbuck described that many Indigenous Pentecostals "embrace Pentecostalism in the conviction that they are becoming, through Jesus, more authentically [Indigenous] ... even as they reject the prevailing religious practices of the tribe."[53] Clatterbuck continued:

> The danger in leveling simplistic accusations of anti-traditionalism ... is that it threatens to obscure the complexities of religious and cultural self-understanding, as well as the spiritual practices that mark the movement today. It also threatens to paint a portrait of duped converts, unwittingly serving as pawns in the hands of a new generation of colonialist Christian missionaries ... Theirs is a story that complicates the issue of post-colonial indigenous religious identity ... Pentecostalism is a movement in which the missionized have eagerly embraced the faith of the missionary, only to reject the institutional hierarchies from which it came.[54]

For example, even in instances where Pentecostal ministers and leaders oppose integration of Indigenous cultural, traditional, and spiritual observances, many Indigenous adherents are attracted to Pentecostal expressions nevertheless, as

> they remind the elders of the old ... traditions ... In these movements they can, as in the old ... tradition, closely associate their daily life practices with religious rules, experiences and values, and express their deep emotions collectively and openly.[55]

Gunner became Kallappa's successor as PAOC Aboriginal Ministries coordinator. Yet this role was not quite the national equivalent to his WOD role as APM director. As the national coordinator, Gunner was first among equals, but he could not determine the various districts' approaches and strategies to ministry among Indigenous people. As the PAOC increasingly affirmed contextualization, Gunner resisted said hierarchies, potentially contributing to his dissociation from the denomination. It is ironic that after decades of opposing Indigenous culture, the PAOC had finally welcomed it, perhaps too much so for Gunner's liking.

Yet if opposition to the PAOC's shifting position regarding contextualization was a motive for Gunner's departure, it was not the only (nor even the main) one. Principally, Gunner wished to pursue self-determination within Aboriginal Ministries. An earlier document intimated his rationale:

> My disappointment at present is with the lack of a First Nations ministry that has an impact nationally. I recently read the comment of a First Nations political leader who stated that you get what you fight for, and if the First Nation people are just looking to fix broken glass and leaky plumbing, we will never dream of a better future. I want to be a leader these young First Nations "Timothys" can look to for an example, and to be an inspiration. God is stirring the faith of young men and women to dream of a better future and giving them a greater vision beyond anything that has been done in First Nations ministry to this point.[56]

Gunner's comments suggest that he had become dissatisfied with the state of affairs within the PAOC's existing Aboriginal Ministries, describing disappointment in the absence of ministry at the national level tailored to Indigenous people. He was also frustrated with PAOC leadership's perceived lack of support.[57] Still, Gunner reports to have first attempted to accomplish his goal of self-determination and a national-level ministry within the structure of the PAOC:

> I believe the Lord gave me that vision to establish a ministry that was national. I spoke with our district superintendent and the executive and I shared our plans [and] our vision … I even went to the national office and said "is there any way that … [s]ome kind of a ministry … would be connected and under the umbrella of the PAOC, yet still national and still be able to be on its own, whether it be at arm's length?" … because I knew it could work. Everybody looked and said "no, it can't."
>
> It came to a point where … I knew I had to leave the position of APM director and step into what I believed the Lord was calling me into. I said "if I stay here I'm going to get frustrated and bitter," because I've seen others that left bitter and angry. And I didn't want to do that. And I said "I want to be able to look at you … and know in my heart that I have nothing against you guys. But I need to do what I feel God is calling me to do." And so that's what we did … and they blessed us. The district executive came in and released us and let us go.[58]

Soon after parting ways with the PAOC, Gunner fulfilled his ministry vision by establishing the Christian Aboriginal Fellowship of Canada (CAFC) in 2014, signalling his inspiration for it in an earlier statement:

> In Aboriginal ministry there is a new generation of young leaders who are looking to fulfil the calling of God in their lives. I believe they are seeking someone they can look up to … someone who will be a mentor, a champion, a model – someone who will be faithful. If there is anything I would like to leave behind, it would be an example of faith that this young First Nations generation could follow. As we have travelled nationally, and as the Lord opened doors for our ministry, we do receive calls from many young First Nations leaders looking for advice, encouragement and direction.[59]

Arguably it is through the CAFC that Gunner provides this model. The organization ordains ministers, and describes itself as originating

> out of a shared desire among Christian Aboriginal leaders across Canada to consolidate under a national and inter-denominational Christian umbrella with a unified vision and

> mandate to ensure a Christian presence in every reserve across Canada … and to advance the raising up and support of Christian Aboriginal leaders to do so. It is a vision of ministry and fellowship inspired by God and given to Aboriginal leaders for their own people.[60]

Regarding the rationale for the CAFC concerning Indigenous self-determination, Gunner continued:

> I think … we're preaching the Gospel the way Jesus wants us to preach it, to where we begin to take over and begin to have control of our own destiny … And it's not then in the hands of those who are over you and saying "you can do this, but you can't do that." I think we can do all things. And that's really what we're trying to do now, to establish with our Christian Aboriginal Fellowship of Canada.[61]

The CAFC describes its intentions as follows:

> Elevating the expectations for excellence in Christian ministry and conduct among the Aboriginal people … [the] CAFC is a national Christian fellowship for Aboriginal people, by Aboriginal people, to the Aboriginal people, and beyond. We are a Spirit-filled ministry that provides Biblical covering for the church.[62]

Described as inter-denominational, the CAFC's reference to biblical covering suggests the organization intends to function as a denomination.

The CAFC has since extended its reach beyond Ontario to western Canada and Quebec, with the potential of expanding into Canada's Maritime provinces. At the time of writing, the CAFC comprises twenty churches – with the prospect of the affiliation of more – and maintains sixty-seven credentialled ministers. The CAFC also operates a First Nations Restoration Centre in Sioux Lookout, Ontario.[63] Although the CAFC does not explicitly bar minister members affiliated with other denominations, presumably those who are already ordained with other denominations would not require CAFC accreditation, as it is an ordaining entity. Commenting on his ministry's position regarding the integration of Indigenous spiritual observances, Gunner reported:

> We've taken a strong stand on the mixing – we call it – of our culture with the Bible, the word of God. We don't believe that we should be doing that, but that we are to be separate from all of that. There is a culture that we believe in. I just went moose hunting … and fishing and all that kind of stuff. That's our culture. But when it crosses over into the spiritual, then I believe that's where we have to draw a line.[64]

Gunner's departure from the PAOC also in a sense fulfilled the premise of the indigenous principle. For Gunner, this meant parting ways with the conventional centre of power in favour of an Indigenous-led, independent church network. Doing so furthermore enabled Gunner to choose which traditional observances to remove or rework into his respective worldview.[65] Indeed the CAFC is truly indigenized and fully autonomous, yet it retains many hallmarks of its antecedent denomination. Presumably some Indigenous, formerly PAOC churches have joined Gunner's breakaway CAFC ministry. Others have integrated into their respective geographic districts. This too might be viewed as the fulfilment of Henry Venn's "Three-Self" policy, in that the Indigenous church has become so self-sufficient that it has integrated into the greater whole, not requiring special aid and attention.[66] While most Indigenous Pentecostal ministers remained affiliated with the PAOC, Gunner's departure left a considerable void. He had been a passionate and effective leader, committed to his convictions and to Indigenous people.[67]

Although PAOC Indigenous church numbers dwindled nationally, under Linklater's and Gunner's leadership the WOD Indigenous churches increased from eleven inherited from the NLM in 1996 (when Gunner was appointed APM associate director) to the APM's twenty-seven churches in 2010. Gunner later reported that at the time of his departure from the PAOC in 2012, the number of APM churches had increased to thirty. Gunner attributes his success as APM director to his application of church growth and leadership principles he had learned while pioneering and pastoring the NLM (and later APM) church in Moose Factory.[68]

To his credit, Gunner grew the WOD-based APM at a time when the Indigenous ministries of other districts were declining in numbers. After Gunner resigned, the WOD executive named Blake Davidson, a Euro-Canadian, as APM interim director. The WOD executive soon established a predominantly Indigenous leadership committee with Robert Linklater (Môsonîw Iliiliw; Moosonee, Ontario), a seasoned minister dating back to the NLM era, as APM committee chair, replacing Davidson.[69] While the WOD-affiliated Indigenous churches generally have remained numerically healthy, in several other PAOC districts there has been observable numeric decline. Indigenous Pentecostalism remains a substantial religious force, but that does not mean that Indigenous Pentecostals always subscribe to the PAOC's brand of Pentecostalism. Although once the denomination of choice for Indigenous Pentecostals, the PAOC is at present one of several Pentecostal organizational options for Indigenous participants.

In the early 1970s, PAOC Missionary Secretary Roy Upton reported the denomination as having reached a peak of "130 Indian congregations ... dedicated to reaching Canada's 300,000 Indians." The figure remained above one hundred into the early 2000s. At the time of writing, however, the number has dropped to fewer than eighty. The reason for the national decline is not entirely clear. Reggie Neeposh describes the challenges in appealing to millennials and younger people, stating: "This younger generation is still seeking. I think one of the problems with the church is that we're not relevant or real to them."[70] There are of course the additional and ongoing realities of denominational and hierarchical rigidity,[71] notwithstanding the significant obstacles overcome throughout the history of Indigenous Pentecostalism. Other contributing factors may include an underlying fluidity of the cited figures, a shortage of leaders trained in the local context (following the closure of most PAOC ministerial training institutions tailored to Indigenous ministerial candidates), and association with non-PAOC, Evangelical denominations led by Indigenous people, and networks such as the CAFC and the Native Evangelical Fellowship of Canada.[72]

Dan Collado offered his perspective on the denominational situation thus:

> In the end, what has really been lacking ... has been the transition of mentor leadership. As of 2019 ... there's a list of seventy-eight [Indigenous Pentecostal] works, and maybe half of them actually had the name of a leader, a pastor associated with that. And of the leaders that were listed, the average age is almost sixty-three. So I'm not so worried about the allegiance to the denomination

> as I am to allegiance to Christ and a commitment to raising up that leadership. The PAOC is going to be fine with our Indigenous leadership if we focus on just leadership development, not so much PAOC allegiance … and let the chips fall as they may, because it's about building up the Kingdom.[73]

Consistent with the above reflections is the precedent for Indigenous, independent, Pentecostal church networks whose influence goes beyond immediate ecclesial circles, also affecting the social and political structure of their communities.[74] These are the networks that Joseph Jolly (Eeyou; Waskaganish, Quebec; raised in Moose Factory, Ontario) refers to as the

> independents, arguably the most indigenous of Native churches … represented by … various independent … Pentecostals. These are churches that espouse a … Pentecostal type of theology and worship – and may even use the word … Pentecostal in their church name – but have no affiliation with any denomination.[75]

Such churches and networks are developing and expanding at an increasing frequency. These individuals', churches', and networks' Pentecostal expression occurring vibrantly, independently, and autonomously from the PAOC potentially points to the fruition of the indigenous principle.

In short: "The market for religion," as Canadian historian of Christianity Robert Burkinshaw reminds us, "is always high. The suppliers will on occasion change."[76] It is also possible that Pentecostalism broadly is now facing a similar track to its denominational forebears, the longer-established churches. They too experienced a rapid initial influx of adherents, gradually building momentum toward religious hegemony, and today their churches frequently strive to maintain a remnant of it. Clinton Westman observed,

> there are many examples of similar situations … in which relatively stable Catholic colonial societies were missionized by … Pentecostal missionaries [who] overwhelm[ed] the Catholic mission … A comparable situation appears to exist in the isolated communities during the postwar period.

Westman's fieldwork points to the tendency of several community members to disassociate from these Pentecostal churches following a preliminary period of strong engagement.[77] Certainly Gunner's grievances with the PAOC echo criticism the Pentecostals once levelled against their longer-established predecessors. Thus it is possible the PAOC's presence within Indigenous communities will be rivalled by ministry originating elsewhere. Gunner's CAFC, with its ministry "for Aboriginal people, by Aboriginal people, to the Aboriginal people," may represent a new trend for twenty-first-century Pentecostalism among Indigenous people.[78]

Still, there remains a strong network of PAOC Indigenous churches, and a committed core of Indigenous leaders nationally who continue to make Pentecostalism Indigenous. Patti Victor (Sto:lo; Cheam First Nation; British Columbia) succeeded Gunner, becoming the first woman to serve as PAOC Aboriginal Ministries coordinator. Victor restored stability to national Aboriginal Ministries, and assisted the PAOC as it addressed the recommendations of the Final Report of the Truth and Reconciliation Commission of Canada (TRC).[79]

Dan Collado succeeded Victor as Indigenous Guiding Group chair, coming to his current position with extensive experience. Collado pastored the NLM church in Weagamow Lake, Ontario, from 1993 to 1995, thereafter pastoring in Rankin Inlet, Northwest Territories (today Nunavut), and Napanee, Ontario. In 2009, Collado became director of the Aboriginal Bible Academy (ABA) in Deseronto, Ontario. The ABA is the PAOC's only remaining Bible college with the specific mandate "to serve all Canadian Aboriginal People (First Nations, Métis & Inuit) with the purpose of helping to train and equip indigenous leadership for Christian ministry." Collado also serves as the PAOC's representative on the Evangelical Fellowship of Canada's Indigenous Advisory Council.[80] Collado reflected on the possibilities for Indigenous Pentecostalism thus:

> I'm excited for what [lies] ahead. Indigenous people make great Pentecostals! They don't need to be convinced concerning the spirit realm which permits them to be naturally supernatural and operate under the unction of the Holy Spirit as a natural extension of their relationship with Christ … They are the "first peoples" of our nation and are the original caretakers of this land … [I]f we believe in praying for God to bless this land and nation of Canada, that blessing, in part,

flows through our Indigenous people and our relationship with them.[81]

Collado's conclusions are consistent with Mark Clatterbuck's findings, his research among Apsáalooke (the exonym for which is Crow) in Montana pointing to an increasingly popular perspective that "indigenous peoples … possess a kind of geospiritual authority over their ancestral homelands, and to them alone belongs 'the true ownership of the spiritual landscape of the continent.'" Clatterbuck's interviewees claimed Indigenous people

> are still the earthly host authority for the land … and the Native believers as new creatures of Christ restored to heavenly authority in the name of Jesus are the only ones who can righteously and permanently deal with any and all ancient issues of iniquity affecting the spiritual and natural landscapes.

Clatterbuck concludes:

> It is no surprise that such a spiritual vision is gaining more and more traction among Pentecostals today as it blends aspects of classic Pentecostal theology, tribal pride, and an empowering sense of indigenous privilege in God's universal salvific plans.[82]

Apsáalooke Pentecostalism mirrors Indigenous Pentecostalism in Canada in additional ways, and may shed light on the movement's possible future. Clatterbuck observed that Apsáalooke Pentecostalism "peaked in the 1980s and early 1990s. After a noticeable decline through the 1990s and early 2000s, the movement is clearly experiencing a resurgence as it approaches its ninetieth anniversary."[83] Perhaps a similar resurgence may be waiting in the wings for Apsáalooke Pentecostalism's counterpart within Indigenous communities in Canada. Or perhaps, as PAOC minister Kyle Mason put it, "Times are changing. What it means to be Aboriginal in Canada is changing. It is time to re-examine our approach to Aboriginal ministry. Let us seek to be a healing presence, witnessing the true gospel of grace, and make a huge impact for the kingdom."[84] With respect to this twenty-first-century cadre of Indigenous Pentecostal ministers, it is clear that the PAOC hopes their ministries will grow and develop as they continue to reach and serve Indigenous people.[85]

CONCLUSION: REFLECTIONS ON THE ROAD TO RECONCILIATION

In 2019 the PAOC celebrated its centenary. Within that century, the PAOC grew to become Canada's largest Evangelical denomination. As such, the PAOC must seriously consider what bearing its past and present have on its future and on Canadian Evangelicalism's future, and specific to the themes developed within this book, the role it continues to play along the road to reconciliation. While historically many Euro-Canadians have been ignorant toward the realities encountered by Indigenous people,[86] at the time of writing, perhaps for the first time in Canadian history, it is nearly impossible to have a casual conversation about issues affecting Canadian public life and society without addressing the injustices endured by Indigenous people. This is not to say that these issues were neither relevant nor known before this time; they most certainly were. This is more a case of the Canadian public's attention now firmly, finally, and irrevocably being directed toward these issues. To be sure, the TRC's release of its Final Report in 2015 brought the conversation to the fore. If the Canadian public's attention is not directed toward these issues, it is not for lack of knowledge.

The PAOC's Apology and Joint Statement on Reconciliation (2012) is still quite recent, and the substance of it has become increasingly relevant considering Canadian current affairs. The tragic events brought to light in May 2021, disclosing the unmarked graves of 215 children at the site of the former Kamloops Indian Residential School in Kamloops, British Columbia, have served to reinvigorate the conversation surrounding formal church apologies. Partially as a result of this event, and after overwhelming public pressure to do so, the Catholic church finally issued a formal papal apology for its role in residential schools, taking place in two parts. The first occurred in the Vatican on 1 April 2022, where before a visiting delegation of Inuit, Métis, and First Nations representatives, Pope Francis apologized for "the deplorable conduct of … members of the Catholic Church" and asked "for God's forgiveness," adding, "I want to say to you with all my heart, I am very sorry. And I join my brothers, the Canadian bishops, in asking your pardon."[87]

On the heels of this event, the Vatican announced that Pope Francis would make an official visit to the Canadian cities of Edmonton, Québec, and Iqaluit, where the second part of the papal apology would be issued to the survivors (and their descendants) of the Canadian Indian Residential Schooling System.[88] Pope Francis spent the final week of July 2022 visiting those cities and stating:

> I am here because the first step of my penitential pilgrimage among you is that of again asking forgiveness, of telling you once more that I am deeply sorry. Sorry for the ways in which, regrettably, many Christians supported the colonizing mentality of the powers that oppressed the Indigenous Peoples.
>
> I am sorry. I ask forgiveness, in particular, for the ways in which many members of the church and of religious communities co-operated, not least through their indifference, in projects of cultural destruction and forced assimilation promoted by the governments of that time, which culminated in the system of residential schools …
>
> In the face of this deplorable evil, the church kneels before God and implores His forgiveness for the sins of her children … I myself wish to reaffirm this, with shame and unambiguously, I humbly beg forgiveness for the evil committed by so many Christians against the Indigenous Peoples.[89]

Pope Francis's "six-day sojourn" constituted the second longest single-country official visit of his papacy. Both parts of Pope Francis's apology were met with a combination of praise, emotion, and disappointment, Dan Collado describing them as "more measured and less detailed than dozens of earlier apologies from Canadian religious orders and bishops dating back more than 30 years." Collado continued: "Some felt the apology was genuine and appropriate, while others remarked that not enough was said. So there was a mix of welcome reception and protest."[90]

These reactions in turn have contributed to ongoing dialogue concerning next steps along the road to reconciliation. Similarly, the revelations that came to light in Kamloops provoked many within the PAOC to pause and reflect on the same process.[91] Collado (in his role of PAOC Indigenous Guiding Group chair), and General Superintendent David Wells responded by co-releasing a joint statement in *Testimony*. The release, titled "A PAOC Response to the Kamloops Tragedy," stated: "The Pentecostal Assemblies of Canada is profoundly moved and grieved at the recent discovery of the loss of life for 215 children under the residential school system … [W]e have all been forced to revisit sins of the past, as though they happened just yesterday." The statement went on to refer to the PAOC's 2012 apology and recommitted the denomination to its "ministry of reconciliation," concluding with the addendum: "We recognize the even greater need to practise what was stated in light of the additional discoveries of unmarked graves still taking place."[92] This final line refers to the recovery of over one hundred unmarked graves at the site of the former Brandon Indian Residential School in Brandon, Manitoba, in June 2021, and of 751 unmarked graves at the site of the former Marieval Indian Residential School in Cowessess First Nation (Anishinaabe, in this instance the exonym for which is Saulteaux, and partially Néhiyaw; Saskatchewan), also in June of 2021. For that matter, as this book was going to press, several reports of suspected unmarked graves at the sites of former residential schools continued to emerge.[93]

While the PAOC's response to these tragic disclosures was appropriate and timely, the events themselves precipitated much soul-searching within the PAOC's ranks. Stephen Kennedy, former editor of *Testimony* from 2007 to 2018, reflected as follows:

> I've been reading the stories of unmarked graves, burial sites that hold the stories of thousands of Indigenous children taken from their parents, never to be seen again. I've been listening, as I hope you have, to the sound of great mourning rising from Indigenous communities. I've been trying, as I hope you have, to imagine the unimaginable – the horrible pain of not knowing what really happened to your child or where their body is. With each new uncovering, the horror grows. This is part of our story as a nation. We have denied it for too long. We *must* think about it. We *must* allow it to cast its shadow on our daily lives and affect the way we live from now on.[94]

Likewise APM, which as of 2021 had been rebranded First Nations Ministries, responded to these events, stating:

> Our heart breaks for our First Nations, Métis and Inuit peoples. As former residential schools are searched, these communities grieve for stolen lives. In this difficult moment, we want to reaffirm our support for our Indigenous First Nations pastors, churches and communities. Please keep them in your prayers.[95]

This time of reflection exposed a general sense of discontent within the PAOC with the fact that at times it appears little action has been taken toward reconciliation since 2012, and that conversation about the 2012 apology really only resurfaces when injustices endured by Indigenous people are raised in the media (and might otherwise be forgotten or at least overlooked). This trend presents some parallels to national-level conversations taking place regarding how few of the TRC's *Calls to Action* have been acted upon (even in light of the recent papal apology).

While it is entirely appropriate for the PAOC to refer to the 2012 apology when realities affecting Indigenous communities and individuals become particularly pronounced, these should not be the only times the apology is invoked. As stated earlier in this chapter, reconciliation must be everyday and ongoing. If working toward reconciliation only happens when the news headlines demand it, then these attempts "can actually cause more harm than healing." Clearly the work of reconciliation has not been accomplished, and may not be accomplished within this generation. Still, effort towards such a goal must not cease. In the words of sociologist Adam Stewart:

> Like Christian social ethics in general, reconciliation is open, ongoing, and un-ended. Like the operation of God's grace in our lives and in the world, reconciliation is a continuous work of dynamic transimmanent cooperation that requires us to be receptive and responsive to where the Holy Spirit is calling us to go, to what the Holy Spirit is calling us to do, to who the Holy Spirit is calling us to be.[96]

One might apply the same rubric to the PAOC and its churches as they address and wrestle with their own legacies respective to the Canadian nation-building project. The recovery of the unmarked graves and the associated despair, trauma, and violence those graves represent both border on the unthinkable. Difficult though this chapter in Canadian public life has been, one outcome is the necessary effect of reorienting the popular opinion yet again back to realities affecting Indigenous people. This certainly can be said of the PAOC and its churches. In response to these findings, many churches acknowledged these events in a significant way. For the first time, hundreds of churches within the denomination designated days of reconciliation. Churches cancelled Canada Day celebrations in solidarity with many

Indigenous people desiring they do so. Some churches went on to commemorate the first National Day for Truth and Reconciliation on 30 September 2021.[97] James and Andrew Thunder (Anishininiwag; Sachigo Lake, Ontario) favourably concluded of these efforts:

> The journey toward reconciliation is a long road, but if we follow Christ's example and the guidance of the Holy Spirit, we can glorify God in our response to the brokenness we see in the world.[98]

Likewise commenting on the road to reconciliation, Collado stated:

> [H]ow you get somewhere is as crucial as where you are going. The journey is just as important as the destination ... Jesus Christ called us to something more when He declared in John 13:3, "By this everyone will know that you are my disciples, if you love one another."[99]

Indeed, perhaps the above-described conciliatory actions are an indication of measurable steps finally being taken on the long road toward reconciliation. Perhaps the PAOC's 2012 apology is in fact alive and well. Perhaps this is evidence at last of non-Indigenous PAOC leadership, clergy, and laity all taking seriously their commitment to remain in right relationship with the Indigenous people also represented within those ranks. On an optimistic note, one might hope that even if the news cycle shifts away from these realities, and if the inclination of some within the PAOC might be to follow suit, the proponents of reconciliation will not allow the journey along the road to reconciliation to cease.

CONCLUSION

Breaking New Ground

Indigenous Pentecostalism in the Twenty-First Century and Its Significance for the Majority World

It has taken some time for scholars of pentecostalism [*sic*] to adjust to a narrative that is not centered in the Global North, but many are now paying attention to the indigenization and contextualization of pentecostalism in non-Western contexts. While this has given rise to a growing body of literature on pentecostalism in the Majority World, it remains the case that comparatively little attention is paid to the relationship between pentecostals and indigenous peoples in Western post-colonial contexts – such as the United States, Canada, Australia and New Zealand. This is of considerable concern given the unavoidable reality that it is often these people groups who are profoundly affected by issues of social concern and change. It is also these people who are often open to, and who offer resources for, indigenizing Pentecostal spirituality.

Michael J. Frost, Alphacruxis College, Auckland[1]

As a British-born, Quebec-raised, Ontario-trained Canadian, with a tinge of Norwegian blood, I longed to be part of a bigger story.

Julia Garratt, PAOC Global Worker[2]

This monograph has focussed on an aspect of the history of Pentecostal mission among Indigenous people. This crucial yet heretofore untold chapter of religious history in Canada has highlighted several developments. It has shown that the predominantly Euro-Canadian Pentecostal Assemblies of Canada (PAOC) missionaries perceived themselves to be proponents of Indigenous autonomy, yet their cultural baggage and predisposition to install Euro-Canadian missionaries often impeded them from fully implementing the indigenous principle. Euro-Canadian Pentecostal missionaries' shortcomings lay not in attracting adherents, which they did, but in failing to trust Indigenous ministers as leaders and subsequently withdrawing as promised. Aboriginal Pentecostal Ministries (APM) emerged from the dissolved Northland Mission (NLM), but only through Indigenous ministers' efforts and determination, rather than from what should have been a proactive and empowering transfer of leadership. When at last the indigenous principle succeeded, it was in spite of and not because of the NLM's methods, notwithstanding the missionaries' intentions otherwise.

The PAOC sought to provide the gospel message unhindered by Euro-Canadian cultural vestiges; they were unsuccessful. The PAOC declared they were training Indigenous acolytes to become clergy, but instead created a ministerial training system that became self-serving, neglecting its obligation to train Indigenous leaders and hand over the ministry to them swiftly. Further, as the third chapter of this monograph demonstrated, the method of procuring ministerial credentials for Indigenous ministers was extremely complicated. Even so, many Indigenous ministry trainees successfully navigated this convoluted educational system. When the denomination finally permitted Indigenous ministers to lead their own ministries, it unloaded on its heirs the resource shortfalls from the Euro-Canadian-dominated era. Despite these denominational shortcomings, many Indigenous Pentecostals desired to remain within the PAOC, demonstrating greater commitment to the indigenous principle than did their Euro-Canadian counterparts.

Pentecostalism's historic success among Indigenous people likely had more to do with Indigenous Pentecostals' agency and determination than Euro-Canadian leadership's intentions. Within the NLM's history, Indigenous ministry hopefuls frequently went overlooked by denominational leaders. With both its finances and its public relations, the PAOC often prioritized filling the needs of Euro-Canadian missionaries over Indigenous ministers. Obtaining their rightful place in leadership required constant persistence and sacrifice on the part of the NLM's Indigenous ministers. Those Indigenous leaders who successfully navigated this process often did so independently, and without the PAOC leadership's full monetary and moral support.

PAOC leadership appeared to be more concerned about an Indigenous minister's purported inability to adapt culturally from one First Nations territory to another than they were for his or her financial wellbeing. Even so, these Indigenous ministers in some cases forfeited government entitlements when they left their own territories to minister in others. Some sacrificed established careers and desirable housing in order to relocate in pursuit of their vocation.[3] Indigenous ministers remained faithful, and persisted, overcoming both denominational prejudice and economic hardship. Having endured these difficulties, Indigenous Pentecostals possibly are poised to become even more effective evangelists than some of their Euro-Canadian missionary predecessors.

Yet into the twenty-first century, the movement's challenges persist. In the final analysis, the PAOC, its history of missionary engagement with Indigenous people, the Indigenous ministers who currently fill the PAOC's ranks (as well as those who have moved on), the PAOC's decreasing number of Indigenous churches, and the seeming shortage of Indigenous ministers poised to assume ministerial leadership, all present the historian with some thoughts for reflection. Perhaps it is most apt to conclude with the words of Angela Tarango, who posited:

> If the core of the indigenous principle is that Christianity has to be realized within the culture of those who are missionized, and if Pentecostalism specifically wants to move beyond the mistakes committed by the Christians who conquered the New World as well as their own problematic history regarding race, then … Pentecostalism can be pushed forward to address the issues of Christian colonization and racism; it can never be detached from that history, because that is a part of its history, yet it can challenge the past and think about what it means to construct a pentecostal [*sic*] identity that accepts all people of all races and backgrounds. It is time for Pentecostalism to reckon with what it really means to be an indigenous person. It is time for the indigenous principle to become truly indigenous.[4]

As it relates to the Indigenous Pentecostal movement in Canada, it would appear that reflection on these very themes remains ongoing. Articulating Pentecostalism's appeal, Levi Samson Beardy (Anishinini; Bearskin Lake, Ontario) explained his embrace of its mission thus:

> It was through the PAOC that Christ chose to minister to our family … It seemed to be the Spirit of God … [that] appeared. So that was the difference … The key is; how can we promote Christ without trying to be converting agents? But to be facilitators for God's Spirit to move within the lives of people. The people become Christians through Christ, without me trying to have to convince them.[5]

Beardy's concluding thoughts point to one of the ways Pentecostalism has indigenized. Beardy's observations also indicate that perhaps the truest fulfilment of the indigenous principle is not only for Indigenous adherents and ministers to lead their own ministries. Perhaps it comes to fruition when Indigenous Pentecostals make the indigenous principle Indigenous as they continually adopt, adapt, and carry Pentecostalism throughout Canada and beyond.[6] Indeed it is on that final point that the historian might ask the question: what significance does Indigenous Pentecostalism have for the rest of the world? Reminiscent of the words of PAOC global worker Julia Garratt transcribed in this conclusion's opening epigraph, there is potential for their experience to contribute to the larger, global story.

THE SIGNIFICANCE OF INDIGENOUS PENTECOSTALISM FOR THE MAJORITY WORLD

The Indigenous Pentecostal movement possessed international ambitions from its inception. Native American participants and leaders within the Holiness and Pentecostal revivals of the early twentieth century frequently crossed borders. In so doing they used speaking in tongues to traverse barriers and forge transnational networks.[7] By the 1960s, on the Mohawk Nation at Akwesasne (Kanien'kehá:ka; straddling the borders of Ontario, Quebec, and New York State) *Testimony* editor Earl Kulbeck recorded, "Indians exercise their treaty rights of going back and forth across the international boundary."[8] Additionally, Indigenous Pentecostals have risen to prominence internationally, and in the United States especially, where Pentecostalism maintains "a strong presence … particularly among the Plains, Basin, and Southwest Indigenous peoples."[9] Andrew Maracle (Kanien'kehá:ka; Six Nations of the Grand River, Ontario) was an early Indigenous Pentecostal pioneer. In 1914, while Maracle was an infant, his mother subscribed to Pentecostalism under the ministry of NLM founding director John Spillenaar's father, Rienhardt Spillenaar. In 1935, Maracle helped build the Pentecostal Church at Tyendinaga Mohawk Territory (Kanien'kehá:ka, Ontario). Maracle later rose to prominence as an evangelist and minister within the Assemblies of God USA (AG USA).[10]

Rodger Cree (Kanien'kehá:ka; Kanesatake, Quebec), during the 1950s, was the NLM's first Indigenous minister. Like Maracle, Cree went on to become very influential within the AG USA. Cree established and pastored several churches, served on the board of the American Indian College, and worked on the translation team for the Mohawk Bible Project. In 1997, the AG USA General Council elected Cree to the General Presbytery (composed of three hundred elected representatives acting as the policy-making body of the AG USA between sessions of the General Council), one of three Indigenous ministers to earn this distinction. Another of the three was Andrew Maracle's nephew, John E. Maracle (Kanien'kehá:ka; Tyendinaga Mohawk Territory, Ontario). In 2007, the AG USA General Council elected John Maracle to the Executive Presbytery (composed of twenty elected members who function as the AG USA's board of directors, equivalent to the PAOC's General Executive). John Maracle, whom Angela Tarango listed among the "Native evangelists ... to break new ground regarding the indigenous principle ... and ... the vanguard of early Native leadership," became the first Indigenous member of this exclusive governing board. Joseph J. Saggio described the event as "a historic first ... elevating Native Christian concerns and giving them a vote at the denominational level."[11]

The NLM's Indigenous ministers carried the missionary mandate introduced by Euro-Canadian Pentecostals. However, this was not merely a message copied verbatim from the missionaries. The Indigenous ministers took full ownership of the Pentecostal message as they spread it among their own people, forming the APM. A central tenant of Classical Pentecostal missiology is its adherence to an "impulse to spread the fire of Spirit Baptism all over the world."[12] Indeed, Pentecostalism among Indigenous people maintains the momentum and evangelistic impulse of its missionary heritage. Within the APM, this can be seen in the continuation of an Indigenous board and leadership. On the global Pentecostal stage, these theological tenets contribute to practices within other post-colonial contexts, catalyzing further expansion of a Pentecostal expression.

It is not surprising, then, that many Indigenous Pentecostal churches operated missions, contributing to the international Pentecostal movement. For instance, in 1995 the pastor from the NLM church in Sioux Lookout reported:

> The past two years I have had the opportunity to take our youth from Sioux Lookout to Mexico and minister in Native churches right across the U.S.A. They've covered over 18,000 kms down many bumpy roads, and ministered in churches, jails and even in the streets ... In August of this year we are planning to travel across the central provinces (prairies) and western Canada (BC), doing drama and music and preaching in our Native churches. We plan to hold services in Saskatoon, Prince George, Prince Rupert and the Queen Charlotte Islands [Haida Gwaii]! The youth have ministered in the north and in Quebec, but now we are breaking new ground as we head out west![13]

By the mid-1990s, the PAOC's National Native Ministries had engaged in transnational relationship with similar ministries. In 1996, then–PAOC National Native Ministries Coordinator James Kallappa (Kwih-dich-chuh-aht; Neah Bay, Washington) combined the PAOC National Native Leadership Council with the AG USA's Convocation of Christian Indian Leaders' meeting in Minneapolis, Minnesota. Similar Canadian-US joint meetings of Indigenous Pentecostal ministries continued throughout the late 1990s.[14]

Pentecostalism continues to develop a uniquely prominent role in Indigenous culture nationally and internationally. As can be seen, Indigenous Pentecostalism in Canada frequently overlaps with its counterpart in the United States. What is more, there are similarities between Indigenous Pentecostalism in North America and Aboriginal Pentecostalism in Australia, presenting scholars with points of comparison.[15] It should not come as a surprise, for example, that Aboriginal Pentecostals in what is now Australia, similar to their Indigenous Pentecostal counterparts in what is now Canada, have experienced some degree of controversy and struggle relating to contextualization of traditional ways into Pentecostal practice.[16]

One might reflect, however, that as significant as Canadian Pentecostalism's contribution has been, the global Pentecostal movement is exponentially larger beyond this country's shores. In fact, the majority of Pentecostals live outside of Australia, Canada, and the

United States, and their rapidly emerging churches are largely indigenous.[17] The expansive growth of indigenous Pentecostal movements in the Majority World has been so great that Pentecostalism is poised to "surpass Catholicism as 'the most predominant form of Christianity in the 21st century.'"[18] The exponential growth of global Pentecostalism provokes the historian to ask not just what Canada's role is in global Pentecostalism, but more specifically: what is the significance of Indigenous Pentecostalism as it relates to the contemporaneous global movement? Accordingly, the history of Indigenous Pentecostalism is not exclusively important within Canada. It has bearing on the global Pentecostal movement generally, and in the Majority World in particular, where Pentecostal expression shares many parallels with Indigenous Pentecostalism.

For example, Joseph Jolly (Eeyou; Waskaganish, Quebec; raised in Moose Factory, Ontario) writes of Indigenous missionaries that had "opportunity to share the gospel message in other countries like China, Philippines, Russia, New Zealand, Australia, Mongolia, South Africa, and even in Israel where Christ was born."[19] Likewise Indigenous Pentecostals frequently recount their Holy Land tours, not a missionary activity, but certainly evidence of the movement's international reach. Reggie Neeposh (Eeyou; Oujé-Bougoumou First Nation, Quebec) explained, "my trip to Israel ... had a special impact on my life – spiritually, physically, emotionally and mentally ... Today when I read the Bible, it comes alive to me because this trip was very inspiring and uplifted my faith."[20]

Simultaneously, Indigenous Pentecostalism resembles global Pentecostal movements throughout the Majority World.[21] Global Pentecostalism and Indigenous Pentecostalism resemble one another spiritually as they both practise oral liturgy, narrative theology and witness, community engagement in worship, dreams and visions, and a unique understanding of the metaphysical as demonstrated in healing through prayer.[22] The resemblance moves from the spiritual to the practical. For example, Indigenous communities in Canada live under the legacy of colonialism, and increasingly find their lives affected by the whims of economic expansion, while their spiritual priorities are often overlooked. Where land and place are sacred subjects to Indigenous cultures, they often represent largely economic and political opportunities to governments and corporations. Similar global economic trends affect indigenous populations elsewhere around the world, where Pentecostalism finds an agreeable audience. It is there – at the place of very oppressive social conditions of economic deprivation – where indigenous Pentecostal leaders are encouraged to establish a "church of the people." These individuals discover an indigenous harmony in the Pentecostal message, as well as the thrust toward the autonomy that it offers.[23] Or, as in the words of professor of Native American Studies Waziyatawin Angela Wilson (Dakota; Virginia, Minnesota):

> With 300 million Indigenous peoples worldwide with common histories of struggle against colonialism and neocolonialism, we have tremendous potential to transform the world. Sharing our stories and linking our voices is one step in achieving a different vision for the world.[24]

Although Indigenous Pentecostals in what is now Canada live in an industrialized, developed country, the realities of reserve life actually display more parallels to the developing, post-colonial Majority World.[25] Increasingly the academy refers to such Pentecostals who engage issues of poverty, inequality, and ecology as "progressive Pentecostals," and Indigenous Pentecostals fall firmly in this category.[26]

Indigenous Pentecostalism and Global Pentecostalism both respond to the social issues that surround their communities of adherents. The experientiality of Pentecostalism allows it to localize both within the Indigenous context in Canada and in many places throughout the Majority World. These contexts facilitate Pentecostal advancement and resemble one another because in both locales, religious traditions prioritize less what an individual believes about the supernatural than they do how the supernatural is experienced in practical and material ways in the world. In so doing, both Indigenous Pentecostalism and Global Pentecostalism uphold traditional ontologies within their respective contexts.[27] There the overlapping dimensions of economics, ethnicity, migration, religion, and politics lend relevance and popularity to Pentecostalism.[28] In its spiritual determination and resourcefulness, the progressive Indigenous Pentecostal movement in Canada mirrors these movements around the world. Although the situations are different, domestic Indigenous socio-economic realities are more similar to those found among the developing countries of the Majority World than they are to much of the rest of the settler-occupied regions of Canada.

Accordingly, Indigenous Pentecostalism reaches far beyond the North American continent. Practical examples are apparent in the accounts of Indigenous Pentecostals such as Absalom Beardy (Anishinini; Bearskin Lake, Ontario, father of Levi Samson Beardy), who on multiple occasions itinerated in both India and the Caribbean, "taking interpreters with him to minister."[29] By 2018, the PAOC Church in Mistissini Cree Nation (Eeyou), Quebec, was regularly sending mission teams and resources to Liberia. *Testimony* reported:

> Helen Petawabano and Charlotte Blacksmith, left the beautiful North and travelled thousands of miles … They ministered in deaf schools, blind schools, nursery schools, and all the way up to high school. They sang, they prayed, they shared, they rejoiced, they laughed, and they loved the beautiful people where God had called them to go … They came from a cool, fresh climate and went to a place with extremely high humidity … One of the local pastors in Liberia said, "My heart is so full when I see our children coming to classes, happy."[30]

A similarly transnational example of Indigenous Pentecostalism's international reach is that of Clarence Dill. Dill, a Caribbean-Canadian evangelist who lived in Ontario before relocating to Alberta, itinerates internationally among Pentecostals in the Majority World, relaying faith stories to his audiences about the "powerful meetings" he shares with Indigenous Pentecostals in Canada's north. "Through these representations, local people are placed as exemplars in a global Christian communion, 'lifting up' church members who see their local ritual life as having larger salience."[31]

American anthropologist Kimberly Jenkins Marshall described Indigenous Pentecostalism's correlation and contribution to the Majority World as follows:

> [I]ndigenous … Pentecostals are not an isolated religious community but are (and have always been) socially connected to a broad range of actors: Native, non-Native … and international. Furthermore, they are socially connected as among equals: they receive visiting evangelists as guests … but they also travel as visiting evangelists across Indian country … and abroad … see[ing] themselves as a missionizing (not missionized) people …

> Rather than seeing themselves as victims of the structural violence of settler-colonialism … [they] see themselves as distinct but equal partners in a global project.[32]

Marshall continued:

> Pentecostalism's spirit-driven theology … has allowed indigenous actors to take control of the faith quite rapidly, fueling its exponential growth. But the influx of spirit-driven preachers has also altered the missionary dynamic, transforming indigenous actors into evangelists for a faith they no longer view as foreign … This change in dynamic is absolutely crucial to understanding the spread of global Pentecostalism.[33]

Elsewhere, Marshall describes how Indigenous Pentecostal ministers "function as fully participating members in the evangelical networks that contribute to growing … Pentecostalism in Native North America and beyond."[34]

In carving out their place within the global Pentecostal movement, Indigenous Pentecostal ministers have forged networks and relationships with similarly minded global Pentecostal evangelists and leaders. These networks have given rise to transnational exchanges and forums of ministry methods and ideas. Within this framework, these Indigenous Pentecostals have accepted the challenge and task of spreading their message to "the nations."[35] These missions and meetings demonstrate the remarkable cultural and religious richness Indigenous Pentecostalism offers to the Majority World. Indigenous Pentecostals have developed a tradition that is unique to their culture and region, while also connected to the broader national and international Pentecostal community. This allows Indigenous Pentecostals from what is now Canada to employ their beliefs as a conduit between cultures.[36]

In an increasingly globalized religious economy, Indigenous Pentecostalism serves as a means by which adherents understand and experience a rapidly changing and transnational world.[37] Accordingly, the key figures who pressured the ethnocentric NLM to develop into the autonomous APM and those who continue to lead Indigenous Pentecostal ministries in Canada have something notable to say to these different yet related global Pentecostal perspectives.[38] The history of Indigenous Pentecostals in Canada thus provides Western-eyed onlookers with a lens other than their own through which to view Pentecostalism globally. As such, the story of Indigenous Pentecostalism, its successes, challenges, and activism, all have bearing on the global dissemination of a progressive Pentecostalism that offers incredible relevance to those on the margins of society throughout the world today, whereby "indigenous Christianity is a barometer for global Christianity in general."[39] Consequently, it is reasonable to conclude that while Indigenous Pentecostalism resembles Majority World Pentecostalism, in the twenty-first century, it maintains the potential to influence the global movement in unique and profound ways.[40] Indeed perhaps it is there that Indigenous Pentecostalism continues to carry out the application and fruition of the indigenous principle, and where the indigenous principle becomes Indigenous.

INDIGENOUS AND PENTECOSTAL

While much has been achieved by Indigenous ministers within the PAOC, there remains an accomplishment yet unattained. Unlike the AG USA, at the time of writing, the PAOC has yet to appoint Indigenous ministers to its most senior positions. There is a degree of irony in the fact that within the AG USA, several of its most predominant Indigenous leaders (Andrew Maracle, Rodger Cree, and John Maracle) originate from what is now Canada, whereas Indigenous Pentecostal leaders are unrepresented on the PAOC's General Executive.[41] The General Executive is one of the PAOC's most influential bodies, second only to the floor of the General Conference. The truest fulfilment of the indigenous principle within the PAOC would be the installation of Indigenous leaders not only within Indigenous ministries, but also at the highest levels of PAOC leadership.

This is not a new observation. As early as the mid-1990s one Indigenous Pentecostal elder recounted the striking absence of Indigenous representation within PAOC denominational leadership. He recalled of a PAOC conference from the period:

> I was just astounded that we don't have any Indian people, Inuit, or Metis people being involved in a setting of that nature ... The responsibility again must lie with the Indian people to save the PAOC. These are the things that we can be responsible for. We are the best ones to handle it and we will do it.[42]

Still, Indigenous Pentecostals are not the only group underrepresented on the General Executive, which, although gradually diversifying, has often been nearly homogeneous along ethnic, gender, and linguistic lines.[43]

Whether in terms of the indigenous principle or simply ecclesial best practices, until very recently PAOC leadership has tended to resist contemporary cultural and demographic trends, as was the case throughout the NLM's history. The PAOC's denominational leadership might otherwise mirror the ever-increasing cultural, ethnic, linguistic, and gender diversity of its local churches. Should there be an absence of such diversity among leadership, an unfortunate fracturing may be the result. This is not a criticism directed toward the General Executive nor the PAOC's executive leadership. To be sure, great strides have been made under the leadership and direction of David Wells. Further, ministers are elected to the General Executive by PAOC clergy. As such, it is the PAOC clergy's responsibility not only to identify this gap, but to respond to it at all levels: local church, district, and national. Doing so will require the PAOC to consider the breadth of perspectives that make up its constituency, and to allow these voices to speak to the PAOC's current context. Michael J. Frost wrote,

> given the importance of indigenization and the centrality of experience to Pentecostal spirituality, indigenous pentecostal experiences and voices should contribute not only to sociological or anthropological analyses, but to the pentecostal *theological* conversation.[44]

In listening to and integrating the diverse voices that fill its ranks at present, the PAOC may learn to contribute to a better future.

As this monograph has demonstrated, decisions made by PAOC leaders, including the missionaries who operated the Northland Mission, contributed to the incomplete transfer of the NLM to Indigenous control, resulting in the mission's ultimate dissolution before its rebirth as the APM. Among the factors that led to this disappointing outcome was a lack of confidence in the emerging Indigenous leadership, demonstrated in such areas as succession planning for leadership, resource management, and empowering candidates for ministry. While this was the case historically, the hope for the next century is that the PAOC may learn from past mistakes.

Responding to the disparity will at the very least require a renegotiation of relationships.[45] Speaking about the broader church's interactions with Indigenous people, Kaitlin B. Curtice (Neshnabé, the exonym for which is Potawatomi; Shawnee, Oklahoma) states: "The important aspect of this relationship is that it is a partnership, a space in which listening really happens, a space in which Indigenous people ... should be heard."[46] As these relationships are redefined, Indigenous Pentecostals indeed may well be poised to lead the necessary diversification and rejuvenation of the PAOC's higher leadership strata. Or, as Benjamin Jacuk (Dena'ina and Sugpiaq; Anchorage, Alaska) put it: "If we take the message of Pentecost seriously, we need to understand and respect the worship and knowledge about God, Native Americans possess."[47] Robert Burkinshaw believes Majority World Pentecostal immigrants to Canada helped PAOC leadership begin to appreciate and embrace Indigenous Pentecostals' input.[48] Similarly, it is possible Indigenous Pentecostals may return the favour and continue to help the PAOC to appreciate the necessity of leadership diversity.[49]

The PAOC's leadership fell short of their attempts to autonomize the denomination's domestic mission during the NLM's life. Nevertheless, NLM Indigenous ministers persevered and withstood, giving birth to their own Aboriginal Pentecostal Ministries. They demonstrated creative and resourceful ways of being part of the larger body, the PAOC, even when they were not always assured of being welcomed for doing so. Ultimately it was their faithfulness and persistence, regardless of their reception, that ensured their position.[50] By virtue of their theology, these ministers made it clear that being Indigenous did not compromise their being Pentecostal, and that being Pentecostal did not compromise their being Indigenous. In so doing, they fought for the indigenous principle. Far from being victims, these leaders forged their identity and cemented their legacy – Indigenous and Pentecostal.

Notes

ACKNOWLEDGMENTS

1 Clatterbuck, "Healing Hills and Sacred Songs," 252.

INTRODUCTION

1 PAOC, 1932, "PAOC General Constitution," PAOC Archives, 48.
2 Barnsley, "National Chief's Religion Cause for Discussion," 2; MacKinnon, "Natives Turn Up Heat"; "Aboriginal Canadians: Matthew Coon Come," *CBC News*, 2 July 2004, https://www.cbc.ca/news2/background/aboriginals/cooncome_interview.html.
3 MacKinnon, "Natives Turn Up Heat."
4 Ibid.
5 Lloyd Mackey, "A Turn in the Road for the Coon Comes," *Christianity.ca: Canada's Christian Library Online*, August 2003, https://www.christianity.ca/page.aspx?pid=10066; Bate, "Evangelical Moonlighting," 5.
6 "Native Christians Have High Hopes for Coon Come Leadership," *Christian Week*, 15 August 2000, https://www.christianweek.org/native-christians-have-high-hopes-for-coon-come-leadership.
7 Barnsley, "National Chief's Religion Cause for Discussion," 2; Crossette, "Indian Chief Miffs Canada."
8 Burkinshaw, "Native Pentecostalism in British Columbia" (presentation paper), 1.
9 Tarango, *Choosing the Jesus Way*, 20.
10 Beninger, "Does the Church Really Care?," 23.
11 Grant, *Moon of Wintertime*, 213; Gibson, "Native Theological Training," 3, 160, Gibson quoting 1991 Statistics Canada census data;

Kirmayer, Tait, and Simpson, "The Mental Health of Aboriginal Peoples in Canada," 23; Deloria, "Vision and Community," 107.

12 Westman, "Pentecostalism among Canadian Aboriginal People," 85–6; Bramadat and Seljak, "Conclusion," 427–9.

13 Gibson, "Native Theological Training," 161, Gibson citing Statistics Canada data.

14 Wilkinson, "Canadian Pentecostalism," 112. There were approximately 372,960 Canadian Pentecostals in 2001. Indigenous people of all religions and no religion account for four per cent of the general population. Westman, "Understanding Cree Religious Discourse," 250–1; Statistics Canada, "2011 National Household Survey: Data Tables," accessed 2 February 2022, https://www12.statcan.gc.ca/nhs-enm/2011/dp-pd/dt-td/Rp-eng.cfm?LANG=E&APATH=3&DETAIL=0&DIM=0&FL=A&FREE=0&GC=0&GID=0&GK=0&GRP=1&PID=107554&PRID=0&PTYPE=105277&S=0&SHOWALL=0&SUB=0&Temporal=2013&THEME=95&VID=0&VNAMEE=&VNAMEF=; Gibson, "Native Theological Training," 21. By way of comparison, in 2006 the total number of Native American adherents within the Assemblies of God USA (AG USA, the PAOC's equivalent and collegial denomination based in the United States) was 40,290, comprising 1.4 per cent of the AG USA's total 2,836,174 adherents. Saggio, "Toward an Indigenous Model of Native American Ministry," 86; Fletcher and Denham, "Moving Towards Healing," 112.

15 Gibson, "Native Theological Training," 11.

16 Burkinshaw, "Native Pentecostalism in British Columbia" (presentation paper), 1; Hageman, "Seven Questions for Reggie Neeposh," 25.

17 McCleary, "An Ethnohistory of Pentecostalism," 118; Westman, "Pentecostalism among Canadian Aboriginal People," 87; Beninger, "The Anglican Church of Canada," 49–51; Preston, "Twentieth-Century Transformations," 216; Guenther, "Ethnicity and Evangelical Protestants in Canada," 391.

18 Guenther, "Ethnicity and Evangelical Protestants in Canada," 372; Tarango, *Choosing the Jesus Way*, 3.

19 Camps, Hoedemaker, Spindler, and Verstralen, "Introduction," 1–3.

20 Warner, "Flying Ambassadors of Goodwill," 3.

21 Grant, *Moon of Wintertime*, 201.

22 Miller, *Canadian Pentecostals*, 213.

23 Northland Mission, circa 1980s, "Preliminary Application for Admission: The Northland Ministries Bible School," PAOC Archives, 1.

24 Alistair Shearer, 26 August 1990, "Preliminary Report Outlining a Program Dealing with Native Offenders and Their Families," PAOC Archives, 1.

25 McClung, "'Try to Get People Saved,'" 31.
26 Whitt, "Developing a Pentecostal Missiology," 135.
27 McClung, "Try to Get People Saved," 32.
28 Miller, *Canadian Pentecostals*, 224.
29 Whitt, "Developing a Pentecostal Missiology," 190.
30 PAOC, 1932, "PAOC General Constitution," 48.
31 Miller, *Canadian Pentecostals*, 17.
32 Tarango, *Choosing the Jesus Way*, 5, 23.
33 Miller, *Canadian Pentecostals*, 224.
34 Whitt, "Developing a Pentecostal Missiology," 191.
35 Tarango, *Choosing the Jesus Way*, 22.
36 Ibid., 32; Whitt, "Developing a Pentecostal Missiology," 68.
37 Neylan, *The Heavens Are Changing*, 69.
38 Nkonge, "The Church Missionary Society's Burden," 23.
39 Whitt, "Developing a Pentecostal Missiology," 45.
40 Beninger, "Does the Church Really Care?," 224–5.
41 Allen, *Missionary Methods*, vii.
42 Kärkkäinen, "Mission in Pentecostal Theology," 8; Tarango, "The Land Is Always Stalking Us," 399.
43 Tarango, *Choosing the Jesus Way*, 35.
44 Neylan, *The Heavens Are Changing*, 70.
45 Beninger, "Does the Church Really Care?," 2–3.
46 Scott, "Cultivating Christians in Colonial Canadian Missions," 36.
47 Grant, *Moon of Wintertime*, 205. It should be noted that where Indigenous agency has occurred within Pentecostalism, it has appeared as a result of Indigenous resilience and in "a vital and creative impulse." Frost, *The Spirit, Indigenous Peoples and Social Change*, 6; Gibson, "Native Theological Training within Canadian Evangelicalism," 81.
48 Stackhouse, "The Protestant Experience," 229.
49 Consistent with Stackhouse's assessment, PAOC missionary Phoebe Spence wrote in 1926, "Our aim … is not to propagate Western civilization … neither [is our aim] to press our creeds upon the heathen." Whitt, "Developing a Pentecostal Missiology," 192–3.
50 LeBlanc continues, "Western use of eschatology is abundantly evident in its mission theology. It is this theology and its praxis that has created the framework for the brokenness in the relationship between Western Christianity and Indigenous peoples – including those who embrace Christian faith and life." LeBlanc, "Toward an Indigenous Eschatology," 234, 246.
51 Newberg, "Said's Orientalism and Pentecostal Views of Islam in Palestine," 197–8. Newburg identifies terms such as "heathen" in the

documentary record as indicating missionaries' colonial biases. This and terms like it were present within Pentecostal parlance of the period, thus intimating association with settler colonial priorities and values. Gibson, "Native Theological Training," 18. Certain missionary records reveal the PAOC's continuity with a settler colonial agenda in the attempt to recruit missionaries to Indigenous territories, such as the following: "Most Canadians are not more than two generations away from their pioneer ancestors, and pioneer blood flows in their veins … [Y]oung men and women will continue to … go to their Indian and Eskimo brothers … There's still room … for you." Brown, *Top of the World*, 183.

52 Tarango, *Choosing the Jesus Way*, 5, 147.

53 Dombrowski, *Against Culture*, 14–15, 154. The Holiness movement of the nineteenth century advocated a post-conversion experience called sanctification, requiring adherents to abstain from dancing, drinking, gambling, smoking, and other forms of entertainment deemed "worldly." Sanchez-Walsh, "Race, Ethnicity, and Gender," 266.

54 Cindy Stephen, "Neo-Pentecostalism Embraced by Cree Community," *Christian Week*, 15 December 2006, https://www.christianweek.org/neo-pentecostalism-embraced-by-cree-community.

55 Westman, "Pentecostalism and Indigenous Culture," 142–3.

56 Stephen, "Neo-Pentecostalism Embraced by Cree Community."

57 Tarango, *Choosing the Jesus Way*, 17, 150. Tarango refers to "an extensive history of Pentecostalism among Canadian first peoples," while lamenting a shortage of academic attention afforded this substantial movement.

58 Tarango, "Native American Christians," 330.

59 Clatterbuck, *Crow Jesus*, jacket description.

60 Any exposition on the history of Christian mission among Indigenous people in what is now Canada typically is a story of encounter. There are several possible outcomes to the tension persisting between adoption of Christianity versus the maintenance of Indigenous culture. Tolly Bradford and Chelsea Horton argue, "Christian missionaries of diverse denominations were deeply imbricated in efforts to alter the lifeways of Indigenous peoples in North America. Moreover, missionary outreach is ongoing in Indigenous Canada, as is the structural and symbolic violence of settler colonialism. At the same time, many Indigenous people continue to interpret and live Christianity in ways meaningful to them, just as others, and sometimes the same people, persist in the practice of specifically Indigenous forms of spirituality. Christianity … has proved a flexible, while always deeply freighted, site of colonial encounter and exchange." Bradford and Horton, "Introduction," 2–3.

61 Smith, *Native Americans and the Christian Right*, jacket description.
62 Whitt, "Developing a Pentecostal Missiology," 135.
63 Miller, *Canadian Pentecostals*, 417.
64 Hodges, *The Indigenous Church*, 7.
65 Tarango, *Choosing the Jesus Way*, 5, 147.
66 Hodges, *The Indigenous Church*, 5.
67 Tapper, *Canadian Pentecostals*, 129.
68 Petersen, "Changing Paradigms," 3.
69 Smith, "Introduction," xvi.
70 Milne, "Diyin God Bizaad," 386–7.
71 Smith, "Introduction," xvi.
72 Zikmund, "Introduction," 6.
73 Austin and Scott, "Introduction," 7. There is evidence of the desire for this sort of exchange. For instance, Pentecostal minister John Maracle (Kanien'kehá:ka; Tyendinaga Mohawk Territory, Ontario) wrote, "The Indian knows the white man's world, but the Indian world to the white man remains a mystery. Yet the Indian world offers so much. It offers Indian solutions to white man's problems. Both worlds are looking for answers, peace and truth that will only come one way – through Christ and God's word." John E. Maracle, Summer 1980, "Information Concerning American Indians to the Missions Committees," Assemblies of God Flower Pentecostal Heritage Center, 7.
74 Twiss, *Rescuing the Gospel from the Cowboys*, 31.
75 Bradford and Horton, "Introduction," 3.
76 Marshall, *Upward, Not Sunwise*, 4–5. Emphasis original.
77 Kovach, *Indigenous Methodologies*, 58; Westman, *Cree and Christian*, xxxi–xxxii.
78 Younging, *Elements of Indigenous Style*, 91.
79 Vowel, *Indigenous Writes*, 10.
80 Jolly, *Christ Is Building His Native Church*, 5.
81 Vowel, *Indigenous Writes*, 13.
82 Gibson, "The Politics of Representation of Other's Spirituality," 6.
83 King, *The Inconvenient Indian*, xii.
84 Dempster, Klaus, and Petersen, "General Introduction," xiv. Quoted from Dana L. Robert.
85 Wilkinson, "Canadian Pentecostalism," 113.
86 Wilson, "They Crossed the Red Sea, Didn't They?," 110–11; Robert, "From Missions to Mission to Beyond Missions," 152.
87 Westman, "Cree Pentecostalism," 396; Vilaça and Wright, "Introduction," 11.

CHAPTER ONE

1 Miller, *Skyscrapers Hide the Heavens*, 4th ed., 119–20.
2 Wilkinson, "Charles W. Chawner," 41.
3 von Rosen, "Three Generations of a Micmac Family Stories and Conversations," 49; Smith, *Sacred Feathers*, xxv–xxvi.
4 Marshall, "Navajo Reservation Camp Meeting a Great Success!," 96.
5 Stewart, *The New Canadian Pentecostals*, 23.
6 Stewart, "From Monogenesis to Polygenesis," 153; Miller, *Canadian Pentecostals*, 28.
7 Reidy, "Holy Ghost Tribe," 376.
8 McGee, *People of the Spirit*, Loc 1270 of 13816.
9 Miller, *Canadian Pentecostals*, 39.
10 Reidy, "Holy Ghost Tribe," 373, 377–9.
11 Stronstad, *The Charismatic Theology of St. Luke*, 68; Miller, *Canadian Pentecostals*, 31.
12 Porter, "Shaping the Missionary Identity," 5, 13, 49.
13 Stewart, "A Canadian Azusa?," 19.
14 Stewart, "From Monogenesis to Polygenesis," 157. Some of the Hebdens' other firsts included: 1) establishment of the first Pentecostal mission in Canada; 2) the first Canadian Pentecostal periodical; 3) the first Canadian Pentecostal camp meeting; 4) the first Canadian Pentecostal convention; and 5) sending the first Canadian Pentecostal missionary.
15 Stewart, "A Canadian Azusa?," 19, 23–4; Miller, *Canadian Pentecostals*, 41, 43.
16 Stewart, "A Canadian Azusa?," 24, 27.
17 Stewart, "From Monogenesis to Polygenesis," 158.
18 Early in the twentieth century, Chicago pastor William H. Durham visited the Azusa Street Mission, taking the Pentecostal practice back to his church. A.H. Argue, a Canadian Pentecostal pioneer from Manitoba, was an associate of Durham. Ease of access via train allowed the two ministers to have frequent interaction. Argue carried Durham's revival from the Windy City to Winnipeg. Wilkinson, *The Spirit Said Go*, 17.
19 Miller, *Canadian Pentecostals*, 35.
20 Ringer, "J. Roswell Flower," 15.
21 McGee, *People of the Spirit*, Locs 1924, 1930, 1943, 2012, 2021, 2030, 2038, 2053, 2061, 2105, 2113, 2127, 2089, 2338, 2343 of 13816.
22 Blumhofer, *The Assemblies of God*, 197–213. The world's earliest classical Pentecostal denomination materialized in 1909, when adherents in the United Kingdom successfully unified to form the Pentecostal Missionary

Union. There were attempts in both the United States and Canada to create equivalent, contemporaneous organizations, but these all came to nothing. McGee, *People of the Spirit*, Locs 1476, 1974 of 13816; Whitt, "Developing a Pentecostal Missiology," 68, 127; Miller, *Canadian Pentecostals*, 105–6, 113–14, 119.

23 Miller, *Canadian Pentecostals*, 58–9, 101, 115–20.

24 Whitt, "Developing a Pentecostal Missiology," 170.

25 Ibid., 130–1.

26 Wilkinson, *Canadian Pentecostalism*, 5; Wilkinson, *The Spirit Said Go*, 17; "District Offices," PAOC website, accessed April 2016, https://paoc.org/family/who-we-are/district-offices; "Fellowship Statistics," PAOC website, accessed April 2020, https://www.paoc.org/docs/default-source/fellowship-services-documents/fellowship-stats-2019-at-9-jan-2020.pdf.

27 Bebbington, "Evangelicalism in Its Settings," 365. Within Evangelicalism there is a movement known as neo-evangelicalism. For instance, the Evangelical Fellowship of Canada (EFC) is a *neo-evangelical* organization. The EFC is the Canadian equivalent of the United States–based National Association of Evangelicals (NAE). Similar founding principles guided both organizations. Rosell, *The Surprising Work of God*, 29; Kydd, "Canadian Pentecostalism," 297–9. The EFC, characterized by neo-evangelical tenets, initially existed only as a loosely organized network of denominations and congregations. Noll, *A History of Christianity in the United States and Canada*, describes the founding of the EFC as having been motivated by denominations such as the PAOC and the Christian Missionary Alliance collaborating to project a public voice equivalent to those of the Catholics and mainstream Protestants (448). Stackhouse, *Canadian Evangelicalism*, 165.

28 World Assemblies of God, "World Assemblies of God Fellowship: Participating Members," accessed August 2017, http://worldagfellowship.org/fellowship/countries.

29 Tapper, *Canadian Pentecostals*, 123–5.

30 Stewart, *The New Canadian Pentecostals*, 2.

31 Grant, *Moon of Wintertime*, 3, 6; Stonechild, "Recovering Ancient Spiritual Paths," 29.

32 Ibid., 9–10.

33 Lewis, *Creating Christian Indians*, 4; McPherson, "A Definition of Culture," 83.

34 Weaver, "Preface," ix–x, Weaver quoting Forbes.

35 LeBlanc, "Being Spiritual Before a Common Creator," 105.

36 Paper, "Aboriginals," 2.

37 Grant, *Moon of Wintertime*, 15, 22–5; Miller, *Skyscrapers Hide the Heavens*, 1st ed., 17–20.
38 Pearson, "Reading Rituals," 22.
39 Greer, "Towards a Comparative Study of Jesuit Missions and Indigenous Peoples," 26; Grant, *Moon of Wintertime*, 28, 31–4, 44, 53.
40 Paper, "Aboriginals," 3, 7. Paper posits that with the exception of Inuit and Northwest Coast nations, many Indigenous people in what is now Canada revered the traditions of: 1) tobacco and/or Sacred Pipe, 2) the Spirit Lodge (colloquially referred to as *sweating*); and 3) belief in ritual power, or *medicine*.
41 Grant, *Moon of Wintertime*, 38–9, 42, 55. Bruce Meyers (Chippewa-Cree; Rocky Boy's Reservation, Montana) is an Assemblies of God USA (AG USA) adherent and maintains that "praying to saints is one reason the Catholic church is more appealing … for many on the reservation since … the practice is roughly analogous to Indians praying to many spirits." Clatterbuck, "Sweet Grass Mass," 98.
42 Lefebvre, "The Francophone Roman Catholic Church," 108.
43 Fletcher, "Canadian Anglicanism and Ethnicity," 160.
44 Laugrand and Oosten, "Shamans and Missionaries," 168; Beninger, "Does the Church Really Care?," 15.
45 Macdonald, "Presbyterian and Reformed Christians and Ethnicity," 173–4.
46 Grant, *Moon of Wintertime*, 71–3, 81, 91; Penner, "The Ojibwe Renaissance," 76.
47 Smith, *Sacred Feathers*, 6.
48 Marshall, "Navajo Reservation Camp Meeting a Great Success!," 97.
49 Grant, *Moon of Wintertime*, 76–7, 87–90; Miller, *Skyscrapers Hide the Heavens*, 3rd ed., 126, 130; Penner, "The Ojibwe Renaissance," 77.
50 Grant, *Moon of Wintertime*, 92–5.
51 Carlson, *Home Is the Hunter*, 106.
52 Beninger, "Does the Church Really Care?," 225.
53 Whitt, "Developing a Pentecostal Missiology," 44–5.
54 Christie and Gauvreau, *Christian Churches and Their Peoples*, 115.
55 Grant, *Moon of Wintertime*, 109–11, 114–15, 191; Miller, *Skyscrapers Hide the Heavens*, 1st ed., 14; Ervin, *The Political and Ecclesiastical History*, 106; Garrett, *My Album of Memories*, 63.
56 Beninger, "Does the Church Really Care?," 15.
57 Bush, *Western Challenge*, 91.
58 Beninger, "Does the Church Really Care?," 44.
59 Miller, *Skyscrapers Hide the Heavens*, 1st ed., 100; Grant, *Moon of Wintertime*, 116–18, 174, 189.

60 Baldridge, "Reclaiming Our Histories," 85.

61 Weaver, "From I-Hermeneutics to We-Hermeneutics," 4, Weaver quoting George Tinker.

62 Beninger, "Does the Church Really Care?," 35–6; Marshall, "Navajo Reservation Camp Meeting a Great Success!," 98.

63 Paper, "Aboriginals," 5.

64 Whitehouse-Strong, "Everything Promised," 26; Lefebvre, "The Francophone Roman Catholic Church," 109. This is not to suggest that reserves should be abolished, but rather that the introduction of the reserves significantly altered Indigenous ways of life during the nineteenth century.

65 Truth and Reconciliation Commission of Canada, *Canada's Residential Schools*, 11.

66 Nelles, *A Little History of Canada*, 118–19.

67 Stonechild, *The Spiritual Seeker*, 40; Neylan, "Choose Your Flag," 207.

68 Bush, "The Presbyterian Church in Canada's Mission," 102; Stonechild, *The Knowledge Seeker*, 15.

69 Lewis, *Creating Christian Indians*, 24.

70 Fletcher, "Canadian Anglicanism and Ethnicity," 160–1.

71 Bush, *Western Challenge*, 103.

72 Hayes, *Anglicans in Canada*, 32, 35.

73 Stonechild, *The Knowledge Seeker*, 117; Bush, "The Presbyterian Church in Canada's Mission," 116, 118.

74 Hayes, *Anglicans in Canada*, 31; Beninger, "The Anglican Church of Canada," 4.

75 Carrington, *The Anglican Church in Canada*, 292–3.

76 McPherson, "A Definition of Culture," 90; Lewis, *Creating Christian Indians*, 100.

77 Lefebvre, "The Francophone Roman Catholic Church," 108; Miller, *Skyscrapers Hide the Heavens*, 3rd ed., 262–3; Beninger, "The Anglican Church of Canada," 1, 4; Paper, "Aboriginals," 5, 23–4.

78 Bush, *Western Challenge*, 12–13.

79 Kelm, *Colonizing Bodies*, 78; Beninger, "Does the Church Really Care?," 16.

80 Grant, *Moon of Wintertime*, 176–89. In 1902, there were one hundred Catholic, eighty-seven Anglican, forty-one Methodist, fourteen Presbyterian, and forty-one nondenominational schools. Miller, *Skyscrapers Hide the Heavens*, 1st ed., 101, 103, 106, 107–8, 112, 189; Miller, *Skyscrapers Hide the Heavens*, 3rd ed., 268; "Pope Says Genocide Took Place at Canada's Residential Schools," *CBC News*, 30 July 2022, https://www.cbc.ca/news/indigenous/pope-francis-residential-schools-genocide-1.6537203.

81 Beninger, "Does the Church Really Care?," 12, 225.
82 Hayes, *Anglicans in Canada*, 12–14.
83 Laugrand and Oosten, "Shamans and Missionaries," 170; Beninger, "The Anglican Church of Canada," 3; Hayes, *Anglicans in Canada*, 16, 30; Grant, *Moon of Wintertime*, 191–2.
84 Beninger, "Does the Church Really Care?," 130.
85 Miller, *Canadian Pentecostals*, 77, 132; Kulbeck, *What God Hath Wrought*, 141–2; Rudd, *When the Spirit Came Upon Them*, 57. Parts of this section appeared previously in Mix-Ross, "The PAOC and Indigenous Peoples," in *Picture This! Reflecting on 100 Years of the PAOC*, edited by David Wells (Mississauga, ON: PAOC, 2018). Used here with permission of the PAOC.
86 Frodsham, *With Signs Following*, 55–6.
87 Rudd, *When the Spirit Came Upon Them*, 114; Frodsham, *With Signs Following*, 56.
88 Gibson, "Two Histories," 8–9.
89 Annie Cressman, 1982, "Northland Mission Report," PAOC Archives, 10.
90 Miller, *Canadian Pentecostals*, 192.
91 McAlister, "The Bible Evidence," 2. This church in Kanesatake was Rodger Cree's (Kanien'kehá:ka, and to be introduced in ch. 2) home church. Kulbeck, "French Bible Institute Holds Graduation Exercises," 4; Dale and Alberta Cummins, 11 March 1977, "Northland Messenger," *Northland Mission Newsletter*, PAOC Archives, 1; DHMBC, 1 September 1988, "Home Missions Executive Committee Meeting Minutes," PAOC Archives, 1–8; Tarango, *Choosing the Jesus Way*, 13, 55, 172; Cree, "Board Reflections," 133–7.
92 Buntain, *The Pentecostal Testimony*, 1 November 1939, 5, 11; Earl N.O. Kulbeck, 28 April 1968, "Consultation on Indian Work; Ottawa, Canada," PAOC Archives, 2–3.
93 Reidy, "Holy Ghost Tribe," 379, 389.
94 Burkinshaw, "Native Pentecostalism in British Columbia," in Wilkinson, 158.
95 Kulbeck, *What God Hath Wrought*, 192.
96 Ruby and Brown, *John Slocum and the Indian Shaker Church*, 171, 175, 181.
97 Burkinshaw, "Native Pentecostalism in British Columbia," in Wilkinson, 143–4.
98 Miller, *Canadian Pentecostals*, 273.
99 Ibid., 214.
100 NNLC, 24 May 1991, "Seventh National Native Leadership Council," PAOC Archives, 1.

101 Atter, *"The Third Force"*, 97.
102 Wilkinson and Ambrose, *After the Revival*, 134.
103 Atter, *"The Third Force"*, 100.
104 Kulbeck, *What God Hath Wrought*, 192.
105 Ibid., 197; Kulbeck, "Consultation on Indian Work," 1. Some Sub-Arctic missionaries employed Dene language in their outreach; Morsch, *Rejoice*, 101; Brown, *Top of the World*, vi, 1, 7, 13, 49, 62–4; Wright, *SickKids*, 178. "Tulita was the long ago name that had been lost and now is found again." Kostelnik, *The White Girl*, 4; Martin, "A Framework," 1.
106 Brown, *Top of the World*, 16–17.
107 Ibid., 17, 21, 23, 36; Westman, *Cree and Christian*, 142; Morsch, *Rejoice*, 112.
108 Bates, "Piety in the American Plains," 208–9; Woodard, "A Light unto the Nations," 32.
109 Miller, *Canadian Pentecostals*, 312; Morsch, *Rejoice*, 103.
110 Miller, *Canadian Pentecostals*, 363; Martin, "A Framework," 1.
111 Westman, "Understanding Cree Religious Discourse," 166.
112 Woodard, "A Light unto the Nations," 32.
113 Grant, *Moon of Wintertime*, 168, 201–2.
114 Brown, *Top of the World*, 68–9, 71.
115 One of the earliest graduates was Burton Ahenakew (Nehiyaw; Ahtahkakoop First Nation, Saskatchewan), who went on to minister with the Sub-Arctic Mission in Hay River, NWT, in 1970. PAOC Saskatchewan District, 1990, "Central Pentecostal College Native Ministries Campus," PAOC Archives, 1; Miller, *Canadian Pentecostals*, 214; Argue, "Home Missions: Indian Fires Burn Brightly," 17.
116 Miller, *Canadian Pentecostals*, 214, 364; Jack Ozard, December 1984, "The Northland Mission Newsletter," PAOC Archives, 1.
117 CPBC, 1 May 1980, "Press Release: First Treaty Indian Graduates from College," PAOC Archives, 1.
118 Northland Bible College, 1993, "Northland Ministries Bible College Graduation 1993," PAOC Archives, 3; PAOC District Superintendents and District Native Ministries Directors, 27 May 1995, "Minutes of the District Superintendents and District Native Ministries Directors meeting," PAOC Archives, 3.
119 Jolly, *Christ Is Building His Native Church*, 88.
120 Miller, *Canadian Pentecostals*, 213.
121 Ibid., 369.
122 Enoch Hall, December 1989, "Native Pentecostal Bible College," PAOC Archives, 1.

123 Hall, "Native Pentecostal Bible College," 6–7.

124 Aldred, LeBlanc, and Jacobs, "Thoughts on Forgiveness," 4; Wilkinson, "Public Acts of Forgiveness," 193.

125 Atter, "*The Third Force*", 259.

126 Carrington, *The Anglican Church in Canada*, 293; Fletcher, "Canadian Anglicanism and Ethnicity," 160.

127 Whitt, "Developing a Pentecostal Missiology," 42; Miller, *Skyscrapers Hide the Heavens*, 3rd ed., 128–30; Neylan, *The Heavens Are Changing*, 23.

128 Preston, "Twentieth-Century Transformations," 213.

129 Grant, *Moon of Wintertime*, 201–2, 205, 213. Grant added: "alienation of many Indians from the traditional churches has been an inevitable result ... expressed in varied ways ... Disillusionment with conventional missions has ... been a significant factor in the spread of Pentecostalism ... that allow[s] more outlets for native initiative."

130 Westman, "Understanding Cree Religious Discourse," 17.

131 Grant, *Moon of Wintertime*, 168.

132 Whitt, "Developing a Pentecostal Missiology," 3. Wilkinson's assessment differs, arguing that the Canadian Pentecostal missionary impulse was in line with that of the longer-established churches. He indirectly rebuts Grant's claim that Canadian Pentecostal missionaries avoided the prevailing missiological trend of trying to assimilate, noting that Pentecostal rhetoric was not as explicit but still sought acculturation. Wilkinson, "Chawner and the Missionary Impulse," 41. Or as American anthropologist Kimberly Jenkins Marshall put it, what Pentecostals "lack in colonial history they make up for in confrontational theology." Marshall, *Upward, Not Sunwise*, 44. The PAOC communicated a distinctly Pentecostal, Euro-Canadian cultural message, seeking to imprint that culture on their Indigenous adherents. PAOC missionaries did their best to ensure their adherents would subscribe to all the movement's tenets wholeheartedly. Simply put, the Pentecostals were not preoccupied with converts' table manners and etiquette, but with their pneumatology. In their dedication to fully acculturate their converts to a Western ecclesial praxis, the PAOC demonstrated parallels to the longer-established churches' missionary enterprises, not least in their gradual but eventual dedication to a mission to Indigenous people. See also Alexander, *Native American Pentecost*, 83; Barde, "Second Coming," 25, 27.

133 Tarango, *Choosing the Jesus Way*, 83.

134 McAlister, "Camp Meetings at 40 Below Zero!," 26.

135 Steed, "Latest Report on the Northland Mission," 3; Erna Alma Peters, 1989, "The History of the Northland Mission," PAOC Archives, 33;

Ostler and Ostler, "Look North Please!," 3; NNLC, 23 May 1992, "Meeting of All Pastors, District Native Directors, Superintendents & Evangelists," PAOC Archives, 1; Miller, *Canadian Pentecostals*, 213; Grant, *Moon of Wintertime*, 113, 168, 229.

136 Westman, *Cree and Christian*, 215. Some Indigenous Christians claimed to have been repulsed by the Catholic church, which had forbidden the practices of burning sweetgrass and drumming. They resorted to Pentecostalism where they installed their own church leaders. Stephen, "Neo-Pentecostalism Embraced by Cree Community." Catholic Charismatic Chippewa-Cree in Montana transitioned to Pentecostalism when Catholic charismatic renewal "lost steam in Catholic missions" following the 1980s. Clatterbuck, "Sweet Grass Mass," 90.

137 Laugrand and Oosten, "Reconnecting People and Healing the Land," 231.

138 Peters, "The History of the Northland Mission," 63.

139 Strong, "Events and Impressions of Northern Ontario," 7.

140 Jack Ozard, December 1984, "The Northland Mission Newsletter," PAOC Archives, 1; PAOC missionary Erna Peters recorded having "had the joy of leading a few Anglican ladies to the Lord but they also stayed in their own church ... [I]t would be nice if they had come our way because that might encourage others to come." Peters, "The History of the Northland Mission," 162.

141 Grant, *Moon of Wintertime*, 91, 186; Beaman, "Aboriginal Spirituality and the Legal Construction," 139–40, 148–9.

142 Gibson, "Two Histories," 13, 19; Beardy, interview by author.

143 Burkinshaw, "Native Pentecostalism in British Columbia," in Wilkinson, 148–9. Burkinshaw likened the rivalry to a turf war, referring to a 1953 skirmish in which some leading Anglicans allegedly pressured the Canadian Federal Department of Indian Affairs and Northern Development (DIAND) to withhold "government relief money" from First Nations elders who continued to attend Pentecostal worship. Indigenous Pentecostal minister James Kallappa (Kwih-dich-chuh-aht; Neah Bay, Washington State) believed that Anglicans feared numeric decline and were intimidated by the Pentecostals' attracting large numbers of Anglicans. In 1963 one PAOC missionary announced his belief that the Anglicans were attempting "to banish us and every Pentecostal believer." These claims led to the 1964 PAOC General Conference's appeal for DIAND's recognition of and permission for PAOC mission work on all reserves. Eventually DIAND granted this recognition. Another PAOC worker exclaimed: "We feel this event constitutes a milestone in our ministry here: helping these dear Indian folk understand that we, in the

sight of God *and* the Law, have the authority to perform marriages; giving them greater sense of security in the Gospel we preach; and imparting to them more boldness to exercise the religious freedom that is rightfully theirs."

144 Brown, *Top of the World*, 38.

145 Ibid., 65.

146 Aboriginal Pentecostal Ministries, 26–7 January 1996, "Aboriginal Pentecostal Ministries Board Meeting Minutes," PAOC Archives, 5.

147 Burkinshaw, "Native Pentecostalism in British Columbia," in Wilkinson, 157.

148 Shepherd, "From Colonization to Right Relations," 159; Bush, *Western Challenge*, 95.

149 Beninger, "Does the Church Really Care?," 210.

150 Miller, *Residential Schools and Reconciliation*, 31.

151 Westman, *Cree and Christian*, 136.

152 Laugrand and Oosten, "Reconnecting People and Healing the Land," 238.

153 Westman, "Pentecostalism and Indigenous Culture," 150. Westman argues that Pentecostalism's spiritual emphasis links directly with Inuit "shamanic traditions." Guenther, "Ethnicity and Evangelical Protestants in Canada," 390.

154 Hodgman, *Light on the Horizon*, 5, 99, 101, 116.

155 One example took place during the late 1950s, when the PAOC demonstrated a small degree of cooperation with the NCEM in their outreach among Dene in the Northwest Territories. Brown, *Top of the World*, 85–6.

156 Although the Mennonite and Baptist movements predate the Methodists, these two denominations remain prominent and visible in Canada, while Methodism became part of the United Church at Church Union in 1925. John Stackhouse noted Mennonites and Baptists were only marginally present in mission among Indigenous people in Canada's north, concluding that the PAOC expended more effort and resources. Stackhouse, "The Protestant Experience," 229.

157 Colwell, "Samuel Stearns Day," 158; Renfree, *Heritage and Horizon*, 99; Miller, *Skyscrapers Hide the Heavens*, 1st ed., 7; Elliott, "Canadian Baptists and Native Ministry," 149.

158 Elliott, "Canadian Baptists," 149–56.

159 Hayes, *Anglicans in Canada*, 32; Elliott, "Canadian Baptists," 156.

160 Renfree, *Heritage and Horizon*, 319; Elliott, "Canadian Baptists," 155.

161 Renfree, *Heritage and Horizon*, 99.

162 Elliott, "Canadian Baptists," 146–9, 153.

163 Westman, *Cree and Christian*, 151.

164 Spillenaar, *Wings of the Gospel*, 132; Miller, *Canadian Pentecostals*, 58–9, 101, 115–20.
165 Loewen, "The Poetics of Peoplehood," 352.
166 Gibson, "Native Theological Training," 49; Loewen, "The Poetics of Peoplehood," 352.
167 Pentecostals and other Evangelicals in Canada have often experienced tension, partially a result of theological differences. However, sociological factors also differentiate Canadian Pentecostals from other Evangelicals. At the 1964 founding of the EFC, Pentecostals were on the fringe of Canadian Evangelicalism. Pentecostals qualified as Evangelicals, yet stood distinct from wider Evangelicalism. John Stackhouse described the upstart EFC as "includ[ing] groups previously isolated in their respective enclave[s], especially Pentecostals." Stackhouse, *Canadian Evangelicalism*, 165. Canadian historian of Christianity Ronald Kydd described the two groups' differences as an aspect of their "mutual exclusion." Kydd theorizes that the PAOC and EFC held one another at arms' length, often pursuing different courses because of an historically all but muted distrust of one another. Kydd, "Canadian Pentecostalism and the Evangelical Impulse," 297–9.
168 Jack Ozard, 1989, "1989 Northland Mission Report to the District Conference," PAOC Archives, 35–8; Northland Mission, 28 March 1983, "Northland Mission Worker's Conference Minutes," PAOC Archives, 2; Robinson, "Oneness Pentecostalism," 39–44; Sanchez-Walsh, 266.
169 NNLC, 18 November 1993, "National Native Leadership Planning Committee Meeting Minutes," PAOC Archives, 2.
170 Tarango, *Choosing the Jesus Way*, 115
171 Pentecostals themselves have perpetuated the mythology of not possessing a colonial agenda, Angela Tarango writing, "Pentecostals like to pride themselves on the fact that they were not a part of the … conquest and colonization of the Americas." Tarango, "The Land Is Always Stalking Us," 398–9.
172 Whitt, "Developing a Pentecostal Missiology," 219, quoting the *Testimony*.
173 Garrett, *My Album of Memories*, 14, 31, 33; Hayes, *Anglicans in Canada*, 31; Grant, *Moon of Wintertime*, 201. The Presbyterian Church continued its missionary efforts among Indigenous people during the late twentieth century, both Euro-Canadian and Korean-Canadian Presbyterians contributing. Macdonald, "Presbyterian and Reformed Christians and Ethnicity," 182, 187; Bush, "The Presbyterian Church in Canada's Mission to Canada's Native Peoples," 115. The Presbyterian Church retained its mission on the Oak Lake-Pipestone Reserve (Dakota Nation,

Manitoba) into the 1990s. As of 2000 the Presbyterian Church continued to minister to the Mistawasis First Nation (Nehiyaw, Saskatchewan); one of the oldest extant Presbyterian missions is Mistawasis Memorial Presbyterian Church (opened in the 1890s) and Birdtail Sioux First Nation (Dakota) in Manitoba. Bush, *Western Challenge*, 100, 118; Beninger, "Does the Church Really Care?," 21.

174 Grant, *Moon of Wintertime*, 111.

175 Ibid., 266.

176 Christie and Gauvreau, *Christian Churches and Their Peoples*, 111.

177 Penner, "The Ojibwe Renaissance," 75. Evans, with assistant John Hessel (Ojibwe Anishinaabe), at Norway House during the 1830s–40s produced early Nêhiyawêwin translations of the Bible and was instrumental in devising the Nêhiyawêwin syllabic writing system still employed today. Garrett, 59, 71; Shepherd, "From Colonization to Right Relations," 157.

178 Bush, *Western Challenge*, 101.

179 Whitt, "Developing a Pentecostal Missiology," 278.

180 Ibid., 278.

CHAPTER TWO

1 Warner, "Flying Ambassadors of Goodwill," 3.

2 Hodgman, *Light on the Horizon*, 170.

3 Austin and Scott, "Introduction," 3.

4 Grant, *Moon of Wintertime*, 215.

5 Christie and Gauvreau, *Christian Churches and Their Peoples, 1840–1965*, 107.

6 Canadian Gospel Music, "Wings of the Gospel," YouTube Video, 16:24, 8 April 2018, https://youtu.be/l_5lTAPHoiY.

7 The Hebden Mission itself served as a missionary-sending entity. Within four years of its initial revival, the young mission sent over twenty-four missionaries to northern and southern Africa, India, Japan, China, and Mongolia, as well as to the Six Nations of the Grand River in Ontario, among other destinations. Whitt, "Developing a Pentecostal Missiology," 98–9; Canadian Gospel Music, "Wings of the Gospel"; Stewart, "A Canadian Azusa?," 27.

8 Saggio, "Toward an Indigenous Model of Native American Ministry within the Assemblies of God," 89, 100. Saggio concludes, "Mohawk Pentecostal Andrew C. Maracle recognized the importance of maintaining his Native language and culture, proudly declaring, 'I maintain my language – I maintain my culture today, and I'm proud of the fact that

I have.'" Andrew Maracle, 1992, "From a Log Cabin: An Autobiography of the Life & Ministry of Rev. Andrew Clifford Maracle," Part 3 of 6, Assemblies of God Flower Pentecostal Heritage Center, 7. Angela Tarango described Andrew Maracle as "a Mohawk missionary to his own people and the uncle of John Maracle, the first American Indian to hold a seat on the AG's Executive Presbytery." Tarango, *Choosing the Jesus Way*, 42–3.

9 Kulbeck, *The Pentecostal Testimony,* August 1958, 12; Spillenaar, *Wings of the Gospel*, 11; Canadian Gospel Music, "Wings of the Gospel."

10 Rudd, *When the Spirit Came Upon Them*, 181.

11 Buntain, *The Pentecostal Testimony*, 1 November 1939, 11; Erna Alma Peters, 1989, "The History of the Northland Mission," PAOC Archives, 4.

12 Canadian Gospel Music, "Wings of the Gospel."

13 Spillenaar, *Wings of the Gospel*, 14–15.

14 Ibid., 16.

15 Ibid., 12–13, 24. Spillenaar completed one year of high school, but he did not attend Bible College, not unusual for the era's Pentecostal workers. However, in the mid-1940s, Spillenaar did take a "prescribed Bible course." The PAOC granted him a licence to preach – an entry-level ministerial credential – before ultimately ordaining him. Ibid., 12–13, 24; PAOC, 5 July 1944, "John Spillenaar's Application for Credentials with the Pentecostal Assemblies of Canada," PAOC Archives, 1–2; PAOC, 7 July 1943, "John Spillenaar's Application for Affiliation into the Fellowship of the Pentecostal Assemblies of Canada," PAOC Archives, 1–2.

16 Upton, "The Call of the North!," 15–16, Upton quoting Spillenaar.

17 Brown, *Fifty Years of Pentecostal History 1933–1983*, 75–6.

18 Nancy R. Oakes, November 2006, "A Life Well Lived: A Tribute to Tyyne Spillenaar," PAOC Archives, 1–2; Canadian Obituaries, "Obits Indexed from the Kitchener Record," accessed September 2017, https://canadianobits.com/obitindex/webbbs_config.pl/read/1071.

19 Spillenaar, *Wings of the Gospel*, 20–1. A decade later, Spillenaar recounted his 1940 visit to the rail-accessible Moosonee, Ontario, but did not specify the Môsoniyi Ililiwak population. Spillenaar, "If I Have Not Vision," 18.

20 Rudd, *When the Spirit Came Upon Them*, 182.

21 Buntain, "Aggressive Christ-Honouring," 12.

22 Spillenaar, *Wings of the Gospel*, 22.

23 Ibid., 23.

24 Miller, *Canadian Pentecostals*, 283.

25 Brown, *Fifty Years of Pentecostal History*, 7.

26 Spillenaar, *Wings of the Gospel*, 24–5, 71–2.

27 Spillenaar, "Missionary Work in Northern Ontario," 7; Spillenaar, "Pioneer Work in Northern Ontario," 16.

28 Brown, *Fifty Years of Pentecostal History*, 67.

29 Spillenaar, "Pioneer Work," 16. Although the couple did not note an Indigenous population in Hearst, the Anishinini community residing at Pagwa River (140 km from Hearst), Ontario, later welcomed the NLM's first Indigenous minister, Rodger Cree (Kanien'kehá:ka; Kanesatake, Quebec). Smith, *The Pentecostal Testimony*, 24 May 1952, 20.

30 Spillenaar, "Pioneer Work," 16.

31 Buntain, "Hitherto the Lord Has Helped Us," 12.

32 Spillenaar, "Missionary Work in Northern Ontario," 7.

33 Buntain, "Pastors across Canada Tell of the Bible Truth," 12; Smith, "News," 15 December 1946, 14.

34 Smith, "News," 1 September 1946, 14.

35 Smith, *The Pentecostal Testimony*, 15 July 1948, 15; Spillenaar, "Missionary Work," 7.

36 Atter, *"The Third Force"*, 203–4.

37 Cunningham, "Revivaltime Released over CKGB Timmins, Ontario," 15.

38 Verlhust, "Burden for Baie Comeau," 11.

39 W.B. Greenwood, 16 August 1962, "Letter to John Spillenaar," PAOC Archives, 1; W.B. Greenwood, 12 June 1963, "Letter to John Spillenaar," PAOC Archives, 1–2; R.A. Bombay, 1963, "Report to District Executive of Northland Mission," PAOC Archives, 1.

40 Gloria Kulbeck, *What God Hath Wrought*, 132; Brown, *Fifty Years of Pentecostal History*, 24. Silver Birches remains a popular summer destination for northern Ontario Pentecostals. Miller, *Canadian Pentecostals*, 190. The economic and subsistence calendars of Môsoniyi Ililiwak, Néhinawak, Anishininiwag, and Ojibweg Anishinaabeg from what is now northern Ontario frequently centre on the hunt, typically a winter activity. As such, though the camp's programming was not particularly tailored to Indigenous participants, Pentecostal members of these nations technically would have been able to attend Silver Birches without their subsistence calendars being negatively affected. This is not always the case for Indigenous Pentecostals of other nations, for whom summer forms the centre of their subsistence calendars, such as the nations of the Pacific Northwest coast. American anthropologist Kirk Dombrowski, whose seminal ethnographic volume *Against Culture* concentrates on Alaska Native Pentecostal communities, was keenly aware of the significance of summer hunting and gathering. As Dombrowski unexpectedly learned on a winter field trip, "Church is a winter event … for many of those who

attended 'radical' Christian churches" because in summer they "pursued subsistence foods." Dombrowski, *Against Culture*, xiv. Robert Burkinshaw notes of the PAOC British Columbia and Yukon District's (BCYD) North Isle Native Pentecostal Camp in Fort Rupert, British Columbia – founded around the same time as Silver Birches – that the district demonstrated cultural awareness, operating the camp during the winter, and tailoring its programming to Indigenous Pentecostals. This allowed campers (predominantly Kwakw'ka'wakw, Nuu-chah-nulth, and Coast Salish) to participate in the camp, while also maintaining regular subsistence work during the summer. North Isle Camp drew hundreds of Indigenous Pentecostals from adjacent areas. Burkinshaw, "Native Pentecostalism in British Columbia," in Wilkinson, 151. Spillenaar's Northwest Territories–based contemporary Ken Gaetz likewise launched the Sub-Arctic Mission's Sandy Creek camp (also referred to as Great Slave Lake Camp) near Hay River, Northwest Territories, during the summer of 1959. Similar to the BCYD's North Isle Native Pentecostal Camp, Sandy Creek maintained an Indigenous emphasis and attracted several Dene and Nehiyawak adherents. Missionary literature described the camp as having "a strong appeal to the Indians who love to move into tents for the summer." The camp closed in the 1970s. Brown, *Top of the World*, 59; Morsch, *Rejoice*, 108; Miller, *Skyscrapers Hide the Heavens*, 1st ed., 6.

41 Kulbeck, *What God Hath Wrought*, 192; Upton, "The Call of the North!," 15–16.

42 Peters, "The History of the Northland Mission," 5.

43 Canadian Gospel Music, "Wings of the Gospel."

44 Warner, "Flying Ambassadors of Goodwill," 3; Elliot, *Through Gates of Splendor*, 92.

45 Spillenaar, "If I Have Not Vision," 18.

46 Spillenaar, *Wings of the Gospel*, 25–34. Toronto's Stone Church Pentecostal Assembly spent $10,000 on the NLM's new Piper Super Cub in 1951. Miller, *Canadian Pentecostals*, 283–4.

47 Jack Ozard, 1983, "The Northland Mission: 1935–1983 – Till Jesus Comes," PAOC Archives, 1.

48 McAlister, "Wings of the Gospel," 19.

49 Atter, *"The Third Force"*, 259.

50 Spillenaar's abrupt shift of focus is consistent with a Pentecostal tradition that accepts simply that missionaries changed direction out of personal conviction. Convinced of God's call to travel north and catalyzed by gaining viable transportation, Spillenaar fully found his Pentecostal vocation and dedicated most of his career to itinerating among the

Indigenous territories he visited. *Testimony* readers would not have been troubled by this change. Pentecostal eschatology and pneumatology fuels a missiological urgency that encourages followers to "act now and theologize later." Such behaviour contributes to the popular perception of Pentecostals being better at action than reflection. Wilson, "They Crossed the Red Sea, Didn't They?," 87; Klaus, "Missiological Reflections on Twentieth-Century Pentecostal Missions," 5; McClung, "Review," 113.

51 Atter, "*The Third Force*", 261.

52 Garrett referred to the Nêhiyawêwin hymnal and William Mason Bible. Garrett, *My Album of Memories*, 20, 30, 36, 59–60.

53 Atter, "*The Third Force*", 261.

54 Gunner, interview by author; Marshall, "Navajo Reservation Camp Meeting a Great Success!," 109.

55 Gibson, "Two Histories," 16.

56 Starblanket, "Foreword," x.

57 Alexander, *Native American Pentecost*, 83; Barde, "Second Coming," 25, 27.

58 Jolly, *Christ Is Building His Native Church*, 88, 97. Jolly describes his and his family's history thus: "The gospel which started in Waskaganish ... eventually reached some of my family members in Moose Factory, Ontario. A group of Native Christians from Waskaganish came to Moose Factory to hold house meetings. My late mother and older brother Allan went to one of their meetings and it was there they trusted Christ as their personal Savior. My mother understood the salvation message that night because she heard it preached in her own Cree language. Eventually my late father accepted the Lord and soon our whole family was saved."

59 Stephen, "Neo-Pentecostalism Embraced by Cree Community."

60 Tanner, "The Origins of Northern Aboriginal Social," 261; Westman, *Cree and Christian*, 26–7, 83, 174, 260–2, 271–3; Stonechild, *The Spiritual Seeker*, 53; Clatterbuck, *Crow Jesus*, 9; Ruby and Brown, *John Slocum and the Indian Shaker Church*, 6; Kim-Cragg, "The Power and Practise of Indigenous Christian Rituals and Ceremonies," 177–8.

61 Milne, "Diyin God Bizaad," 473, 495.

62 Westman, *Cree and Christian*, 194. At the very least, many post-war-period Indigenous Pentecostals were children of the previous generation of practitioners of Indigenous traditional spiritualities. The practice of Indigenous traditional spiritualities continued alongside the rise of Christianity among Indigenous people. The term "previous" is used here to denote that many present practitioners of Indigenous traditional spiritualities are participants in the resurgence of Indigenous

traditional spiritualities which had been interrupted and intercepted (but not entirely arrested) by Christian mission. Paper, "Aboriginals," 1, 5. Still, and considering the above, it is important to note that although the late nineteenth and early twentieth centuries saw a significant rise in the degree of Indigenous people's adherence to Christianity, this trend alone does not intimate that Indigenous traditional spiritualities ceased altogether to be practised – some being maintained by Indigenous adherents of Christianity. Or, in the words of Mark Clatterbuck, "the appearance of a name on a baptismal record or list of converts among a tribe does not necessarily mean that traditional ceremonies, even those publicly condemned by the church's hierarchy, were abandoned by those church members." Clatterbuck, *Crow Jesus*, 48; Tarango, "Jonathan Edwards, Pentecostals, and the Missionary Encounter with Native Americans," 209.

63 Kracht, *Religious Revitalization among the Kiowas*, 225; Brown, *Top of the World*, 46, 55.

64 Spillenaar, *Wings of the Gospel*, 78.

65 Beaman, "Aboriginal Spirituality and the Legal Construction of Freedom of Religion," 137.

66 Spillenaar, *Wings of the Gospel*, 35.

67 Ibid., 50.

68 Kulbeck, *What God Hath Wrought*, 190–1.

69 Spillenaar, *Wings of the Gospel*, 65.

70 Clatterbuck, *Crow Jesus*, 215; Lewis, *Creating Christian Indians*, 13.

71 Spillenaar, *Wings of the Gospel*, 65.

72 Hodgman, *Light on the Horizon*, 243; Garrett, *My Album of Memories*, 12–14, 17, 29, 42, 51, 72–4, 77.

73 Ervin, *The Political and Ecclesiastical History of the Anglican Church of Canada*, 112.

74 Grant, *Moon of Wintertime*, 190, 198.

75 Beninger, "The Anglican Church of Canada," 32, 47–8; Hodgman, *Light on the Horizon*, 19–20, 37–8.

76 Garrett, *My Album of Memories*, 72–4.

77 Spillenaar, *Wings of the Gospel*, 71–2.

78 Ng, "The United Church of Canada," 229; Carrington, *The Anglican Church in Canada*, 293.

79 Garrett, *My Album of Memories*, 26.

80 Spillenaar, *Wings of the Gospel*, 122.

81 Hodge, "Navaho Pentecostalism," 82; Gibson, "Two Histories," 16; David Mainse, 1976, "Turning Point: The Charles Lee Story," Assemblies of God Flower Pentecostal Heritage Center, 11–12.

82 Milne, "Diyin God Bizaad," 483, 609–10; McCleary, "An Ethnohistory of Pentecostalism," 130; Fletcher and Denham, "Moving towards Healing," 112–13; Tarango, "Jonathan Edwards, Pentecostals, and the Missionary Encounter with Native Americans," 208.

83 Milne, "Diyin God Bizaad," 439–40, 474. Kimberly Jenkins Marshall explains: "In contrast to other forms of Christianity, Pentecostalism ... emphasizes experientiality. Whereas rational Protestantism concerns itself with questions of belief ... Pentecostalism places a significant value on 'practice theology.'" Marshall, "Non-Human Agency," 399.

84 Swain, *Oka*, 21.

85 Westman, "Cree Pentecostalism and Its Others," 414; McCleary, "Akbaatashee," 51; Milne, "Diyin God Bizaad," 352. Within Indigenous Pentecostalism, a leader's legitimacy inside their community might also be reinforced by the individual's experience of Pentecostalism, knowledge base of Indigenous traditions, and demonstration of acts of healing. McCleary, "An Ethnohistory of Pentecostalism," 121; Marshall, *Upward, Not Sunwise*, 57.

86 Spillenaar, *Wings of the Gospel*, 157–8.

87 Tarango, *Choosing the Jesus Way*, 14, 56; Spillenaar, *Wings of the Gospel*, 66, 78–9; Burkinshaw, "Native Pentecostalism in British Columbia," 154–63; Grant, *Moon of Wintertime*, 202; Laugrand and Oosten, "Reconnecting People and Healing the Land," 233, 237; Westman, "Pentecostalism and Indigenous Culture," 144, 147–8.

88 Spillenaar, *Wings of the Gospel*, 50–1. Spillenaar's association between Jesus's blood and Indigenous expression may be neither unintentional nor coincidental. Mark Clatterbuck's interview of Native American Pentecostal pastor Kenneth Pretty On Top (Apsáalooke; Crow Agency, Montana) points to the perceived correlation, Pretty On Top proposing: "What makes you Crow? Here's the answer: blood. You got Crow blood. Anybody can dance. Anybody can wear feathers ... But bein' a Crow is you got that Crow blood. The blood. And then you can turn that and say, 'What makes you a Christian?' The blood of Jesus." Clatterbuck, *Crow Jesus*, 125.

89 Cummins, "Christian Education," 16; Milne, "Diyin God Bizaad," 438.

90 McCleary, "Akbaatashee," 72, 83; McCleary, "An Ethnohistory of Pentecostalism," 133; Gibson, "Native Theological Training," 74–5.

91 Grant, *Moon of Wintertime*, 199–201; Bush, "The Presbyterian Church in Canada's Mission to Canada's Native Peoples, 1900–2000," 117.

92 Kulbeck, "People and Activities," July 1957, 15.

93 Strong, "Events and Impressions of Northern Ontario," 7; Stiller, "North with 'Wings of the Gospel,'" 1.

94 Argue, "Home Missions," April 1968, 10; Klaus, "Missiological Reflections," 4.

95 Argue, "Home Missions," April 1968, 10.

96 Carson Latimer, *Dominion Outreach*, April–June 1966, 3; Miller, *Canadian Pentecostals*, 214.

97 Argue, "Wings of the Gospel: And Hope for Scattered Canadians," 10; Spillenaar, *Wings of the Gospel*, 148, 151.

98 Miller, *Canadian Pentecostals*, 213.

99 PAOC, 1932, "PAOC General Constitution," PAOC Archives, 48.

100 Kulbeck, "Northern Lights," 8.

101 Johnstone, "Panorama of Home Missions across Canada," 1962, 10.

102 Spillenaar, "The Proposed Courses of Study for MPBS," 22; Spillenaar, *Wings of the Gospel*, 98.

103 Spillenaar, *Wings of the Gospel*, 35, 38–9. Spillenaar recounted that his remote location prevented communication with his family near Timmins. He described that in the five days between the murder attempt and Spillenaar's contact with his family, popular opinion held that the missionary had been killed, with the press carrying the false news.

104 W.B. Greenwood, 30 December 1957, "Letter to John Spillenaar," PAOC Archives, 1; Victor G. Brown, 21 October 1958, "Memo to PAOC General Executive," PAOC Archives, 1; George R. Upton, 10 December 1953, "Letter to W.B. Greenwood," PAOC Archives, 1–2; Kulbeck, *The Pentecostal Testimony*, April 1962, 16; PAOC, 1 March 1975, "Minutes of the Standing Home Missions Committee," PAOC Archives, 2.

105 R.M. Argue, *Dominion Outreach: Home Missions and Bible Colleges Bulletin of the Pentecostal Assemblies of Canada*, January–March 1963, 3.

106 Peters, "The History of the Northland Mission," 36.

107 Scott, "Cultivating Christians in Colonial Canadian Missions," 21–2, 35.

108 Austin and Scott, "Introduction," 8.

109 Peters, "The History of the Northland Mission," 22.

110 Ibid., 22–3.

111 George R. Upton, 10 December 1953, "Letter to W.B. Greenwood," PAOC Archives. 1–2.

112 Kulbeck, *What God Hath Wrought*, 192.

113 Canadian Gospel Music, "Wings of the Gospel."

114 Spillenaar, *Wings of the Gospel*, 59–60, 109.

115 Kulbeck, "Northern Lights," 8; Spillenaar, *Wings of the Gospel*, 47–8, 94, 112–13; Brown, *Fifty Years of Pentecostal History*, 13.

116 Peters, "The History of the Northland Mission," 38, 54.

117 Spillenaar, *Wings of the Gospel*, 152.

118 Prankard, "Foreword," 6; Spillenaar, *Wings of the Gospel*, 8.

119 Spillenaar, *Wings of the Gospel*, 9, 119–20. Reflecting on the Pentecostal pattern of attributing success to Providence, Michael Wilkinson and Linda Ambrose wrote: "Saying that it was all the Spirit's doing is a cultural repertoire, utilized in a particular way to carry on the internal culture of the movement within the structures of the organization." Wilkinson and Ambrose, *After the Revival*, 181.

120 Spillenaar, "Northland Missionary Saves a Life, and God Saves a Soul," 4.

121 For the sake of comparison, it would appear that Spillenaar's Northwest Territories–based contemporary Ken Gaetz suffered as many mishaps aboard his boats as Spillenaar did aloft in his aircraft. Likewise Gaetz's correspondence along with the denominational literature of the period afforded disproportionate attention to the missionary's adventures and misadventures. Brown, *Top of the World*, 29.

122 Said, *Culture and Imperialism*, xii. Emphasis original.

123 Stackhouse, "By Their Books Ye Shall Know Them," 58.

124 Ibid., 58.

125 Tarango, *Choosing the Jesus Way*, 63.

126 McAlister, *The Pentecostal Testimony*, July 1953, 14. Spillenaar, *Wings of the Gospel*, 73, 135–6, 140–1; Neely, "Church Growth – Toronto's Stone Church," 27; Kracht, *Religious Revitalization among the Kiowas*, 62. When he inquired again to upgrade his aircraft, the Home Missions Department's administration informed Spillenaar: "John, you have the most costly piece of equipment of all our missionaries. You have a good plane, so be satisfied with what you have!" Peters, "The History of the Northland Mission," 36, 49.

127 Gibson, "Native Theological Training," 135–6, Gibson paraphrasing anonymous First Nations elder.

128 Tanner, "The Origins of Northern Aboriginal Social Pathologies," 259–60.

129 Indeed there is precedent for this, as historian of Presbyterian mission Bonnie Sue Lewis wrote, "In the 1860s and 1870s conversions numbered in the hundreds among the Dakotas and the Nez Perces. Native leaders were instrumental in the harvest of souls ... The birth of Indigenous Christianity among the Dakotas and the Nez Perces allowed a means of responding to change while affirming native identity in these two tribes." Lewis, *Creating Christian Indians*, 22.

130 Milne, "Diyin God Bizaad," 531; McCleary, "An Ethnohistory of Pentecostalism," 120.

131 Austin and Scott, "Introduction," 7; Garrett, *My Album of Memories*, 20. But for rival denominations' infrastructure and presence, as well as the

Hudson's Bay Company, the NLM initially would not have had facilities to host their outreaches to Indigenous people.

132 Stiller, "The Northland," *Dominion Outreach*, July–September 1963, 1; Marks, "Called to a Cold Spot," 24; Neely, "Church Growth – Toronto's Stone Church," 27. Pentecostal women were a missionary tour de force within the NLM and beyond, contributing to the PAOC's other ministries to Indigenous people. Grace Veale served with the PAOC's Sub-Artic Mission in the Northwest Territories where she learned and became proficient in the Dene language. Veale was instrumental in the preservation of audio recordings of Dene Pentecostals' testimonies, and contributed to the work of translating scripture into the Dene language. Brown, *Top of the World*, 79, 84–7, 179.

133 Ambrose, "Zelma and Beulah Argue," 102. Unfortunately the challenges are not simply those of the past and in fact continue into the present. PAOC pastor and Bible college instructor William Sloos likewise wrote: "Although women were eventually granted ordination in 1984, these gender-biased undercurrents still exist today, especially at the local church level. I have witnessed these prejudicial realities first-hand while teaching in Peterborough. Female students in my third-year Pentecostal History course still struggle to reconcile being part of a Spirit-empowered movement with such a long history of gender suppression." Sloos, "Book Review," 27.

134 Peters, "The History of the Northland Mission," 10.

135 PAOC, 27 August 1984, "General Conference Minutes," PAOC Archives, 16.

136 Wilkinson and Ambrose, *After the Revival*, 90, 74.

137 Gibson, "Women of Faith," 80.

138 Ambrose, "Zelma and Beulah Argue," 101.

139 Ibid., 104.

140 Atter, *"The Third Force"*, 100.

CHAPTER THREE

1 Nkonge, "The Church Missionary Society's Burden," 20.

2 Peters, *The Contribution to Education by the Pentecostal Assemblies of Canada*, 62.

3 Sombrero, "Black Robes," 177.

4 John Spillenaar, 1 December 1953, "The Northland Newsletter," PAOC Archives, 1.

5 Peters, *The Contribution to Education*, 62. Peters taught school in Manitoba from 1938 to 1978. In 1970, Peters wrote her M.Ed. thesis,

"The Contribution to Education by the Pentecostal Assemblies of Canada," self-publishing it in 1971. As a layperson, Peters supported mission. Her husband Ed died in 1978, and in February 1979 she moved to Liberia as a missionary teacher with the PAOC's Seniors' Overseas Service. By late 1981 Peters had moved to continue teaching in Kenya. She returned to Canada in October 1982 and began working for the NLM in December 1984. Hansell, "Mother with a Missionary Heart," 3; Peters, "Christ on the Cross," 26; Peters, "The Responsibility of the Local Church to Missions," 23; Erna Alma Peters, 1989, "The History of the Northland Mission," PAOC Archives, 202–3.

6 R.M. Argue, "An Indigenous Work Needed," 1.

7 Peters, "The History of the Northland Mission," 16.

8 Ibid., 8.

9 Spillenaar, *Wings of the Gospel*, 70.

10 Miller, *Canadian Pentecostals*, 213.

11 Brown, *Fifty Years of Pentecostal History*, 167; Spillenaar, *Wings of the Gospel*, 70; Jack Ozard, 1983, "The Northland Mission: 1935–1983 – Till Jesus Comes," PAOC Archives, 1.

12 John Spillenaar, March 1955, "The Northland Newsletter," PAOC Archives, 1.

13 John Spillenaar, 1962, "The Nikinona Moosonee Pentecostal Bible School Yearbook," PAOC Archives, 2. The yearbook title, Nikinona, is the Nêhiyawêwin word for "call." Students chose this name because they had "felt the need of their people and have answered God's CALL." Peters, *Contribution to Education*, 63.

14 John Spillenaar, September 1959, "The Northland Newsletter," PAOC Archives, 1.

15 Peters, "The History of the Northland Mission," 16.

16 Elizabeth Fraser, 1 September 1959, "Letter to Rev. and Mrs. Greenwood," PAOC Archives, 1–2; Peters, "The History of the Northland Mission," 10, 25–8.

17 Peters, "The History of the Northland Mission," 16.

18 Spillenaar, *Wings of the Gospel*, 71.

19 Tarango, *Choosing the Jesus Way*, 128; Milloy, *A National Crime*, 116–17; Bush, *Western Challenge*, 113; John Spillenaar, 1962, "The Nikinona Moosonee Pentecostal Bible School Yearbook," PAOC Archives, 5.

20 PAOC Home Missions, "The Moosonee Bible School," 1.

21 John Spillenaar, 1960, "The Proposed Courses of Study for MPBS," PAOC Archives, 21; Peters, *Contribution to Education*, 63; PAOC, 1968, "1968 PAOC General Constitution & By-Laws," PAOC Archives, 31.

22 Peters, "The History of the Northland Mission," 41.
23 Ibid., 22; Jack Ozard, 1983, "Northland Mission Report," PAOC Archives, 2; Jack Ozard, September 1984, "The Northland Mission Newsletter," PAOC Archives, 3.
24 Peters, "The History of the Northland Mission," 20.
25 Eddie Gilles, 1962, "Nikinona Moosonee Pentecostal Bible College Yearbook," PAOC Archives, 11–13.
26 Dale Cummins, 1981, "Presentation Script," PAOC Archives, 2.
27 Clinton Westman observed: "Pentecostalism contributes strongly to the maintenance of the Cree language, mainly through its emphasis on orality, but also through the development and distribution of media including a printed corpus of songs, scriptures, and other Cree writings ... [and] there remains a strong emphasis on doctrine, scripture, and text in Pentecostal practice." Westman, "Understanding Cree Religious Discourse," 15.
28 John Spillenaar, 1962, "Nikinona Moosonee Pentecostal Bible College Yearbook," PAOC Archives, 17.
29 John Spillenaar and James Barkman, 1962, "Nikinona Moosonee Pentecostal Bible College Yearbook," PAOC Archives, 12.
30 Peters, "The History of the Northland Mission," 25. In 1970 the average age of English-speaking students was fifteen years.
31 PAOC, September 1987, "Teaching Opportunity," PAOC Archives, 1.
32 John Spillenaar, 1962, "Nikinona Moosonee Pentecostal Bible College Yearbook," PAOC Archives, 2–7.
33 Johnstone, "General Conference Report," 8.
34 Peters, "The History of the Northland Mission," 16.
35 Ibid., 68.
36 McAlister, "Who's Who in the C.A's," 14.
37 Smith, "News!," September 1946, 14; Smith, "Hundreds of Canada's Children Have Decided for Christ Jesus," 12; McAlister, "Who's Who," 14; Kulbeck, "Camp Roundup," 34; Kulbeck, "People and Activities," April 1965, 15.
38 Stiller, "Indigenous Methods in Moosonee," 11.
39 Ibid., 11. These Môsoniyi Ililiwak Pentecostals employed an expression of denominationally Christian tradition (in this instance a funerary practice) as a means of asserting and maintaining their own cultural stability. Marshall, *Upward, Not Sunwise*, 4. In many Nehiyawak communities, a Pentecostal funeral "is a central illustration of the efforts by Pentecostals to portray their faith as the leading public religion." Westman, *Cree and Christian*, 203.
40 Kulbeck, "Indians Accept Christ," 10; PAOC, 31 August 1959, "Minutes of the Standing Home Missions Committee," PAOC Archives, 3.

41 Earl N.O. Kulbeck, 28 April 1968, "Parliamentary Consultation on Indian Work; Ottawa, Canada," PAOC Archives, 2.
42 Howarth, "Tragedy in the North," 3.
43 Stiller, "Indigenous Methods in Moosonee," 11.
44 Robert, "The 'Christian Home' as a Cornerstone of Anglo-American Missionary Thought and Practice," 140, 165. A later NLMBC student handbook contained the following requirements: "The student's appearance and conduct will reflect upon the local church, and therefore a clean look and good behaviour is essential." Northland Ministries, 1991, "Student Handbook," PAOC Archives, 4–11. Around 1988 the PAOC increasingly referred to the Northland Mission as Northland Ministries. Beyond the NLM, a missionary of the PAOC's Northwest Territories–based Sub-Arctic Mission continued the civilizing axiom, critiquing what she perceived to be Dene people's excessive generosity within their giving traditions, stating: "They will give or share what they have until nothing is left ... A custom that was essential to a primitive society has become a burden today to those who would try to get ahead. The only solution is in Christianity. The truly Christian Indian is industrious, clean and reliable." Brown, *Top of the World*, 89.
45 Northland Ministries, 1 May 1995, "Native Board Meeting," PAOC Archives, 1–3.
46 R.M. Argue, *Dominion Outreach*, January–March 1962, 4; Peters, "The History of the Northland Mission," 20; Howarth, "Greetings from Moosonee," 2.
47 Peters, "The History of the Northland Mission," 20; Sonnenberg, "Window on the World," 17.
48 Peters, "The History of the Northland Mission," 21.
49 Howarth, "Indian Bible School a Success," 4.
50 Peters, "The History of the Northland Mission," 21.
51 Peters, *Contribution to Education*, 64, 66; Gibson, "Native Theological Training within Canadian Evangelicalism," 111.
52 John Spillenaar, *Dominion Outreach*, October–December 1964, 1; Peters, *Contribution to Education*, 66–7.
53 Howarth, "Indian Bible School a Success," 4.
54 Spillenaar, *Dominion Outreach*, October–December 1964, 1.
55 Steed, "Latest Report on the Northland Mission," 3; Spillenaar, *Wings of the Gospel*, 123; Atter, "*The Third Force*", 261; Peters, *Contribution to Education*, 63.
56 Peters, "The History of the Northland Mission," 44.

57 Kervan Chalmers, 23 November 1993, "History of Northern Bible College, Sioux Lookout," PAOC Archives, 2.
58 Peters, "The History of the Northland Mission," 68.
59 Argue, "Home Missions – Resourcefulness," 10.
60 Ozard, "The Northland Mission: 1935–1983," 1. Once in Nakina, Bible College Principal Harold Howarth again reported challenges with language, including cultural and linguistic differences and nuances between Nêhiyawêwin and Ojibwemowin Anishinaabemowin. To Howarth's credit, while fulfilling the duties of principal he also dedicated his time to "supply the Indian people with religious literature and Bible helps in their own language." Peters, "The History of the Northland Mission," 25–8; Peters, *Contribution to Education*, 68.
61 Cummins, "Christian Education," 15.
62 Peters, "The History of the Northland Mission," 27, 86; Spillenaar, *Wings of the Gospel*, 88.
63 Peters, "The History of the Northland Mission," 75.
64 Birch, "New Strategy for Nakina Bible School," 10.
65 Heather D. Martin posits that such a production-oriented educational model invariably results in pedagogical shortcomings, where investment in mentorship and relationship is forfeited in the pursuit of achievement of outcomes. Martin, "A Framework for Theological Lifelong Learning in the Northwest Territories," 54.
66 Peters, "The History of the Northland Mission," 18; Argue, "Exciting News from Here and There," 10.
67 Peters, "The History of the Northland Mission," 28.
68 Myrah, "Moosonee Native Bible School," 1; Argue, "Exciting News from Here and There," 10; Birch, "New Strategy for Nakina Bible School," 10; PAOC, 1972, "PAOC General Conference Meeting Minutes," PAOC Archives, 156–7.
69 Spillenaar, *Wings of the Gospel*, 88.
70 Spillenaar, "Graduation Moosonee Pentecostal Bible School 1966," 10.
71 Spillenaar, *Wings of the Gospel*, 88.
72 Peters, "The History of the Northland Mission," 14.
73 Hunter, "'T.E.E. Off' in Ontario's Northland," 4–5; Ozard, "The Northland Mission: 1935–1983," 1; Peters, "The History of the Northland Mission," 30, 32.
74 Tom Johnstone, June 1961, "Letter to PAOC Pastors," PAOC Archives, 1–2; Peters, "The History of the Northland Mission," 32.
75 Hunter, "'T.E.E. Off,'" 14.

76 Peters, "The History of the Northland Mission," 78. The NLM printed a Nêhiyawêwin hymnal titled *Cree English Hymns*. Hunter, "'T.E.E. Off,'" 4–5; PAOC, 23–27 August 1974, "PAOC General Conference Meeting Minutes," PAOC Archives, 19; PAOC, 1974, "PAOC General Constitution & By-Laws," PAOC Archives, 32–3, 37.
77 Smith, "Introduction," xxi.
78 Northland Ministries, 1 May 1995, "Native Board Meeting," PAOC Archives, 2.
79 Spillenaar, *Wings of the Gospel*, 161–2.
80 Spillenaar, *To the Regions Beyond*, 1.
81 Tarango, *Choosing the Jesus Way*, 48–9. The ideal of a "Three-Self" church would require a fully indigenized clergy. In subsequent years, Indigenous ministers' desire for ordination became even more apparent.
82 Grosshans and Cummins, "Pickle Lake Preview," 26; Spillenaar, *To the Regions Beyond*, 1–3.
83 Jack Ozard, 1983, "Northland Mission Report," PAOC Archives, 1; Jack Ozard, 14 June 1995, "Letter to Evangel Pentecostal Tabernacle," PAOC Archives, 1.
84 Howard D. Honsinger, 23 December 1976, "Letter to Rev. Charles Yates," PAOC Archives, 1–2.
85 Charles Yates, 16 December 1976, "Letter to Howard Honsinger," PAOC Archives, 1.
86 Jack Ozard, 1983, "1983 Northland Mission Report," PAOC Archives, 1.
87 Peters, "The History of the Northland Mission," 15.
88 Laugrand and Oosten, "Reconnecting People and Healing the Land," 233, 237; Gibson, "Two Histories," 11; Westman, "Pentecostalism and Indigenous Culture," 233; Spillenaar, *To the Regions Beyond*, 155.
89 John Spillenaar, 20 September 1995, "Letter to PAOC General Executive," PAOC Archives, 1.
90 Reuben Schmunk, 9 November 1995, "Letter to John Spillenaar," PAOC Archives, 1.
91 On his final tour Spillenaar even baptized by immersion an Anglican minister, who allegedly proceeded to join the local Pentecostal church thereafter. John Spillenaar, 1995, "Arctic Trip," PAOC Archives, 1. Still, another account reports Spillenaar's association with the non-PAOC, Canadian Independent Assemblies of God International during the final two decades of his ministry. "Arctic Mission Outreach Trust Fund Newsletter: Winter 2003–2004," accessed December 2021, http://www.odyssey.on.ca/~david.ellyatt/arcticmissionsKeepUp/2004winter.htm.

92 Grosshans and Cummins, "Pickle Lake Preview," 27; Cummins, "Christian Education," 17; Chalmers, "History of Northern Bible College," 2.

93 Spillenaar, *Wings of the Gospel*, 133–4, 136, 157.

94 Jack Ozard, 1983, "1983 Northland Mission Report," PAOC Archives, 2.

95 Chalmers, "History of Northern Bible College," 2.

96 Peters, "The History of the Northland Mission," 74; Gibson, "Native Theological Training," 112.

97 Wayne Scott and Northland Ministries, circa 1980s, "Preliminary Application for Admission: The Northland Ministries Bible School," PAOC Archives, 1; Dale Cummins, 1981, "Presentation Script," PAOC Archives, 5.

98 Northland Mission, February 1984, "Vision North, February – March 1984," PAOC Archives, 2.

99 Dale and Alberta Cummins, June 1981, "The Northland Mission Newsletter," PAOC Archives, 1. John Mekenak went on to assist teaching at NLMBC. Jack Ozard, June–July 1982, "The Northland Mission Newsletter," PAOC Archives, 3.

100 Jack Ozard, April 1983, "The Northland Mission Newsletter," PAOC Archives, 3.

101 Cummins, "Christian Education," 17; Peters, "The History of the Northland Mission," 118.

102 Harbridge, "The Growing Northland Mission," 10–11.

103 Dale and Alberta Cummins, May 1980, "Northland Mission Report for 1979," PAOC Archives, 1–2.

104 Hugh Munro, 1981, "The Northland Newsletter," PAOC Archives, 1; Harbridge, "The Growing Northland Mission," 10–11; Jack Ozard, September 1983, "The Northland Newsletter," PAOC Archives, 2.

105 Jack Ozard, 2 November 1981, "Letter to Northland Mission Supporters," PAOC Archives, 2; Jack Ozard, 10 December 1981, "Northland Newsletter," PAOC Archives, 1.

106 Homer Cantelon, 20 March 1980, "Letter to Jerry Harbridge," PAOC Archives, 2–3.

107 Harbridge, "The Growing Northland Mission," 10.

108 WOD Executive, 1980, "Excerpts from District Executive Meetings Re: The Northland Mission," PAOC Archives, 8; DHMBC, 1981, "Job Description – Overseer of Pickle Lake Training Centre," PAOC Archives, 1; WOD Executive, 1981, "Excerpts from District Executive Meetings Re: The Northland Mission," PAOC Archives, 1–3; Dale and Alberta

Cummins, 18 September 1981, "The Northland Newsletter," PAOC Archives, 2.

109 Jack Ozard, 2 November 1981, "Letter to Northland Mission Supporters," PAOC Archives, 1; Cummins, "Where Is the Prophet's Roar?," 25; Cummins, "Christian Education," 17.

110 Peters, "History of The Northland Mission," 148; Northland Mission, 28 March 1983, "Northland Mission Worker's Conference Minutes," PAOC Archives, 2; Spillenaar, *Wings of the Gospel*, 131.

111 Gunner, interview by author; Collado, interview by author.

112 Peters, "The History of the Northland Mission," 28; Kulbeck, "Indians Accept Christ," 10; Cantelon, "Letter to Jerry Harbridge," 1–3; Dale and Alberta Cummins, 18 September 1981, "The Northland Newsletter," PAOC Archives, 1–2.

113 Gunner, interview by author.

114 Ibid.

115 Northland Mission, 1983, "Job Description – Overseer of Pickle Lake Training Centre," PAOC Archives, 1. Such was consistent with the era's mission practices. Truth and Reconciliation Commission of Canada, *Canada's Residential Schools – The History, Part 1 Origins to 1939*, 37.

116 DHMBC, 5 October 1981, "Requests and Information Needed for Ian Winter," PAOC Archives, 1.

117 Peters, "The History of the Northland Mission," 167; Jack Ozard, 1984, "Northland Mission Indian Bible School," PAOC Archives, 1–2; Northland Ministries, "Student Handbook," 4–11; Northland Mission, "Preliminary Application for Admission," 1; NLMBC, 16 December 1985, "Course Calendar," PAOC Archives, 1.

118 Jack Ozard, December 1984, "The Northland Newsletter," PAOC Archives, 1.

119 Guy Campeau, "North of the 50th," 1985, 1; Jack Ozard, 1985–1986, "The Northland Mission," PAOC Archives, 1; Northland Ministries, "Northern Bible College Handbook," 3; Peters, "The History of the Northland Mission," 142.

120 Jack Ozard, 1986, "The Northland Mission Report," PAOC Archives, 1; NLM BC, 199?, "NLM Bible College Student Handbook," PAOC Archives, 3; Campeau, "North of the 50th," 1; Jack Ozard, October–November 1984, "The Northland Newsletter," PAOC Archives, 2; Peters, "The History of the Northland Mission," 132. PAOC literature referred to Mishkeegogamang as Osnaburgh.

121 Gibson, "Editorial," 4.

122 Gibson, "Native Theological Training within Canadian Evangelicalism," 1.

123 Hansell, "Bible College Graduates – 1981," 11; Northland Ministries, "Northern Bible College Handbook," 3; Jack Ozard, 1987, "Northland Mission Report," PAOC Archives, 1.

124 Jack Ozard, March 1982, "Northland Newsletter," PAOC Archives, 1; Jack Ozard, 30 December 1982, "The Northland Newsletter," PAOC Archives, 1; Jack Ozard, May–June 1982, "The Northland Newsletter," PAOC Archives, 1; Jack Ozard, March–April 1983, "The Northland Newsletter," PAOC Archives, 5; PAOC National Bible College Committee, 26–27 May 1986, "Meeting Minutes," PAOC Archives, 2. There is some discrepancy between sources regarding peak enrolment during Gibson's tenure. Denominational records point to the higher number of thirty-five, while Gibson recorded only fifteen. Said students contributed to extracurricular college life by offering translation and teaching services. Gibson, "Native Theological Training," 113.

125 Ozard, "Northland Ministries Audio Visual Presentation," 3.

126 Jack Ozard, May 1991, "The Northland Newsletter," PAOC Archives, 2.

127 Northland Ministries, 1991, "Student Handbook," PAOC Archives, 2; Miller, *Canadian Pentecostals*, 213.

128 Jack Ozard, June–July 1982, "The Northland Newsletter," PAOC Archives, 3.

129 NLMBC, 1988, "Northland Ministries Bible College Graduation Program," PAOC Archives, 2.

130 Northland Mission, circa 1980s, "Preliminary Application for Admission," PAOC Archives, 1.

131 NLMBC, 1993, "Northland Ministries Bible College Graduation," PAOC Archives, 3.

132 Gibson, "Native Theological Training," 82.

133 Jack Ozard, October–November 1984, "The Northland Newsletter," PAOC Archives, 3; Jack Ozard, April 1984, "The Northland Newsletter," PAOC Archives, 4; Kervan Chalmers, 30 June 1992, "Letter to Jack Ozard," PAOC Archives, 1; Westman, *Cree and Christian*, 246–7; McCleary, "An Ethnohistory of Pentecostalism," 132.

134 Ruth Skunk (Ojibwe Anishinaabe; Mishkeegogamang, Ontario) affirmed that being at NLMBC had "done a great deal for my life, gives me more knowledge to be able to recognize the real need for souls to Jesus … without Him. And … set good examples for the Lord." Jack Ozard and Ruth Skunk, April 1984, "The Northland Newsletter," PAOC Archives, 4; Dale and Alberta Cummins, June 1981, "The Northland Newsletter," PAOC Archives, 2.

135 Shepherd, "From Colonization to Right Relations," 159; Stackhouse, "The Protestant Experience," 229; Miller, *Skyscrapers Hide the Heavens*, 1st ed., 100; Grant, *Moon of Wintertime*, 116–18, 168, 174, 189, 201–2.

136 CPBC, 1 May 1980, "Press Release: First Treaty Indian Graduates from College," PAOC Archives, 1; Gordon Upton, 2 January 1985, "Letter to Pastor Roger Ratt," PAOC Archives, 1–2.

137 Northland Ministries, 1991, "Northland Ministries Report & Recommendations to the Western Ontario Executive," PAOC Archives, 1. The NLMBC eventually offered theological courses in contextualization, which Gibson referred to as "'Native' courses, never taught by aboriginals … [which] were not sufficient to offset the EuroCanadian [*sic*] cultural bias of the curriculum as a whole." Gibson, "Native Theological Training," 116.

138 Gibson, "Native Theological Training," 89–90, 98, Gibson quoting Bible college administrator, brackets original. Levi Samson Beardy (Anishinini; Bearskin Lake, Ontario) attended EPBC from 1990–1993, earning a Bachelor of Theology. Beardy attested to conversation within the college regarding PAOC ministry to Indigenous people that frequently detailed socio-economic challenges affecting Indigenous communities rather than focusing on positive accounts of ministry taking place. Beardy, interview by author.

139 PAOC Standing Committee on Mission, 1968, "Proposal to the PAOC General Executive," quoted in Northland Mission, 29 March 1983, "Northland Mission Worker's Conference Meeting Minutes," PAOC Archives, 4; PAOC Standing Committee on Mission, 1968, "Proposal to the PAOC General Executive," quoted in Northland Mission, 29 March 1983, "Northland Mission Worker's Conference Minutes," PAOC Archives, 4.

140 Skinner, "Ordination of Native Minister," 20–1.

141 Northland Ministries, 1993, "Northern Bible College Handbook," PAOC Archives, 3. In the mid-1990s those colleges were still in operation and comprised: the Northland Mission Bible College (WOD) in Sioux Lookout, Ontario; Canadian Native Bible College (British Columbia and Yukon District) in Vancouver, British Columbia; Central Pentecostal Bible College, Native Ministries Campus (Saskatchewan District) in Saskatoon, Saskatchewan; Native Pentecostal Bible College (of the EOQD) in Chibougamau, Quebec; and Pentecostal Sub-Arctic Leadership Training College (Alberta and Northwest Territories District) in Fort Smith, Northwest Territories. Gibson, "Native Theological Training," 86.

142 NNLC, 20–1 March 1984, "Minutes of the Native Leadership Council," PAOC Archives, 8.

143 WOD, 1994, "Interview of Wally McKay by William Morrow and Jack Ozard," PAOC Archives, 1.

144 Ian Winter, 18 February 1985, "Letter to Gordon Upton," PAOC Archives, 1; Skinner, "Newslines," 15; Miller, *Canadian Pentecostals*, 362; PAOC, 1988, "General Constitution and By-Laws and Essential Resolutions," PAOC Archives, 51; PAOC National Bible College Committee, 25–26 November 1985, "Minutes of the National Bible College Committee," PAOC Archives, 3; PAOC National Bible College Committee, December 1986, "The National Bible College Standard of the PAOC," PAOC Archives, 5–9; Gordon Upton, 28 February 1985, "Letter to Ian Winter," PAOC Archives, 1–2; Ian Winter, 7 October 1987, "Letter to Gordon Upton," PAOC Archives, 1; Gordon Upton, 22 December 1987, "Letter to Ian Winter," PAOC Archives, 1; PAOC, 23–28 August 1990, "PAOC General Conference Meeting Minutes," PAOC Archives, 41–2; NNLC, 1992, "Meeting of All Pastors, District Native Directors, Superintendents and Evangelists," PAOC Archives, 1.

145 PAOC, 1986, "PAOC General Constitution & By-Laws," PAOC Archives, 38.

146 Peters, "The History of the Northland Mission," 178; PAOC General Executive, 17 September 1985, "General Executive Report, Department of Home Missions and Bible Colleges," PAOC Archives, 2; Roy Upton, "Canadian Missionary Outreach," *World Pentecost*, 1972, 2–3; PAOC General Executive, 25 February 1986, "Meeting Minutes," PAOC Archives, 8; Pierre Bergeron, 24 October 1988, "NBCC Standard – Two-Year Native Ministerial Diploma Course," PAOC Archives, 1; PAOC National Bible College Committee, 26–27 May 1986, "National Bible College Committee Meeting Minutes," PAOC Archives, 2; PAOC General Executive, 6 February 1985, "PAOC General Executive Meeting Minutes," PAOC Archives, 13–14; Gordon Upton, May 1990, "Mission Canada," PAOC Archives, 1–8.

147 PAOC, 1986, "PAOC General Constitution & By-Laws," 38.

148 Peters, "The History of the Northland Mission," 192.

149 PAOC, 23–8 August 1990, "PAOC General Conference Meeting Minutes," PAOC Archives, 6–8.

150 Pierre Bergeron, 8 September 1988, "Letter to Graham Gibson," PAOC Archives, 1; Upton, "Pierre Bergeron Joins National Home Missions Department," 19.

151 Chalmers, "History of Northern Bible College," 3. Ian Winter described students' loneliness and isolation as a major issue. Ian Winter, 28 December 1989, "Letter to Gordon Upton," PAOC Archives, 1.

152 Northland Ministries, 1991, "Northland Ministries Report & Recommendations to the Western Ontario Executive," PAOC Archives, 1; Graham and Linda Gibson, 10 January 1991, "Letter to Jack Ozard and Western Ontario District Executive," PAOC Archives, 1.

153 Jack Ozard, 1991, "Northland Mission Report to the 1991 District Conference," PAOC Archives, 32.

154 PAOC General Executive, 6 February 1985, "PAOC General Executive Meeting Minutes," PAOC Archives, 14; Gibson, "Native Theological Training," 114.

155 Chalmers, "History of Northern Bible College," 3.

156 The WOD also spent tens of thousands of dollars on electrical generators and subsequently funded and constructed a seven-mile electric power line from the town of Pickle Lake to the remote NLM headquarters. Jack Ozard, February 1982, "The Northland Mission Newsletter," PAOC Archives, 1–4; Jack Ozard, December 1983, "The Northland Mission: The Miracle of the Hydro Line," *The Challenge:* PAOC *Western Ontario District Bulletin*, PAOC Archives, 10–11.

157 Gibson, "Native Theological Training," 112; Kervan Chalmers, 1992, "Report for the Western Ontario District Conference," PAOC Archives, 31.

158 Gibson, "Native Theological Training," vii, 113.

159 Ibid., 114–15. An NLMBC student handbook from Pickle Lake laid out strict requirements: "Each Friday afternoon you will be taken to town to look at the stores, make any long distance phone calls, etc. Three good meals will be provided at the school but any snacks or treats, or baby supplies must be bought by students when they go to town. There will be no special trips to town made unless someone is sick. Also if students do not have their school work done they will not be allowed the trip to town until it is completed." The handbook added: "Students encouraged to bring chainsaws and axes." Northland Mission, 1983, "Northland Mission Indian Bible School," PAOC Archives, 2. Students would have used the chainsaws and axes for harvesting firewood for warmth.

160 Graham Gibson, 13 February 1991, "Letter to William Morrow," PAOC Archives, 1–2. Gibson recalled: "I have heard personal accounts of several Native adults who have come through the experience of ministerial training under the supervision of EuroCanadian [*sic*] missionaries, teachers, and administrators. Some aspects of their stories are not altogether different from those of their younger counterparts of

the residential schools." Gibson, "Native Theological Training," 53. The NLM's disciplinary heavy-handedness continued into the 1990s, with NLMBC leadership instructing students: "Attendance is required in all classes in which the student is enrolled. Failure to attend any class without previous permission granted by the principal will result in a meeting of the student with the Discipline Committee to explain the absence." NLMBC, 1991, "NLMBC Student Handbook," PAOC Archives, 10. Absence from class is generally unadvisable, but few colleges require a disciplinary hearing for a single absence. Such stringent requirements and close supervision at the very least indicate an environment within which students would be uncomfortable, and which prospective students would be hesitant to attend. Following further studies at Wilfrid Laurier University and the University of Toronto, Gibson became a professor at EPBC (as of the late 1990s called Master's College and Seminary), and continues to teach there at the time of writing. Gibson's research and writing at the graduate level reflected insightfully upon the NLM and Indigenous Pentecostalism, contributing to and expanding this discipline of study. Gibson, "Canadian Bible Colleges," 22. From 2006–07, Linda Gibson served as editor of *Testimony*.

161 Northland Mission, 1981, "Job Description – Overseer of Pickle Lake Training Centre," PAOC Archives, 1; WOD Executive, 1980, "Excerpts from District Executive Meetings Re: The Northland Mission," PAOC Archives, 6; Northland Ministries, 27 October 1992, "Northland Ministries Bible College Meeting of the Board of Administration," PAOC Archives, 4; PAOC, 1 March 1980, "Minutes of the Standing Home Missions Committee," PAOC Archives, 3.

162 Northland Mission, "1984 Budget," PAOC Archives, 1; Graham Gibson, 1990, "Report for 1990 District Conference," PAOC Archives, 1; Jack Ozard, April-May 1982, "The Northland Mission Newsletter," PAOC Archives, 2; Jack Ozard, 24 November 1982, "The Northland Mission Newsletter," PAOC Archives, 4; Western Ontario District of the PAOC, 1993, "Northland Bible College Statement of Income," PAOC Archives, 1; Northern Bible College, 1994, "Disbursements," PAOC Archives, 1.

163 Special Committee to Study Native Ministerial Training, 24 October 1994, "Meeting Minutes," PAOC Archives, 3; Gunner, interview by author.

164 Airhart, *A Church with the Soul of a Nation*, 205.

165 Beninger, "Does the Church Really Care?," 16.

166 In several instances, bands and councils funded Christian elementary schools led by college graduates. Likewise those schools were clearly Christian, but they were led by Indigenous people. Jack Ozard,

February 1996, "Aboriginal Pentecostal Ministries Newsletter," PAOC Archives, 1; Miller, *Residential Schools and Reconciliation*, 5. The NLMBC's restrictive living procedures differed from typical college residences, providing a Euro-Canadian-infused religious education exclusively to Indigenous youths, while permitting few freedoms. PAOC, February 1993, "Report on Native Bible Colleges," PAOC Archives, 2; Kervan Chalmers, 10 March 1994, "Letter to Jack Ozard," PAOC Archives, 1.

167 Beninger, "The Anglican Church of Canada," 20–2; Hayes, *Anglicans in Canada*, 35, 41. One NLMBC graduate believed bands and councils withheld funding for students because they perceived "that the Native communities aren't benefitting from Bible school students." Gibson, "Native Theological Training," 123. George Gunner (Moose Cree First Nation; Moose Factory, Ontario) later decried that government funding was withheld for Indigenous Pentecostals' ministerial training, but granted to educational programs outside of the Christian tradition. Gibson, "Two Histories," 21.

168 Jack Ozard, May 1991, "The Northland Newsletter," PAOC Archives, 3. Graham Gibson points to the NLMBC's relocation to Sioux Lookout as having been an influential factor in attracting Indigenous faculty members to the college. Gibson, "Native Theological Training," 115.

169 Gibson, "Native Theological Training," 131. Gibson interviewed an anonymous Pentecostal First Nations elder who advocated for "a Native principal 'that went through it'… and so is better equipped than a EuroCanadian [*sic*] 'to go at those things in leaps and bounds.'"

170 Ozard, "Northland Ministries Audio Visual Presentation," 2.

171 Jack Ozard, 1991, "Northland Mission Report to the 1991 District Conference," PAOC Archives, 33; Alistair Shearer, 26 August 1990, "Preliminary Report Outlining a Program Dealing with Native Offenders and Their Families," PAOC Archives, 5.

172 Northland Ministries, 1991, "Northland Ministries Report & Recommendations to the Western Ontario Executive," PAOC Archives, 1; Northland Ministries, 1990, "Dean of Students at NMBC," PAOC Archives, 1; District Native Directors and Superintendents, 24 May 1990, "Annual Meeting Minutes," PAOC Archives, 1; Ozard, "Northland Ministries Audio Visual Presentation," 2.

173 Jack Ozard, 1994, "Recommendations Re: The Northland Ministries," PAOC Archives, 4.

174 Northland Ministries, "Report & Recommendations," 1.

175 Kulbeck, "77 Graduates," 8; Kulbeck, "91 Graduates," 9; Hornby, "Canada for Christ Crusade," 8; Beselt, "A Christian's Career in Scarlet," 3;

Lynn, "Bungoma Church Dedication," 24; Chalmers, "Progress through Building," 30; Hansell, "Visit to Kenya," 4; Duncalfe, "Turkana Country," 15; Skinner, "Newslines of the Fellowship," 13.

176 Jack Ozard, 1992, "Northland Mission Report to the 1992 District Conference," PAOC Archives, 30.

177 Kervan Chalmers, 30 June 1992, "Letter to Jack Ozard," PAOC Archives, 2.

178 Chalmers, "History of Northern Bible College," 4.

179 Jack Ozard, May 1992, "The Northland Newsletter," PAOC Archives, 1.

180 Northland Ministries, "Report & Recommendations," 1–2.

181 Jack Ozard, May 1992, "The Northland Newsletter," PAOC Archives, 1.

182 Kervan Chalmers, 30 June 1992, "Letter to Jack Ozard," PAOC Archives, 2.

183 Northland Ministries, "Meeting of the Board of Administration," 1.

184 Jack Ozard, Summer 1994, "Northland Ministries Newsletter," PAOC Archives, 1. The establishment of the Christian school in Lac Seul came at the invitation of the Lac Seul Band Council. The Christian school in Moose Factory received funding from the Moose Factory Band Council. Jack Ozard, February 1996, "Aboriginal Pentecostal Ministries Newsletter," PAOC Archives, 1.

185 Northland Ministries, "Meeting of the Board of Administration," 1.

186 Jack Ozard, Summer 1994, "The Northland Newsletter," PAOC Archives, 1; Jack Ozard, August 1995, "The Northland Newsletter," PAOC Archives, 2.

187 Shearer, "Preliminary Report," 7; Northland Ministries, "Meeting of the Board of Administration," 1.

188 Jack Ozard, May 1992, "The Northland Newsletter," PAOC Archives, 1.

189 Kervan Chalmers, 21 July 1992, "Letter to Terry Corvanick," PAOC Archives, 1; Chalmers, "History of Northern Bible College," 3; Northland Ministries, "Northern Bible College Handbook," 3.

190 Kervan Chalmers, 7 November 1991, "Letter to William Morrow," PAOC Archives, 1–2.

191 Kervan Chalmers, 10 January 1994, "Letter to Kenneth Birch," PAOC Archives, 1–2.

192 Kenneth Birch, 1 February 1994, "Letter to Kervan Chalmers," PAOC Archives, 1.

193 Kervan Chalmers, 7 February 1994, "Letter to Jim Minor of Arrowhead Ministries," PAOC Archives, 1.

194 Northland Ministries, "Meeting of the Board of Administration," 4.

195 In 1990, Upton (unsuccessfully) asked Tom Siddon, then Progressive Conservative Minister of DIAND, to help fund PAOC Indigenous ministerial training institutions. Gordon Upton, 3 December 1990, "Letter to

Tom Siddon," PAOC Archives, 1–2; Tom Siddon, 19 February 1991, "Letter to Gordon Upton," PAOC Archives, 1. Meanwhile the WOD executive member attempted to secure provincial accreditation and recognition of the NLM Bible College. Jack Ozard, 1985, "The Northland Mission Report – 1985," PAOC Archives, 2.

196 Chalmers met with the Northern Nishnawbe Education Council and the Sioux Lookout Area Aboriginal Management Board to seek funding for students, with little success. He lamented that the Northern Nishnawbe Education Council, which represented and provided educational funding for twenty-five Indigenous communities surrounding Sioux Lookout, declined requests to fund the NLMBC. The principal implied the Councils were biased against the NLMBC as it was an outright Christian institution. The Councils relayed that they had suffered from recent federal government cutbacks in educational funding, and their organizations were intended only to fund official post-secondary students. This impeded Chalmers's attempts at funding, as many NLMBC students had not graduated secondary school. PAOC, February 1993, "Report on Native Bible Colleges," PAOC Archives, 2; Kervan Chalmers, 14 June 1993, "Letter to William Morrow," PAOC Archives, 1; Kervan Chalmers, 10 March 1994, "Letter to Jack Ozard," PAOC Archives, 1. According to 1986 Canadian census reports, 37 per cent of the adult Indigenous population reported having less than a Grade 9 education. Graham Gibson opined that one rationale for the establishment of the NLMBC was "the general lack of academic qualifications amongst aboriginal candidates for entry into mainstream schools; the number of Native graduates of Grade 12 or possessing post-secondary academic skills is considerably lower than the Canadian average." Gibson, "Native Theological Training," 56, 111. In remote, northerly regions, the rate of secondary school graduation is disproportionately low. For instance, in the Northwest Territories, only 45 per cent of Indigenous people over the age of fifteen possess a secondary school diploma and on average only 34 per cent of Indigenous students graduate from secondary school. Martin, "A Framework," 8, 20. Additionally, DIAND experienced budgetary limitations throughout the 1980s, contributing to a trickle-down effect whereby Indigenous territories also saw decreased federal funds. Swain, *Oka*, 32.

197 Brown, "'Watchmen' Graduate at E.P.B.C.," 10. Maracle was known to work with the PAOC Eastern Ontario and Quebec District (EOQD), and on at least one occasion taught at the Indian Pentecostal Mission Camp in Senneterre, Québec. Kulbeck, "The Pentecostal Assemblies of

Canada 1971 Camp Slate," 9; PAOC District Indian Directors and Superintendents, 29 March 1985, "Meeting Minutes," PAOC Archives, 10; "Aboriginal Bible Academy: A Leadership Training Centre," accessed April 2017, http://www.aboriginalbibleacademy.ca/about-us; Collado, "Aboriginal Bible Academy," 13.

198 Collado, interview by author, 24 November 2021; Jolly, *Christ Is Building His Native Church*, 56.

199 Peters, "The History of the Northland Mission," 192; Kervan Chalmers, 30 July 1992, "Letter to Jack Ozard," PAOC Archives, 1; Northland Ministries, "Meeting of the Board of Administration," 1.

200 EOQD, 10 October 1991, "Standing Native Ministries Committee Meeting Minutes," PAOC Archives, 3; Northland Ministries, "Meeting of the Board of Administration," 1.

201 Collado, interview by author.

202 Northland Ministries, 1 May 1995, "Native Board Meeting," PAOC Archives, 2.

203 Kervan Chalmers, 27 August 1992, "Letter to Jack Ozard," PAOC Archives, 2.

204 Kervan Chalmers, 16 August 1995, "Letter to William Morrow," PAOC Archives, 1–2.

205 PAOC Special Committee to Study Native Ministerial Training, 24 October 1994, "Meeting Minutes," PAOC Archives, 1–3.

206 Peters, "The History of the Northland Mission," 49.

207 Erna Peters noted that "80+ year old Gilbert Thunder and 75 year old Eli Mickenack ... stayed true all these years and have pastored the greater part of that time." Peters, "History of the Northland Mission," 150.

208 Gibson, "Native Theological Training," 124, Gibson quoting an anonymous NLMBC graduate.

209 PAOC Native Educational Leaders, 26 May 1994, "Summary of Discussion of Native Educational Leaders Consultation," PAOC Archives, 1–4.

210 Kervan Chalmers, 1 February 1995, "Letter to Northern Bible College Supporters," PAOC Archives, 1.

211 Kervan Chalmers, 14 September 1995, "Letter to Mike Davis," PAOC Archives, 1; Jack Ozard, April 1996, "Aboriginal Pentecostal Ministries Newsletter," PAOC Archives, 2.

212 Northland Mission, "Preliminary Application for Admission," 1.

213 Whitt, "Developing a Pentecostal Missiology" 136.

214 PAOC Aboriginal Pentecostal Ministries, 15–16 November 2000, "National Standing Committee Meeting Minutes," PAOC Archives, 1.

CHAPTER FOUR

1 Neylan, *The Heavens Are Changing*, 9.
2 Jolly, "A Native View of Self Government," 55.
3 Bear-Barnetson, *Introduction to First Nations Ministry*, 67. Cheryl Bear (Dakelh; Nadleh Whut'en First Nation, British Columbia) is "distinctively and unashamedly a Pentecostal scholar [and] … exercises a Native Pentecostal hermeneutic that is integrated with redemptive analogy." Alexander, *Native American Pentecost*, 29.
4 Twiss, *Rescuing the Gospel from the Cowboys*, 31, 40, 242. Of Twiss, Terry LeBlanc, Ray Aldred, and Bear (Indigenous theologians broadly referred to as "the contextualists"), Corky Alexander noted, "almost all … have connections to Pentecostalism, if not being Pentecostal themselves." Alexander further identified a "growing body of Pentecostal scholarship that features dimensions that can also be found in an indigenous theology. They include discernment from a spiritual approach rather than a solely scriptural approach, oral liturgy, narrative theology, inclusion of dreams and visions, and the use of sacred objects. For Pentecostals, sacred objects include anointing oil, water for footwashing, and prayer cloths." Alexander, *Native American Pentecost*, 24. Bear described many Euro-Canadian missionaries as apprehensive of Indigenous culture, believing "that all things indigenous are, at the very least, suspicious and, at the very worst, evil." Bear-Barnetson, *Introduction to First Nations Ministry*, 31.
5 Gibson, "Native Theological Training," 143.
6 Kracht, *Religious Revitalization among the Kiowas*, xv.
7 Ibid., 14; Weaver, "Foreword," xii. Elsewhere Weaver distinguishes religious dimorphism from syncretism, with the former denoting a process "whereby a person participates in Christianity but also still participates in his or her traditional culture and ways without mixing the two." Weaver, "From I-Hermeneutics to We-Hermeneutics," 19. Others might add that the embrace of Indigenous cultural practices within Pentecostal worship serves to solidify the indigenization of ministries. Today some Indigenous Pentecostals (many in western Canada) readily adopt aspects of Indigenous traditional spiritualities, integrating them into Pentecostal devotion as meditative aides. Waugh, "Conflicting Ethics," 173.
8 Lewis, *Creating Christian Indians*, 180–1.
9 Kracht, *Religious Revitalization*, 19; Hodge, "Navaho Pentecostalism," 88, 91.
10 Tarango, "Native American Christians," 329.

11 Tarango, *Choosing the Jesus Way*, 54–5, 93; Mesa New Life Assembly of God, "Memorial for Rodger Cree," YouTube Video, 1:04:05, 27 July 2020, https://www.youtube.com/watch?v=syDRFf2QYnU.
12 Kulbeck, "French Bible Institute," 4; Dale and Alberta Cummins, 11 March 1977, "The Northland Newsletter," PAOC Archives, 1; DHMBC, 1 September 1988, "Home Missions Executive Committee Meeting Minutes," PAOC Archives, 1–8; Peters, *The Contribution to Education by the Pentecostal Assemblies of Canada*, 58; Tarango, *Choosing the Jesus Way*, 54–5, 93; DHMBC, "Testimonies from British Columbia and Quebec," 2; Erna Peters, 1989, "The History of the Northland Mission," PAOC Archives, 37, 55.
13 Spillenaar, *Wings of the Gospel*, 70.
14 Cree, "Pagwa River Dedicates New Church," 26.
15 Ibid., 26; DHMBC, 1 September 1988, "Home Missions Executive Committee Meeting Minutes," PAOC Archives, 1–8.
16 John Spillenaar, 9 December 1953, "Letter to W.B. Greenwood," PAOC Archives, December 2014, 1. Cree earned only $30.00 per month for his efforts, but received Spillenaar's high praise. John Spillenaar, 1 December 1953, "The Northland Newsletter," PAOC Archives, 1.
17 John Spillenaar, March 1955, "The Northland Newsletter," PAOC Archives, 1.
18 Tarango, *Choosing the Jesus Way*, 55.
19 Lewis, *Creating Christian Indians*, 24.
20 Rodger Cree, 1987, "Open Letter Concerning Native American Ministry," Assemblies of God Flower Pentecostal Heritage Center, 1–2.
21 Dale and Alberta Cummins, 11 March 1977, "The Northland Newsletter," PAOC Archives, 1; Kulbeck, "People and Activities," November 1958, 15; Kulbeck, "Three Indian Works," 33; DHMBC, 1 September 1988, "Home Missions Executive Committee Meeting Minutes," PAOC Archives, 1–8; Tarango, *Choosing the Jesus Way*, 13, 55, 172; Cree, "Board Reflections," 133–7; Alexander, *Native American Pentecost*, 49; Marshall, *Upward, Not Sunwise*, 84.
22 Kulbeck, "Canadian," 14; Kulbeck, *What God Hath Wrought*, 336.
23 Cree, "Board Reflections," 133–4.
24 Tarango, "Native American Christians," 329.
25 Kulbeck, "People and Places," March 1960, 32.
26 Saggio, "Toward an Indigenous Model," 101–2.
27 Dale and Alberta Cummins, 11 March 1977, "The Northland Newsletter," PAOC Archives, 1; DHMBC, 1 September 1988, "Home Missions Executive Committee Meeting Minutes," PAOC Archives, 1–8;

Tarango, *Choosing the Jesus Way*, 13, 55, 172; Saggio, "Toward an Indigenous Model," 91, 97, 101–2; Cree, "Board Reflections," 133–7.

28 Mesa New Life Assembly of God, "Memorial for Rodger Cree."

29 Knott, "Testimony of a Young Indian," 10.

30 John Spillenaar, circa 1960, "The Proposed Courses of Study for MPBS," PAOC Archives, 23.

31 Kulbeck, *The Pentecostal Testimony*, October 1960, 9; Kulbeck, *What God Hath Wrought*, 132.

32 Regarding missionary displays of Indigenous people's wares, Austin and Scott argued such presentations "were not value-neutral, sentimental souvenirs, but were graphic, almost toxic 'representations' of 'heathen customs.'" Austin and Scott, "Introduction," 16. While Spillenaar's donning of Inuit regalia was not intended to be toxic, the lack of sensitivity in such culturally misappropriated displays is clear, especially since it would appear no Inuk person was present to wear the regalia in its ceremonial fashion.

33 King, *The Inconvenient Indian*, 55.

34 Kulbeck, "People and Activities," January 1958, 15; Moody, "You Are What You Eat," 25; Kulbeck, "Northern Lights," 8; Kulbeck, "Indians Accept Christ," 10.

35 Peters, "The History of the Northland Mission," 46–7. Peters quoting *The Northland Newsletter*.

36 Tarango, *Choosing the Jesus Way*, 107.

37 Peters, "The History of the Northland Mission," 47; Dombrowski, *Against Culture*, 124; Marshall, *Upward, Not Sunwise*, 21; Westman, "Understanding Cree Religious Discourse," 305; Milne, "Diyin God Bizaad," 432.

38 Strong, "Events and Impressions of Northern Ontario," 7; Smith, "Introduction," xxi; Peters, "The History of the Northland Mission," 56.

39 Brown, *Top of the World*, 151–62.

40 Ibid., 151–62.

41 Grace Priest, March 1958, "Our Mission to Fort Severn," PAOC Archives, 1.

42 John Spillenaar, 1 December 1953, "The Northland Newsletter," PAOC Archives, 1.

43 John Spillenaar, March 1955, "The Northland Newsletter," PAOC Archives, 1.

44 Priest, "Our Mission to Fort Severn," 1–2.

45 Beninger, "Does the Church Really Care?," 210.

46 McKay and Silman, *The First Nations*, 26–7.

47 Priest, "Our Mission to Fort Severn," 1–2.

48 Ibid., 3.
49 Brown, *Top of the World*, 154–62.
50 John Spillenaar, 1 December 1953, "The Northland Newsletter," PAOC Archives, December 2014, 1; John Spillenaar, March 1955, "The Northland Newsletter," PAOC Archives, December 2014, 1.
51 Morsch, *Rejoice*, 106.
52 Kostelnik, *The White Girl*, 39–40.
53 Brown, *Top of the World*, 166.
54 DHMBC, "Our Land," 1; Brown, *Top of the World*, 104.
55 Peters, "The History of the Northland Mission," 87.
56 Gibson, "Women of Faith," 70.
57 Canadian Obituaries, "Obits Index," accessed July 2017, https://canadianobits.com/obitindex/webbbs_config.pl/noframes/read/1071.
58 "Arctic Mission Outreach Trust Fund Newsletter: Winter 2003–2004," accessed December 2021, http://www.odyssey.on.ca/~david.ellyatt/arcticmissionsKeepUp/2004winter.htm.
59 Brown, *Fifty Years of Pentecostal History*, 179.
60 Gunner, interview by author.
61 Milne, "Diyin God Bizaad," 56, 99, 100.
62 McCleary, "An Ethnohistory of Pentecostalism," 124; Clatterbuck, "Sweet Grass Mass," 89; Marshall, "Navajo Reservation Camp Meeting a Great Success!," 96. Additionally, Indigenous Pentecostal ministers typically are more outspokenly opposed to Indigenous traditional spiritualities and what is perceived to be syncretizing with Pentecostalism than are Indigenous Pentecostal laity. Milne, "Diyin God Bizaad," 445.
63 Gunner, interview by author; Clatterbuck, *Crow Jesus*, 183, 223; Marshall, "Soaking Songs," 150.
64 Alexander, *Native American Pentecost*, 126. It might be further added that there is a comparable counter-trend with some adherents of Indigenous traditional spiritualities opposing the integration of Christianity into Indigenous traditional spiritualities, who observe "Christianity's encroachment into Native ceremonies with grave concern." Clatterbuck, *Crow Jesus*, 114, 246; Milne, "Diyin God Bizaad," 585–6.
65 Martin, "A Framework," 78.
66 Mason, "Christian Witness," 87.
67 Milne, "Diyin God Bizaad," 529, 624.
68 Ibid., 591. Contrastingly, to a practitioner of Indigenous traditional spiritualities, Pentecostal practice might "appear simple and unelaborated." Academics interpret Pentecostalism's integration with Indigenous culture

differently. American anthropologist Kirk Dombrowski argued that Indigenous Pentecostalism opposes Indigenous traditional spiritualities. Canadian anthropologist Clinton Westman claimed Indigenous Pentecostalism embraces Indigenous traditional spiritualities. Westman noted "a strong interest, or even deep compatibility, between Cree culture and Pentecostalism." He also maintains that "Cree Pentecostal practice is consistent with many elements of Cree culture ... [and] that Pentecostalism has the potential to support or renovate, rather than tear down, Aboriginal social structures." American anthropologist Kimberly Jenkins Marshall argued that Diné Pentecostalism resonates with Indigenous traditional spiritualities, whilst also ambiguously existing in rupture with it. American anthropologist Derek Brothers Milne posits that Diné Pentecostalism maintains an opposing but ongoing dialogue with Indigenous traditional spiritualities, explaining: "Pentecostals, who disdain what they see as the traditional, thus have a very interesting relationship to this ideology, contesting it with their own interpretations and counterideology." Milne argues that it is typically the denomination rather than the individual that draws the line between Pentecostalism and Indigenous traditional spiritualities. While "anti-syncretism" continues at the institutional level, such is not always the case with individual Indigenous Pentecostals, for whom "practicing both traditions is a common choice and the group that does so is both sizeable and stable (that is, not getting smaller in numbers)." Milne concludes, "Becoming Pentecostal means accepting the espoused ideologies of that movement and while those can be quite critical of other religious practices, the reality is one where such practices occur alongside of Pentecostalism." Dombrowski, *Against Culture*, 14; Westman, "Pentecostalism and Indigenous Culture in Northern North America," 142, 144; Westman, "Understanding Cree Religious Discourse," 14; Alexander, *Native American Pentecost*, 61; Marshall, "Soaking Songs," 75–7; Barde, "Second Coming," 27–31; Milne, "Diyin God Bizaad," 510, 625, 635.

69 Westman, "Cree Pentecostalism," 411; Marshall, "Soaking Songs," 152.

70 Peters, "The History of the Northland Mission," 73, 151, 159, 172.

71 Ibid., 86.

72 Ibid., 77.

73 Ibid., 91–2.

74 Ibid., 93.

75 Hansell, "Who/What: News about People and Events in the Pentecostal Assemblies of Canada," 10.

76 Peters, "The History of the Northland Mission," 76.

77 Hansell, "Who/What: News about People and Events in The Pentecostal Assemblies of Canada District Conferences – 1977: 50 Years for Two," 12.
78 Peters, "The History of the Northland Mission," 126–7.
79 Carlson, *Home Is the Hunter*, 122–3, 129. Mekenak's and McKay's exegetical exchange was quite significant for the Pentecostal historical record. Carlson continued, "hunting must be connected to Christianity in some meaningful way, and, given that hunting occurred out on the land and away from the missionaries and the traders, it is almost impossible to find this connection in the written record."
80 Preston, "Twentieth-Century Transformations," 208.
81 Westman, "Understanding Cree Religious Discourse," 82.
82 Weaver, "From I-Hermeneutics to We-Hermeneutics," 19.
83 Peters, "The History of the Northland Mission," 87.
84 Clarke, "Summer Is Coming," 16–17.
85 Cummins, "Christian Education," 15.
86 Preston, "Twentieth-Century Transformations," 205; McCleary, "Akbaatashee," 9.
87 McKay and Silman, *The First Nations*, 26–7.
88 Lewis, *Creating Christian Indians*, 46.
89 Clatterbuck, *Crow Jesus*, 73.
90 Bear-Barnetson, *Introduction to First Nations Ministry*, 73.
91 Peters, "The History of the Northland Mission," 130.
92 Ibid., 130.
93 Nadeau, *Unsettling Spirit*, 248; Bear-Barnetson, *Introduction to First Nations Ministry*, 85.
94 Barde, 27; Hayes, *Anglicans in Canada*, 31; Beninger, "The Anglican Church of Canada," 1.
95 Westman, "Cree Pentecostalism," 405.
96 Vilaça and Wright, "Introduction," 13; Tanner, "The Origins of Northern Aboriginal Social Pathologies," 266.
97 Peters, "The History of the Northland Mission," 100.
98 Ibid., 105.
99 Westman, "Cree Pentecostalism and Its Others," 414.
100 Clatterbuck, *Crow Jesus*, 241.
101 Peters, "The History of the Northland Mission," 132.
102 Gibson, "Native Theological Training," 17, Gibson quoting John Stott.
103 Peters, "The History of the Northland Mission," 95. Cheryl Bear noted: "Many Christians feel skeptical about Native traditions ... There are dozens of questions that Native people are forced to answer about their culture and sometimes it can get tiring ... While many Native people

continue to answer the questions, some simply withdraw … from the prying questions … [P]eople are ethnocentric" and prefer "that to which they are accustomed." If "anybody trifles with their stable lives, they get upset. That is unfortunate because Native people do not need validation from the church to feel Native or to be accepted by the Church. They will just leave … There should be unity in the body of Christ and First Nations should be accepted as they are." Bear-Barnetson, *Introduction to First Nations Ministry*, 70.

104 Peters, "The History of the Northland Mission," 131–2.
105 Alexander, *Native American Pentecost*, 4, 75; Westman, "Understanding Cree Religious Discourse," 109.
106 Gibson, "Native Theological Training," 134, Gibson quoting anonymous First Nations minister.
107 Clatterbuck, "Healing Hills and Sacred Songs," 249.
108 Peters, "The History of the Northland Mission," 157.
109 Jack Ozard, September 1983, "The Northland Mission Newsletter," PAOC Archives, 2; Jack Ozard, Fall 1995, "The Northland Newsletter," PAOC Archives, 2; Jack Ozard, August 1995, "The Northland Newsletter," PAOC Archives, 1; Jack Ozard, May 1995, "The Northland Newsletter," PAOC Archives, 1; Jack Ozard, August 1996, "Aboriginal Pentecostal Ministries Newsletter," PAOC Archives, 1; Northland Ministries, 1993, "Northland Ministries Bible College Graduation," PAOC Archives, 2; Peters, "The History of the Northland Mission," 140.
110 Carlson, *Home Is the Hunter*, 110.
111 Peters, "The History of the Northland Mission," 83.
112 The nearby North Spirit Lake First Nation (Anishinini) maintained a popular and prominent Mennonite church that practised some contextualization. Grant, *Moon of Wintertime*, 213–14.
113 Hodgman, *Light on the Horizon*, 205.
114 Gibson, "Two Histories," 12.
115 Peters, "The History of the Northland Mission," 95.
116 Dale and Alberta Cummins, May 1980, "Northland Mission Report for 1979," PAOC Archives, 1–2; Peters, "The History of the Northland Mission," 111, 114.
117 Carlson, *Home Is the Hunter*, 117.
118 Peters, "The History of the Northland Mission," 95.
119 Westman, *Cree and Christian*, 283.
120 Peters, "The History of the Northland Mission," 99.
121 Gibson, "Native Theological Training," 114.
122 Jack Ozard, 198?, "Itineration Presentation," PAOC Archives, 2.

123 Peters, "The History of the Northland Mission," 92, 95, 150.

124 Frost, *The Spirit, Indigenous Peoples and Social Change*, 5.

125 Peters, "The History of the Northland Mission," 84.

126 Maracle, "Goodbye, Snauq," 217; Alexander, *Native American Pentecost*, 61–2; Westman, *Cree and Christian*, xxxi–i. On Pentecostal holiness codes, Canadian sociologist Michael Wilkinson and Canadian historian Linda Ambrose write, "Pentecostals have a long history of requiring holiness, which included a range of restrictions. Over time, those restrictions have changed, but they included things like not drinking alcohol or smoking cigarettes. Restrictions revolved around where sacred bodies could be found and especially where they could not be found, including theatres and dance halls." Wilkinson and Ambrose, *After the Revival*, 125.

127 Tarango, *Choosing the Jesus Way*, 85.

128 In the late 1970s Dale and Alberta Cummins, sponsored by American Mennonite missionary friends, took a two-week language course. At its end, "They didn't feel they had learned the language but felt it was soft, musical, expressive and very complex with refinements that we lack in English." Peters, "The History of the Northland Mission," 99.

129 Cummins described the NLM as a PAOC "outreach ... to Canadian Indians living in the most remote parts of Ontario ... Our purpose is to see established strong indigenous native churches, *self-governing, self-supporting, self-propagating* and culturally relevant to this different world within Ontario borders ... Today the Mission is mainly concerned with Indian communities inaccessible except by airplane. Responsibility is particularly felt for places where PAOC churches were begun but where full development was stunted by lack of teaching and training a responsible Christian ministry or leadership." Peters, "The History of the Northland Mission," 73.

130 Peters, "The History of the Northland Mission," 78; Cummins, "Home Mission," 16–17; Cummins, "Somebody Prayed," 6. Cummins recorded a 1977 incident when NLM workers brought Nêhiyawêwin Bibles to Fort Hope, an Ojibwe Anishinaabe town, resulting in language challenges. Alberta and Dale Cummins, 11 March 1977, "The Northland Newsletter," PAOC Archives, 2. NLM missionaries also lamented "the dearth of Scripture and gospel literature in the various dialects of the north ... The Ojibway ... people have only the New Testament in their language." Peters, "The History of the Northland Mission," 28. Notwithstanding, some Indigenous Pentecostals exercise linguistic mutual intelligibility, moving between Nêhiyawêwin and Ojibwemowin Anishinaabemowin, both spoken and read, pointing to the fact that such

linguistic oversight might not have been as problematic as suggested. Westman, "Understanding Cree Religious Discourse," 77–8.

131 Peters, "The History of the Northland Mission," 105–7. It should be noted that the PAOC's desire for Indigenous people's allegiance was not uncommon among denominations. Neither was it unusual for Indigenous laity to identify for example as both Catholic and Pentecostal at the same time, many viewing elements of multiple religious traditions as compatible with one another, much to the chagrin of missionaries. Westman, "Cree Pentecostalism," 397.

132 Cummins, "Christian Education,"16.

133 DHMBC, 5 October 1981, "Requests and Information Needed for Ian Winter," PAOC Archives, 1.

134 WOD Executive, 1980, "Excerpts from District Executive Meetings Re: The Northland Mission," PAOC Archives, 2; WOD Executive, 1981, "Excerpts from District Executive Meetings Re: The Northland Mission," PAOC Archives, 1–2.

135 Peters, "The History of the Northland Mission," 71.

136 Alexander, *Native American Pentecost*, 106, 127.

137 Canadian Obituaries, "Obits Index," accessed July 2017, http://canadianobits.com/obitindex/webbbs_config.pl/noframes/read/685.

138 Lewis, *Creating Christian Indians*, 44.

139 Hodgman, *Light on the Horizon*, 68–9.

140 Whitt, "Developing a Pentecostal Missiology," 193.

141 Ibid., 292.

142 Moir, *Enduring Witness*, 158.

143 WOD Executive, 1981, "Excerpts from District Executive Meetings Re: The Northland Mission," PAOC Archives, 6.

144 Jack Ozard, 1986, "The Northland Mission," PAOC Archives, 1; Griffin, *The Pentecostal Testimony*, 21; Jack Ozard, 1990, "Northland Mission Report," PAOC Archives, 25.

145 Jack Ozard, March 1982, "Northland Mission Newsletter," PAOC Archives, 1.

146 Jack Ozard, March–April 1983, "The Northland Mission Newsletter," PAOC Archives, 4.

147 McKay and Silman, *The First Nations*, 26–7.

148 Jack Ozard, September 1983, "The Northland Newsletter," PAOC Archives, 2.

149 Jack Ozard, 1984, "The Northland Newsletter," PAOC Archives, 4.

150 Jack Ozard, September 1984, "The Northland Newsletter," PAOC Archives, 3.

151 Ibid.; Jack Ozard, October–November 1984, "The Northland Newsletter," PAOC Archives, 3.

152 Jack Ozard, May 1991, "The Northland Newsletter," PAOC Archives, 1–2.

153 Clarke, "Summer Is Coming," 17.

154 Jack Ozard, May 1995, "The Northland Newsletter," PAOC Archives, 1; Ian Winter, 1994, "Northland Ministries Report," PAOC Archives, 1.

155 Jack Ozard, December 1984, "The Northland Newsletter," PAOC Archives, 3.

156 Peters, "The History of the Northland Mission," 161.

157 Ibid., 163. Exceptionally few residential schools offered secondary education. Although residential schools had ceased operation, negative sentiments toward the schools were being expressed.

158 Grant, *Moon of Wintertime*, 202–14.

159 Bear-Barnetson, *Introduction to First Nations Ministry*, 15–16, 23.

160 Peters, "The History of the Northland Mission," 165.

161 Hodge, "Navaho Pentecostalism," 83.

162 Milne, "Diyin God Bizaad," 535, 537. Within a Pentecostal context, this linguistic conciliatory capacity is additionally aided through the advent of tongues-speaking. Reidy, "Holy Ghost Tribe," 379.

163 Gibson, "Native Theological Training," 133. Gibson quoting an anonymous First Nations minister.

164 Westman, "Cree Pentecostalism," 402.

165 Simpson, *Dancing on Our Turtle's Back*, 85.

166 Lewis, *Creating Christian Indians*, 92.

167 Posterski and Nelson, *Future Faith Churches*, 85, 93–4.

168 Gibson, "Native Theological Training," 83–4. Gibson quoting and paraphrasing Doolittle.

169 Jack Ozard, May–June 1984, "The Northland Newsletter," PAOC Archives, 1.

170 Dan Doolittle, May–June 1984, "The Northland Newsletter," PAOC Archives, 2.

171 Jack Ozard, 1986, "The Northland Mission Report," PAOC Archives, 3, emphasis added. Ozard was not ignorant of the indigenous principle, but only halfway embraced it. Prior to the above statement, the executive member had appealed to mission supporters: "Workers are needed! – Native Workers, trained, yes, but also *white workers* who are willing to come north." Jack Ozard, 1983, "The Northland Mission Report," PAOC Archives, 1, emphasis added.

172 Barker and Lowman, "Ways of Knowing and Being," 45.

173 Simpson, *Dancing On Our Turtle's Back*, 33.

174 Stonechild, *The Knowledge Seeker*, 9.
175 Gibson, "Native Theological Training," 122–3, punctuation original.
176 McCleary, "Akbaatashee," 61–2.
177 McPherson, "A Definition of Culture," 94.
178 Martin, "A Framework," 46, Martin quoting Lori Lambert.
179 Simpson, *Dancing On Our Turtle's Back*, 31.
180 Gibson, "Native Theological Training," 123–4.
181 Barker and Lowman, "Ways of Knowing and Being," 46.
182 Lewis, *Creating Christian Indians*, 180–1.
183 Milne, "Diyin God Bizaad," 626, 628.
184 Lewis, *Creating Christian Indians*, xiii.
185 PAOC Aboriginal Ministries Guiding Group, 21 January 2011, "Conference Call Meeting Minutes," PAOC Archives, 23–4.
186 Wilkinson, "Public Acts of Forgiveness," 186.
187 Jack Ozard, May–June 1982, "The Northland Newsletter," PAOC Archives, 2.
188 Dale and Alberta Cummins, June 1981, "The Northland Newsletter," PAOC Archives, 2–3.
189 Jack Ozard, 24 November 1982, "The Northland Newsletter," PAOC Archives, 2. One explanation for the missionaries' lament was that it served as a sort of Euro-Canadian "cultural narrative" of its own. Maintaining a connection with their wider social circles and Euro-Canadian friends and family helped to provide meaning for the missionaries' work, as well as enabling them to impose their social and moral values upon Indigenous Pentecostals. Carlson, *Home Is the Hunter*, 118.
190 Jack Ozard, 1984, "1984 Northland Mission Report," PAOC Archives, 1; District Indian Directors and District Superintendents, 29 March 1985, "District Indian Directors' and Superintendents' Meeting," PAOC Archives, 1.
191 Jack Ozard, 24 November 1982, "The Northland Newsletter," PAOC Archives, 2–3.
192 Northland Mission, 28 March 1983, "Northland Mission Worker's Conference Minutes," PAOC Archives, 2.
193 Northland Ministries, 27 October 1992, "Northland Ministries Bible College Meeting of the Board of Administration," PAOC Archives, 3.
194 Ian Winter, 1994, "Northland Ministries Report," PAOC Archives, 1.
195 Pat Linklater, 5 April 1984, "Pentecostal Mission Church Report," PAOC Archives, 1.
196 Jack Ozard, April 1984, "The Northland Newsletter," PAOC Archives, 4.

197 Tarango, *Choosing the Jesus Way*, 85; Woodard, "A Light unto the Nations," 32.

198 Peters, "The History of the Northland Mission," 175.

199 Bear-Barnetson, *Introduction to First Nations Ministry*, 24.

200 Jack Ozard, 1989, "Northland Report," PAOC Archives, 36; Ian Winter, 1989, "The Northland Director's Report," PAOC Archives, 27; Jack Ozard, 1993, "Northland Ministries Report," PAOC Archives, 36.

201 Kervan Chalmers, 20 September 1995, "Letter to Marg Sanders," PAOC Archives, 2.

202 Jack Ozard, August 1996, "Aboriginal Pentecostal Ministries Newsletter," PAOC Archives, 1.

203 Aboriginal Pentecostal Ministries, 16 November 1995, "Conference Call – Board Meeting Minutes," PAOC Archives, 2–3.

204 Aboriginal Pentecostal Ministries, "Conference Call," 2–3.

205 Peters, "The History of the Northland Mission," 134–7, 172–3, 175; Jack Ozard, 24 November 1982, "The Northland Newsletter," PAOC Archives, 2.

206 Lewis, *Creating Christian Indians*, 120.

207 Jack Ozard, Fall 1995, "The Northland Newsletter," PAOC Archives, 2.

208 Jack Ozard, 1995, "Northland Ministries Report," PAOC Archives, 1.

209 Johnson, "Contextualization," 17.

210 Ng, "The United Church of Canada," 233–4.

211 Jack Ozard, Summer 1994, "Northland Ministries Newsletter," PAOC Archives, 1.

212 NNLC, 25 October 1994, "National Native Leadership Planning Committee Meeting," PAOC Archives, 1.

CHAPTER FIVE

1 Deloria, *Custer Died for Your Sins*, 112.

2 Boyd, "National Native Leadership Council," 1, Boyd quoting Kallappa.

3 Northland Ministries, 12–15 October 1995, "Northland Leadership Conference," PAOC Archives, 1.

4 TEDx Talks, "Decolonization Is for Everyone | Nikki Sanchez | TEDx-SFU," YouTube Video, 13:18, 12 March 2019, https://www.youtube.com/watch?v=QP9x1NnCWNY.

5 Jack Ozard, 1985, "The Northland Mission Report," PAOC Archives, 3.

6 Martin, "A Framework," 2.

7 Earl N.O. Kulbeck, 28 April 1968, "Parliamentary Consultation on Indian Work; Ottawa, Canada," PAOC Archives, 2.

8 Miller, *Canadian Pentecostals*, 283.
9 Mix-Ross, "The PAOC and Indigenous Peoples," 130.
10 Porterfield, email message to author; "Sanderson Reginald: Winnipeg Free Press Passages," *Winnipeg Free Press*, 1 November 2005, https://passages.winnipegfreepress.com/passage-details/id-101627/SANDERSON_REGINALD.
11 PAOC, 15 August 1970, "Minutes of the Standing Home Missions Committee," PAOC Archives, 1.
12 Erna Peters, 1989, "The History of the Northland Mission," PAOC Archives, 150.
13 DHMBC, "Native Leadership in Canada," 1.
14 Gibson, "Native Theological Training," 144.
15 Peters, "The History of the Northland Mission," 150.
16 Jack Ozard, 1996, "Northland Ministries Report," PAOC Archives, 2.
17 Gibson, "Native Theological Training," 117.
18 Jack Ozard, 1994, "Recommendations Re: The Northland Ministries," PAOC Archives, 4; Jack Ozard, April 1996, "Aboriginal Pentecostal Ministries Newsletter," PAOC Archives, 2.
19 Saggio, "Toward an Indigenous Model," 94, Saggio quoting Cree.
20 Aboriginal Pentecostal Ministries, 1996, "Aboriginal Pentecostal Ministries (Development) Timeline," PAOC Archives, 1.
21 Jack Ozard, 1993, "Northland Ministries Report," PAOC Archives, 35. Ozard quoting Richard Long, then Executive Director of the Alberta Native Council. Davis Inlet was a predominantly Naskapi community in Labrador. The year prior to Ozard's report, six children died in a house fire while their parents attended a party. Fifty community residents died from alcohol abuse between 1973 and 1995. Teenage suicide was also a leading cause of death in the community. Press, "Davis Inlet in Crisis," 201.
22 Younging, *Elements of Indigenous Style*, 60.
23 Jolly, "A Native View of Self Government," 56.
24 Dickason and Newbigging, *Indigenous Peoples within Canada*, 328–9.
25 King, *The Inconvenient Indian*, 135; Dickason and Newbigging, *Indigenous Peoples within Canada*, 329.
26 Peach, "The Power of a Single Feather," 6.
27 Smith, *Sacred Feathers*, xxv–i.
28 King, *The Inconvenient Indian*, 178.
29 Peach, "The Power of a Single Feather," 5, 11, 12.
30 Ibid., 5, 12; Monahan, *Meech Lake*, xiii, xvi, 1, 5–6, 8–9, 12, 33, 200, 234; Stryker, "A Sin of Omission," 292–5.

31 Taylor, "A Blurry Image," 224, 230, 234–5.

32 Guenther, "Ethnicity and Evangelical Protestants in Canada," 392; Smith, *Native Americans and the Christian Right*, 92. Reflecting on Maracle's unique suitability to serve as negotiator at Oka, Dan Collado (Kanien'kehá:ka; Tyendinaga Mohawk Territory, Ontario) observed, "He was a person for that time for sure." Collado, interview by author.

33 Peach, "The Power of a Single Feather," 19, Peach paraphrasing Coon Come.

34 Elijah Harper, 1995, "Letter to Participants in Sacred Assembly '95," PAOC Archives, 1; James Kallappa, 15 October 1995, "Letter to James MacKnight," PAOC Archives, 2; Jack Ozard, Fall 1995, "Northland Ministries Newsletter," PAOC Archives, 3; Wilkinson, "Public Acts of Forgiveness," 193.

35 Gibson, "Native Theological Training," 101–2, Gibson quoting Bergeron.

36 Ernie Linklater, 13 June 1997, "Letter to William Morrow," PAOC Archives, 1–2.

37 Peach, "The Power of a Single Feather," 2.

38 Hayes, *Anglicans in Canada*, 41; Smith, *Native Americans and the Christian Right*, 104, Smith quoting Diamond; Dickason and Newbigging, *Indigenous Peoples within Canada*, 324–5; Beninger, "The Anglican Church of Canada," 49–51, 58–60. Subsequent convocations occurred in 1993 and 1997. Guenther, "Ethnicity and Evangelical Protestants in Canada," 391. In 1975 the Presbyterian Church stated its intention to hold consultations with Indigenous leaders, and to train Indigenous clergy. Beninger, "Does the Church Really Care?," 56, 219, 226–7.

39 Airhart, *A Church with the Soul of a Nation*, 211, 227, 231–2; Beninger, "Does the Church Really Care?," 3.

40 Beninger, "Does the Church Really Care?," 229–31.

41 Ibid., 210, 213.

42 PAOC District Native Directors and District Superintendents, 25 May 1989, "Annual Meeting of District Native Directors and District Superintendents," PAOC Archives, 3.

43 Peters, "The History of the Northland Mission," 150.

44 Gordon Upton, 1 April 1984, "Letter from Gordon R. Upton to Pastors," PAOC Archives, 1. Joseph Jolly (Eeyou; Waskaganish, Quebec; raised in Moose Factory, Ontario) articulated an Evangelical position on self-determination: "This principle of indigenous missions is similar to principles being advocated in native self-government. Ownership and self-government are just two characteristics of an indigenous church." Jolly, "A Native View of Self Government," 55.

45 Upton, "Window on the World," 16.
46 Sonnenberg, "Window on the World," 17.
47 PAOC District Native Directors, District Superintendents, Pastors and Evangelists, 29 May 1993, "NNLC Meeting of District Native Directors, District Superintendents, Pastors, and Evangelists," PAOC Archives, 1; Klaus Sonnenberg, 19 July 1993, "Letter to the Assembly of First Nations," PAOC Archives, 1.
48 Ozard, "Recommendations Re: The Northland Ministries," 1.
49 Gordon Upton, 19 June 1990, "Letter to Billy Diamond," PAOC Archives, 1; Clinton N. Westman, "Pentecostalism among Canadian Aboriginal People," 93.
50 Northland Mission, 15 January 1990, "NLM Northern Board Meeting," PAOC Archives, 1.
51 District Native Directors and District Superintendents, 24 May 1990, "Annual Meeting," PAOC Archives, 1.
52 Northland Mission, 28 March 1983, "Northland Mission Worker's Conference Minutes," PAOC Archives, 1; Northland Mission, "Northland Mission Worker's Conference Minutes," 2; Northland Mission, February 1984, "The Northland Newsletter," PAOC Archives, 2; Skinner, *Pentecostal Testimony*, 27; Jack Ozard, 199?, "Northland Ministries Audio Visual Presentation," PAOC Archives, 3; Upton, "The Canadian Scene," 35–6; Upton, "Indifferent Attitude," 5.
53 NNLC, 24 May 1991, "Seventh National Native Leadership Council," PAOC Archives, 1; Peters, "The History of the Northland Mission," 133.
54 Jack Ozard, May 1994, "Northland Ministries Newsletter," PAOC Archives, 1; Jack Ozard, Fall 1995, "Northland Ministries Newsletter," PAOC Archives, 1; Gunner, interview by author.
55 Ozard, "Recommendations Re: The Northland Ministries," 1.
56 Ibid., 2.
57 Jack Ozard, October 1994, "Northland Ministries Newsletter," PAOC Archives, 1–2; Northland Ministries, 12–15 October 1995, "Northland Leadership Conference, Timmins, Ontario," PAOC Archives, 1. George Gunner established the NLM church in Moose Factory in 1989. In reference to his subscription to the Pentecostal message, Gunner described it as "something that … I knew was real and that Jesus was the answer. Not only for me, but for anyone. For all our people. And I had a desire to let everyone know. I wanted our people to know there is an answer out of what we are facing; the poverty we are in, the problems. It's the same thing today. Jesus is still the answer." Gunner, interview by author.

58 Northland Mission, 6 January 1995, "Native Leadership Committee Meeting," PAOC Archives, 1.
59 Northland Mission, 7 January 1995, "Native Leadership Committee Meeting," PAOC Archives, 5.
60 WOD, 1994, "Interview of Wally McKay by William Morrow and Jack Ozard," PAOC Archives, 1.
61 WOD, "Interview of Wally McKay," 1.
62 Northland Ministries, 1 May 1995, "Native Board Meeting," PAOC Archives, 1–2.
63 Gunner, interview by author.
64 Gibson, "Native Theological Training," 120.
65 Northland Mission, 6 January 1995, "Native Leadership Committee Meeting," PAOC Archives, 1.
66 Northland Ministries, 1 May 1995, "Native Board Meeting," PAOC Archives, 3. Levi Beardy is not the same person whose interview is referenced elsewhere in this monograph, and who is referred to as Levi Samson Beardy.
67 Ibid., 3.
68 Ibid., 1.
69 PAOC District Superintendents and District Native Ministries Directors, 27 May 1995, "Meeting Minutes," PAOC Archives, 2.
70 Jack Ozard, Summer 1994, "Northland Ministries Newsletter," PAOC Archives, 2; Jack Ozard, February 1995, "Northland Ministries Newsletter," PAOC Archives, 2.
71 Jack Ozard, February 1995, "Northland Ministries Newsletter," PAOC Archives, 2.
72 Northland Mission, 12–15 October 1995, "Northland Leadership Conference," PAOC Archives, 1.
73 Jack Ozard, 1993, "Northland Ministries Report," PAOC Archives, 36; Jack Ozard, May 1994, "Northland Ministries Newsletter," PAOC Archives, 1.
74 Northland Ministries, 12–15 October 1995, "Northland Leadership Conference," PAOC Archives, 2.
75 Northland Ministries, "Native Board Meeting," 1–3.
76 Ibid., 1–3.
77 Northland Ministries, "Northland Leadership Conference," 3.
78 Kervan Chalmers, 1 February 1995, "Letter to Northern Bible College Supporters," PAOC Archives, 1.
79 Northland Ministries, 26 July 1995, "Native Board of Directors Meeting," PAOC Archives, 1–2.

80 Northland Ministries, "Northland Leadership Conference," 2.
81 Ibid., 2.
82 Northland Ministries, 26 July 1995, "Native Board of Directors Meeting," 1–2.
83 Ibid., 5.
84 Ibid., 5.
85 Aboriginal Pentecostal Ministries, 10 October 1997, "Board Meeting," PAOC Archives, 4; Northland Ministries, "Northland Leadership Conference," 9. Likewise Indigenous Pentecostal trailblazer Rodger Cree lamented the general trend of Indigenous Pentecostal ministers enduring inadequate funding, exclaiming: "Many Indian pastors do not have adequate support to provide the basic necessities of life for their families." Saggio, "Toward an Indigenous Model," 94, Saggio quoting Cree.
86 Northland Ministries, "Northland Leadership Conference," 3; Gunner, interview by author.
87 Northland Ministries, "Native Board of Directors Meeting," 5.
88 Northland Ministries, "Northland Leadership Conference," 2.
89 WOD, "Interview of Wally McKay," 2.
90 Jack Ozard, April 1996, "Aboriginal Pentecostal Ministries Newsletter," PAOC Archives, 2.
91 Northland Ministries, "Northland Leadership Conference," 1, 7.
92 Kervan Chalmers, 15 September 1995, "Aboriginal News," PAOC Archives, 1.
93 DHMBC, 199?, "Native Canada Today," PAOC Archives, 2, 7.
94 Jack Ozard, February 1996, "Aboriginal Pentecostal Ministries Newsletter," PAOC Archives, 1.
95 Aboriginal Pentecostal Ministries, 1996/1997, "Aboriginal Pentecostal Assemblies Constitution," PAOC Archives, 3.
96 Ibid., 7.
97 Kervan Chalmers, 14 September 1995, "Letter to Mike Davis," PAOC Archives, 2.
98 Ian Winter, 19 May 1995, "Letter to Supporting Pastors of the Northland Ministries," PAOC Archives, 1.
99 Jack Ozard, August 1996, "Aboriginal Pentecostal Ministries Newsletter," PAOC Archives, 1; Northland Ministries, 8 October 1994, "Native Leadership Meeting," PAOC Archives, 1–2.
100 Smith's Funeral Home: Your Life Moments, "Reverend Jack Ozard Obituary," accessed July 2017, http://www.yourlifemoments.ca/sitepages/obituary.asp?oid=557117; Budgell Funeral Home, "Donald

Kervan Chalmers Obituary," accessed April 2019, https://www.budgellfuneralhome.ca/obituary/donald-kervan-chalmers.

101 James Kallappa, 15 April 1996, "Fax to Kenneth Birch," PAOC Archives, 1.

102 Jack Ozard, Summer 1994, "Northland Ministries Newsletter," PAOC Archives, 1.

103 Jack Ozard, August 1996, "Aboriginal Pentecostal Ministries Newsletter," PAOC Archives, 2.

104 Aboriginal Pentecostal Ministries, 1996, "Aboriginal Pentecostal Ministries (Development) Timeline," PAOC Archives, 2; Brown, *Fifty Years of Pentecostal History*, 7.

105 Ernie Linklater, 13 June 1997, "Letter to William Morrow," PAOC Archives, 1–2; Hageman, "Seven Questions for Reggie Neeposh," 28.

106 Northland Ministries, 12–15 October 1995, "Northland Leadership Conference," PAOC Archives, 4.

107 Aboriginal Pentecostal Ministries, 2 December 1997, "Board Meeting Minutes," PAOC Archives, 3.

108 Aboriginal Pentecostal Ministries, 10 October 1997, "Board Meeting," PAOC Archives, 4; Aboriginal Pentecostal Ministries, 1997, "Board Meeting Minutes," PAOC Archives, 1–2.

109 Jack Ozard, 1994, "Recommendations Re: The Northland Ministries," PAOC Archives, 3.

110 PAOC Aboriginal Ministries National Standing Committee, 15–16 November 2000, "Committee Meeting Minutes," PAOC Archives, 3–6; PAOC Aboriginal Ministries National Standing Committee, 30 May 2001, "Committee Meeting Minutes," PAOC Archives, December 2015, 1–2; PAOC Mission Canada Aboriginal Guiding Group, 2–3 November 2010, "Meeting Minutes," PAOC Archives, 3; Gunner, interview by author; WOD, 2007, "Aboriginal Pentecostal Ministries," PAOC Archives, 1.

111 Preston, "Twentieth-Century Transformations of East Cree Spirituality and Autonomy," 216.

112 PAOC General Executive, 2001, "Special Announcement," PAOC Archives, 1; Hiebert, "Fellowship Notes," 20.

113 Kennedy, "Apology, Forgiveness, and Reconciliation," 22.

114 Gunner, interview by author; WOD, 2007, "Aboriginal Pentecostal Ministries," PAOC Archives, 1.

115 Mission Canada Aboriginal Council, 3–5 January 2007, "Letter to Invitees to Planning Meeting in Vancouver," PAOC Archives, 1; PAOC General Executive, 1989, "Home Missions Committee Restructuring Proposal,"

PAOC Archives, 1; "Aboriginal Canadians," PAOC Mission Canada, accessed March 2017, https://paoc.org/canada/priorities/aboriginal; WOD, 2007, "Aboriginal Pentecostal Ministries," PAOC Archives, 1.

CHAPTER SIX

1 Wilkinson, "Public Acts of Forgiveness, 193–4, Wilkinson quoting LeBlanc.
2 Wilkinson, "Public Acts of Forgiveness," 192, Wilkinson quoting Aldred.
3 McKenzie, "From the Editor," 3.
4 Gunner, interview by author.
5 Burkinshaw, "Native Pentecostalism in British Columbia" (presentation paper), 1; Kenneth Birch, 4 June 1993, "Letter to Matthew Coon Come, Grand Chief/Chairman Cree Nation," PAOC Archives, 1.
6 Smith, *Native Americans and the Christian Right*, 104, Smith quoting Coon Come.
7 MacKinnon, "Natives Turn Up Heat, Elect Aggressive New Chief."
8 Dees, 284; Dickason and Newbigging, *Indigenous Peoples within Canada*, 341.
9 Dickason and Newbigging, *Indigenous Peoples within Canada*, 340.
10 Ministry of Indigenous and Northern Affairs of Canada, "Statement of Apology to Former Students of Indian Residential Schools," accessed December 2017, http://www.aadnc-aandc.gc.ca/eng/1100100015644/1100100015649.
11 *100 Huntley Street*, "First Nations Follow Up."
12 Wilkinson, "Public Acts of Forgiveness," 186, 192.
13 PAOC Aboriginal Ministries Guiding Group, 21 January 2011, "Conference Call Meeting Minutes," PAOC Archives. 1.
14 "News," PAOC website, accessed May 2016, http://paoc.org/about/news?nID=902.
15 Ibid. The PAOC's reconciliation statement is included in its entirety in this monograph with the permission of the PAOC (copyright May 2012). It is available for viewing at https://paoc.org/docs/default-source/paoc-family/letter-of-apology-between-the-paoc-and-its-aboriginal-leadership-final-gc2012.pdf?sfvrsn=9073f56a_0.
16 Bush, "The Canadian Churches' Apologies," 47.
17 Wilkinson, "Public Acts of Forgiveness," 186. The PAOC apology addresses residential schools, not for their operation, but for the PAOC's "failure to address the hurt and harmful practices" therein. "News," PAOC website, accessed May 2016, http://paoc.org/about/news?nID=902.
18 Mason, "Christian Witness," 87.

19 Beninger, "The Primacy of Justice," 9–10.
20 Bush, "The Canadian Churches' Apologies," 48, 51.
21 Beninger, "Does the Church Really Care?," 218.
22 Bush, "The Presbyterian Church in Canada's Mission to Canada's Native Peoples, 1900–2000," 119.
23 Ibid., 119.
24 Beninger, "Does the Church Really Care?," 224.
25 Miller, *Residential Schools and Reconciliation*, 4.
26 "Pope Francis Apologizes for Forced Assimilation of Indigenous Children at Residential Schools," *CBC News*, 25 July 2022, https://www.cbc.ca/news/canada/edmonton/edmonton-pope-alberta-apology-1.6530947.
27 Beninger, "Does the Church Really Care?," 226–35.
28 Ibid., 210–11.
29 Bush, "The Canadian Churches' Apologies," 49, 52–6, 64; Heinrichs, "An Indigenous Intrusion Troubles the House," 26.
30 Gunner, interview by author.
31 Collado, interview by author.
32 Aldred, LeBlanc, and Jacobs, "Thoughts on Forgiveness and Aboriginal Residential Schools," 4.
33 Wilkinson, "Public Acts of Forgiveness," 193.
34 Ibid., 193–4.
35 Bush, "The Canadian Churches' Apologies," 55, 68. Bush quoting the Anglican Church of Canada's General Synod Communications.
36 Davidson, "What's Up with APM?," 18; PAOC, 2013, "PAOC Credential Change Report," PAOC Archives, March 2017, 2; "House of All Nations," accessed March 2017, http://hoan.ca/home. Gunner continues to pastor his church in North Bay, Ontario. Christian Aboriginal Fellowship of Canada, "CAFC's Vision, Mission and Goals," accessed September 2019, http://www.christianaboriginalfellowship.ca/about-us.
37 *100 Huntley Street*, "House of All Nations."
38 Aboriginal Pentecostal Ministries, 18 February 1997, "Board Meeting Minutes," PAOC Archives, 3. Incidentally, in 2000, James Kallappa's brother George Kallappa (Kwih-dich-chuh-aht; Neah Bay, Washington State), working for the Native Christian Resource Center in Mesa, Arizona, likewise drafted a document for the AG USA, supporting "the use of Native culture 'for the purposes of worship and evangelism.'" Smith, *Native Americans and the Christian Right*, 85.
39 James Kallappa, 13 September 2000, "Dear Companion in Ministry," PAOC Archives, 1; NNLC, 25 May 1998, "Native Summit Meeting Minutes," PAOC Archives, 3.

40 Hageman, "Seven Questions for Reggie Neeposh," 28–9, Hageman quoting Neeposh. These internal reactions are akin to processes which sociologist Bruce F. Ryan termed "social conflict" and "ideological competition." Kracht, *Religious Revitalization*, 13, Kracht quoting Ryan.
41 Beardy, interview by author.
42 Ibid.
43 Dickason and Newbigging, *Indigenous Peoples within Canada*, 329.
44 Mix-Ross, "The PAOC and Indigenous Peoples," 134–5, Mix-Ross paraphrasing Beardy.
45 Beardy, interview by author, Beardy paraphrasing Revelation 8.
46 Woodard, "A Light unto the Nations," 32.
47 Gunner, interview by author.
48 James Kallappa, 13 September 2000, "Dear Companion in Ministry," PAOC Archives, 1.
49 *Aboriginal Peoples Television Network National News*, "APTN Investigates."
50 Gibson, "Two Histories," 22, Gibson quoting Gunner.
51 Tanner, "The Origins of Northern Aboriginal Social Pathologies," 267.
52 Milne, "Diyin God Bizaad," 625.
53 Clatterbuck, "Healing Hills and Sacred Songs," 272.
54 Ibid., 274.
55 Laugrand and Oosten, "Shamans and Missionaries," 183.
56 Gunner, "Aboriginal Ministry that Endures," 73–4.
57 PAOC Mission Canada Aboriginal Guiding Group, 2–3 November 2010, "Meeting Minutes," PAOC Archives, 3.
58 Gunner, interview by author.
59 Gunner, "Aboriginal Ministry that Endures," 70, 73–4.
60 "Christian Aboriginal Fellowship of Canada," accessed December 2017, http://www.christianaboriginalfellowship.ca.
61 Gunner, interview by author.
62 "Christian Aboriginal Fellowship of Canada."
63 Aboriginal Peoples Television Network National News, "APTN Investigates"; Gunner, interview by author.
64 Gunner, interview by author.
65 Tarango, "Native American Christians," 338.
66 Nkonge, "The Church Missionary Society's Burden," 23.
67 Gordon Upton, 1991, "Mission Canada National Update," PAOC Archives, 1.
68 Daniels, "North American Pentecostalism," 81, 91; PAOC Western Ontario District, 2007, "Aboriginal Pentecostal Ministries," PAOC Archives, 1; *100 Huntley Street*, "House of All Nations"; Mission Canada Aboriginal

Guiding Group, 2–3 November 2010, "Meeting Minutes," PAOC Archives, 3; Gunner, interview by author. Some of the increase in the number of APM churches came through the affiliation of pre-existing churches, rather than exclusively through the establishment of new churches.

69 Davidson, "What's Up with APM?," 18; Aboriginal Pentecostal Ministries, "APM Leadership Council," accessed July 2017, https://north1515.wordpress.com/apm-leadership-council; PAOC Western Ontario District, "Contact," accessed December 2017, http://www.wodistrict.org/contact.

70 Upton, "Canadian Missionary Outreach," 2–3; Jack Ozard, 1984, "1984 Northland Mission Report," PAOC Archives, 1. The contemporary trend of millennials' and younger people's congregational disassociation is similarly observable in many of the PAOC's historically settler Canadian churches. Neeposh's church has demonstrated healthy growth numerically, and at the time of writing comprises over one hundred adherents. Hageman, "Seven Questions for Reggie Neeposh," 25, 28–9. By way of comparison to the number of Indigenous Pentecostal churches within the PAOC, in 1955 there were 36 "Native churches" in the AG USA. By 2006 the total number of "Indian AG churches" had risen to 190. From 1989 to 2004, there was a 27 per cent increase in the number of "Native pastors" leading AG USA churches in the New Mexico and Arizona Districts. Saggio, "Toward an Indigenous Model," 86, 92.

71 Clatterbuck, "Sweet Grass Mass," 112.

72 For his part, Gunner attests that he does not desire for the CAFC to compete with the PAOC. Gunner, interview by author. The Native Evangelical Fellowship of Canada (NEFC), incorporated on 1 April 1971, exists separate from the larger Evangelical Fellowship of Canada (EFC). The NEFC maintains its "primary purpose … as a Native Church is to promote the gospel message in all lawful ways and to bring lost souls to a saving knowledge of Jesus Christ." Jolly, *Christ Is Building His Native Church*, 154.

73 Collado, interview by author.

74 Upton, "Canadian Missionary Outreach," 2–3; Jack Ozard, 1984, "1984 Northland Mission Report," PAOC Archives, 1; PAOC, "Fellowship Statistics," accessed August 2017, https://paoc.org/docs/default-source/fellowship-services-docs/fellowship-stats.pdf?sfvrsn=10; Guenther, "Ethnicity and Evangelical Protestants in Canada," 390.

75 Jolly, *Christ Is Building His Native Church*, 60; McCleary, "Akbaatashee," 2.

76 Burkinshaw, "Native Pentecostalism in British Columbia," in Wilkinson, 161, Burkinshaw quoting Rodney Stark and Roger Finke.

77 Westman believes that "Pentecostalism may play a steadily decreasing role ... Pentecostalism can be a response to stress or crisis, but ... it is also strongly associated with a long term rise in the proportion of those espousing 'no religion' ... possibly sowing the seeds of its demise." Westman, "Understanding Cree Religious Discourse," 17–18, 176, 178–9.

78 "Christian Aboriginal Fellowship of Canada."

79 Mix-Ross, "The PAOC and Indigenous Peoples," 137.

80 Collado, interview by author; Aboriginal Bible Academy, "About Us," accessed June 2017, http://www.aboriginalbibleacademy.ca/about-us. The ABA is the continuation of Ross Maracle's National Native Bible College. Affiliated with the PAOC Eastern Ontario District, at the time of writing the ABA enrolls "over 80 students stretching from northern Labrador all the way to B.C., with several points in between." Collado, "Aboriginal Bible Academy," 13.

81 Mix-Ross, "The PAOC and Indigenous Peoples," 138–9, Mix-Ross quoting Collado.

82 Clatterbuck, *Crow Jesus*, 29.

83 Ibid., 241.

84 Mason, "Christian Witness," 92.

85 Kennedy, "Apology, Forgiveness, and Reconciliation," 22; PAOC Mission Canada, "Aboriginal Canadians," accessed March 2017, https://paoc.org/canada/priorities/aboriginal. At the time of writing, Victor is on faculty at Trinity Western University in British Columbia as: University Siya:m, Co-Director of the Institute of Indigenous Issues & Perspectives, Indigenous Elder, and Instructor of Education. Trinity Western University, "Patricia Victor, M.A.L.," accessed March 2022, https://www.twu.ca/profile/patricia-victor.

86 Simpson, "Liberated Peoples, Liberated Lands," 56.

87 Olivia Stefanovich, "Pope Francis Apologizes to Indigenous Delegates for 'Deplorable' Abuses at Residential Schools," *CBC News*, 1 April 2022, https://www.cbc.ca/news/politics/pope-francis-responds-indigenous-delegations-final-meeting-1.6404344.

88 Olivia Stefanovich, "Vatican Announces Late July Visit by Pope Francis to Canada," *CBC News*, 12 May 2022, https://www.cbc.ca/news/politics/pope-canada-visit-vatican-announcement-1.6448229.

89 The Canadian Press, "'I Am Deeply Sorry': Full Text of Residential School Apology from Pope Francis," *CBC News*, 25 July 2022, https://www.cbc.ca/news/canada/edmonton/pope-francis-maskwacis-apology-full-text-1.6531341.

90 Thomson Reuters, "Pope Francis Asks for 'Forgiveness in the Name of the Church' for Abuses at Residential Schools," *CBC News*, 3 August 2022, https://www.cbc.ca/news/world/pope-francis-general-audience-canada-residential-schools-1.6539562; Collado, "History Made," 38.

91 Courtney Dickson and Bridgette Watson, "Remains of 215 Children Found Buried at Former B.C. Residential School, First Nation Says," *CBC News*, 27 May 2021, https://www.cbc.ca/news/canada/british-columbia/tk-eml%C3%BAps-te-secw%C3%A9pemc-215-children-former-kamloops-indian-residential-school-1.6043778.

92 Wells and Collado, "A PAOC Response to the Kamloops Tragedy," 2.

93 Ian Froese, "Team Investigating Brandon's Former Residential School for Graves Turns to Elders for Clues," *CBC News*, 20 June 2021, https://www.cbc.ca/news/canada/manitoba/team-investigating-brandon-former-residential-school-help-model-follow-1.6073118; *CBC News*, "Survivors, Community Honour 751 Unmarked Graves at Sask. Residential School Site with Vigil," *CBC News*, 27 June 2021, https://www.cbc.ca/news/canada/saskatoon/survivors-community-honour-751-unmarked-graves-at-sask-residential-school-site-with-vigil-1.6082063; Karin Larsen, "National Gathering Calls for Records to Help in Search for Missing Residential School Children," *CBC News*, 17 January 2023, https://www.cbc.ca/news/canada/british-columbia/national-gathering-calls-records-search-missing-residential-school-children-1.6716629.

94 Kennedy, "The Other Boys of Bethlehem," 9. Emphasis original.

95 FNIM PAOC, "wodfirstnations" Instagram post, 25 June 2021, https://www.instagram.com/p/CQi3GQCJrS4; WOD, "First Nations Ministries," accessed January 2022, https://wodistrict.org/here-to-serve/first-nations-ministries.

96 Stewart, "The Unfinished Work of Reconciliation," 102, 106.

97 Thunder and Thunder, "Reconciliation with Indigenous Peoples," 11.

98 Ibid., 13–14.

99 Collado, "History Made," 39.

CONCLUSION

1 Frost, *The Spirit, Indigenous Peoples and Social Change*, 1.

2 Garratt and Garratt, *Two Tears on the Window*, 3.

3 Dale and Alberta Cummins, June 1981, "The Northland Newsletter," PAOC Archives, 2; Gibson, "Native Theological Training," 113.

4 Tarango, "The Land Is Always Stalking Us," 405–6.

5 Beardy, interview by author.

6 Jack Ozard, May 1995, "Northland Ministries Newsletter," PAOC Archives, July 2016, 2; Bonney Lake Christian Academy, "Kallappa, James & Jeanne," accessed November 2017, http://www.blcc.org/go/missionaries/kallappa,-james--jeanne.html; James Kallappa, June 1995, "The National Native Counsel," Newsletter, PAOC Archives, October 2015, 1–2; Davies, "The Men of Mistissini," 24.

7 Reidy, "Holy Ghost Tribe," 377.

8 Earl N.O. Kulbeck, 28 April 1968, "Consultation on Indian Work; Ottawa, Canada"; Presentation on behalf of the PAOC to Parliamentary Committee, PAOC Archives, October 2015, 2–3.

9 Bates, "Piety in the American Plains," 189.

10 Andrew Maracle, 1992, "From a Log Cabin: An Autobiography of the Life & Ministry of Rev. Andrew Clifford Maracle," Assemblies of God Flower Pentecostal Heritage Centre, 7.

11 Tarango, *Choosing the Jesus Way*, 53, 171; Merino, "Staff Reflections," 345, 349; Washburn, "Trail to the Tribes," 78; J. Saggio and Dempsey, *A Witness to the Tribes*, 398; AG USA General Council, 3–7 August 2015, "Minutes of the 56th Session of the General Council of the Assemblies of God With Revised Constitution and Bylaws," Assemblies of God USA website, 101–2, accessed July 2017, https://ag.org/-/media/AGORG/Downloads/Constitution-and-Bylaws/GCM-08-2015-Constitution-and-Bylaws-with-Minutes-and-Index.pdf; AG USA, "Executive Presbytery," accessed July 2017, https://ag.org/About/Leadership-Team/Executive-Presbytery; Iroquois Caucus, 3–4 July 2013, "Record of Decisions – Final," 1, accessed July 2017, http://www.iroquoiscaucus.com/wp-content/uploads/2014/02/ROD-July-3-4-2013.pdf; Tarango, "Native American Christians," 332; Wikipedia, "Assemblies of God USA," accessed January 2023, https://en.wikipedia.org/wiki/Assemblies_of_God_USA; Saggio, "Toward an Indigenous Model," 93.

12 Wilkinson, "Charles W. Chawner," 41–2.

13 Jack Ozard, May 1995, "Northland Ministries Newsletter," PAOC Archives, 2.

14 PAOC District Superintendents and District Native Ministries Directors, 27 May 1995, "Minutes of the District Superintendents and District Native Ministries Directors Meeting," PAOC Archives, 3.

15 Yong, "Improvisation, Indigenization, and Inspiration," 280, 283.

16 Riches, *Worship and Social Engagement*, 20.

17 Chetty, "Towards a Postcolonial Pentecostal Historiography," 337.

18 Marshall, *Upward, Not Sunwise*, 183, Marshall quoting José Casanova.

19 Jolly, *Christ Is Building His Native Church*, 86.

20 Hageman, "Seven Questions for Reggie Neeposh," 29. Some Indigenous Pentecostals express points of similarity with "the ten Lost Tribes of Israel," identifying "ties … between ancient Judaism and Indian religion … [with] the Sun Dance lodge as a 'type' of the ancient Hebrews' tabernacle," with others even claiming linguistic commonality. Clatterbuck, "Healing Hills and Sacred Songs," 258. Others identify instead with the ancient Hebrews' rivals, reading "the Exodus stories with Canaanite eyes." Warrior, "Canaanites, Cowboys, and Indians," 95; Clatterbuck, "Sweet Grass Mass," 97.

21 Laugrand and Oosten, "Reconnecting People and Healing the Land," 237; Tarango, *Choosing the Jesus Way*, 2.

22 Chetty, "Towards a Postcolonial Pentecostal Historiography," 341.

23 McClung, "Review," 114; Dombrowski, *Against Culture*, 181; Steve Hubrecht, "Supreme Court of Canada Dismissed Ktunaxa Case against Jumbo: Ruling Made Thursday, November 2nd," *The Columbia Valley Pioneer*, 8 November 2017, https://www.columbiavalleypioneer.com/news/supreme-court-of-canada-dismissed-ktunaxa-case-against-jumbo.

24 Smith, *Native Americans*, xxvii. Smith quoting Wilson's volume *Remember This!*

25 Wilkinson, "Public Acts of Forgiveness," 192.

26 Wilkinson and Studebaker, "Pentecostal Social Action," 2, 4, 11, 17.

27 Marshall, "Non-Human Agency," 399, 407.

28 Sarat, *Fire in the Canyon*, 3–4, 6, 11, 22, 34, 103. Leah Sarat, Assistant Professor of Religion in the School of Historical, Philosophical, and Religious Studies at Arizona State University, specifically refers to the Maya migrants of the Totonicapán region of Guatemala and the Otomí migrants of the El Alberto region of Mexico, for whom Pentecostal expressions such as fasting, prophecy, and prayer greatly influence their practice of migration in the regions straddling the United States and Mexico called the borderlands. Sarat explains: "Pentecostalism in many ways entails a continuation of rather than a radical break with indigenous cosmologies. Pentecostalism's non-dualistic approach to the body resonates with traditional hñähñu conceptions of illness and healing, just as indigenous notions of personhood and agency continue to play out within Pentecostal spiritual warfare." These themes are in keeping with insights regarding other commonalities between Indigenous Pentecostalism and Majority World Pentecostalism. Sarat continues to describe how Pentecostals' "stories brim with indigenous Mesoamerican elements," such as "the … concept of the nahual, and the notion … [of] hñähñu popular" Christianity.

29 Beardy, interview by author. Absalom Beardy spoke primarily in Anishininiimowin, thus the interpreters who travelled with him presumably were Anishininiwag also.

30 Davies, "The Men of Mistissini," 24.

31 Westman, *Cree and Christian*, 271.

32 Marshall, *Upward, Not Sunwise*, 182–3.

33 Ibid., 187–8.

34 Marshall, "Navajo Reservation Camp Meeting a Great Success!," 111.

35 There is also the reality that an Indigenous Pentecostal cosmology bears similarity to the various Majority World Pentecostal cosmologies. Compared to Euro-Canadian Pentecostal cosmology, Indigenous Pentecostal cosmology generally operates with a more tangible perception of the immediacy and accessibility of the spiritual world. Put another way, "within a totalizing Pentecostalist framework ... God is daily engaged in battles with demonkind, a drama played out among the lives of individual humans." Marshall, *Upward, Not Sunwise*, 188–9, 191–2.

36 Westman, "Understanding Cree Religious Discourse," 326.

37 Sarat, *Fire in the Canyon*, 109.

38 Tarango, *Choosing the Jesus Way*, 176.

39 Tarango, "Native American Christians," 338.

40 Gibson, "Native Theological Training," 149.

41 Maracle, "From a Log Cabin," 7; Tarango, *Choosing the Jesus Way*, 53, 171; Merino, "Staff Reflections," 345, 349; Washburn, "Trail to the Tribes," 78; J. Saggio and Dempsey, *A Witness to the Tribes*, 398; AG USA General Council, 3–7 August 2015, "Minutes of the 56th Session of the General Council of the Assemblies of God With Revised Constitution and Bylaws," 101–2; Assemblies of God USA, "Executive Presbytery," accessed July 2017, https://ag.org/About/Leadership-Team/Executive-Presbytery; Iroquois Caucus, 3–4 July 2013, "Record of Decisions – Final," accessed July 2017, http://www.iroquoiscaucus.com/wp-content/uploads/2014/02/ROD-July-3-4-2013.pdf, 1; PAOC, "General Constitution and By-Laws," 9, 20, accessed July 2017, https://paoc.org/docs/default-source/fellowship-services-documents/constitutions/2016/2016-general-constitution-and-by-laws.pdf?sfvrsn=eb66196a_2.

42 Gibson, "Native Theological Training," 136–7, Gibson quoting an anonymous Indigenous Pentecostal elder.

43 PAOC, "General Executive," accessed July 2017, https://paoc.org/family/who-we-are/general-executive; PAOC, "Fellowship Statistics," https://paoc.org/docs/default-source/fellowship-services-docs/fellowship-stats.pdf?sfvrsn=10.

44 Frost, *The Spirit, Indigenous Peoples and Social Change*, 11, emphasis original.
45 Wilkinson and Ambrose, *After the Revival*, 149.
46 Curtice, *Native*, 123.
47 Jacuk, "Native Americans, Land and the Spirit," 8.
48 Burkinshaw, "Native Pentecostalism in British Columbia" (presentation paper), 41.
49 Wilkinson, "Canadian Pentecostalism," 114; Guenther, "Ethnicity and Evangelical Protestants in Canada," 392–3; Tarango, *Choosing the Jesus Way*, 3.
50 Lewis, *Creating Christian Indians*, 164, 180.

Bibliography

ARCHIVAL SOURCES

Archival sources held at the Flower Pentecostal Heritage Center, the General Council of the Assemblies of God, Springfield, MO.

Archival sources held at the Pentecostal Assemblies of Canada Archives, PAOC International Office, Mississauga, ON.

BROADCASTS

100 Huntley Street. "First Nations Follow Up." Featuring Ron Mainse, Kathy Mainse, and George Gunner. Aired 25 January 2012 on Christian Television Service.

– "House of All Nations." Featuring Moira Brown, George Gunner, and Pauline Gunner. Aired 21 December 2011 on Christian Television Service.

Aboriginal Peoples Television Network National News. "APTN Investigates: Between the Feather and the Cross." Featuring Todd Lamirande and Melissa Ridgen. Aired 7 November 2014 on Aboriginal Peoples Television Network.

INTERVIEWS AND CORRESPONDENCE

Beardy, Levi Samson. Interview by author. 17 October 2017.

Collado, Dan. Interview by author. 24 November 2021.

Gunner, George. Interview by author. 29 October 2021.

Porterfield, Andrew. Email message to author. 10 October 2019.

OTHER SOURCES

AG USA General Council. "Minutes of the 56th Session of the General Council of the Assemblies of God with Revised Constitution and Bylaws." 3–7 August 2015. Assemblies of God USA.

Airhart, Phyllis D. *A Church with the Soul of a Nation: Making and Remaking the United Church of Canada*. Montreal and Kingston: McGill-Queen's University Press, 2014.

Aldred, Ray, Terry LeBlanc, and Adrian Jacobs. "Thoughts on Forgiveness and Aboriginal Residential Schools." *Indian Life Newspaper: News from Across Native North America*, June 2010.

Alexander, Corky. *Native American Pentecost: Praxis, Contextualization, Transformation*. Cleveland, TN: Cherohala Press, 2012.

Ambrose, Linda M. "Zelma and Beulah Argue: Sisters in the Canadian Pentecostal Movement." In *Winds From the North: Canadian Contributions to the Pentecostal Movement*, edited by Michael Wilkinson and Peter Althouse, 99–128. Leiden, Netherlands, and Boston, MA: Brill, 2010.

Argue, R.M. *Dominion Outreach*, January-March 1962.

– "Exciting News from Here and There." *Pentecostal Testimony*, September 1971.

– "Home Missions." *Pentecostal Testimony*, April 1968.

– "Home Missions: Indian Fires Burn Brightly." *Pentecostal Testimony*, April 1967.

– "Home Missions – Resourcefulness." *Pentecostal Testimony*, October 1968.

– "Wings of the Gospel: And Hope for Scattered Canadians." *Pentecostal Testimony*, October 1968.

Atter, Gordon F. *"The Third Force": A Pentecostal Answer to the Question So Often Asked by Both Our Own Young People and by Members of Other Churches – "Who Are the Pentecostals?"* Peterborough, ON: College Press, 1970.

Austin, Alvyn, and Jamie S. Scott. "Introduction." In *Canadian Missionaries, Indigenous Peoples: Representing Religion at Home and Abroad*, edited by Alvyn Austin and Jamie S. Scott, 3–18. Toronto: University of Toronto Press, 2005.

Baldridge, William. "Reclaiming Our Histories." In *Native and Christian: Indigenous Voices on Religious Identity in the United States and Canada*, edited by James Treat, 83–92. New York and London: Routledge, 1996.

Barde, Joel. "Second Coming: Inside the Controversial US Evangelical Movement Targeting Indigenous People in Canada." *Walrus: Canada's Conversation*, November 2017.

Barker, Adam J., and Emma Battell Lowman. "Ways of Knowing and Being: The Imperative of Understanding Indigenous Ontologies." In *Quest For Respect: The Church and Indigenous Spirituality*, edited by Jeff Friesen and Steve Heinrichs, 45–7. Winnipeg: Mennonite Church Canada, 2017. A special issue of *Intotemak*, Spring 2017, and part of Commonword's *Intotemak Trilogy*.

Barnsley, Paul. "National Chief's Religion Cause for Discussion." *Windspeaker* 18, no. 5 (2000).

Bate, Michael. "Evangelical Moonlighting? Matthew Coon Come: Soul Man." *Frank Magazine*, 3 April 2002.

Bates, Eric. "Piety in the American Plains: The Politics of Identity and Pentecostalism on the Blackfeet Indian Reservation." In *Indigenous People and the Christian Faith: A New Way Forward*, edited by William H.U. Anderson and Charles Muskego, 189–213. Wilmington, DE: Vernon Press, 2020.

Beaman, Lori G. "Aboriginal Spirituality and the Legal Construction of Freedom of Religion." *Journal of Church and State* 44, no. 1 (Winter 2002): 135–49.

Bear-Barnetson, Cheryl. *Introduction to First Nations Ministry*. Cleveland, TN: Cherohala Press, 2013.

Bebbington, David. "Evangelicalism in Its Settings: The British and American Movements since 1940." In *Evangelicalism: Comparative Studies of Popular Protestantism in North America, the British Isles, and Beyond, 1700–1990*, edited by Mark A. Noll, David W. Bebbington, and George A. Rawlyk, 365–88. New York: Oxford University Press, 1994.

Beninger, Carling. "The Primacy of Justice: Ted Scott, Social Justice, and the Anglican Church of Canada." *The Ecumenist* 53, no. 2 (Spring 2016): 8–13.

Beninger, Carling C. "The Anglican Church of Canada: Indigenous Policies." MA thesis, Trent University, Peterborough, ON, 2011.

– "'Does the Church Really Care?': The Indigenous Policies of the Anglican, Presbyterian, and United Churches of Canada, 1946–1990." PhD diss., University of Saskatchewan, Saskatoon, SK, 2018.

Beselt, Art. "A Christian's Career in Scarlet." *Pentecostal Testimony*, July 1973.

Birch, Kenneth. "New Strategy for Nakina Bible School." *Pentecostal Testimony*, November 1971.

Blumhofer, Edith. *The Assemblies of God: A Chapter in the Story of American Pentecostalism*, vol. 1: *To 1941*. Springfield, MO: Gospel Publishing House, 1989.

Boyd, David P. "National Native Leadership Council." *Action Magazine*, Summer 1985.

Bradford, Tolly, and Chelsea Horton. "Introduction: The Mixed Blessings of Encounter." In *Mixed Blessings: Indigenous Encounters with Christianity in Canada*, edited by Tolly Bradford and Chelsea Horton, 1–18. Vancouver: University of British Columbia Press, 2016.

Bramadat, Paul, and David Seljak. "Conclusion: The Discourse of Loss and the Future of Christianity and Ethnicity in Canada." In *Christianity and Ethnicity in Canada*, edited by Paul Bramadat and David Seljak, 415–35. Toronto: University of Toronto Press, 2008.

Brown, Mildred Grace. *Top of the World: The Story of Ken and Sarah Gaetz, Dan and Grace Priest and Many Other Missionaries in the Northwest Territories*. Saskatoon, SK: Modern Press, 1977.

Brown, Victor G. *Fifty Years of Pentecostal History: 1933–1983*. Burlington, ON: Western Ontario District of the PAOC, 1983.

– "'Watchmen' Graduate at E.P.B.C." *Pentecostal Testimony*, July 1967.

Buntain, Daniel N. "Aggressive Christ-Honouring: Canada's Home." *Pentecostal Testimony*, 1 July 1943.

– "Hitherto the Lord Has Helped Us." *Pentecostal Testimony*, 15 November 1943.

– "Pastors across Canada Tell of the Bible Truth." *Pentecostal Testimony*, 1 September 1944.

– *Pentecostal Testimony*, 1 November 1939.

Burkinshaw, Robert. "Native Pentecostalism in British Columbia." Paper presented at the Canadian Pentecostal Research Network Symposium, Langley, BC, October 2006.

Burkinshaw, Robert K. "Native Pentecostalism in British Columbia." In *Canadian Pentecostalism: Transition and Transformation*, edited by Michael Wilkinson, 142–70. Montreal and Kingston: McGill-Queen's University Press, 2009.

Bush, Peter. *Western Challenge: The Presbyterian Church in Canada's Mission on the Prairies and North, 1885–1925*. Winnipeg: Watson and Dwyer, 2000.

Bush, Peter G. "The Canadian Churches' Apologies for Colonialism and Residential Schools, 1986–1998." *Peace Research: The Canadian Journal of Peace and Conflict Studies* 47, nos. 1–2 (2015): 47–70.

– "The Presbyterian Church in Canada's Mission to Canada's Native Peoples, 1900–2000." *International Bulletin of Missionary Research* 36, no. 3 (July 2012): 115–20.

Campeau, Guy. "North of the 50th." *The Challenge: PAOC Western Ontario District*, February 1985.

Camps, A., L.A. Hoedemaker, M.R. Spindler, and F.J. Verstralen. "Introduction: What Do We Mean by 'Missiology'?" In *Missiology: An Ecumenical Introduction; Texts and Contexts of Global Christianity*, edited by A. Camps, L.A. Hoedemaker, M.R. Spindler, and F.J. Verstralen, 1–8. Grand Rapids, MI: Eerdmans, 1995.

Carlson, Hans M. *Home Is the Hunter: The James Bay Cree and Their Land*. Vancouver: University of British Columbia Press, 2008.

Carlson Cumbo, Enrico. "'Your Old Men Will Dream Dreams': The Italian Pentecostal Experience in Canada, 1912–1945." *Journal of American Ethnic History* 19, no. 3 (Spring 2000): 35–81.

Carrington, Philip. *The Anglican Church in Canada: A History*. Toronto: Collins, 1963.

Chalmers, D. Kervan. "Progress through Building." *Pentecostal Testimony*, February 1978.

Chetty, Irvin G. "Towards a Postcolonial Pentecostal Historiography: Ramblings from the South." *Studia Historiae Ecclesiasticae* 35, no. 2 (October 2009): 337–51.

Christie, Nancy, and Michael Gauvreau. *Christian Churches and Their Peoples, 1840–1965: A Social History of Religion in Canada*. Toronto: University of Toronto Press, 2010.

Clarke, Wilson. "Summer Is Coming." *Pentecostal Testimony*, December 1977.

Clatterbuck, Mark. *Crow Jesus: Personal Stories of Native Religious Belonging*. Norman, OK: University of Oklahoma Press, 2017.

– "Healing Hills and Sacred Songs: Crow Pentecostalism, Anti-Traditionalism, and Native Religious Identity." *Spiritus: A Journal of Christian Spirituality* 12, no. 2 (2012): 248–77.

– "Sweet Grass Mass and Pow Wows for Jesus: Catholic and Pentecostal Missions on Rocky Boy's Reservation." *U.S. Catholic Historian* 27, no. 1 (2009): 89–112.

Collado, Dan. "Aboriginal Bible Academy: Equipping, Educating, Establishing." *Testimony and Enrich: Lifestyle and Leadership*, Summer 2019.

– "History Made: Reflections on Pope Francis' Visit to Canada." *Testimony and Enrich: Lifestyle and Leadership*, Winter 2023.

Colwell, Judith. "Samuel Stearns Day: First Canadian-Born Baptist Missionary." In *Memory and Hope: Strands of Canadian Baptist History*, edited by David T. Priestly, 155–70. Waterloo, ON: Wilfrid Laurier University Press, 1996.

Cree, Rodger. "Pagwa River Dedicates New Church." *Pentecostal Testimony*, February 1955.

Cree, Rodger A., Sr. "Board Reflections: Rodger A. Cree, Sr." In *American Indian College: A Witness to the Tribes*, edited by Joseph J. Saggio and Jim Dempsey, 133–8. Springfield, MO: Gospel Publishing House, 2008.

Crossette, Barbara. "Indian Chief Miffs Canada, Not Sparing Indians." *New York Times*, 31 October 2001.

Cummins, Dale. "Christian Education among the Native Peoples of Northern Ontario." *Source Magazine: A Journal of Christian Education*, June 1982.

– "Home Mission: As Dale Cummins Sees It." *Pentecostal Testimony*, October 1980.

– "Somebody Prayed – Was It You?" *Action Magazine*, September 1977.

– "Where Is the Prophet's Roar?" *Pentecostal Testimony*, January 1982.

Cunningham, Robert C. "Revivaltime Released over CKGB Timmins, Ontario." *The Pentecostal Evangel: Official Voice of the Assemblies of God*, 4 April 1965.

Curtice, Kaitlin B. *Native: Identity, Belonging, and Rediscovering God*. Grand Rapids, MI: Brazos Press, 2020.

Daniels, David D., III. "North American Pentecostalism." In *The Cambridge Companion to Pentecostalism: Cambridge Companions to Religion*, edited by Cecil M. Robeck, Jr, and Amos Yong, 73–92. Cambridge, UK: Cambridge University Press, 2014.

Davidson, Blake. "What's Up with APM?" *Connections Magazine: The Western Ontario District of the Pentecostal Assemblies of Canada*, Summer 2014.

Davies, Donna. "The Men of Mistissini: How a Cree Nation Is Impacting Liberia." *Testimony Magazine*, May-June 2018.

Dees, Sarah. "Religion and US Federal Indian Policy." In *A Companion to American Religious History*, edited by Benjamin E. Park, 276–86. Hoboken, NJ: Wiley Blackwell, 2021.

Deloria, Vine, Jr. *Custer Died for Your Sins: An Indians Manifesto*. Norman, OK: University of Oklahoma Press, 1988.
– "Vision and Community: A Native American Voice." In *Native and Christian: Indigenous Voices on Religious Identity in the United States and Canada*, edited by James Treat, 105–14. New York and London: Routledge, 1996.
Dempster, Murray W., Byron D. Klaus, and Douglas Petersen. "General Introduction." In *The Globalization of Pentecostalism: A Religion Made to Travel*, edited by Murray W. Dempster, Byron D. Klaus, and Douglas Petersen, xiii–xvii. Oxford, UK: Regnum Books International, 1999.
Dickason, Olive Patricia, and William Newbigging. *Indigenous Peoples within Canada: A Concise History*. 4th ed. Don Mills, ON: Oxford University Press, 2019.
Dombrowski, Kirk. *Against Culture: Development, Politics and Religion in Indian Alaska*. Lincoln: University of Nebraska Press, 2001.
Duncalfe, John R. "Turkana Country." *Pentecostal Testimony*, August 1980.
Elliot, Elisabeth. *Through Gates of Splendor: The Event That Shocked the World, Changed a People, and Inspired a Nation*. Peabody, MA: Hendrickson, 2011.
Elliott, David R. "Canadian Baptists and Native Ministry in the Nineteenth Century." *Canadian Society of Church History Historical Papers 2000* (2000): 145–63.
Emmons, D.A. "Forgotten Sacrifice." *Dominion Outreach*, January–March 1968.
Ervin, Spencer. *The Political and Ecclesiastical History of the Anglican Church of Canada*. Ambler, PA: Trinity Press, 1967.
Fletcher, Christopher, and Aaron Denham. "Moving towards Healing: A Nunavut Case Study." In *Aboriginal Healing in Canada: Studies in Therapeutic Meaning and Practice*, edited by James B. Waldram, 93–129. Ottawa: Aboriginal Healing Foundation, 2008.
Fletcher, Wendy. "Canadian Anglicanism and Ethnicity." In *Christianity and Ethnicity in Canada*, edited by Paul Bramadat and David Seljack, 138–67. Toronto: University of Toronto, 2008.
Frodsham, Stanley Howard. *With Signs Following: The Story of the Pentecostal Revival in the Twentieth Century*, revised ed. Springfield, MO: Gospel Publishing House, 1946.
Frost, Michael J. *The Spirit, Indigenous Peoples and Social Change: Māori and a Pentecostal Theology of Social Engagement*. Leiden, Netherlands, and Boston, MA: Brill, 2019.

Garratt, Julia, and Kevin Garratt. *Two Tears on the Window: An Ordinary Canadian Couple Disappears in China*. Victoria: First Choice Books, 2018.

Gibson, Graham S. "Native Theological Training within Canadian Evangelicalism: Three Case Studies." MA thesis, Wilfrid Laurier University, Waterloo, ON, 1994.

– "The Politics of Representation of Others' Spirituality: The Challenge of Non-Native Study of Aboriginal Pentecostalism." Paper presented at the 39th annual meeting of the Society for Pentecostal Studies, North Central University, Minneapolis, MN, Assemblies of God Flower Pentecostal Heritage Center, March 2009.

– "Two Histories of Pentecostal Missionization of Aboriginal Peoples in Northern Canada: A Study of Fairford, Manitoba and Weagamow, Ontario." Paper presented at the 45th annual meeting of the Society for Pentecostal Studies, Life Pacific College, San Dimas, CA, Assemblies of God Flower Pentecostal Heritage Center, March 2016.

Gibson, Linda. "Editorial: Transformed Together." *Testimony Magazine*, November 2006.

– "Women of Faith." In *Picture This! Reflecting on 100 Years of the PAOC*, edited by David Wells, 68–83. Mississauga, ON: PAOC, 2018.

Graham, Roger. "Canadian Bible Colleges." *Pentecostal Testimony*, October 2000.

Grant, John Webster. *Moon of Wintertime: Missionaries and the Indians of Canada in Encounter since 1534*. Toronto: University of Toronto Press, 1984.

Greer, Allan. "Towards a Comparative Study of Jesuit Missions and Indigenous Peoples in Seventeenth-Century Canada and Paraguay." In *Native Christians: Modes and Effects of Christianity among Indigenous People of the Americas*, edited by Aparecida Vilaça and Robin M. Wright, 21–32. London and New York: Routledge: 2016.

Griffin, William A. *Pentecostal Testimony*, October 1982.

Grosshans, George, and Dale Cummins. "Pickle Lake Preview." *Pentecostal Testimony*, August 1976.

Guenther, Bruce L. "Ethnicity and Evangelical Protestants in Canada." In *Christianity and Ethnicity in Canada*, edited by Paul Bramadat and David Seljak, 365–414. Toronto: University of Toronto Press, 2008.

Gunner, George. "Aboriginal Ministry that Endures." In *Tenacious: Inspiration & Encouragement from Those Who Persevere*, edited by David Wells and Stacey McKenzie, 69–74. Mississauga, ON: PAOC, 2011.

Hageman, Jordan. "Seven Questions for Reggie Neeposh: Life Lessons from the Former Chief of the Oujé-Bougoumou Cree Nation." *Testimony and Enrich: Lifestyle and Leadership*, Fall 2020.

Hansell, Joy E. "Bible College Graduates – 1981." *Pentecostal Testimony*, July 1981.

– "Mother with a Missionary Heart: Erna Peters." *Pentecostal Testimony*, May 1972.

– "Visit to Kenya: The Testimony Interviews General Superintendent R.W. Taitinger." *Pentecostal Testimony*, April 1978.

– "Who/What: News about People and Events in the Pentecostal Assemblies of Canada." *Pentecostal Testimony*, October 1978.

– "Who/What: News about People and Events in the Pentecostal Assemblies of Canada District Conferences – 1977 50 Years for Two." *Pentecostal Testimony*, August 1977.

Harbridge, Gerald E. "The Growing Northland Mission." *Action Magazine*, May 1981.

Hayes, Alan L. *Anglicans in Canada: Controversies and Identity in Historical Perspective*. Urbana and Chicago: University of Illinois Press, 2004.

Heinrichs, Steve. "An Indigenous Intrusion Troubles the House: A Call to Decolonization." In *Buffalo Shout, Salmon Cry: Conversations on Creation, Land Justice, and Life Together*, edited by Steve Heinrichs, 13–30. Waterloo, ON, and Harrisonburg, VA: Herald Press, 2013.

Hiebert, Rick. "Fellowship Notes: New Appointment." *Testimony Magazine*, April 2001.

Hodge, William H. "Navaho Pentecostalism." *Anthropological Quarterly* 37, no. 3 (July 1964): 73–93.

Hodges, Melvin. *The Indigenous Church*. Springfield, MO: Assemblies of God, 1953.

Hodgman, Rollie. *Light on the Horizon: Northern Canada Evangelical Mission's Fifty Years of Ministry to Canada's First Peoples*. Prince Albert, SK: Northern Canada Evangelical Mission, 1996.

Holy Bible. New International Version Anglicized. Grand Rapids, MI: Zondervan, 2011.

Hornby, Allon E. "Canada For Christ Crusade Centennial Thrust." *Pentecostal Testimony*, February 1967.

Howarth, Harold. "Greetings from Moosonee." *Dominion Outreach*, July-September 1967.

– "Indian Bible School A Success." *Dominion Outreach*, October-December 1967.

– "Tragedy in the North." *Dominion Outreach*, October–December 1968.

Hunter, E.S. "'T.E.E. Off' in Ontario's Northland." *Action Magazine*, December 1974.

Iroquois Caucus. "Record of Decisions – Final." 3–4 July 2013.

Jacuk, Benjamin. "Native Americans, Land and the Spirit: A Red Theology of Liberation." Paper presented at the 48th annual meeting of the Society for Pentecostal Studies, William Seymour College, Hyattsville, MD, Assemblies of God Flower Pentecostal Heritage Center, March 2019.

Johnson, Van. "Contextualization: An Introduction." In *His Witnesses: Christian Witness in a Multi-Religious World*, edited by David Wells and Van Johnson, 13–19. Mississauga, ON: PAOC, 2013.

Johnstone, Tom. "General Conference Report by Executive Director of Home Missions and Bible Colleges." *Pentecostal Testimony*, November 1962.

– "Panorama of Home Missions across Canada." *Pentecostal Testimony*, October 1962.

Jolly, Joseph. *Christ Is Building His Native Church: Strategies and Methods for Planting Indigenous Churches*. Cleveland, TN: Cherohala Press, 2019.

– "A Native View of Self Government." In *Shaping a Christian Vision for Canada: Discussion Papers on Canada's Future*, edited by Aileen Van Ginkel, 53–9. Markham, ON: Faith Today Publications, 1992.

Kärkkäinen, Veli-Matti. "Mission in Pentecostal Theology." *International Review of Mission* 107, no. 1 (June 2018): 5–22.

Keller, O.C., and Mrs O.C. Keller. "Missionary News: Outline of Work at Nyangori Mission Station British East Africa." *Pentecostal Testimony*, March 1932.

Kelm, Mary-Ellen. *Colonizing Bodies: Aboriginal Health and Healing in British Columbia 1900–50*. Vancouver: University of British Columbia Press, 1998.

Kennedy, Stephen. "Apology, Forgiveness and Reconciliation." *Testimony Magazine*, August-September 2012.

– "Apology, Forgiveness, and Reconciliation: PAOC and Aboriginal Representatives Exchange Historic Reconciliation Statements." *Testimony Magazine*, Spring 2012.

– "The Other Boys of Bethlehem: Living in the Shadow of an Ancient Story." *Testimony and Enrich: Lifestyle and Leadership*, Fall 2021.

Kim-Cragg, HyeRan. "The Power and Practise of Indigenous Christian Rituals and Ceremonies." In *Honouring the Declaration: Church*

Commitments to Reconciliation and the United Nations Declaration on the Rights of Indigenous Peoples, edited by Don Schweitzer and Paul L. Gareau, 159–82. Regina: University of Regina Press, 2021.

King, Thomas. *The Inconvenient Indian: A Curious Account of Native People in North America*. Toronto: Doubleday Canada, 2012.

Kirmayer, Laurence J., Caroline L. Tait, and Cori Simpson. "The Mental Health of Aboriginal Peoples in Canada: Transformations of Identity and Community." In *Healing Traditions: The Mental Health of Aboriginal Peoples in Canada*, edited by Laurence J. Kirmayer and Gail Guthrie Valaskakis, 3–35. Vancouver: University of British Columbia Press, 2009.

Klaus, Byron D. "Missiological Reflections on Twentieth-Century Pentecostal Missions: North American Perspectives." *Pneuma: The Journal of the Society for Pentecostal Studies* 16, no. 1 (Spring 1994): 3–10.

Knott, John Daniel. "Testimony of a Young Indian." *Pentecostal Testimony*, November 1964.

Kostelnik, Dawn. *The White Girl: True North Stories*. Whitehorse: Author, 2015.

Kovach, Margaret. *Indigenous Methodologies: Characteristics, Conversations and Contexts*. Toronto: University of Toronto Press, 2009.

Kracht, Benjamin R. *Religious Revitalization among the Kiowas: The Ghost Dance, Peyote, and Christianity*. Lincoln: University of Nebraska Press, 2018.

Kulbeck, Earl N.O. "77 Graduates from Our Canadian Pentecostal Bible Colleges." *Pentecostal Testimony*, July 1963.

– "91 Graduates from Our Canadian Pentecostal Bible Colleges." *Pentecostal Testimony*, July 1964.

– "Canadian: Alumni Meet of Canadian Colleges at World Conference." *Pentecostal Testimony*, November 1958.

– "French Bible Institute Holds Graduation Exercises." *Pentecostal Testimony*, July 1952.

– "Indians Accept Christ." *Pentecostal Testimony*, July 1962.

– "Missionary News." *Pentecostal Testimony*, June 1957.

– "Northern Lights." *Pentecostal Testimony*, October 1959.

– "The Pentecostal Assemblies of Canada 1971 Camp Slate." *Pentecostal Testimony*, May 1971.

– "People." *Pentecostal Testimony*, September 1959.

– "People and Activities." *Pentecostal Testimony*, July 1957.

– "People and Activities." *Pentecostal Testimony*, January 1958.

– "People and Activities." *Pentecostal Testimony*, November 1958.
– "People and Places." *Pentecostal Testimony*, March 1960.
– *Pentecostal Testimony*, April 1958.
– *Pentecostal Testimony*, August 1958.
– *Pentecostal Testimony*, October 1960.
– *Pentecostal Testimony*, October 1963.
– "Three Indian Works." *Pentecostal Testimony*, September 1964.

Kulbeck, Gloria. *What God Hath Wrought: A History of the Pentecostal Assemblies of Canada*. Toronto: PAOC, 1958.

Kydd, Ronald A.N. "Canadian Pentecostalism and the Evangelical Impulse." In *Aspects of the Canadian Evangelical Experience*, edited by George A. Rawlyk, 289–300. Montreal and Kingston: McGill-Queen's University Press, 1997.

Latimer, Carson. *Dominion Outreach*, April–June 1966.

Laugrand, Frédéric, and Jarich Oosten. "Reconnecting People and Healing the Land: Inuit Pentecostal and Evangelical Movements in the Canadian Eastern Arctic." *Numen: International Review for the History of Religions* 54 (2007): 229–69.

Laugrand, Frédéric B., and Jarich G. Oosten. "Shamans and Missionaries: Transitions and Transformations in the Kivalliq Coastal Area." In *Native Christians: Modes and Effects of Christianity Among Indigenous People of the Americas*, edited by Aparecida Vilaça and Robin M. Wright, 167–86. London and New York: Routledge: 2016.

LeBlanc, Terry. "Being Spiritual Before a Common Creator." In *Quest For Respect: The Church and Indigenous Spirituality*, edited by Jeff Friesen and Steve Heinrichs, 105–8. Winnipeg: Mennonite Church Canada, 2017. A special issue of *Intotemak*, Spring 2017, and part of Commonword's *Intotemak Trilogy*.

– "Toward an Indigenous Eschatology: Caution, Circle Ahead." In *Indigenous People and the Christian Faith: A New Way Forward*, edited by William H.U. Anderson and Charles Muskego, 229–46. Wilmington, DE: Vernon Press, 2020.

Lefebvre, Solange. "The Francophone Roman Catholic Church." In *Christianity and Ethnicity in Canada*, edited by Paul Bramadat and David Seljack, 101–37. Toronto: University of Toronto Press, 2008.

Lewis, Bonnie Sue. *Creating Christian Indians: Native Clergy in the Presbyterian Church*. Norman: University of Oklahoma Press, 2003.

Loewen, Roydon. "The Poetics of Peoplehood: Ethnicity and Religion among Canada's Mennonites." In *Christianity and Ethnicity in Canada*, edited by Paul Bramadat and David Seljack, 330–64. Toronto: University of Toronto Press, 2008.

Lynn, Lowana. "Bungoma Church Dedication." *Pentecostal Testimony*, October 1977.

Macdonald, Stuart. "Presbyterian and Reformed Christians and Ethnicity." In *Christianity and Ethnicity in Canada*, edited by Paul Bramadat and David Seljack, 168–203. Toronto: University of Toronto Press, 2008.

MacKinnon, Mark. "Natives Turn Up Heat, Elect Aggressive New Chief." *Globe and Mail*, 13 July 2000.

Maracle, Lee. "Goodbye, Snauq." In *Our Story: Aboriginal Voices on Canada's Past*, edited by Cardinal Tantoo, 201–20. Toronto: Anchor Canada, 2004.

Marks, Pauline. "Called to a Cold Spot." *Pentecostal Testimony*, February 1982.

Marshall, Kimberly Jenkins. "'Navajo Reservation Camp Meeting a Great Success!' The Advent of Diné Pentecostalism after 1950." *Ethnohistory: The Journal of the American Society for Ethnohistory* 62, no. 1 (January 2015): 95–117.

– "Non-Human Agency and Experiential Faith among Diné Oodlání, 'Navajo Believers.'" *Anthropologica: Canadian Anthropology Society* 57, no. 2 (2015): 397–409.

– "'Soaking Songs' Versus 'Medicine Man Chant': Musical Resonance among Diné Oodlání (Navajo Believers)." In *The Spirit of Praise: Music and Worship in Global Pentecostal-Charismatic Christianity*, edited by Monique M. Ingalls and Amos Yong, 148–62. University Park: Pennsylvania State University Press, 2015.

– *Upward, Not Sunwise: Resonant Rupture in Navajo Neo-Pentecostalism*. Lincoln: University of Nebraska Press, 2016.

Martin, Heather D. "A Framework for Theological Lifelong Learning in the Northwest Territories." DMin diss., Providence Theological Seminary, Otterburne, MB, 2007.

Mason, Kyle. "Christian Witness: Where Aboriginal Meets Urban." In *His Witnesses: Christian Witness in a Multi-Religious World*, edited by David Wells and Van Johnson, 85–92. Mississauga, ON: PAOC, 2013.

McAlister, R.E. "The Bible Evidence." *Pentecostal Testimony*, November 1925.

McAlister, Walter E. "'Camp Meetings at 40 Below Zero!'" *Pentecostal Testimony*, May 1955.

– *Pentecostal Testimony*, July 1953.

– "Wings of the Gospel: Gospel Plane Flying Again in Northland." *Pentecostal Testimony*, October 1953.

McCleary, Timothy P. "Akbaatashee: The Oilers Pentecostalism among the Crow Indians." MA thesis, University of Montana, Missoula, MT, 1993.

– "An Ethnohistory of Pentecostalism among the Crow Indians of Montana." *Wicazo Sa Review: A Journal of Native American Studies* 15, no. 1 (2000): 117–35.

McClung, L. Grant. "'Try to Get People Saved': Revisiting the Paradigm of Urgent Pentecostal Missiology." In *The Globalization of Pentecostalism: A Religion Made to Travel*, edited by Murray W. Dempster, Byron D. Klaus, and Douglas Petersen, 30–51. Oxford, UK: Regnum Books International, 1999.

McClung, L. Grant, Jr. "Review: Murray W. Dempster, Byron D. Klaus and Douglas Petersen, ed., Called & Empowered: Global Mission in Pentecostal Perspective." *Pneuma: The Journal of the Society for Pentecostal Studies* 15, no. 1 (Spring 1993): 113–15.

McGee, Gary B. *People of the Spirit: The Assemblies of God*. Springfield, MO: Gospel Publishing House, 2014.

McKay, Stan, and Janet Silman. *The First Nations: A Canadian Experience of the Gospel-Culture Encounter*. Geneva, Switzerland: World Council of Churches Publications, 1995.

McKenzie, Stacey. "From the Editor." *Testimony and Enrich: Lifestyle and Leadership*, Summer 2021.

McPherson, Dennis. "A Definition of Culture: Canada and First Nations." In *Native American Religious Identity: Unforgotten Gods*, edited by Jace Weaver, 77–98. Maryknoll, NY: Orbis Books, 1998.

Merino, Donald P. "Staff Reflections: Donald P. Merino (Maidu/Wintun) Director of Plant Operations." In *American Indian College: A Witness to the Tribes*, edited by Joseph J. Saggio and Jim Dempsey, 343–9. Springfield, MO: Gospel Publishing House, 2008.

Miller, J.R. *Residential Schools and Reconciliation: Canada Confronts Its History*. Toronto: University of Toronto Press, 2017.

– *Skyscrapers Hide the Heavens: A History of Indian-White Relations in Canada*. 1st ed. Toronto: University of Toronto Press, 1989.

– *Skyscrapers Hide the Heavens: A History of Indian White Relations in Canada*. 3rd ed. Toronto: University of Toronto Press, 2000.

– *Skyscrapers Hide the Heavens: A History of Native-Newcomer Relations in Canada*. 4th ed. Toronto: University of Toronto Press, 2018.

Miller, Thomas William. *Canadian Pentecostals: A History of the Pentecostal Assemblies of Canada*. Mississauga, ON: Full Gospel Publishing House, 1994.

Milloy, John S. *A National Crime: The Canadian Government and the Residential Schooling System, 1879 to 1986*. Winnipeg: University of Manitoba Press. 1999.

Milne, Derek Brothers. "Diyin God Bizaad: Tradition, Change and Pentecostal Christianity among the Navajo." PhD diss., University of California Los Angeles, Los Angeles, 2011.

Mix-Ross, Aaron. "The PAOC and Indigenous Peoples: 'They Will Soar on Wings Like Eagles.'" In *Picture This! Reflecting on 100 Years of the* PAOC, edited by David Wells, 124–39. Mississauga, ON: PAOC, 2018.

Moir, John S. *Enduring Witness: A History of the Presbyterian Church in Canada*. Toronto: Bryant Press, 1974.

Monahan, Patrick J. *Meech Lake: The Inside Story*. Toronto: University of Toronto Press, 1991.

Moody, W.H. "You Are What You Eat." *Pentecostal Testimony*, January 1958.

Morsch, Shirley J. *Rejoice: A History of the Pentecostal Assemblies of Alberta and the Northwest Territories*. Edmonton: Alberta and Northwest Territories District of the PAOC, 1983.

Myrah, Eunice. "Moosonee Native Bible School." *Dominion Outreach*, January–March 1966.

Nadeau, Denise M. *Unsettling Spirit: A Journey into Decolonization*. Montreal and Kingston: McGill-Queen's University Press, 2020.

Neely, Lois. "Church Growth – Toronto's Stone Church: The Gospel Either Works Downtown or It Doesn't Work at All." *Pentecostal Testimony*, December 1988.

Nelles, H.V. *A Little History of Canada*. Don Mills, ON: Oxford University Press, 2011.

Newberg, Eric N. "Said's Orientalism and Pentecostal Views of Islam in Palestine." *International Bulletin of Missionary Research* 36, no. 4 (2012): 196–9.

Neylan, Susan. "'Choose Your Flag': Perspectives on the Tsimshian Migration from Metlakatla, British Columbia, to New Metlakatla, Alaska, 1887." In *New Histories for Old: Changing Perspectives on Canada's Native Pasts*, edited by Theodore Binnema and Susan Neylan, 196–219. Vancouver: University of British Columbia Press, 2008.

– *The Heavens Are Changing: Nineteenth-Century Protestant Missions and Tsimshian Christianity*. Montreal and Kingston: McGill-Queen's University Press, 2003.

Ng, Wenh-In Greer Anne. "The United Church of Canada: A Church Fittingly National." In *Christianity and Ethnicity in Canada*, edited by Paul Bramadat and David Seljack, 203–46. Toronto: University of Toronto Press, 2008.

Nkonge, Dickson K. "The Church Missionary Society's Burden: Theological Education for a Self-Supporting, Self-Governing, and Self-Propagating African Anglican Church in Kenya, 1844–1930." *Anglican and Episcopal History* 83, no. 1 (2014): 20–41.

Ostler, John, and Betty Ostler. "Look North Please!" *Dominion Outreach*, October–December 1968.

PAOC Department of Home Missions and Bible Colleges (DHMBC). "Native Leadership in Canada." *Action Magazine*, Winter 1987.

– "Our Land – Our People – Our Commission." *Action Magazine*, April–May 1982.

PAOC Home Missions. "The Moosonee Bible School." *Dominion Outreach*, September 1964.

Paper, Jordan "Aboriginals." In *The Religions of Canadians*, edited by Jamie S. Scott, 1–31. Toronto: University of Toronto Press, 2012.

Peach, Ian. "The Power of a Single Feather: Meech Lake, Indigenous Resistance and the Evolution of Indigenous Politics in Canada." *Review of Constitutional Studies* 16, no. 1 (2011): 1–29.

Pearson, Timothy. "Reading Rituals: Performance and Religious Encounter in Early Colonial Northeastern North America." In *Mixed Blessings: Indigenous Encounters with Christianity in Canada*, edited by Tolly Bradford and Chelsea Horton, 21–37. Vancouver: University of British Columbia Press, 2016.

Penner, Robert. "The Ojibwe Renaissance: Transnational Evangelicalism and the Making of an Algonquin Intelligentsia, 1812–1867." *American Review of Canadian Studies* 45, no. 1 (2015): 71–92.

Peters, Erna Alma. "Christ on the Cross." *Pentecostal Testimony*, April 1978.

– *The Contribution to Education by the Pentecostal Assemblies of Canada*. Homewood, MB: Author, 1971.

– "The Responsibility of the Local Church to Missions." *Pentecostal Testimony*, November 1981.

Petersen, Douglas. "Changing Paradigms: An Introductory Overview." In *The Globalization of Pentecostalism: A Religion Made to Travel*, edited by Murray W. Dempster, Byron D. Klaus, and Douglas Petersen, 3–7. Oxford, UK: Regnum Books International, 1999.

Porter, David K. "Shaping the Missionary Identity of the Pentecostal Assemblies of Canada: Spirit Baptism and Eschatology in the Writings of George A. Chambers and Robert E. McAlister." ThM thesis, Wycliffe College, Toronto, 1999.

Posterski, Don, and Gary Nelson. *Future Faith Churches: Reconnecting with the Power of the Gospel for the 21st Century*. Kelowna, BC: Wood Lake Books, 1997.

Prankard, Bill. "Foreword." In *Wings of the Gospel: The Story of Canada's Northland Missionary Pilot*, by John Spillenaar, 6. Caledonia, ON: ACTS Books, 1976.

Press, Harold. "Davis Inlet in Crisis: Will the Lessons Ever Be Learned?" *Canadian Journal of Native Studies* 15, no. 2 (1995): 188–209.

Preston, Richard J. "Twentieth-Century Transformations of East Cree Spirituality and Autonomy." In *Indigenous Peoples and Autonomy: Insights for a Global Age*, edited by Mario Blaser, Ravi De Costa, Deborah McGregor, and William D. Coleman, 195–217. Vancouver: University of British Columbia Press, 2010.

Reidy, Skyler. "'Holy Ghost Tribe': The Needles Revival and the Origin of Pentecostalism." *Religion and American Culture: A Journal of Interpretation* 29, no. 3 (Fall 2019): 361–90.

Renfree, Harry A. *Heritage and Horizon: The Baptist Story in Canada.* Mississauga, ON: Canadian Baptist Federation, 1988.

Riches, Tanya. *Worship and Social Engagement in Urban Aboriginal-led Australian Pentecostal Congregations: (Re)imagining Identity in the Spirit*. Leiden, Netherlands, and Boston, MA: Brill, 2019.

Ringer, David. "J. Roswell Flower: Pentecostal Servant and Statesman," *Assemblies of God Heritage: The Official Magazine of The Assemblies of God Flower Pentecostal Heritage Center*, 2012.

Robert, Dana L. "The 'Christian Home' as a Cornerstone of Anglo-American Missionary Thought and Practice." In *Converting Colonialism: Visions and Realities in Mission History, 1706–1914*, edited by Dana L. Robert, 134–65. Grand Rapids, MI: Eerdmans, 2008.

– "From Missions to Mission to Beyond Missions: The Historiography of American Protestant Foreign Missions since World War II." *International Bulletin of Missionary Research* 18 (1994): 146–62.

Robinson, Thomas A. "Oneness Pentecostalism." In *Canadian Pentecostalism: Transition and Transformation*, edited by Michael

Wilkinson, 39–57. Montreal and Kingston: McGill-Queen's University Press, 2009.

Rosell, Garth M. *The Surprising Work of God: Harold John Ockenga, Billy Graham, and the Rebirth of Evangelicalism*. Grand Rapids, MI: Baker Academic, 2008.

Ruby, Robert H., and John A. Brown. *John Slocum and the Indian Shaker Church*. Norman: University of Oklahoma Press, 1996.

Rudd, Douglas. *When the Spirit Came upon Them: Highlights from the Early Years of the Pentecostal Movement in Canada*. Mississauga, ON: PAOC, 2002.

Saggio, Joseph J. "Toward an Indigenous Model of Native American Ministry within the Assemblies of God." *Pneuma: The Journal of the Society for Pentecostal Studies* 31, no. 1 (2009): 85–104.

Saggio, Joseph J., and Jim Dempsey, eds. *American Indian College: A Witness to the Tribes*. Springfield, MO: Gospel Publishing House, 2007.

Said, Edward W. *Culture and Imperialism*. New York: Alfred A. Knopf, 1993.

Sanchez-Walsh, Arlene M. "Race, Ethnicity, and Gender among Early Pentecostals." In *A Companion to American Religious History*, edited by Benjamin E. Park, 266–75. Hoboken, NJ: Wiley Blackwell, 2021.

Sarat, Leah. *Fire in the Canyon: Religion, Migration, and the Mexican Dream*. New York: New York University Press, 2013.

Scott, Jamie S. "Cultivating Christians in Colonial Canadian Missions." In *Canadian Missionaries, Indigenous Peoples: Representing Religion at Home and Abroad*, edited by Alvyn Austin and Jamie S. Scott, 21–45. Toronto: University of Toronto Press, 2005.

Shepherd, Loraine MacKenzie. "From Colonization to Right Relations: The Evolution of United Church of Canada Missions within Aboriginal Communities." *International Review of Mission* 103, no. 1 (April 2014): 153–71.

Simpson, Leanne. "Liberated Peoples, Liberated Lands." In *Buffalo Shout, Salmon Cry: Conversations on Creation, Land Justice, and Life Together*, edited by Steve Heinrichs, 50–7. Waterloo, ON, and Harrisonburg, VA: Herald Press, 2013.

Simpson, Leanne Betasamosake. *Dancing on Our Turtle's Back: Stories of Nishnaabeg Re-Creation, Resurgence and a New Emergence*. Winnipeg: ARP Books, 2011.

Skinner, Robert J. "Newslines: Canada's First National Native Leadership Council." *Pentecostal Testimony*, October 1985.

– "Newslines of the Fellowship: Eighteen Hundred Attend Western Ontario Retreats." *Pentecostal Testimony*, December 1983.
– "Ordination of Native Minister." *Pentecostal Testimony*, February 1984.
– *Pentecostal Testimony*, April 1989.
Sloos, William. "Book Review: After the Revival." *Testimony and Enrich: Lifestyle and Leadership*, Summer 2021.
Smith, Andrea. *Native Americans and the Christian Right: The Gendered Politics of Unlikely Alliances*. Durham, NC: Duke University Press, 2008.
Smith, C. Bannerman. "Hundreds of Canada's Children Have Decided for Christ Jesus." *Pentecostal Testimony*, 15 September 1945.
– "News!" *Pentecostal Testimony*, September 1946.
– "News." *Pentecostal Testimony*, 15 December 1946.
– *Pentecostal Testimony*, 15 July 1948.
– *Pentecostal Testimony*, 24 May 1952.
Smith, Donald B. *Sacred Feathers: The Reverend Peter Jones (Kahkewaquonaby) and the Mississauga Indians*. 2nd ed. Toronto: University of Toronto Press, 2013.
Smith, Keith D. "Introduction." In *Strange Visitors: Documents in Indigenous-Settler Relations in Canada from 1876*, edited by Keith D. Smith, xv–xxiv. Toronto: University of Toronto Press, 2014.
Sombrero, Tweedy. "Black Robes: Native Americans and the Ordination Process." In *Native American Religious Identity: Unforgotten Gods*, edited by Jace Weaver, 173–9. Maryknoll, NY: Orbis Books, 1998.
Sonnenberg, Klaus. "Window on the World: Native Church Leaders Confront Issues of the 90's." *Pentecostal Testimony*, November 1992.
Spillenaar, John. *Dominion Outreach*, October–December 1964.
– "Graduation Moosonee Pentecostal Bible School 1966." *Pentecostal Testimony*, November 1966.
– "If I Have Not Vision." *Pentecostal Testimony*, 15 February 1950.
– "Missionary Work in Northern Ontario." *Pentecostal Testimony*, 1 December 1948.
– "Northland Missionary Saves a Life, and God Saves a Soul." *Pentecostal Testimony*, 1 April 1952.
– "Pioneer Work in Northern Ontario." *Pentecostal Testimony*, 1 September 1946.
– *To the Regions Beyond*. Burlington, ON: Acts Books, 1992.
– *Wings of the Gospel: The Story of Canada's Northland Missionary Pilot*. Caledonia, ON: Acts Books, 1976.

Stackhouse, John G. "By Their Books Ye Shall Know Them: Books that Have Shaped American Evangelicals in the Last 40 Years." *Christianity Today: Theology, Church, Culture*, 16 September 1996.

– *Canadian Evangelicalism in the Twentieth Century: An Introduction to Its Character*. Vancouver, BC: Regent College Publishing, 1999.

– "The Protestant Experience in Canada since 1945." In *The Canadian Protestant Experience 1760–1990*, edited by George Rawlyk, 198–252. Burlington, ON: Welch, 1990.

Starblanket, Noel. "Foreword." In *The Knowledge Seeker: Embracing Indigenous Spirituality*, by Blair Stonechild, ix–xi. Regina: University of Regina Press, 2016.

Steed, Brian. "Latest Report on the Northland Mission." *Dominion Outreach*, July-September 1967.

Stewart, Adam. "A Canadian Azusa? The Implications of the Hebden Mission for Pentecostal Historiography." In *Winds from the North: Canadian Contributions to the Pentecostal Movement*, edited by Michael Wilkinson and Peter Althouse, 17–38. Leiden, Netherlands, and Boston, MA: Brill, 2010.

– "From Monogenesis to Polygenesis in Pentecostal Origins: A Survey of the Evidence from the Azusa Street, Hebden, and Mukti Missions." *PentecoStudies: An Interdisciplinary Journal for Research on the Pentecostal and Charismatic Movements* 13, no. 2 (2014): 151–72.

– *The New Canadian Pentecostals*. Waterloo, ON: Wilfrid Laurier University Press, 2015.

– "The Unfinished Work of Reconciliation: The Truth and Reconciliation Commission of Canada, Neoliberal Liability Amelioration, and Nimi Wariboko's Pentecostal Principle." *The Journal of* NAIITS*: An Indigenous Learning Community* 16, no. 1 (2018): 95–107. EPUB.

Stiller, C.H. "Indigenous Methods in Moosonee." *Pentecostal Testi mony*, July 1965.

– "The Northland." *Dominion Outreach*, July-September 1963.

– "North with 'Wings of the Gospel.'" *Dominion Outreach*, July–September 1965.

Stonechild, Blair. *The Knowledge Seeker: Embracing Indigenous Spirituality*. Regina: University of Regina Press, 2016.

– "Recovering Ancient Spiritual Paths." In *Quest For Respect: The Church and Indigenous Spirituality*, edited by Jeff Friesen and Steve Heinrichs, 28–31. Winnipeg: Mennonite Church Canada, 2017. A special issue of *Intotemak*, Spring 2017, and part of Commonword's *Intotemak Trilogy*.

Strong, Alec. "Events and Impressions of Northern Ontario." *The Challenge:* PAOC *Western Ontario District*, October 1969.

Stronstad, Roger. *The Charismatic Theology of St. Luke*. Peabody, MA: Hendrickson, 1984.

Stryker, Alyssa. "A Sin of Omission and Misrecognition: Representations of the Oka Crisis in Three Canadian History Textbooks." *Our Schools / Our Selves* 19, no. 3 (Spring 2010): 291–302.

Swain, Harry. *Oka: A Political Crisis and Its Legacy*. Toronto: Douglas & McIntyre, 2010.

Tanner, Adrian. "The Origins of Northern Aboriginal Social Pathologies and the Quebec Cree Healing Movement." In *Healing Traditions: The Mental Health of Aboriginal Peoples in Canada*, edited by Laurence J. Kirmayer and Gail Guthrie Valaskakis, 249–71. Vancouver: University of British Columbia Press, 2009.

Tapper, Michael A. *Canadian Pentecostals, The Trinity, and Contemporary Worship Music: The Songs We Sing*. Leiden, Netherlands, and Boston, MA: Brill, 2017.

Tarango, Angela. *Choosing the Jesus Way: American Indian Pentecostals and the Fight for the Indigenous Principle*. Chapel Hill, NC: The University of North Carolina Press, 2014.

– "Jonathan Edwards, Pentecostals, and the Missionary Encounter with Native Americans." In *Pentecostal Theology and Jonathan Edwards*, edited by Steven M. Studebaker and Amos Yong, 197–209. London: T&T Clark, 2019.

– "'The Land Is Always Stalking Us': Pentecostalism, Race and Native Understandings of Sacred Land." *Pneuma: The Journal of the Society for Pentecostal Studies* 36, no. 3 (2014): 397–406.

– "Native American Christians and the Varieties of Modern Pentecostalism." In *A Companion to American Religious History*, edited by Benjamin E. Park, 229–40. Hoboken, NJ: Wiley Blackwell, 2021.

Taylor, Drew Hayden. "A Blurry Image on the Six O'Clock News." In *Our Story: Aboriginal Voices on Canada's Past*, edited by Cardinal Tantoo, 221–44. Toronto: Anchor Canada, 2005.

Thunder, Jimmy, and Andrew Thunder. "Reconciliation with Indigenous Peoples: A Road Map for Healing and Restoration." *Testimony and Enrich: Lifestyle and Leadership*, Winter 2022.

Truth and Reconciliation Commission of Canada. *Canada's Residential Schools – The History, Part 1 Origins to 1939: The Final Report of the Truth and Reconciliation Commission of Canada*, vol. 1. Montreal and Kingston: McGill-Queen's University Press, 2015.

Twiss, Richard. *Rescuing the Gospel from the Cowboys: A Native American Expression of the Jesus Way*. Downers Grove, IL: IVP Books, 2015.

Upton, Gordon. "The Call of the North!" *Pentecostal Testimony*, April 1953.

– "The Canadian Scene: Decade of Destiny for Native Canada." *Pentecostal Testimony*, November 1990.

– "Indifferent Attitude." *Pentecostal Testimony*, November 1987.

– "Pierre Bergeron Joins National Home Missions Department." *Pentecostal Testimony*, June 1988.

– "Secretary's Corner." *Pentecostal Testimony*, March 1953.

– "Window on the World: Native Canada on the Move." *Pentecostal Testimony*, October 1991.

Upton, Roy. "Canadian Missionary Outreach." *World Pentecost*, 1972.

Verlhust, Carl. "Burden for Baie Comeau." *Pentecostal Testimony*, July 1963.

Vilaça, Aparecida, and Robin M. Wright. "Introduction." In *Native Christians: Modes and Effects of Christianity Among Indigenous People of the Americas*, edited by Aparecida Vilaça and Robin M. Wright, 1–19. London and New York: Routledge: 2016.

Von Rosen, Franziska. "Three Generations of a Micmac Family: Stories and Conversations." Paper prepared as part of the Research Program of the Royal Commission on Aboriginal Peoples. December 1993. https://publications.gc.ca/collections/collection_2016/bcp-pco/Z1-1991-1-41-41-eng.pdf.

Vowel, Chelsea. *Indigenous Writes: A Guide to First Nations, Métis & Inuit Issues in Canada*. Winnipeg: Highwater Press, 2016.

Warner, Wayne. "Flying Ambassadors of Goodwill: The Story of Two Converted World War II Planes." *Assemblies of God Heritage Magazine*, Winter 1985–86.

Warrior, Robert Allen. "Canaanites, Cowboys, and Indians: Deliverance, Conquest, and Liberation Theology Today." In *Native and Christian: Indigenous Voices on Religious Identity in the United States and Canada*, edited by James Treat, 93–104. New York and London: Routledge, 1996.

Washburn, Alta M. "Trail to the Tribes." In *American Indian College: A Witness to the Tribes*, edited by Joseph J. Saggio and Jim Dempsey, 17–121. Springfield, MO: Gospel Publishing House, 2008.

Weaver, Jace. "From I-Hermeneutics to We-Hermeneutics: Native Americans and the Post-Colonial." In *Native American Religious*

Identity: Unforgotten Gods, edited by Jace Weaver, 1–25. Mary Knoll, NY: Orbis Books, 1998.

– "Foreword." In *Crow Jesus: Personal Stories of Native Religious Belonging*, by Mark Clatterbuck, xi–xiv. Norman: University of Oklahoma Press, 2017.

– "Preface." In *Native American Religious Identity: Unforgotten Gods*, edited by Jace Weaver, ix–xiii. Mary Knoll, NY: Orbis Books, 1998.

Wells, David, and Dan Collado. "A PAOC Response to the Kamloops Tragedy." *Testimony and Enrich: Lifestyle and Leadership*, Summer 2021.

Westman, Clinton N. *Cree and Christian: Encounters and Transformations*. Lincoln: University of Nebraska Press, 2022.

– "Cree Pentecostalism and Its Others." Paper presented at the 40th Algonquin Conference, Minneapolis, 2008.

– "Pentecostalism among Canadian Aboriginal People: A Political Movement?" In *A Liberating Spirit: Pentecostals and Social Action in North America*, edited by Michael Wilkinson and Steven M. Studebaker, 85–111. Eugene, OR: Wipf and Stock, 2010.

– "Pentecostalism and Indigenous Culture in Northern North America." *Anthropologica: Canadian Anthropology Society* 55, no. 1 (2013): 141–56.

– "Understanding Cree Religious Discourse." PhD diss., University of Alberta, Edmonton, 2008.

Whitehouse-Strong, Derek. "'Everything Promised Had Been Included in the Writing': Indian Reserve Farming and the Spirit and Intent of Treaty Six Reconsidered." *Great Plains Quarterly* 27, no. 1 (2007): 25–37.

Whitt, Irving Alfred. "Developing a Pentecostal Missiology in the Canadian Context (1867–1944): The Pentecostal Assemblies of Canada." DMin diss., Fuller Theological Seminary, Los Angeles, 1994.

Wilkinson, Michael. "Canadian Pentecostalism: A Multicultural Perspective." *Canadian Society of Church History Historical Papers 2008* (2008): 104–19.

– "Charles W. Chawner and the Missionary Impulse of the Hebden Mission." In *Winds from the North: Canadian Contributions to the Pentecostal Movement*, edited by Michael Wilkinson and Peter Althouse, 39–54. Leiden, Netherlands, and Boston, MA: Brill, 2010.

– "Public Acts of Forgiveness: What Happens When Canadian Churches and Governments Seek Forgiveness for Social Sins of the Past?" In *Forgiveness, Reconciliation and Restoration: Multidisciplinary Studies from a Pentecostal Perspective*, edited by Martin William Mittelstadt and Geoffrey William Sutton, 177–96. Eugene, OR: Pickwick Publications, 2010.

– *The Spirit Said Go: Pentecostal Immigrants in Canada*. New York: Peter Lang, 2006.

Wilkinson, Michael, and Linda M. Ambrose. *After the Revival: Pentecostalism and the Making of a Canadian Church*. Montreal and Kingston: McGill-Queen's University Press, 2020.

Wilkinson, Michael, and Steven M. Studebaker. "Pentecostal Social Action: An Introduction." In *A Liberating Spirit: Pentecostals and Social Action in North America,* edited by Michael Wilkinson and Steven M. Studebaker, 1–22. Eugene, OR: Wipf and Stock, 2010.

Wilson, Everett A. "They Crossed the Red Sea, Didn't They? Critical History and Pentecostal Beginnings." In *The Globalization of Pentecostalism: A Religion Made to Travel*, edited by Murray W. Dempster, Byron D. Klaus, and Douglas Petersen, 85–115. Oxford, UK: Regnum Books International, 1999.

Woodard, Joe. "A Light unto the Nations: Pentecostals Apologize to Natives, But Not for the Gospel." *The Alberta Report* 20, no. 18 (April 1993).

Wright, David. *SickKids: The History of the Hospital for Sick Children*. Toronto: University of Toronto Press, 2016.

Yong, Amos. "Improvisation, Indigenization, and Inspiration: Theological Reflections on the Sound and Spirit of Global Renewal." In *The Spirit of Praise: Music and Worship in Global Pentecostal-Charismatic Christianity*, edited by Monique M. Ingalls and Amos Yong, 279–88. University Park: Pennsylvania State University Press, 2015.

Younging, Gregory. *Elements of Indigenous Style: A Guide for Writing by and About Indigenous Peoples*. Edmonton: Brush Education, 2018.

Zikmund, Barbara Brown. "Introduction: Using Jamestown in 1607 to Stimulate Questions about Christian Mission in 2007." In *Remembering Jamestown: Hard Questions about Christian Mission*, edited by Amos Yong and Barbara Brown Zikmund, 1–11. Eugene, OR: Pickwick Publications, 2010.

Index